Reading for the Law

Victorian Literature and Culture Series

Jerome J. McGann and Herbert F. Tucker, Editors

Reading for the Law

British Literary History and Gender Advocacy

CHRISTINE L. KRUEGER

University of Virginia Press
CHARLOTTESVILLE AND LONDON

University of Virginia Press

Printed in the United States of America on acid-free paper

First published 2010

9 8 7 6 5 4 3 2 1

Library of Congress Cataloging-in-Publication Data

Krueger, Christine L.
Reading for the law : British literary history and gender advocacy / Christine L. Krueger.
p. cm. (Victorian literature and culture series)
Includes bibliographical references and index.
ISBN 978-0-8139-2893-7 (cloth : alk. paper)—ISBN 978-0-8139-2897-5 (e-book)
1. English literature—History and criticism. 2. Legal stories, English—History and criticism. 3. Law and literature—Great Britain—History. 4. Law in literature. 5. Female offenders in literature. 6. Women—Legal status, laws, etc.—Great Britain—History. 7. Sex discrimination against women—Law and legislation—Great Britain—History. 8. Feminist jurisprudence—Great Britain. I. Title.
PR830.L43K78 2010
823.009'3554—dc22

2009032569

For my father, William R. Krueger,
and my teacher and friend, Bertrand A. Goldgar

Contents

Acknowledgments

A LONG-TERM PROJECT like this one benefits from, and is sustained by, many mentors, colleagues, students, and friends. While I was still working on women preachers, Margaret Anne Doody and Jeffrey Spear turned my mind to crime. Catherine McClenahan, Claudia Johnson, Andrew Elfenbein, and Susan Sage Heinzelman read my early work on women and the law and set me on the right path. I have benefited greatly from the support of Martha Nussbaum, Susan Staves, and Richard Stein. My fellow fellows at the Huntington Library, especially Barbara Donagan, Kevis Goodman, Richard Kaueper, and Jessie Matz, gave me wise and learned advice, and lots of laughs. Wai-Chee Dimock and Judith Resnick offered encouragement and direction at a crucial stage in the project. Alison Booth provided essential publication advice. Conversations with Nancy Snow, Jan-Melissa Schramm, Rohan McWilliam, Simon Petch, William Cohen, Josephine McDonaugh, David Wayne Thomas, Joseph Kestner, George Justice, Devoney Looser, Cliff Spargo, Amelia Zurcher, Krista Ratcliffe, and Mary Catherine Bodden were enlightening and challenging. Sharing a Way Klingler Interdisciplinary Teaching Award with Shirley Wiegand of the Marquette University Law School gave me an opportunity to learn firsthand how lawyers teach literature, and to try out my arguments on law students.

Mary Jean Corbett and an anonymous reader for the University of Virginia Press went above and beyond the call of duty in their careful reading and insightful suggestions for revisions. Cathie Brettschneider, humanities acquisitions editor at the University of Virginia Press, offered enthusiastic support, sensible advice, and an expeditious editorial process. Book production was gracefully managed by Mark Mones and Morgan

Myers. Colleen Romick Clark was an astute and tactful copyeditor. Readers for *Victorian Studies* and *Mosaic* were enormously helpful in refining my arguments, as were Michael Freeman and Andrew D. E. Lewis for Oxford University Press.

I am grateful to colleagues who have invited me to share my work at their institutions: Sue Lonoff at Harvard, Emory Elliott at the University of California–Riverside, and Andrew Elfenbein at the University of Minnesota–Twin Cities. Thomas Wortham and the UCLA English department graciously hosted me during a sabbatical. Students and research assistants who have made heroic contributions to this project include Maria Keaton, Sarah Stefanko, Colleen Willenbring, Kaye Wierzbicki, and Elizabeth Wawrzyniak.

Throughout, two groups have solved cruxes, provided key pieces of information, and patiently thought through this project as it evolved. They are members of Interdisciplinary Nineteenth-Century Studies, particularly Johanna Smith, Teresa Mangum, Anca Vlasapolos, Deborah Morse, Mary Jean Corbett, Ellen Rosenman, Mark Schoenfield, and Claire Simmons, and the St. Pancras Research Group (formerly the Tivoli Research Group): A. R. Braunmuller, Bertrand Goldgar, Anne Goldgar, Charlotte Morse, J. Paul Hunter, F. J. Levy, Cynthia Wall, the late Lee Bliss, and the late Joseph Levine. The inspiration that brought this work to completion came from Margaret Bloom and colleagues in the Association of American Colleges and Universities Shared Futures project. Despite all this help, I doubtless could have used more, and I acknowledge all errors as my own.

Reading for the Law has been generously supported by the National Endowment for the Humanities, the Huntington Library, the Bradley Foundation, and the Committee on Research, the Graduate School, and the Klingler College of Arts and Sciences at Marquette University. Dr. Jeanne Hossenlopp, interim dean of Arts and Sciences, and Dr. William Wiener, vice provost for research and dean of the Graduate School, stepped in with additional funding at a crucial juncture. I am especially grateful to Fr. Thaddeus Burch, S.J., former dean of the Graduate School, for his sustained interest in my research.

I owe a great debt to the staff at the Huntington Library (especially its director of research, Roy Ritchie, and Caroline Powell, Susie Krasnoo, and Mary Robertson); the Public Records Office, UK; the British Library; the Folger Shakespeare Library; the Clark Library; and the Marquette University Library.

Al, Bill, Chris, and Kip provided the best reasons to keep working, as well as the most compelling distractions.

Portions of this book originally appeared in the following publications: "Naming Privates in Public: Indecent Assault Depositions, 1830–60," *Adversaria: Special Issue on Law and Literature* of *Mosaic, a Journal for the Interdisciplinary Study of Literature* 27.4 (December 1994): 121–40; "Witnessing Women: Trial Testimony in Novels by Tonna, Gaskell and Eliot," in Susan Sage Heinzelman and Zipporah Batshaw Wiseman, eds., *Representing Women: Feminism, Literature, and Law* (Durham, NC: Duke University Press, 1994), 337–55; "Literary Defenses and Medical Prosecutions: Representing Infanticide in Nineteenth-Century Britain," *Victorian Studies* 40 (Winter 1997): 271–94; "Victorian Narrative Jurisprudence," Michael Freeman and Andrew D. E. Lewis, eds., *Law and Literature: Current Legal Issues* (Oxford: Oxford University Press, 1999), 2:437–461; "Legal Uses of Victorian Fiction: Infant Felons to Juvenile Delinquents," in Christine L. Krueger, ed., *Functions of Victorian Culture at the Present Time* (Athens: Ohio University Press, 2002), 115–33; and "*Vox Populi, Vox Vulgari: Pro Se* Representation in the Victorian Popular Imagination," *Nineteenth Century Studies* 21 (2009). I am grateful to Duke University Press, Ohio University Press, Oxford University Press, *Mosaic: A Journal of the Interdisciplinary Study of Literature, Victorian Studies,* and *Nineteenth Century Studies* for permission to reprint these materials.

Reading for the Law

Introduction

Theory, Advocacy, and History

I TAKE THE TITLE for this book from the British term for legal study, "to read for the law." The principal question I address is how "reading for the law" as literary history can contribute to the progressive educational purposes for which the Law and Literature movement was founded. I intend a sympathetic critique of Law and Literature from the perspective of literary and legal history, one meant to supply evidence for more robust and judicious appeals to literature and law for both scholarship and teaching. At a time when the field of literary scholarship was first registering its marginalization in the academy and in the culture generally, the field of law and literature promised both a meaningful purpose and an influential new audience—the law professors and their students, who enjoyed relatively more prestigious status within universities and who appeared to offer a route by which literary study could transform the inequitable power relationships that were the subject of our critiques.[1]

Despite enormous productivity on law and literature, by legal and literary scholars alike, the field met two obstacles to its influence. The first has been extensively discussed by legal scholars, *viz.*, the rise of Law and Economics, which eclipsed Law and Literature as the interdisciplinary approach to legal studies favored in American law schools.[2] The second, which is my concern here, is the failure to create a sustained dialogue between law and literature and historical literary scholarship. Beyond studies of copyright law, which directly connect histories of law and literature, literary historians produced volumes of scholarship on historical interconnections between literature and law with little attention to their implications for contemporary legal advocacy, while legal scholars continued to treat their literary examples in New Critical or formalist fashions, abstracted from the historical conditions under which they had been produced. Symptomatic of this disconnect is Robert Weisberg's and Guyora Binder's encyclopedic survey of the field in *Literary Criticisms of the Law.* Weisberg and Binder analyze every other major literary critical approach to law in great detail; however, they give cursory attention to literary history, largely collapsing it into the practice of cultural studies. More than just a missed opportunity, this disconnect prevents literary historians from making substantive contributions to legal advocacy and handicaps legal scholars in making nuanced and defensible claims about the literary examples they draw from the past. Ironically, the result can be a new bifurcation of law and literature. Both legal and literary scholars (excepting, perhaps, literary historians) have tended to theorize law as an authoritarian, rule-bound, patriarchal disciplinary discourse in need of the antidote of multivoiced, subjective, and oppositional literary discourse. Alternatively, law and literature, particularly in New Historicist literary criticism and in Critical Legal theory, are understood as equally complicit in maintaining patriarchal bourgeois hegemony.

Reading for the Law argues that a multidisciplinary "historical narrative jurisprudence" strengthens narrative legal theorists' claims for the transformative powers of stories by replacing an ahistorical opposition between literature and law with a history of their interdependency, and their embeddedness in print culture. Focusing on gender and feminist advocacy in the long nineteenth century, I will demonstrate the relevance of literary history to feminist jurisprudence and suggests how literary history might contribute to other forms of "outsider jurisprudence." The argument is developed across discussions of key jurisprudential concepts: precedent, agency, testimony, and motive. Evidence is drawn from a wide range of literary, legal, and historical sources, from the early modern period through the Victorian, as well as from contemporary literary, feminist, and legal theory.

Using literary history to read for the law, I will argue, provides the context necessary for educating scholars and students in both disciplines in a manner that enables the interdiscipline to fulfill its promise. The import of literary history to this project has many facets. It demonstrates the historically contingent political impact of legal and literary texts for outsider advocacy. Rather than characterizing either discourse as progressive, or construing both as hegemonic, it enables a nuanced account of their strategic value to outsider advocacy under particular historical conditions. By restoring the exigencies of print culture, especially commodification, to literary production, literary history presents serious challenges to the celebration of narrative—even autobiography—as intrinsically suited to outsider advocacy. Yet historical scholarship can also provide viable accounts of literary advocacy that, under specific circumstances, moved forward legal recognition for excluded groups. In addition, it can reveal instances in which literary advocacy was efficacious only because new legal rights had been granted to literary authors, as well as instances in which literary writing impeded progressive legal reforms. This complex and dynamic history is not merely a curiosity, however, but part of the evolution of precedents, literary traditions, and disciplinary cultures that has shaped the practices and dictated the categories that structure the current relationship between law and literature, in scholarship, and in the culture beyond the academy. Above all, what literary history makes obvious is that reading for the law must be multidisciplinary if it is to transform the way we think about how our scholarship and teaching contribute to the common good. It challenges all of us, and our students, to become literate in multiple forms of representation, evidence, and advocacy.

Reading for the Law is not meant to be a comprehensive argument on behalf of this thesis. Rather, it illustrates the practice for law and literature I am advocating by focusing on gender and feminist advocacy. Following Jürgen Habermas, who takes the feminist movement from the late eighteenth century to the present to be paradigmatic of efforts to secure legal recognition, I seek to demonstrate the relevance of literary history to feminist jurisprudence not only to forward its ongoing project of advocacy for women but also to suggest how literary history might contribute to other forms of "outsider jurisprudence," which advocate for justice for legally disadvantaged sexual, racial, ethnic, and religious groups. Though they are analyzed in terms of gender advocacy—for female and male subjects of the law—the concepts on which I focus, and their related theoretical cruxes, are central to any outsider jurisprudence: precedent (the subject of part 1); agency (the subject of part 2); testimony (the subject of part 3); and motive, or *mens rea* (the subject of part 4). I hope that the general claims I make regarding the value of literary history as the basis for a sympathetic critique of narrative legal theory as a tool for progressive social change could be adapted to other emancipatory projects.

In order to demonstrate both diachronic and synchronic uses of literary history to inform an account of feminist advocacy, part 1 of *Reading for the Law* traces gender within the dialectic between English law and print culture regarding witchcraft prosecutions from the late sixteenth century to the nineteenth century. Parts 2, 3, and 4 take up particular legal concepts and literary developments that attain special significance in the context of concerted gender advocacy in the nineteenth century. In each of these sections, I also discuss how contemporary critical practices have framed our understanding of the issues at hand, and how that understanding can be enhanced by attention to historical evidence. Neither the diachronic nor the synchronic parts of this study purport to be exhaustive. What I have tried to do in the diachronic history of part 2 is to demonstrate how the long arms of both legal precedent and print culture reach across traditional boundaries of historical periodization and compel us to look beyond our fields of specialization to scholarship in earlier and later periods. In the synchronic sections of the book, I have tried to select some of the most salient points of contact among a variety of phenomena, typically studied in distinct disciplines. In order to lend coherence to the diachronic and synchronic histories, I have focused on English law and literature, though important parallels with other countries' histories could certainly be drawn.

After describing the theoretical rationale for historical jurisprudence below, I begin part 1 with common law's fundamental historical concept—precedent—and examine how gender came to be constituted within law through the burgeoning controversial literature spawned by early modern witchcraft trials. Rather than debating the misogynistic motives of witchcraft prosecutors, which has led to methodological and ideological impasses in historiographies of witchcraft trials, historical narrative jurisprudence shifts the grounds of argument to gendered legal precedents as a problem of the emergence of legal historicism in print culture. I pursue this phenomenon through eighteenth- and nineteenth-century histories of witchcraft trials that are constrained to grapple with the gender problem as a challenge to rationalist and progressivist historiographies of the law. I frame this argument with a narrative of feminist historical realism—Elizabeth Gaskell's *Lois the Witch* (1859)—as an example of how Victorian literary techniques enabled a reconceptualization of gender in legal history that embraced at once empirical evidence, retrospective justice, and an ethnographic understanding of historical change.

Because the history of witchcraft prosecution so strikingly foregrounds the production of deviance, its relevance to outsider jurisprudence should be clear. What may not be so obvious is the significance of this history of deviance for current debates about rationality and emotion, objectivity and empathy, empiricism and constructivism, propositional and narrative reasoning in law. Poststructuralist critiques of objectivity and historical evidence in contemporary feminist historiography seem to sustain rather than challenge these traumatic features of legal precedent, encouraging obsessive repetition in the absence of psychic resources or cultural conditions enabling transformation. Nineteenth-century realism, I will argue, offered an alternative literary "solution" to this problem. Gaskell's novella responds to traumatic history in a way that challenges many assumptions about literature as a therapeutic technique and about narrative evidence, or storytelling, as an antidote to the violence of legal reasoning. Rather than theorize the legal system as a tool of patriarchal interests, Gaskell historicizes witchcraft prosecutions, in this case emphasizing the material and political conditions of her setting in 1690s Salem. Additionally, she acknowledges women's agency in witch trials as storytellers: witnesses, inspectors, and plaintiffs. But instead of deriving skeptical conclusions from this analysis, she turns on the anti-rationalist ideology of the Salem elite, which she blames for authorizing psychosexual pathologies—of women as well as men—as "spectral" evidence in courts of law. In so doing, Gaskell posits a standard of rationality and realist historical narrative as defenses against legalized misogyny.

Seeking legal recognition under the conditions of Enlightenment political theory and social formations is the subject of part 3, which traces gendered agency from the conception of the reasonable person of Enlightenment narrativity to the Married Women's Property Act. Through discussions of two novels treating the loss of civil rights by incarceration in a lunatic asylum, Mary Wollstonecraft's novel *Maria; or, The Wrongs of Woman* (1798) and Charles Reade's *Hard Cash* (1863), along with narratives supplied to the Commissioners in Lunacy as part of the mid-Victorian asylum inspection scheme to identify sane persons wrongfully incarcerated, I test Robin West's claim that equal treatment under the law depends upon a return to "Enlightenment narrativity."[3] By this term West means ownership of one's own stories, which would entail, she argues, not only the right to complain of harm but also the recognition of that harm by someone obliged to prevent or cease to cause that harm. West's theory is promising in its acknowledgement of both narrative and history, but its Enlightenment property-rights model of narrative fails to deal with the intersubjective element of storytelling or with how the conditions of reading (or listening) are inflected by the dynamics of the literary public sphere.

Current deconstructions of equal treatment have a complex history in at least two principal strands of argument about procedural democracy.

One strand has construed equal treatment as an epistemological and evidentiary problem, of ascribing rational decision making to other minds. The other strand has emphasized equality as a function of the conferral of legal rights and obligations. These two strands are focused in the development of *compos mentis* as a legal and medical concept. The significance of gender in this history has been misrecognized. Foucauldian and psychoanalytic accounts of lunacy in nineteenth-century Britain, which stress techniques of disciplining deviance through the medicalization of madness, have obscured the relationship between rationality as the prerequisite of legal agency and property law. While historians have given considerable attention to the rise of the insanity defense, lunacy was primarily a matter of civil—not criminal—law, and as such, became the object of legislative and judicial action principally when property was at stake. By privileging sexual deviance as the object of discipline, we disregard the way gender was constructed in both Chancery writs *de lunatico inquirendo* and the Lunacy Acts. These were the principal sites of popular agitation on the part of men as well as women, at which the informal and formal political spheres impinged upon one another to forge procedural mechanisms for equal treatment and legal recognition.

Wollstonecraft's critique of "partial law" in her posthumously published novel *The Wrongs of Woman* dramatizes a woman's wrongful incarceration in a lunatic asylum by her dissolute husband as merely the logical extension of her abject dispossession of property and agency under coverture. Reade's *Hard Cash* was based upon an actual case of a son incarcerated in a lunatic asylum by his father, which fueled public fears and returned attention to lunacy commissions as an issue of male competition. These works, by a major feminist theorist of universal reason and a trained barrister with a strong interest in gendered evidence, interpellate propertied male readers into narratives of legal dispossession and show how liberal reformers of both sexes sought to comprehend gender difference within the evidentiary rules drawn from shared class values—common sense as opposed to expert testimony. Yet, as is demonstrated by the pathetically inefficacious attempts of government-appointed inspectors to win release for women they believed to be wrongfully incarcerated in lunatic asylums by bringing their stories before the Commissioners in Lunacy, it was the legal and social conditions of *listening*—or *reading*—that required change before positive arguments for legal agency could be effective. Importantly, it was not a change in lunacy laws, but in property law, that enabled women to defend their competency in courts of law: the Married Women's Property Act had the unanticipated consequence of enabling women, such as Georgina Weldon, for instance, to represent themselves in court against their husbands and the medical professionals who had sought to incarcerate them. As such, it is a key instance of what Rosemary Coombe argues that a cultural criticism of law should discover: its "sporadic and arbitrary acknowledgements of the social production of meaning."[4]

Following on this discussion of the unevenness of law's recognition of agency in the development of equal treatment procedures, I turn to the question of testimony in part 3. "Voice," and its antithesis "silence," have come to metaphorize legal recognition and its denial in much feminist and political theory, as well as in literary criticism. I challenge several contentions associated with this metaphorization, including the equation of law with silencing women's speech (in the Lacanian concept of "the law of the father"); the corollary argument, that literature is, by contrast, more amenable to female speech; and finally, that "forensic eloquence" is either inaccessible to female speakers or necessarily contrary to their aims. The nineteenth century saw major changes in rules governing the competency of witnesses, culminating in the Criminal Evidence Act of 1898, which first granted the accused the right to testify under oath. The impotency of persons legally disqualified as witnesses to represent themselves, which is a crucial element in Wollstonecraft's and Reade's attacks on lunacy laws, becomes a common trope of women's writing in the nineteenth century. Time and again, as in the novels of Charlotte Elizabeth Tonna, Elizabeth Gaskell, and George Eliot that I discuss, the failure of women's testimony is used to thematize women's disenfranchisement and legal disabilities. That is, women's legal nullity is narrated as their literal silencing or misconstrual before the representative institution of patriarchal authority: a court of law. But importantly, many of the same narratives generated by female writers reemerge in the testimony and depositions of men, both those who are accused of indecently assaulting other men and those who prosecute them. Ironically, the protests of nineteenth-century women against their silencing have been used, in twentieth-century feminist literary criticism, to contribute to the "metaphorization of law," in Rosemary Coombe's terms. That is, seen not as historically specific challenges to legal exclusion, they are grounds for extrapolating a theory of the totalized oppression of women by patriarchy, for which law provides the governing metaphor.

On the one hand, this fungibility of emancipatory narrative forms, their availability to the privileged as well as the victimized, points away from narrative itself as an essential source of emancipatory strategies and returns us to the positionality of authors as the salient variable in recognition. Though, as Alexander Welsh has argued, the growing preference for circumstantial evidence imported fundamentally literary considerations into judgments of probity, Pierre Bourdieu has reminded us that the competency of speakers to employ a given narrative is a feature of social relations.[5] On the other hand, we must consider the appropriateness of courts of law as the paradigmatic representative of women's disenfranchisement in women's narratives. If a persuasive figure of beset manhood could be drawn from women's narratives for use in actual criminal proceedings, might these narratives be seen as mystifying the true sources of women's oppression and demonizing the law in favor of private moral reform? That is, do these literary critiques of law *on behalf of women* participate in the fundamentally conservative aestheticization of reform so strikingly exemplified by Dickens's attack on Chancery in *Bleak House*? Counterexamples to these overdetermined failures of representation are afforded by Charles Reade's dissemination of legal literacy in *Griffith Gaunt,* a virtual "how-to" guide to *pro se* representation by women, and the remarkable success of Georgina Weldon's *pro se* litigations in the wake of the Married Women's Property Act. Unlike his canonical contemporaries, Dickens and Eliot, Reade maintained faith in the law's capacity to hear and respond justly to the arguments of the disenfranchised, and sought to equip readers with the forensic and procedural literacy to make their cases. Still, it took a transformation in women's legal status to realize this hope.

Part 4, on motive, returns to the figure of the witch and the unintended consequences of exposing *mens rea* through a feminist epistemology that privileges women's knowledge and the empathic powers of literary narrative. In a chapter of *Technologies of Gender* entitled "Gaudy Rose," Theresa de Lauretis juxtaposes the woman burned as a witch in Umberto Eco's *The Name of the Rose* with Dorothy Sayers's novel of detection and women's education, *Gaudy Night,* to expose the mechanisms by which technologies of knowledge reproduce and enforce gender hierarchy. De Lauretis offers sophisticated deconstructions of the masculinist epistemologies that render women's knowledge incomprehensible, just as the screams of the burning peasant woman are gibberish to Eco's male narrator. But the pitfalls of a distinctively feminist epistemology as a strategy of legal advocacy are evident in Mary Carpenter's misappropriation of narrative based on literary constructions of female expertise and fictional access to *mens rea* through omniscient narration. Carpenter was recognized as the preeminent expert on the causes of juvenile delinquency, and an influential proponent of empirical evidence—including verbatim reports of incarcerated children's stories—as the basis of humane legal responses to child crime. Nevertheless, she was susceptible to a narrative that purported to offer access to the *mens rea* of incarcerated women, taken in by the power of omniscient narration coupled with assumptions about female empathy. After a career of countering sensationalistic novels celebrating a life of crime for gullible young readers with the voices of real children, Carpenter herself could not resist the expertise in others' minds afforded only by fiction. What she believed to be the authentic memoirs of a prison matron, who brought her feminine powers of empathy to bear on reporting the thoughts of female charges, was revealed to have been written by Frederick William Robinson, the author of scores of pulp novels, none of which ever achieved the popularity or sales of the Prison Matron's narratives.

In the remainder of chapter 8, I juxtapose with Carpenter's fictional quest for knowledge of other minds an alternative strategy of literary advocacy aimed at concealing the motives of women accused of infanticide. Nineteenth-century legal reforms, decisions by judges and juries, doctors' testimony, and later, police practice, all belied a desire to shield women from prosecution and punishment for infanticide. Literary treatments of infanticide (including romantic ballads and novels such as *Adam Bede*) contributed to this effort to protect women from the state by elaborating a representation of infanticide that insisted on its private character—a strategy that remains successful, if limiting, in securing reproductive rights today.[6] The success of this representational strategy, demanding cooperation among the professions of law, medicine, and literature—which have been theorized as constituting themselves through the disciplinary objectification of women—complicates arguments regarding the violence of representation. Thanks in large part to Foucault's analyses of nineteenth-century medical discourses and their broad impact on social policies, we are well aware of the power of what Mary Poovey has termed "anatomical realism" to objectify, scrutinize, and discipline the social body.[7] But greater attention must be paid to the fact that resistance to scientific investigation of the social body came not only from the disenfranchised but also from within institutions and privileged classes simultaneously defending their own interests and those of victimized women with the aid of literary narratives.

In the concluding chapter, this possibility is even more strikingly illustrated by the 1871 trial of Boulton and Park for conspiracy to commit sodomy. The success of the cover story used in their defense depended upon the tacit agreement among various privileged males to conceal certain forms of evidence from speculatory technologies, and pitted them against the rising professions of medicine and forensic science. As such, they focus particular attention on what Barbara Shapiro has termed the "black box" of legal history—jury decision making, which is at once crucial to gauging the success of various forms of outsider advocacy and utterly unavailable to historical research. In order to suggest how we might read for cover stories in legal cases, I juxtapose the transcript of *Regina v. Boulton, et al.* with Trollope's *Orley Farm* (1862), a novel about a female forger, whose omniscient narrator gives us access not only to *mens rea* but also to the motives of legal decision makers on whose sympathetic tacit cooperation "motherhood," as a forged identity necessary to bourgeois social relations, depends. Analogous to Carlo Ginzburg's strategy of reading between the lines in witchcraft trials to infer the voices of the accused, the omniscient narration of realist novels affords indirect evidence of jury decision making and how oppositional solidarity could be formed tacitly by privileged men sitting in judgment of their peers. This context sheds new light on the Labouchère Amendment, "the blackmailer's charter," which threatened to reveal a criminalized *mens rea* against the interests of extralegal solidarities.

My choice of these cautionary tales about gendered advocacy as the endpoint of *Reading for the Law* is in part logistical. It will take another volume, and other expertise, to pursue this argument into the twentieth century when women attain suffrage. But it is also intrinsic to my thesis regarding the relevance of historical scholarship, and to my contention that the conditions of the dynamic between literature and law change for women when literature is no longer their primary or, indeed, their sole method of engagement with the political sphere. The great imponderable raised by my argument is whether the preponderance of Victorian realist novels adduced in Law and Literature scholarship is a form of nostalgia not only for a romanticized literary public sphere but also for a time before classic liberal remedies for injustice were tried and, perhaps, found wanting. That is, as Habermas remarks, feminism in the twentieth century has exposed the gap between *de jure* and *de facto* legal recognition.[8] While it remains to be seen whether the literary imagination can assist legal decision makers and advocates alike in achieving *de facto* legal recognition for women—and others—the account of literary and legal history I offer here is intended to inform our assessment of this proposition. Historical narrative jurisprudence needs to be part of a feminist, legal, and literary education.

It is a truism of interdisciplinary study that human problems do not fit neatly into disciplinary categories. Nevertheless, attention to the practices of discrete disciplines provides not only carefully honed methodologies and forms of evidence but also crucial critiques of other disciplines' assumptions. I am aware of the demands interdisciplinary scholarship places on readers' patience, as groundwork from a familiar discipline is laid for the benefit of scholars in other fields, or where mistakes (inevitable, perhaps) are made in translating concepts or evidence from one discipline into another. But the risks incurred by the interdisciplinary scholar are, I believe, worthwhile. I can only hope that my readers find their patience rewarded.

Toward a Historical Narrative Jurisprudence

At the stage in his *Lectures on the Relation between Law and Public Opinion in England* where he addressed the political consequences of historical jurisprudence produced by the great legal scholars Sir Frederick Pollock and Frederic William Maitland, A. V. Dicey disparagingly remarked: "Historical research . . . tends to quench the confident enthusiasm necessary for carrying out even the most well approved and the most beneficial among democratic innovations."[9] Like Sir Henry Sumner Maine before them, Pollock and Maitland challenged the positivist jurisprudential theory of Dicey's hero, John Austin, dragging law back into the mire of precedent and historical processes against Austin's efforts to liberate it as a science. Though Maitland, at least, believed legal history had utility in that it taught the "lesson that each generation has an enormous power of shaping its own law," Dicey saw historicism as undermining faith in legislative change and abetting the conservative mystification of law.[10] For Dicey, history was both theoretically and practically incompatible with the efficacious advocacy of legal reform.

My contention in *Reading for the Law* is that a multidisciplinary "historical narrative jurisprudence" would strengthen the claims of narrative legal theorists for the transformative powers of stories by replacing an ahistorical opposition between literature and law with a history of their mutual dependency, and the embeddedness of stories in material culture, specifically print culture.

Whereas historicism is no longer characterized as antithetical to progressive political change, as Dicey viewed it, substantial barriers remain to the uses of literary history in the democratic project to extend legal recognition. Some of these are ideological, but many, too, stem from confusion over the diverse meanings of history and historicism in various disciplines. In law, history may be restricted to the significance of precedent, or it may be associated with the Marxism of the early Critical Legal Studies movement. In feminist legal advocacy, it can be adduced for evidence of a pattern of oppression, whereas some feminist theorists counter such empiricist historiography with psychoanalytic trauma theory. In literary criticism, it may refer to scholarship on such disparate topics as influence or publication conditions, or it may signal a New Historicist preference for "thick history" and historical rupture.

Narrative legal theory has proposed storytelling as a solution to the problem of attaining legal recognition on the grounds that it allows for testimony regarding "life contexts," or alternative realities, excluded by normative rules of evidence, and that it enables privileged legal decision makers to empathize with people whose experiences and constraints may be very different from their own. Some practitioners have taken a formalist tack, insisting on the probative force of narrative sequencing and "realistic" detail, while others have promoted autobiographical writing as unmediated self-expression. But narrative legal theory has been hampered by its ahistorical appeals to stories. As critics of Victorian culture well appreciate, narrative is not removed from politics and the marketplace, off in some autonomous Kantian category of the aesthetic. Neither should it be construed as offering some uniquely efficacious means of advocacy or an "antidote" to law, understood as positivistic, rule-bound, and oppressive. Indeed, as Jane B. Baron has cautioned, we should not seek to empty law of its imaginative and interpretive elements.[11] By claiming history as a productive meeting ground for feminist advocacy, legal theory, and literary history, I am not proposing to replace law or literature with history as yet a new privileged discourse. History does not have some unique explanatory power, nor does it offer a perfect solution to the conceptual and ideological difficulties we face in trying to secure social justice. Indeed, I define the historical scope of each section as I do in order to argue that literary history supplies a critique of both law and literature as privileged tools of feminist advocacy if it proceeds from two premises: (1) the validity of continuous history and (2) the inextricability of storytelling in modernity from the history of democratic social formation, capitalism, and mass culture technologies, a link forged in the nineteenth century. In these respects, historical jurisprudence avoids the pitfalls of cultural studies, as advocated by Binder and Weisberg, which ultimately denies the historian's—and legal theorist's—own embeddedness by detaching the historical anecdote from the processes of which it is a part and inviting us to "choos[e] what kind of culture we hope to have and what identities we hope to foster."[12] Feminist advocates and narrative legal theorists alike must insist that individual choice is constrained, and that we work provisionally within institutional, technological, and discursive processes that make us as we make them.

Historical narrative jurisprudence can delineate the residual elements in the project of Law and Literature, both as an impetus to critique and as a source of unrecognized strengths. Our inherited conceptions of justice have been imagined across a variety of discourses, literature and law each making distinctive contributions and offering salutary mutual critiques. A historical narrative jurisprudence must acknowledge not only the historical integration of propositional and narrative reasoning, objectivity and sympathy, rationality and imagination, in emancipatory projects, but also the ways in which storytelling is implicated in a history of the politics of print culture—above all, the uneven distribution of narrative capital and the commodification of storytelling. In addition to its critical value, this literary history demonstrates how communicative action has functioned to recognize the other, not by pitting the literary imagination against propositional reasoning, but by forging a more comprehensive rationality necessary for imagining the institutions and practices of a democratic state. Finally, the literary history of the long nineteenth century in particular also enables us to accord narrative jurisprudence an important place in the "*achievement* of [our] own history" and helps to restore the position of jurisprudence in public debate.[13]

Historical literary criticism, with its focus on the interrelations among authorial and reading practices and material conditions, offers a point of engagement between narrative jurisprudence and its critics. While it is doubtless galling that the discussion of Law and Literature once seemed preoccupied with such unsympathetic critiques as Richard Posner's *Law and Literature*, it might also be argued that the continuing engagement between the two late-twentieth-century manifestations of the aesthetic-rationalist dialectic has produced some salutary revisions, including by Judge Posner himself.[14] In Martha C. Nussbaum's view, the literary imagination supplements rule-based reasoning and, I would add, is dialectically related to other forms of knowing, including the analysis of empirical data and logical deduction.[15] When one of the founders of the Law and Literature movement, Richard Weisberg, turns to the Holocaust, he reminds us of the enduring importance of what Elizabeth Gaskell, speaking of the historical traces of witchcraft prosecutions, termed "hard facts."[16] Maintaining the negotiations between the world of words and the world of things is a hallmark of both nineteenth-century literary realism and liberal democratic theory. Rather than demonize legal reasoning and forms of evidence as the enemy of emancipatory narratives, we might remember our common goals and encourage a popular legal culture that engages the public imagination in representations of the full scope of human experience.

The value of this more capacious historical account of narrative may be illustrated by contrast with the practice recommended by Guyora Binder and Robert Weisberg in their *Literary Criticisms of Law*. In their comprehensive, well-informed critique of the major strains of the movement, these legal theorists analyze a broad range of the reading strategies and theoretical positions that legal scholars have borrowed from literary study—hermeneutics, narrative theory, rhetorical criticism, deconstruction—criticizing them for everything from sentimentality to cynicism, misconceptions to misrepresentations. They conclude not by dismissing the relevance of literary criticism, or at least the linguistic turn, to legal reform, but rather by vigorously endorsing cultural criticism as the appropriate paradigm for a transformative legal scholarship. A cultural criticism of the law, as Binder and Weisberg put it, "is part of the work—at once political and aesthetic—of choosing what kind of culture we hope to have and what identities we hope to foster."[17]

The examples of cultural criticism with which Binder and Weisberg illustrate their claims, drawn as they are from diverse historical periods and cultures, immediately suggest two questions to a critic of nineteenth-century literature.[18] First, in practicing aesthetic analyses of social texts, would cultural critics of the law necessarily take literary discourses as their subject matter? Though literary criticism is closely associated with cultural criticism, both in its origins and current practice, there is no necessary connection between the two, and literature is hardly the prerequisite subject matter of cultural criticism.[19] Indeed, for some cultural critics, to speak of the "literary" is to reinstate the very transcendent categories of Kantian aesthetics that cultural criticism aims to deconstruct. New Historicism comes in for praise from Binder and Weisberg, and its emergence in literary criticism—especially the work of Stephen Greenblatt—is recognized, but only insofar as it has contributed to the elaboration of cultural criticism, where literature holds no special place.[20] And second, why should the cultural critic of law with the aspirational goals cited above choose to practice her art on the cultural artifacts of one historical period rather than another? What, that is, governs the relationship between cultural history and contemporary legal reform? Binder and Weisberg are well aware of the varieties of cultural criticism and reject both the "'Romantic' critique of modernization" and its project of demystification, suggesting instead a third, which aims "not to recover virtues of the heroic age but to fashion new ones."[21] But what remains to be elaborated in their model is a theory of the history of aesthetics and politics that explains its usefulness and consequences. This is a task literary historians, particularly of nineteenth-century British culture, are well suited to perform.

The one striking deficiency in Binder and Weisberg's survey of literary criticisms of law is the absence of any systematic attention to historical narrative scholarship. *Literary Criticisms of Law* opens with a brief history of the relationship between law and literature, anemic by contrast with the robust analyses of literary theories in the rest of the volume. Law and Literature, in this account, is inescapably tainted with the origins of "literature" as an autonomous category in the contemplative, subjectivist, and naïve thought of British and American Romanticism.[22] The history of literature, as they present it, serves mainly to disqualify literature from participation in the legal and political domains.[23] Like Binder and Weisberg, I too have criticized the ahistorical formalism of much Narrative Legal Theory.[24] I would not, however, so hastily abandon the claims that aspects of literary form have particular cognitive and phenomenological import, as narrative ethicists have also argued. Nor would I uncritically embrace (as Weisberg and Binder apparently do) the historiographic principles implicit in some forms of cultural criticism, which might militate against accounts of continuity in favor of anecdote and disjunction and obscure the processes by which disenfranchised groups engage in the ongoing project of attaining recognition. Literary discourse has played a crucial role in this process as a principal means by which disenfranchised and even criminalized people participated in the formation of an informal political sphere.[25]

Rather than analyzing literature's claims to transcendence as itself a *political* phenomenon—an antidemocratic reaction against radical and feminist political theory, as David Simpson has argued, and a crucial example of literature's inescapable embeddedness in economics, professional culture, technological developments, and so on—Binder and Weisberg seem to take one Romantic conception of literature as a fait accompli. Scholars of nineteenth-century culture might think they have missed a golden opportunity to point to a historical moment when literary discourse had become so profoundly influential a tool of political transformation that political adversaries sought to claim exclusive rights to its use. What is more, merely by locating the historical origins of some forms of the Law and Literature argument, Binder and Weisberg cannot by fiat undo their own place within this history. If cultural criticism is to be a genuinely useful, and a genuinely *literary* criticism of law, then it must make the case that the decision to approach the law through literature was not accidental, or misguided, but implicated in the historical relationship between the two forms of discourse and as such historically meaningful.

Of course, cultural criticism itself owes much to scholars of nineteenth-century British literature and culture, notably Raymond Williams and E. P. Thompson.[26] It should not be surprising that there has been a remarkable outpouring of interdisciplinary studies of law in nineteenth-century literature by literary critics. The scholarship of Brook Thomas, Wai-Chee Dimock, and Laura Hanft Korobkin has extended the arguments about law in nineteenth-century American literature first put forward by Robert A. Ferguson.[27] Alexander Welsh's *Strong Representations: Narrative and Circumstantial Evidence in England* played a similarly germinal role in British studies, and recent scholarship on nineteenth-century British literature and law has yielded new insight into the related ethical functions of equity law and literary discourse (Dieter Paul Polloczek), constructions of testimonial evidence in law, literature, and theology (Jan-Melissa Schramm), the interplay between narrative form and legal reasoning (Kieran Dolin), and the impact of censorship rulings on theories of culture in the age of mass publication (Barbara Leckie).[28] I share the dissatisfaction Binder and Weisberg express with the skepticism of some forms of cultural criticism, and I concede that much work on eighteenth- and nineteenth-century culture, especially that produced from within a Foucauldian model of the rise of the carceral state, might be seen to "quench the confident enthusiasm necessary for carrying out even the most well approved and the most beneficial among democratic innovations." The hermeneutics of suspicion have caused literary critics to retreat from celebratory claims to more cautious, if not downright cynical, positions about the politics of literary representation. Realist literature figures prominently in arguments promoting the benefits of storytelling in law, but it does not resemble many literary critics' historicized version of realism as a set of conventions particularly suited to the disciplinary aims of bourgeois patriarchy in a phase of liberalism and capitalism.[29] Familiar texts such as Dickens's *Hard Times* seem foreign when we encounter them in arguments extolling their power to effect sympathetic identification because we have been alerted to their interpellation of readers into bourgeois ideology in the guise of advocacy for the disenfranchised. It should be noted here as well that autobiography, central to the project of outsider narrative jurisprudence, likewise carries with it an ethically ambiguous history. Aware of the constructed nature of this popular genre, not to mention the coercive features of confession, we must hesitate before claims that outsiders should be invited to share their life stories in courts of law.[30] Ruling-class interest in the stories of the disenfranchised has gone hand in hand with a desire to possess them, or as Judith R. Walkowitz terms it (speaking of Victorian social investigators such as Henry Mayhew), to achieve "intrapsychic incorporation."[31] These assertions regarding the historical complicity in oppressive practices of the very narrative genres to which narrative jurisprudence typically appeals contain the basis for poststructuralist legal theorists' critiques of narrative jurisprudence, and as such, they must be addressed.[32]

The challenge is to establish the unique import for narrative legal theory of this historical literary scholarship, what David Simpson in a related context identifies as the "strong continuities" between nineteenth-century British culture and our own.[33] Kieran Dolin remarks upon the absence from most cultural histories of law and literature of a discussion of "the interrelation of the two disciplines in specific societies, as practiced by Ferguson and Thomas, or Weisberg in his studies of Vichy France."[34] That interrelation for narrative jurisprudence in contemporary Anglo-American legal scholarship itself has a history in the formation of democratic states. The many revisions of Jürgen Habermas's account of an eighteenth-century informal public sphere created through literary discourse suggest the folly of locating an absolute origin for the interdiscipline of Law and Literature.[35] Still, for anyone committed to making legal systems more responsive to women, to racial, sexual, and ethnic minorities, or to the economically disadvantaged, the nineteenth century, which saw an astonishing growth in literacy and authorship by these groups, must be seen as continuous with current practices.

We might begin by historicizing narrative jurisprudence itself, the project of reading law as a social text embedded in the matrix of narratives by which society is organized. Kathryn Abrams associates the turn to narrative in legal scholarship with the postmodern critiques of objectivity in the history of science and philosophy, replacing objective proofs with strategies of persuasion.[36] But we might instead see narrative jurisprudence as an extension of the process of articulating and legitimating a view of the state wherein order would be produced not through abject obedience to awful power but through sympathy and sensibility—fundamentally aesthetic faculties. As William Roscoe put the problem in 1819, "The question would no longer be, whether stripes and bloodshed can prevail against guilt and ignorance, but whether sympathy, prudence, and compassion, have lost their influence on the moral feelings of mankind."[37] Citing Roscoe, Randall McGowen claims that nineteenth-century legal reform was directly related to aestheticization, the promulgation of "an ideal of social union founded upon subjective feelings" wherein "sympathetic bonds were expected to produce a social order far more smoothly regulated than that of any preceding civilization."[38] On this view, public opinion, and eventually representational democracy, would necessarily take on new significance, since laws could be legitimated only in terms of their general benefit.

Narrative would play a crucial role in making mass democracy in the course of the nineteenth century by providing what Patrick Joyce has termed "political subjectivities which created agency and legitimacy."[39] Noting that "the 'contractual' and 'institutional' capacity of literary genres implicitly attributes to them an explanatory function that is both epistemological and social," Michael McKeon asserts that "genres provide a conceptual framework for the mediation (if not the 'solution') of intractable problems, a method for rendering such problems intelligible."[40] For twentieth-century narrative jurisprudence, as for the first theorists of representational democracy within bourgeois capitalism, those intractable problems center on representation itself and its functions of mediating between facts and values, dominant and subordinate social groups, social constructions and the world outside of words.

In light of these "strong continuities," it should not be surprising that law and literature scholars have relied so extensively—if not self-consciously—on nineteenth-century literary texts to bolster their claims. Although narrative legal scholars regularly discuss other texts—notably, Plato's dialogues, *The Merchant of Venice,* and *Measure for Measure*—nineteenth-century novels seem to have special attractions. Richard Weisberg devotes a chapter to Dickens's lawyers in his germinal study *Poethics,* where he claims that "fiction about law continues to uncover better than any other medium the private lives of lawyers . . . and compels us to recognize that lawyers' private lives directly affect their public performances."[41] Both Richard Rorty and Martha Nussbaum use Dickens to illustrate how the imagination and emotions assist in just decision making. Rorty names

Dickens among the authors whose novels provide "the details about kinds of suffering being endured by people to whom we had previously not attended," a reason why the novel is among "the principal vehicles of moral change and progress."[42] Dickens's *Hard Times* figures prominently in Nussbaum's book *Poetic Justice,* where she writes: "I defend the literary imagination precisely because it seems to me an essential ingredient of an ethical stance that asks us to concern ourselves with the good of other people whose lives are distant from our own."[43]

Not only are acknowledged poets of interest to narrative jurisprudence, however, but so are "outsiders"—women, workers, people of color—the very groups whose stories began to enter into public discourse in significant numbers in the nineteenth century.[44] Whereas Richard Weisberg and James Boyd White (like Rorty and Nussbaum) turn to canonical texts to educate the legal imagination, another group of narrative jurisprudence advocates, such as Kathryn Abrams and Richard Delgado, privileges the stories of historically disenfranchised authors. For these feminist and Critical Race theorists, narrative jurisprudence must encompass storytelling generally if it genuinely seeks knowledge of "people to whom we had previously not attended," for their stories may not be recognizable as "literature" at all. Once again, historians of nineteenth-century culture find themselves on familiar ground, since our domain has comprehended not only William Wordsworth and Matthew Arnold but also Mary Wollstonecraft and George Eliot, William Cobbett and Hannah More, Elizabeth Barrett Browning and Ellen Johnston (the "Factory Girl" poet), as well as the texts of so-called popular culture, from *Reynolds's Newspaper* (for the working classes) to melodramas such as *Black-eyed Susan.* Narrative jurisprudence appears committed to nineteenth-century politico-aesthetic projects, such as that set out by Thomas Carlyle, who urged his reform-minded contemporaries to inquire into working men's beliefs. To the question "What is just?" Carlyle wrote in *Chartism* (1840): "The words they promulgate are notable by way of answer, and their actions are still more notable. Chartism with its spikes, Swing with its tinderbox, speak a loud though inarticulate language."[45] Familiar with historical versions of such arguments, we are sympathetic to the claim that outsiders' stories enable typically privileged decision makers to empathize with subjects whose constraints and needs are unfamiliar.

While both Terry Eagleton and John McGowan analyze a phenomenon of "high culture," perhaps the most remarkable result of the integration of rational and aesthetic reasoning is the burgeoning popular legal culture of the nineteenth century. Lawrence M. Friedman, discussing contemporary America, uses the term "popular legal culture" to refer to "the mind-set of the people who interact with legal institutions—lay people, bankers, merchants, policemen, women who want a divorce, and so on."[46] Carol J. Clover emphasizes the global impact of American popular legal culture in the form of film, television, and novelistic treatments of legal processes, noting that "Swedes and Spanish [*sic*] know more about the American legal system than their own."[47] Popular legal culture is arguably coincident with legal culture itself, but the peculiar features of modern popular legal culture evolve with the bourgeois state, wherein the literary and legal, the rational and aesthetic, are wholly intertwined. No less an observer of democratic institutions than de Tocqueville believed that trial by jury "extends the habit [of legal thought] to all classes. The language of the law thus becomes, in some measure, a vulgar tongue; the spirit of the law, which is produced in the schools and courts of justice, gradually penetrates beyond their walls into the bosom of society, where it descends to the lowest class, so that at last the whole people contract the habits and tastes of the judicial magistrate."[48] In the nineteenth century, to an unprecedented degree, a wide range of laypeople spoke back to the law and represented the law to itself in the form of published documents—pamphlets, ballads, melodramas, novels—which came to be called public opinion. The Queen Caroline affair, the Tichborne Claimant movement, or the Armstrong case arising out of "The Maiden Tribute of Modern Babylon" are only a few of the most celebrated examples of a new mass popular legal culture, in which arises what Dror Wahrman has called "the metapolitical jurisdiction of 'public opinion.'"[49] That new jurisdiction results from, among other things, the specific conditions that enabled engagements between the legal and literary.

Furthermore, it reveals the dialectical relationship between lawyers and laypersons mediated through narratives. If the law had ever been an autonomous institution, as Sir Edward Coke had imagined, it certainly ceased to be under these conditions. If anything, the more centralized the legal system became, the more new economic and social practices and new technologies conspired to reinstate the face-to-face engagement that had characterized local justice. What is more, the evidence of an evolving literate popular legal culture demonstrates the fallacy of a category of subjects incapable of legal agency. Douglas Hay's analysis of malicious prosecutions brought by the poor against their masters in the eighteenth and nineteenth centuries is relevant to popular legal culture generally. Hay claims that only "naïve sociology, or uncritical jurisprudence, or unimaginative history" denies legal agency to all but a ruling elite. Speaking of the poor and middling ranks who went to law, Hay concludes that "when they could, they used [the law], or least what parts of it they knew and could afford. . . . And when they succeeded in those purposes, parts of the law, its rhetoric, its instruments, acquired a legitimacy they otherwise would not have had."[50] Hay's remark also reminds us that when laypeople become legal actors, they both shape, and are shaped by, legal culture. Indeed, as Martha Vicinus has argued, the very literary forms imposed on working-class writers who wished to engage public opinion required them to "struggle to create and sustain a distinctive literature in the face of bourgeois economic and cultural control."[51] The dialectics of popular legal culture—lawyers with laypeople, literature with law—involved all its participants in one another's belief systems and discourses.

This picture of the history of narrative jurisprudence includes a decision-making elite prone to aestheticism and sentimentality and disenfranchised storytellers who resort to narrative in order to get a hearing for their empirically verifiable claims. It is hardly for trivial reasons, then, that nineteenth-century writers were interested in the law, or that contemporary narrative legal scholars so often recur to them. How is it, then, that we have come to see storytelling and legal reasoning as mutually exclusive, so much so that a whole movement now devotes itself to reconnecting them? And, remembering the circumstances under which they were once joined, why—if they are now separated—should we desire their reunion?

Urging a historicist perspective on cultural legal critics, Rosemary Coombe has argued that we "attend to the various ways in which the terms [law and culture] have been historically articulated, while recognizing the political stakes of their current destabilizations and restabilizations in struggles enacted in multiple forums." She continues,

> Rather than definitively and authoritatively elaborate the appropriate form of their intersection, we might become more critically cognizant of the historical forces always already at work in the world articulating this relationship. We might position ourselves to address how relationships between law and culture have been established and maintained in the world, effecting new distributions of wealth and new inequalities of power, legitimating some identities and delegitimating others, recognizing some communities of self-fashioning while prohibiting others, provoking new identifications and disrupting others.

Coombe argues that "this endeavor will demand more than an abstract or linguistically modeled 'constitutivism.' . . . To do so would be to recognize culture as signification, but also to address its materiality: to recognize both the signifying power of law and law's power over signification as evidenced in concrete struggles over meaning and their political consequence."[52]

What I wish to develop in the chapters that follow is a practice of historical narrative jurisprudence that heeds Coombe's advice. I seek to make historical narrative jurisprudence more "critically cognizant of the historical forces always already at work in the world articulating [its own] relationship" between law and literature and to establish the material and discursive conditions of nineteenth-century print culture as a position from which narrative jurisprudence can engage "concrete struggles over meaning and their political consequence." As I have suggested above, the various roles of literature in nineteenth-century emancipatory movements afford an important *critical* perspective on contemporary narrative legal theory. But it is also *positive*. The peculiar saliency of the heritage of nineteenth-century literary culture includes its place in an Anglo-American politico-legal tradition that produces the very conditions of cultural legal critics' aspirations for meaningful social transformation in modern, multicultural democracies. As with Habermas's notion of "constitutional patriotism," the loyalty that a culturally diverse citizenry accords democratic institutions and procedures because they are "the *achievement* of their own history," this cultural heritage is a history to which every citizen of modern, multicultural societies should stake a claim.[53] It is a key context in which the institutions of modern democracy—political bodies and legal procedures as well as schools, the press, public opinion, special interest groups—were formed, and a still powerful source of narratives about rationality, agency, rights, and *social change*, or history itself. Engagement with this history affords a critical self-consciousness, but it also provides a uniquely valuable perspective from which we can judge "what kinds of culture we hope to have and what kind of identities we hope to foster," since many of the aspirations of nineteenth-century emancipatory projects have yet to be realized.

PART ONE

Precedent

CHAPTER ONE

Historiographies of Witchcraft for Feminist Advocacy

Historical Justice in Elizabeth Gaskell's *Lois the Witch*

PRECEDENT AND TRAUMA are historiographic concepts describing continuity or persistence of a phenomenon over time. Both theorize how even the distant past may remain—for better or worse—a living force. Neither, however, accounts for change, attaching instead to acts of obsessive repetition. The prosecution of witches may seem a topic remote from any aspect of gender advocacy on which Victorianist literary critics and narrative legal theorists might productively converse. Felony sorcery legislation was repealed in Britain just over a century before Victoria ascended the throne. And yet, as precedent and trauma, witchcraft prosecution survived, not only into the nineteenth century but also into our own time. Elizabeth Gaskell's 1859 story *Lois the Witch* illustrates a host of interconnected reasons why a study of literature and law arguments appealing to Victorian texts needs to be historicized by examining earlier trends and critiquing our own ideological investments in the past.

First, *Lois the Witch* is an example of historical fiction, a major Victorian subgenre that would reward greater attention from narrative legal theorists. Women writers used historical fiction as a form of advocacy to denaturalize culturally and legally constructed gender roles by identifying the particular circumstances that produced them.[1] Second, *Lois the Witch* contributes to a significant body of work—literary, legal, and historical—that attempts to explain the motives of witchcraft prosecution, especially whether witch-hunting was woman-hunting. Third, it treats an instance of witchcraft prosecution that foregrounds its most challenging feature for historians, *viz.*, its sporadic occurrence under Anglo-American law. Statute law and its applications in common law create precedents that should conform to a relatively continuous history, and critics of witchcraft prosecutions from the early modern period onward certainly feared the precedents set by their anomalous rules of evidence. Defying conventional historical paradigms, however, witchcraft prosecutions occurred in clusters between the first English legislation in 1542 and its repeal in 1736, putting extraordinary pressure on historians to account for the distinctive local causes of each spate of prosecutions, as well as long periods of quiescence. Fourth, the principal sources of historical evidence of witchcraft prosecution are not legal documents, few of which are extant, but literary ones, including treatises, controversial literature, popular "true crime" literature, ballads, plays, and histories. As such, the witchcraft prosecution and attempts to explain it are profoundly influenced by the dynamics of print culture, from the explosion of printed matter that coincided with the first witchcraft legislation, to antiquarian reprintings of witchcraft literature in the eighteenth and nineteenth centuries, to the rise of documentary history, New Historicism, and feminist theory. Finally, theories as to the motives, occurrences, and targets of witchcraft prosecution, based largely on literary evidence, have produced wildly competing claims right down to our own time. These theories often tell us as much about the gender politics of the period in which they were produced as they do about witchcraft prosecution as a historical phenomenon. Powerful among those theories is one that poses witchcraft prosecution as the paradigmatic event defining women's relationship with the law as traumatic. Gaskell's story intervenes in the historiographic debates of her own time and their implications for feminist advocacy; examining her strategies in the context of the history she inherited allows us to critique the ideological claims and historiographic methods of our contemporaries.

Witches have a secure home in the history of gender advocacy. In its effort to exclude them from legitimate community—indeed, to define community in contradistinction to witchcraft—the law wrote witches into its precedents. For their part, witches have lived up to their reputation as troubling and troublesome guests, generating problems of evidence, interpretation, and advocacy since early modern Englishmen first tried them in courts of law. How early modern English witchcraft prosecution set a precedent for advocacy based on gender is far from obvious, however. Skeptical critiques of witchcraft prosecution, beginning with Reginald Scot's 1584 *The Discoverie of Witchcraft,* are among the original instances of gender advocacy in Britain. Scot was the first to advocate for the abolition of witchcraft prosecution because, among other reasons, it victimized poor old women. Despite Scot's anecdotal evidence of a gender bias in witchcraft prosecution, his strategy of gender advocacy was enormously influential. Following Scot, virtually all writers on witchcraft prosecution—pro and con—repeated the assumption that women made up the bulk of defendants in witchcraft trials. Historical jurisprudence, an approach to law credited with encouraging rational progressive reform, was founded by Sir Matthew Hale, who presided at the 1662 trial in which two women were convicted of witchcraft and executed. Every subsequent legal historian and theorist celebrating Hale's contribution has been forced to address this "anomaly." In 1718, eighteen years prior to the repeal of the felony sorcery legislation, Royal Society member Sir Henry More branded critics of witchcraft prosecution "Hag-Advocates." Nevertheless, it is far from clear that gender advocacy was anything more than a strategy in an argument that was entirely about things other than "hags": politics, the monarchy, and professional rivalries between men, as well as the dynamics of print culture itself.

Anthropological, Marxist, psychoanalytic, ethnographic, as well as feminist theories have been used to interpret the substantial body of documents generated by prosecutions under the felony sorcery legislation. "We suffer from no lack of theoretical positions as we continue our attempts to understand witchcraft," writes James Sharpe; "the issue . . . is to get to grips with the phenomenon as it was experienced in the past."[2] Or, as Bernard Rosenthal remarks regarding the Salem witch trials, the subject of *Lois the Witch,* "They resist being subsumed under a single, overall theory; but when elements of the narrative are pieced together, they reveal a comprehensible tale. . . . The methodological challenge is to find reasonable conclusions, generalizations at times, that do more than impose one more myth upon the Salem witch trials."[3] On no point is the methodological challenge more vexing than on the significance of gender.

Engaging this challenge enables literary critics and legal scholars to examine their disciplines' historiographic assumptions and commitments as they have determined the course of gender advocacy. Without an understanding of their historiographic differences, literary and legal scholars are apt to talk past one another and miss common ground. In the rich literature of the witch trials, storytelling and interpretation, normative, empirical, rational, and empathic modes of legal reasoning, discursive constructions of gender and deviance, and the law's relationship to elite and popular belief systems, all conjoin. The questions we are apt to pose to contemporary cultures of evidence resonate with the witchcraft prosecutions as well in such a way as to denaturalize any assumptions about the emancipatory or subversive qualities of narrative or the exclusionary and oppressive effects of rule-based or empirical reasoning.

The history of gender advocacy in witchcraft controversies bears more directly on the intersections between Victorian literature and narrative legal theory, however. By tracing legal and literary precedents and traumatic repetitions of witchcraft narratives from the early modern period to Victorian realism, it is possible to discern how specifically Victorian phenomena, including the rise of historical jurisprudence, feminist anthropology, and folklore studies, and the proliferation of antiquarian reprinting projects within the context of mass-circulation print culture, required mediation of a debilitating legacy of misogyny through the evidentiary conventions of realism. Understandably, Victorianists have concentrated on Enlightenment and Romantic precursors, and it is not surprising, therefore, that legal theorists appealing to Victorian literature have ignored that the early modern precedents governing their discipline might exert power over literary narratives as well. To illustrate the significance of Victorian realism as an antidote to the obsessive repetitions that mark much historical witchcraft literature as well as contemporary efforts to theorize it, I begin this chapter by offering a reading of Elizabeth Gaskell's *Lois the Witch* as a example of the complex—and therapeutic—response to the legal and literary legacy of the witchcraft trials afforded by realism. Unlike Enlightenment feminism, the subject of part 2 of this book, Gaskell's realist treatment of witchcraft prosecution engages history, comprising legal precedent, psychic trauma, and the interpretation of historical and forensic evidence, all necessary to moving beyond the obsessive repetition of what had grown to become a defining experience of women and the law. By recovering this history, and Gaskell's realist response to it, narrative legal theorists can better understand their own epistemological and political commitments—particularly their reliance on Victorian realist literature. At the same time it more fully explains the appeal of Victorian realism to narrative legal theorists. Contextualizing Victorian narrative within this long history, paralleling such well-established accounts of the rise of the novel as J. Paul Hunter's, Michael McKeon's, and Ian Watt's, enriches Victorianists' appreciation of realism as a progressive political force. It can also provide new perspectives from which feminists can face the history of women and the law.

Elizabeth Gaskell made only brief use of a nom de plume, though one that deserves as much scrutiny as "George Eliot" or "Currer Bell." Gaskell's first fiction appeared under the name of Cotton Mather Mills, an odd juxtaposition of a seventeenth-century colonial Puritan with a nineteenth-century Manchester industry. The proximity of the two worlds comprised in this name seems designed to unsettle, evoking on the one hand spiritual fanaticism, delusions, and witchcraft trials, and on the other materialism, political economy, and exploited labor. As we will see in chapters 2 and 3, for historians, from Mather's contemporaries to Gaskell's, the phenomenon of the witchcraft trials posed a haunting problem, challenging fundamental propositions regarding reasonable belief, rules of evidence, and the progress from superstition to enlightenment. Gaskell specialized in the use of narrative to demonstrate and examine ideological and historical complexities, particularly with respect to gender.[4] Her story about the Salem witchcraft trials affords us an important example of realist historiography regarding a defining feature of women's experience with the law.

In applying realist technique to the historiography of witch trials, Gaskell was bucking the mainstream of nineteenth-century literature. Witches abounded, but of the gothic, or romantic spectacle, variety: Coleridge's Christabel, Tennyson's Vivian, or the hundreds of witches soaring over Victorian productions of *Macbeth*—the largest "hanging" of witches in British history. *Lois the Witch* departs from this trend and is illuminating of the dialectic realism enabled between cultures of evidence. Jenny Uglow, who notes Gaskell's particular interest in witchcraft trials, suggests that the story "depicts a cast of mind which might make itself manifest any time, anywhere, clothed in a shape to fit the age."[5] Gaskell analyses witch-hunting, however, not as a transhistorical misogynistic conspiracy or feature of the male psyche. Rather, she treats it as a practice that could be better understood—and thereby combated—by means of detailed historical investigation that remained theoretically self-critical.

A hallmark of realistic fiction is the presentation of evidence in a form modeled on legal argument. Full-blown trial scenes appear frequently in Victorian fiction, and women writers of the period used such scenes to dramatize a condition of legal disability or erasure, as we shall see in chapter 6. Whether or not actual witchcraft trials proceeded in this manner (and the scholarship I will adduce in the next chapter suggests that often they did not), our sense of the witch trial, with its foregone conclusions, its harassment of witnesses, its conspiracy of virulent prejudice, and the impotence of defendants and their sympathizers, corresponds with representations of the law in trial scenes by George Eliot, Frances Trollope, Elizabeth Gaskell, and others. Still, whereas male novelists, such as

Sir Walter Scott in *The Heart of Mid-lothian* (1818), Thomas Gaspey in *The Witch-finder* (1824), and William Harrison Ainsworth in *The Lancashire Witches* (1849), produced notable critiques of the witch persecutions, female writers seemed reluctant to connect their own legal and political situation to that of the witch.

Perhaps these women were too close to the times of persecution to risk identifying with the witch. Indeed, a few years before Gaskell wrote *Lois the Witch,* her friends William and Mary Howitt translated and edited Joseph Ennemoser's *The History of Magic* (1854), which articulates an ethnographic approach to witchcraft. In her preface, Mary Howitt recounted a telepathic experience between her husband and her, commenting nervously that "the mind of the Translator being occupied at the time by the peculiar views of Ennemoser, predisposed it for occult impressions."[6] As Alex Owen and Diana Basham have documented, women's interests in spiritualism and the occult, particularly as they provided political leverage and authorized them as agents, all too often became evidence for lunacy commitments and other forms of persecution, as I will discuss in part 2. Furthermore, these women may have worried that their period's interest in the history of witchcraft prosecutions concealed a degree of sadistic misogyny behind its disinterested rationalism or, indeed, its Romantic sympathy. Or was their own rationalistic feminism an obstacle to understanding witch-hunting as woman-hunting? To put it another way, was it necessary to repress the history of the witchcraft trials in order to sustain a faith in rationalistic, liberal feminist reform?

Elizabeth Gaskell, who in her first social-problem novel, *Mary Barton* (1848), had announced her plan to speak for the dumb masses of the laboring poor, seems to have developed a more sophisticated sense of storytelling politics through her own encounters with the public controversy that met her three social-problem novels.[7] This is evident in *Lois the Witch.* Set in Salem during the 1691–92 trials, the story focuses on the danger of public sentiment informed by storytelling, and its power to override legal processes to the detriment of "outsiders." Gaskell incorporates the rich historiography of witchcraft in this tale of a young orphaned English woman sent to live with her Salem relatives, including the Romantic tendency to aestheticize witchcraft. She advocates storytelling not, however, as an explanatory technique where rational analysis has failed, but as a prompt to the empirical imagination.

Importantly, Gaskell shares to a significant degree the historiographic commitments of her sources, William Howitt's *Popular History of Priest-*

craft (1833) and Charles Upham's *Lectures on Witchcraft* (1831), to retelling the tale of witch prosecutions in order to prevent their repetition. But whereas Upham and Howitt decry the superstitions of a deluded, unenlightened community, Gaskell stresses the correspondences between the citizens of Salem in 1691–92 and her readers, and where differences exist, she invites her readers to understand the conditions under which cruelty and prejudice can be made to appear acceptable. Gaskell brought a number of salient experiences and engagements to her subject. There was her commitment to both rationality and religious belief, central to her Unitarian theology, which suffuses much of her fiction, but is especially formative of her views of history. From her girlhood acquaintance with the Reverend William Turner, a founding member of the Newcastle Literary and Philosophical Society, through her adult associations with Unitarians engaged in antiquarian studies, Gaskell understood historical study as a means of negotiating relationships among peoples of differing beliefs—the beliefs of the living with those of a causally integrated past. Much of Gaskell's historical fiction narrates the stories of the losers, whose beliefs were not irretrievably obliterated by the winners' histories, but could be significantly, if imperfectly, reconstructed through research. At the same time, Gaskell was keen to analyze history as a process that so often turned victims into persecutors. However sympathetically Gaskell sought to enable her readers to enter into the past through her narratives, she tried to maintain criteria by which cruelty and injustice could be identified and condemned. It was in this manner that Gaskell's realism also contributed to an analysis of gender in the witch trials.

Lois the Witch involves several historical personages, including Cotton Mather and the Reverend Tappau, in whose family the accusations of bewitchment originated. It centers, however, on a fictional creation, a young orphaned English woman, Lois Barclay. Her mother's deathbed wish was that her daughter go to live with her Salem relatives. Lois leaves England hoping that her suitor, Hugh Lucy, will eventually overcome his wealthy father's objections to the penniless Lois and return her to her homeland to become his wife. This romantic heroine possesses a complex religious and political identity, however. As the daughter of a Jacobite Anglican clergyman, Lois is put off by the habits of her mother's Puritan relatives. Her aunt, Grace Hickson, born and raised in Salem and proclaimed a "godly woman" by Cotton Mather himself, is openly hostile to her sister-in-law's child. Many of the story's characters come similarly equipped with a strong sense of history—familial, political, and providential. It is not an exaggeration to say that Gaskell's characters display the complex and contradictory group identities so often stressed in Habermas's theories of selfhood and political affiliation.

These characters also display an obsession with history that produces it own kind of curse. Cast in terms of divine Providence, history is scrutinized with passionate interest for signs of God's approval or correction. From Cotton Mather to the Hickson's Indian servant, Nattee, characters demand certainty in historical interpretation, and where certainty is lacking, they attempt to supply it. Many of the story's characters have recourse to divination, native spells, and visions in order to interpret their histories and influence future events. Lois's cousin, Manasseh Hickson, declares that through divination and visions, God has revealed that Lois is to be his wife, a prospect Lois firmly rejects. Rather than spurn the hated girl as a suitable wife for her son, Grace Hickson shocks Lois by urging her to accept Manasseh, but not because she credits his vision. Rather, she seeks a "medicine" for the young man's troubled mind. Manasseh's sister, Faith, has been forced to conceal her affections for the Reverend Nolan because he is a rival to her mother's favorite, the Reverend Tappau. In desperation, she has turned to Nattee's divination rituals to determine Nolan's heart, and then encourages Nattee to bewitch him. When Nolan unexpectedly returns to Salem, Faith scorns Lois's attempts to bring Faith and Nolan together out of guilt over her sinful recourse to magic. Nolan turns his attentions to Lois, and Faith becomes viciously jealous. The youngest daughter, Prudence, engages in various behaviors aimed at eliciting attention in this loveless family, rising to a climax with a hysterical fit, which, in imitation of the notorious Tappau children, she blames on Lois's witchcraft. While the Hickson family espouses a belief in the reality of witchcraft, none of them seems entirely convinced by Prudence's testimony, yet each has private motives for failing to defend Lois. Only Manasseh expresses a desire to defend her.

Importantly, Manasseh's defense is entirely consistent with Puritan belief. He reasons with Cotton Mather that, because Lois's execution for witchcraft has been revealed to Manasseh in a vision, "it must have been foredoomed in the councils of God. If so," he continues, "why punish her for doing that in which she had no free will?"[8] Mather cautions Manasseh that he is verging on blasphemy, but he persists, and "even Dr. Mather felt himself on the point of being worsted in the very presence of this congregation, who but a short half-hour ago, looked upon him as all but infallible" (175). But the congregation rises up "as one man" against Manasseh, with Mather smiling grimly over them. They are prevented from stoning Manasseh only by his mother's cry, "My son, my only son, is mad" (176). Manasseh's pleas on Lois's behalf are immediately converted into evidence against Lois, who is then accused of bewitching him as well. Having discovered a contradiction at the heart of witch persecution, Manasseh must be confined as a madman.

Gaskell seeks to criticize the outcome of these beliefs on their own terms, and without making a distinction between elite and vulgar belief. What makes these beliefs potentially lethal is the demand for certainty and control, and the suppression of contradiction. Sustaining belief in the face of internal contradiction requires not only a selective but also a circular standard of evidence, as Lois's trial dramatizes. Gaskell constructs that trial from historical accounts of Salem, but supplements her material with Lois's point of view. The accused are made to stand before the judges while the accusers demonstrate signs of bewitchment. Lois pauses in her recitation of the Lord's Prayer, and the crowded courtroom declares her a witch. All of the accused are condemned by the judges, Mr. Hathorn and Mr. Curwin, and Lois is led back to her cell, too exhausted to plead her innocence or even to weep. Left alone, she is tempted to believe that she deserves condemnation—that she is indeed a witch. But she refuses to confess, fearful that such a lie would condemn her soul. Gaskell deplores this process not because it violates a universal standard of rationality, but because it applies a self-ratifying standard of evidence. The accusation and the judgment are, in effect, the same. But the question remains: How can the combination of historical hostilities and immediate anxieties present in some form in all societies erupt in these spectacular persecutions and then, seemingly as inexplicably, recede?

Running throughout *Lois the Witch* are incidents of storytelling and interpretation. Gaskell's characters tell stories not only to create continuity between generations but also to pass on political commitments and assert current political claims. When Lois first arrives in Boston, Captain Holderness, with whom she had sailed, takes her to the lodging house of the Widow Smith. This woman enjoys an authority unusual for women of her community, the narrator tells us: because of her goodness of heart, she is "allowed a liberty of speech which was tacitly denied to many, under penalty of being esteemed ungodly if they infringed certain conventional limits" (111–12). Over dinner, the Elder Hawkins and Smith's daughters repeat tales of threatening Indians and suspected supernatural goings-on. The girls tell of an attack on Marblehead by French pirates, who took a woman prisoner. Despite the woman's cries for help, no one attempted a rescue and she died. During the crisis, an old blind and deaf woman stood up and pronounced a curse on the people of Marblehead and their descendants for their cowardly abandonment of the woman. According to the story, the people still hear the woman's cries in the marsh: "Lord Jesu! have mercy on me! Save me from the power of man O Lord Jesu!" (113).

What is the proper purpose for telling this tale? The Smith girls are more impressed with its sensational elements than with its record of cowardice and cruelty. The Elder Hawkins attempts to erase both gender and injustice from the account and treat it as an example of Satan's efforts to test the people of Marblehead. His displacement prompts a direct contradiction from the Widow: "It was no vision," she retorts; "they were real living men who went ashore, men who broke down branches and left their footmarks on the ground" (114). The Widow Smith cites forensic details—the broken branches and the footprints—as evidence that a real crime has taken place against a real woman. These facts resist appropriations of the story into a totalizing historical scheme. Insofar as the people of Marblehead are cursed, it is in the commitment of storytellers—specifically, female witnesses and storytellers—to recalling precisely what happened.

Lois has her own story of a witch's curse. "They are fearful creatures, the witches! and yet I am sorry for the poor old women, whilst I dread them," Lois remarks. She goes on to recount a witch-ducking she witnessed as a child. The woman accused of witchcraft corresponds with the stereotypical victim of persecution as described by witchcraft skeptics since Reginald Scot. She is old, poor, begs for her food, and has only a cat for company in her mud hut. The four-year-old Lois is an innocent witness to the woman's drowning, but it remains a traumatic memory. "I only know I got a sick fright on that afternoon," she says.

> I hid my face, I know, as soon as I saw the fearsome sight, for her eyes met mine as they were glaring with fury—poor, helpless, baited creature!—and she caught the sight of me, and cried out, "Parson's wench, parson's wench, yonder, in thy nurse's arms, thy hath never tried for to save me, and none shall save thee when thou art brought up for a witch." Oh! the words rang in my ears, when I was dropping asleep, for years after. I used to dream that I as in that pond, all men hating me with their eyes because I was a witch; and at times, her black cat used to seem living again, and say over those dreadful words.

The narrator remarks that "all had reason, before many months had passed over, to remember the words which Lois spoke in answer" (115).

Lois's traumatic memory is itself determinative. The crowd's motives for persecuting Hannah remain a mystery to Lois: "I never heard much about it," she says, "for my father said it was ill talking about such things" (115). A conspiracy of silence imposed by one whose convictions and position should lead him to speak up against a crowd intent on cruelty perpetuates a practice that Hannah voices as a curse. Gaskell reminds us that the beliefs of seventeenth-century society were not monolithic. Because dissenters failed to resist dominant beliefs, Lois is trapped by the curse of history.

This curse, according to Gaskell, can be lifted neither by mythologizing the witchcraft persecution, nor by imposing a transhistorical standard of rationality, but rather by subjecting stories to the critical analyses available within a culture's belief structures. Lois herself puts the key question to these storytellers when Elder Hawkins asserts that the painted Indians are Satan's children: "Is it true?" she asks. Her question prompts Captain Holderness to offer an account of New England's political situation, notable for its refrain: "Who knows?"

> "My wench," said the old sailor, "thou hast come to a country where there are many perils, both from land and from sea. The Indians hate the white men. Whether other white men" (meaning the French away to the north) "have hounded on the savages, or whether the English have taken their lands and hunting-grounds without due recompense, and so raised the cruel vengeance of the wild creatures—who knows? But it is true that it is not safe to go far into the woods, for fear of the lurking painted savages; nor has it been safe to build a dwelling for from a settlement; and it takes a brave heart to make a journey from one town to another, and folk do say the Indian creatures rise up out of the very ground to waylay the English; and then other affirm they are all in league with Satan to affright the Christians out of the heathen country over which he has reigned so long. Then, again, the seashore is infested by pirates, the scum of all nations: they land, and plunder, and ravage, and burn, and destroy. Folk get affrighted of the real dangers, and in their fright imagine, perchance, dangers that are not. But who knows? Holy Scripture speaks of witches and wizards, and of the power of the Evil One in desert places; and even in the old country we have

> heard tell of those who have sold their souls for ever for the little power they get for a few years on earth." (115)

For Gaskell, there is comfort—or at least some hope—in hard facts. Rather than dismissing her as a naïve positivist, it is worth understanding what she means by this term.

When Lois first arrives in Boston, exhausted, lonely, and fearful, Captain Holderness attempts to cheer her by "talk[ing] on about the hard facts, connected with the life that lay before her . . . and perhaps," the narrator comments, "Lois was more brightened by this style of conversation, and the new ideas it presented to her, than she would have been by the tenderest woman's sympathy" (108). A history made up of "hard facts" in Gaskell's sense is valuable because it warns us of present danger, but it does not mythologize the danger and thereby rob us of effective agency. Indeed, such a myth would participate in the very claims to certainty that make all our evidence point to foregone conclusions.

Gaskell resists any universalizing history, including one that equates witch-hunting with woman-hunting to the exclusion of a whole complex of motives that may never have been fully apparent. "Who knows?" is the refrain of her characters, faced with incomplete evidence and faulty explanations. This is not the smug Whiggishness so often associated with nineteenth-century historiography, but the circumspection we appropriately learn from the limited evidence of history. To historians who would fill in the gaps in the historical record with universalized theories of gender, Gaskell would answer that it is precisely in pointing out and investigating the gaps and contradictions in universalizing ideologies that the most effective means of resisting violence and injustice lays. That is why Captain Holderness continues to tell Lois's story, as well as the story of the Salem Elders' repentance. Hugh Lucy, Lois's suitor, responds despairingly to this story: "All this will not bring my Lois to life again, or give me back the hope of my youth" (192). Though Gaskell closes the story with a statement of forgiveness, she is also careful, as is her wont, to confirm the justice of Lucy's resentment. Captain Holderness does not chide Lucy; rather, he shakes his head, "for what word could he say, or how dispute what was so evidently true?" (192).

Gaskell's position arises out of realism itself, which gestures to a world outside itself by marking the artificiality of its own coherent form. Whereas Drucilla Cornell, or Roberto Unger, sees the aesthetic in the moment of social commitment, Elizabeth Gaskell, herself a disenfranchised Victorian woman and an advocate for the downtrodden, sees an encounter with brute embodied experience as the foundation of commitment and fears the aestheticization of cruelty, power, and fanaticism.[9] She interrupts her story, as George Levine puts it in speaking of realism generally, "to avoid the inevitable conventionality of language in pursuit of the unattainable unmediated reality." By so doing, Levine continues, "the realistic novel persistently drives us itself to question not only the nature of artificially imposed social relations, but the nature of nature, and the nature of the novel."[10]

Gaskell's story acquires significance for gender advocacy in light of both contemporary epistemological debates regarding evidence and of the inescapable precedents of gender advocacy in the history of witchcraft prosecution since the early modern period. Though it is neither a monumental work of realist literature nor an authoritative treatise of legal history, it demonstrates the complexity of historical analysis Victorian realism afforded to a progressive woman writer in coming to grips with a potentially traumatic past that continued to ramify in the present. Realist fiction, as its many theorists have argued, developed to negotiate various apparently incompatible demands, preeminently those of emerging representative democracy, *viz.,* that between individual desire and the aggregate public interest.[11] In the case of a woman writing in the context of feminist agitation and sensational fiction, of rational utilitarianism and romantic nostalgia for a paternalistic past, of an uneven course, that is, toward what might constitute *de facto* recognition for legal outsiders, realism's dialectic between empathy and judgment enabled Gaskell to achieve a striking synthesis. In subsequent chapters I will delineate this context more thoroughly. What I wish to stress here is that her realist technique emerges from—and is the best analytical tool for understanding—a long history of both the fundamental and the trivial place of gender in cultures of evidence, whose most salient legacy for feminist advocacy is lodged in the historiography of witchcraft trials. Perhaps less a synthesis than a salutary suspension, Gaskell's story manages to convey both the reality of female agency and the constructedness of gendered identity; the authority of both intimate, first-person narrative and historical hindsight; the living legacy of the past and the urgency of our aspirations to forge new, and more just, social relations. Storytelling will necessarily play a role, but without critique, literature—as much as law—can simply reproduce past injustices and create new traumas. The full import of these claims will emerge from the consideration of contemporary historiographic debates about witchcraft prosecution, to which I now turn. Furthermore, the goals of justice must be historically informed and cannot afford to confine themselves to any one mode of representation or faculty of human understanding. As I will argue in the next two chapters, this is what the conditions of modern print culture, emerging along with witchcraft trials in the early modern period and evolving in the long nineteenth century in tandem with democratic political theory, teach us.

Historiographies of Witchcraft and Feminist Advocacy

Just as Gaskell's treatment of witchcraft prosecution is marked by her own historical position, so too do the methodological and ideological disputes that dominate the study of the witchcraft prosecution throw into relief the profound influence of modern historical events and politics on our vision of the past. Early modern witchcraft prosecution provided twentieth-century political critique with one of its central tropes. The first usage recorded by the *OED* for "witch hunt" as meaning "a single-minded and uncompromising campaign against a group of people with unacceptable behavior, *spec.* Communists; *esp.* one regarded as unfair or malicious prosecution" occurs in twentieth-century Spain: George Orwell, writing in *Homage to Catalonia* (1938), decried the "senseless witch-hunt" for Trotskyists.[12] Witch-hunting represented for Orwell the fundamental threat to democratic freedoms and processes posed by totalitarian states. The witch trial may symbolize not merely an abuse of legal power, but the illegitimacy of an entire legal system or of the state itself. "Law" can be seen as cloaking domination with rationality and justifying the force of the state brought to bear against the criminalized other—women, racial minorities, gays and lesbians, religious and political minorities, and so forth.

For radical feminist historiography, the methodological anxiety surrounding witchcraft prosecution is merely a form of mystification, a way of employing history to deny what its practitioners take to be the obvious explanation for a legally sanctioned persecution. For Mary Daly, or Marianne Hester (who subtitles her *Lewd Women and Wicked Witches* "a study of the dynamics of male domination"), historical research can at best contextualize, but never explain, witchcraft prosecutions without a theory of power wherein gender hierarchy is determinative.[13] In *The Witch in History,* Diane Purkiss has provocatively claimed that the radical feminist critique of empiricist witchcraft histories as guilty misrepresentations manifests an investment in what she terms a feminist "holocaust of one's own." Purkiss refers to a position in feminist witchcraft studies that rejects conventional historiographic methods and evidence in favor of a story of genocidal misogyny. In this view, research following empiricist historiographic conventions (Gaskell's "hard facts") is pernicious, forming a more insidious resistance to recognizing witch-hunting for what it was: woman-hunting. Purkiss remarks that "usually this has nothing to do with poststructuralism or even solipsism: the more flagrant a radical feminist writer's disregard for the rules of evidence, the more dogmatic her own truth-claims are likely to be."[14]

By contrast with the Orwellian usage, radical feminist jurisprudence, like radical feminist historiography, offers its own uncomplicated account of the law as always and everywhere the tool of male domination. In this manner the "witch hunt" trope has contributed to the more general tendency in cultural studies to "metaphorize the law," culminating, as Rosemary J. Coombe has complained, in the psychoanalytic formulation "the Law of the Father."[15] Within a psychoanalytic historiography, the witch trials are construed as a traumatic event, with all that implies about narrative evidence. To subject witch trials to the scrutiny of empiricist historical analysis is to violate once again the victims of patriarchal oppression. Instead, the appropriate approach to the witch trials as the metaphorization of the psychic trauma women experience before "the Law of the Father" is through therapeutic narratives of memory.

When Purkiss attributes to some feminist historians of witch trials the desire to appropriate a "holocaust of one's own," she reminds us of the principal context in which trauma theory has been elaborated for historiography in recent decades: Holocaust studies. For contemporary feminist historians to render the witchcraft trials as a holocaust of women is to announce broader ideological claims about the uses of history. As Kerwin Lee Klein has argued in an attack on the "memory industry," "It is no accident that our sudden fascination with memory goes hand in hand with postmodern reckonings of history as the marching black boot and of historical consciousness as an oppressive fiction. Memory can come to the fore in an age of historiographic crisis precisely because it figures as a therapeutic alternative to historical discourse."[16] The implication for a history of women and the law is that the witchcraft trials are rendered as a "limit event" in the formation of female subjectivity, incommensurable with any other historical precedent and off-limits to critical historical analysis. If both law and history are the tools of fascist, patriarchal oppression, then neither can serve women's interests. Women should not seek emancipation as a matter of legal recognition, but should undergo psychic therapy by means of subjective narratives.

The route by which the trauma theory elaborated in Holocaust studies has entered into discussions of witch trials is complicated, however, and owes much to the evolution of twentieth-century cultures of evidence in the wake of the Holocaust. Research for Christina Larner's *Enemies of God,* the earliest example of an empirical historical investigation into the significance of gender in the prosecution of witchcraft, was funded by the Columbus Centre, founded, in the words of its director, Norman Cohn, for "the comparative study of the dynamics of persecution and extermination." In a foreword to *Enemies of God,* Cohn explicitly connected the "great witch-hunt" with the Holocaust as the "two specific historical problems at the very core of [the center's] program of research."[17]

Cohn looked to the great European witch hunt in the hope of explaining an example of twentieth-century cruelty where there is at least some plausible basis for imputing a unitary motive. But the account of witch prosecutions in early modern Scotland that Larner produced on the basis of her archival research did not lead to a unified theory of persecution motives but rather pointed up evidence of key disparities between the persecution of witches in early modern Europe (indeed, the diversity of behaviors among various European countries) and any twentieth-century events. Still, the profound pressure exerted on historiography by demands to explain the West's most traumatic event of the twentieth century has had its impact throughout the field, and it cannot be surprising that many feminist historians of witchcraft, invited to draw parallels with the persecution of Jews, would embrace the holocaust model to represent the persecution of women.

But is this assimilation of the holocaust into feminist analysis akin to experiencing sympathetic symptoms? Is it a false memory? This is precisely the sort of question ruled out of court by the very critique of empirical evidence and standards of rational inference used to produce the myth of the burning times in the first place. Consider, for example, the legacy of Christina Larner's scholarship. Larner is generally credited with being the first historian to give extended attention to the significance of gender as a factor in the witchcraft trials. In *Enemies of God,* Larner posed the question, Was witch-hunting woman-hunting? She concluded that the phenomenon was gender-related, but that gender was not the defining characteristic of the trials. Rather, Larner emphasized the coincidence of the Reformation political crisis in England and the rise of witchcraft legislation, signaling its place within a matrix of law-and-order measures designed to reconsolidate religious and legal authority in the state. Research by James Sharpe and Clive Holmes tended to bear out Larner's assessment.[18] Yet Larner's refusal to identify gender as the fundamental principle operating in the witchcraft prosecutions, rather than as one of many causal factors, has been the source of some scandal. "Larner's conclusions are the most disappointing of all," Anne Llewellyn Barstow complained in 1988, "for she had a keen awareness of how the oppression of women works in history."[19] Larner has been blamed for failing to appreciate women's agency in the witchcraft prosecutions, either as accusers or as self-acknowledged witches. Deborah Willis criticizes Larner for representing the female accuser as "one-dimensionally complicit with early modern patriarchy, an enforcer of a normalizing code of woman's 'proper' behavior, at bottom, little more than a patriarchal male in drag."[20]

Larner did not predict such a state of affairs in feminist historiography, but she did warn of the effects of any "general theory" of witchcraft, by implication distinguishing early modern witchcraft prosecutions from other examples of institutionalized persecution as well. Despite the characterization of her work by some feminist critics, both in *Enemies of God* and her later work *Witchcraft and Religion: The Politics of Popular Belief*, Larner elaborated on the various ways in which European witch-hunting *was* woman-hunting, *viz.*, a way of policing female sexuality, suppressing direct challenges to patriarchal authority, and acting out men's fear of women's reproductive power. But she was also concerned that any unified theory of witchcraft would have to rely on a very low common denominator indeed. She had in mind the tendency to merge historical, anthropological, and sociological studies of witchcraft, but her caution seems prescient regarding feminist historiography: "There is a danger that we will continue to push in the same direction," she wrote, "ensuring that new empirical studies will be tailored to one procrustean theoretical bed."[21] She alerted us to any narrowing of the kinds of questions put to evidence of witch hunts, which would include the essentializing of gender as a category of historical analysis. Gaskell would have concurred.

In *Gender and the Politics of History,* Joan Wallach Scott asks, "Does the presence of women always call for gender analysis?"[22] She reviews the contributions of feminist activism and scholarship toward "expos[ing] the ways in which seemingly neutral classification has masked the exclusion of women." Key among them is the feminist critique of the theory of universal rights constituted as it historically has been through the exclusion of women: "Autonomy and independence, the power of self-representation and the possession of rights were figured as phallic functions, attributed to those with a biological penis. And the birth of the nation (the bringing to life of the social contract) demonstrated the generative potential of the phallus: politics was entirely men's labor" (209–10). From this insight follows two distinct lines of feminist arguments regarding rights, each articulated by feminist lawyers. One concludes that universalism is "Western patriarchalism in disguise," as Catherine Mackinnon, for example, argues. The other maintains, as Patricia Williams writes, that "for the historically disempowered, the conferring of rights is symbolic of all the denied aspects of their humanity: rights imply a respect that places one in the referential range of self and others, that elevates one's status from human body to social being."[23] Scott sees the feminist historian as having a role in mediating this debate among gender advocates.

First, feminist theory can reconceptualize universalism in a way that reclaims it from its gendered past: "It is not possession but aspiration that provides common ground," Scott writes.

> Women's claims for rights, from this vantage, would be analyzed as an insistence on their (symbolic and actual) position as desiring subjects, individuals whose desire rested not on their possession of some physical trait or the performance of a specified biological function, but on the lack associated with the very constitution of their being: a being conceptualized through an other's recognition, necessarily expressed in words that are always inadequate for the full representation of the self and that, therefore, leave one yearning for completeness. (216–17)

This reconceptualization leads Scott to examine the individual as the possessor of rights, a move that engages questions of gender difference as it invites the critical distance of historical perspective. Far from limiting investigation to a unified theory of gender difference, Scott poses a series of questions regarding a range of differences:

> How did "rights" come to be understood as something individuals possessed? How did gender figure in the articulation of this possessive individualism? What, historically and cross-culturally, have been the relationships between notions of possession and representations of sexual difference? How did the fantasy of political egalitarianism (the democratic vision) interact with (supplement? challenge? contradict?)

> the fantasies of human origin that, at least in the West, make sexual difference fundamental to individual identities? . . . If political and social identities always operate reductively, the question becomes how? . . . What are the stakes in such reductions? Have they been contested? How? And by whom? (217–18)

Scott concludes by insisting that these questions must be asked in terms of specific historical and cultural examples and so that, by historicizing the category of gender itself, "we can establish a certain reflexivity on our own stakes and intentions. . . . In this way, we open ourselves to history, to the idea and possibility that things have been, and will be, different from what they are now" (218).

I have quoted at length from Scott both because of the leading role she plays in feminist activism and feminist historiography and because her peroration, though proceeding from a context apparently remote from the historiography of witch hunts (i.e., the theory of rights), does, in fact, lead back not only to Larner's critical empiricism but also to Gaskell's historical realist strategies. Larner may have embraced a list of questions regarding the witch trials very like that proposed by Scott, and may have welcomed Scott's insight that "the physical presence of females is not always a sure sign that 'women' are a separate political category, that they have been mobilized as women. . . . The projection of a separate women's interest into a situation where it is not operating naturalizes 'women,' since their interest is taken to predate the political context of the crowd's action and the terms of its mobilization" (212).

To be open to history in the way Scott is suggesting requires us to consider that forms of misremembering—both denial and obsession—are symptoms of a traumatic experience elevated to the status of a theoretical commitment. Larner remarked that, despite some strong parallels, "the way in which the term 'witch-hunt' is applied to contemporary political phenomena [e.g., the Holocaust or the McCarthy hearings] plays down some aspects of the historical hunt—notably the fact that about 80 per cent of the suspects were women."[24] Ignoring what must certainly be the principal feature of witches in the popular imagination, from the early modern period to the present—namely, that they are *women*—suggests that authors such as Orwell, or Arthur Miller, who appropriated the witch hunt to denounce the persecution of the left, erase material particularity in favor of the ideological construct of the victim as feminized other. In so doing, they eerily revise a strategy of witch trial critics beginning with

Reginald Scot in 1584, who sought to discredit prosecutions that, as we shall see, threatened the rights of propertied males on the grounds that they disproportionately victimized poor women.

But whereas the Orwellian view of witch-hunting upholds factual evidence and objectivity as violated norms, another accords obsessive priority to gender as the defining characteristic of witch hunts and deconstructs empiricist historical method in order to insist on woman hunts as the archetypal form of persecution. In exploring Purkiss's connection between recent feminist responses to empirical historical study and Holocaust studies, I have invited examination of feminist historiography as a symptom of trauma. Purkiss reads the desire to assert a "holocaust of one's own" as entailing the rejection of conventional rules of evidence and replacing academic legitimating strategies with authentication by victimization. If rational argument and objective evidence could be used to condemn women as witches in courts of law, then these forms of persuasion must themselves be renounced as misogynistic and replaced by representational forms valuing—not demonizing—female experience. Narrative, literary, or imaginative forms of discourse—whether on the basis of *écriture feminine,* feminist linguistics and gendered rationalities, or feminist poststructuralism—have been urged as uniquely suited to representing women's interests, and it is in these forms that the myth of the burning times is promulgated. The strategic value of such forms of representation is both offensive and defensive—they deconstruct the grounds of opposing arguments and repel criticism proceeding from incommensurate assumptions. But their very imperviousness enables endless repetition, a pathological compulsion that prevents the traumatic event from being represented to the conscious mind, even symptomatic, perhaps, of a survivor neurosis.

This would seem a particularly anxious, debilitating form of historical memory. Importantly, its critique of empirical methods runs counter to the imperative to acknowledge documentary and material evidence of Jewish deaths at the hands of Nazis.[25] If anything, scholarship on witchcraft trials, unlike Holocaust scholarship, threatens to dissipate into a bewildering array of special cases. Surely one obvious motive for flattening out these distinctions is simply to hold the general phenomenon of witchcraft prosecution coherently in mind. If there is indeed a traumatic past displaced onto this narrative, however, hedging that narrative round with defensive moves—construing all counterevidence as *prima facie* masculinist—would only serve to perpetuate the trauma's destructive force.

At this point it would be well to note Purkiss's observation that a significant body of that story is produced outside of any academic paradigm and bespeaks a psychic investment on the part of women deeply alienated from political and social institutions, some of whom are self-identified witches. Their story is threatening to academic historians, Purkiss argues, including feminist historians. Still, there seems little reason to assume that there is in principle so unbridgeable a gap between what is in effect popular feminism and academic feminism as Purkiss implies. First, ignoring the shared origins in the rise of anthropological and myth study of academic radical feminist discourse on witchcraft and those of a popular discourse treats the latter as if it were some pre-scripted women's folk law. The nineteenth-century folklorists and antiquarians, who began researching and recording popular beliefs, were amateurs, some of whom were women, barred from professional study.[26] As with other forms of representation under conditions of mass literacy, those records reenter popular discourse, as is demonstrated by the continuing popularity of Margaret Murray's theory (now discredited among academic historians) that witches were practitioners of an ancient fertility religion, brutally put down by Christianity.[27] Popular and academic treatments of witchcraft may influence one another through complex mediations, but they are hardly unrelated.[28]

Second, if the similarities in methodology demonstrate the desire of radical feminists to create solidarity with nonacademic women by embracing methods of representation that reject traditional rules of evidence, then the value of that strategy should be scrutinized by narrative legal theorists, especially those who wish to gain women full recognition in the law. If this method would turn out to be a counterproductive mystification, one that obscures women's agency and ethical complexity and encourages their disaffection from political as legal institutions as alienated others, it would have significant implications for any adoption of anti-empirical, anti-rational representational strategies by/for outsiders. Embracing narrative evidence as an "antidote" to traditional historiography has the effect of enshrining the myth of the burning times as a kind of women's folk law, reproducing women's outlaw status in a kind of self-fulfilling prophecy. When such popular and academic feminist intersections are acknowledged, the relevance of the traumatic history of gender in the witch trials to contemporary feminist jurisprudence and narrative legal theory can be brought into representation.

If the witch hunt itself were not in fact the trauma fantasized by the myth of the burning times, does that myth in its resistance to alternative explanations help to conceal different traumatic experiences? That this myth arises and is nurtured coincident with, for example, women's enfranchisement, the *de jure* (if not *de facto*) recognition of equal rights, and presence within legal institutions and governments, suggests that it may address an anxiety tied directly to another coincident phenomenon: the emergence of the masculinist witch-hunt analogy adduced by Orwell, one peculiarly embedded in the history of the democratic constitutional state. It seems to internalize women's historic betrayal by progressive, democratic, and socialist movements as a universal characteristic of women as legal subjects. Not only does it deny the ambiguous legal agency of women even within witch trials themselves but it also demonizes the law in such a way as to persuade women to eschew legal power as essentially linked with masculine interests. Is *this* a narrative likely to bring about greater justice for women? If not, how should it be challenged?

Given the understandable preoccupation of historians, particularly feminist historians, with the motives of witch prosecutors, the temptation clearly exists to underplay the exigencies of documentary evidence, to convert necessity into virtue and elevate what is both a practical and theoretical problem to the status of an evidentiary principle by taking the "linguistic turn." By construing all evidence in textual terms, gaps, mediation, and contradictions are subsumed under axioms of theory even when they proceed from the physical existence—or nonexistence—of historical records. Carlo Ginzburg has challenged this position in his readings of court records of Continental witch trials. He distinguishes between two sorts of historical practice. One, represented by Jules Michelet in his influential study of witchcraft, *La Sorcière* (1862), enabled historians to overcome both the paucity of evidence and the unconventionality of their subject matter by adopting novelistic narrative devices. The other is the "inverted positivism" of "contemporary skeptics who regard [textual evidence] as a wall, which by definition precludes any access to reality."[29] "Even if we reject positivism," Ginzburg argues, "we must still confront ourselves with notions like 'reality,' 'proof,' and 'truth.'"[30]

The critical methods Ginzburg advocates to make inferences about the people who appear in court records align him with Gaskell's realism. They should also apply to our analyses of the authors and producers of textual evidence of witch trials, including historians. Should it matter that the contention that witches were an organized protest movement of medieval serfs—which underpins their representation as women subverting patriarchy—was first popularized in Jules Michelet's hastily written, sensationalistic *La Sorcière*? Arguably, Michelet is the first of many radicals to co-opt the persecution of witches to narrate their own political traumas. From Michelet's text, James Sharpe traces an interpretive tradition that adopted his story of political persecution, despite its lack of documentary evidence.[31] The suffragists Elizabeth Cady Stanton and Matilda Joslyn Gage, rationalists both, decried the religious superstitions that fueled the witch hunts at the same time that Gage in *Women, Church, and State* (1893) presented her own theory of witches as folk-healers executed by rival male practitioners.[32] Gage likely originated the claim that the number of women executed as witches in Europe from 1484 could be computed from historical sources to be nine million.[33] Apprised of documentary evidence that fails to support her belief—evidence she could not have known—would Gage have revised her hypothesis or rejected such evidence as an antifeminist assault on an enabling narrative?

Recalling the reasons I listed at the beginning of this chapter for attending to *Lois the Witch,* I would argue that scholarship which seeks to advance viable strategies of gender advocacy must be informed not only by the historical conditions that produced Victorian exemplars but also by the more capacious historical record that constituted the Victorians' precedents and traumas. At the very least, we need to know something about the kinds of evidence upon which Victorian and contemporary accounts of gender advocacy are based. Before turning to that evidence in chapters 2 and 3, I wish to make several points that provide further incentive for Victorianists and legal scholars alike to venture into the unfamiliar territory of witchcraft literature from the early modern period.

The historiographic debate over witchcraft prosecution surveyed above is contested largely on the basis of literary evidence, since relatively little legal evidence of crime in early modern England survives. The legal evidence that might supply clues to the features of witchcraft prosecution and its motives would be court documents from the assize circuits, where witchcraft was tried along with homicide, grand larceny, burglary, highway robbery, and rape.[34] Criminal procedure required a substantial paper trail of depositions, indictments, pleas, verdicts, and sentences, but apart from indictments for the Home Circuit, few materials from the period before 1645 survive.[35] The paucity of petty sessions records further impedes investigation into the prosecution of crime in the sixteenth and early seventeenth centuries, the period that saw the greatest interest in trying witches.[36] Accusations turned back by magistrates before they could reach grand juries left no trace, making it impossible to gauge reliably the enthusiasm of ordinary subjects or magistrates for legal responses to witchcraft or any other disturbance.[37] Christina Larner's conclusions regarding the causes of the witch trials in Scotland were drawn on the basis of the far more complete Scottish legal archives and should imply for the study of English witch trials the value of attending to the particularities of distinct legal systems and local politics.[38]

The statute record remains: though sorcery was already being tried in English ecclesiastical courts, witchcraft entered the history of English secular law as a felony with a parliamentary act passed in 1542 (33 Hen. 8, c. 8).[39] That legislation was repealed in 1547. A new law was enacted in 1563 (5 Eliz., c. 16), and its provisions strengthened in 1580–81 (23 Eliz., c. 2). In contrast with Continental and Scottish witchcraft legislation, these laws evinced the Common Law preoccupation with crimes against persons and property, with the 1580–81 act reflecting as well anxiety over supernatural efforts to predict—or hasten—the aging Elizabeth's natural end. The Act of 1604 (1 Jac. 1, c. 12), introducing from Continental theory into English law the notion of a demonic pact, or contract, between the witch and Satan, remained in force until 1736. But a mere chronology of these statutes tells us little about patterns of prosecution or the motives of prosecutors.

Literary and legal historians alike have offered contestable conclusions not only about who should be blamed for witchcraft prosecutions but also about the numbers of women prosecuted as well. Historians working from court records estimate the total of European executions at 50,000 and English executions at 1,000, and locate the peak period of prosecutions as having come during the reign of Elizabeth I, 1580–1600.[40] Keith Thomas reports that there were periods when prosecutions peaked in specific jurisdictions: in 1582 fourteen people were convicted in Essex; in Lancashire, twenty-one in 1612 and twenty in 1633. The greatest number of convictions came in the wake of the Civil War when normal assize structures were interrupted and detection was professionalized by Matthew Hopkins, who achieved a record-high 42 percent conviction rate in the period of 1645–47.[41] Approximately half of all executions for witchcraft in England took place in East Anglia during these two years.

Had there been a steady decline in prosecutions across the seventeenth century, progress from "superstition" to rationality would be a plausible historical narrative. Alternatively, a constant level of prosecution would confirm feminist historians' claim of unremitting misogyny. Instead, the puzzlingly sporadic occurrence of witch trials between 1542 and 1712 has baffled historians from the eighteenth century to the present. Metaphors historians typically use to describe clusters of prosecutions, such as "outbreaks," "crazes," "contagions," "epidemics," and "spasms," beg the question of causality and resist a coherent historical narrative. It would be foolish to propose that a complete legal record could explain key features of the history of prosecutions. Instead, evidence of the sporadic and localized nature of prosecution under witchcraft legislation helps to thwart attempts to impose a single interpretation on the motives of the Crown, Parliament, the courts, legal functionaries, juries, and accusers over nearly two centuries.

In addition, witch trials were both products of evidentiary dilemmas and occasions for their elaboration. Witchcraft was classified as *crimen exceptum,* along with clandestine murder, infanticide, secret poisoning, and sorcery. Later, Matthew Hale would add rape to that list.[42] To our eyes, what binds these crimes together is gender; what early moderns saw—or said they saw—were crimes that did not admit of direct proof. As such, ordinary rules of evidence were themselves on trial in prosecuting these crimes, allowing for a greater emphasis on presumptive evidence, hearsay, and circumstantial evidence, demanding, that is, a lower standard of proof for a conviction, but perhaps also accounting for the high rate of acquittal. Evidence ranged in kind from the crudely empirical—notably, the witch's mark or teat—to the decidedly metaphysical—apparitions and other forms of so-called spectral evidence. That *crimen exceptum* registered the fundamental inability of male jurors and judges to have direct knowledge of female bodies is evident in two features of witchcraft prosecutions: the uniquely high percentage of female witnesses and the official use of trustworthy women to examine female prisoners for signs of the witch's mark. Witchcraft prosecutions occasioned both the production of gender-specific knowledge and its incorporation within legal norms.

How can we—Victorian literary critics, legal theorists, feminist historians—read this difficult, uneven, and unfamiliar evidence? How can we learn from this evidence to build a historical narrative jurisprudence for gender advocacy? Gaskell's strategies in *Lois the Witch,* like those of Carlo Ginzburg and Joan Wallach Scott, offer some guidance. As I have noted, historians of the novel have argued that the genre's success from the eighteenth century is owing to its capacity to negotiate precisely the kinds of cruxes represented by the legacy of the witchcraft trials. Bakhtin's notion of heteroglossia identifies a narrative practice that accommodates multiple logics, or forms of argument. While this is an important element in the development of a historiography that negotiates with the past, women writers reserved the right to judge the abuses of women in the past, to engage, that is, in historical "hag-advocacy." What literary techniques supplied were methods of historical narrative that invited a self-consciousness of anachronistic value judgments combined with a critique of institutions and practices that enjoyed a transhistorical authority, and that could be rationalized by current ideology. That narrative had also to negotiate between objective evidence and the social construction of evidence, without vitiating either.

Two preliminary conclusions for a historical jurisprudence of gender advocacy might be drawn. Information becomes intelligible, narratable, readable as a story because, in Bernard S. Jackson's phrase, it can be placed within a "framework of existing social knowledge."[43] But whereas the writers on witchcraft trials I take up in subsequent chapters, from Reginald Scot to William Godwin, as well as the theorists discussed above, achieved that intelligibility at the expense of excluding contradiction and historically contingent causality, Gaskell's tale draws attention to the inadequacies of "frameworks of existing social knowledge." In lieu of sentimentalization, rationalization, aestheticization, or theorization, this insistence on the "hard facts"—i.e., the unassimilatable instances of human suffering and motives that controvert those frameworks (be they patriarchal or feminist)—is what the realistic imagination affords our efforts at *de facto* recognition of difference. If narrative jurisprudence seeks to transform those frameworks, what it might consider valuing about storytelling is neither its coherence, nor an artful postmodern incoherence, but how stories gesture outside themselves toward a history they cannot accommodate. Insofar as Gaskell's realism eschews totalizing explanations, it insists on the contingency of closure ("for what could he say . . . ?") and calls into question "existing social knowledge." Gaskell's realistic imagination functions as a fundamentally pragmatic discourse of negotiation on the subject of witchcraft prosecution, neither replacing one authoritative interpretation with another, nor abandoning questions of justice. Rather, it insists on the "hard facts" of physical existence (especially the consequences of human decision making) while acknowledging the contingency of our interpretations of those facts, be they legal interpretations or literary. The second is that a historicized narrative jurisprudence should afford feminist advocacy not an antidote to an allegedly masculinist mode of legal reasoning, nor an unmediated account of the "hard facts" of women's lives. As the history of witchcraft literature demonstrates, no mode of representation enjoys special powers of advocacy. Rather, techniques of literary narrative that arose within the conditions of historical self-consciousness, mass literacy, and democratic theory compel us to use literature as critically as we do the law. Above all, Gaskell would have us notice that her literary treatment of the history of witchcraft trials is not an autonomous aesthetic object, but is itself historically contingent. She would not have us enshrine it as an ideal, as some law and literature scholars have the works of her contemporaries. Instead, Gaskell's story reacts to a moment in the history of feminism wherein women's access to politics and history was preeminently through literary means. Her version of realism, then, exhibits not only the powers of literature for gender advocacy but also its political limitations.

The vast literature on witch trials, which I can only survey in the next two chapters, can hardly be credited with arousing a skeptical critique of witchcraft legislation or dispelling belief in witchcraft. Publicity had an ambiguous effect on belief formation at the origins of print culture as much as it did in Bentham's time, at the advent of mass circulation publication media. Indeed, as Owen Davies has shown, the dissemination of literature about witchcraft to an increasingly literate population helped to keep witchcraft belief alive into the twentieth century, to the dismay of elite church theologians.[44] The kind of imaginative identification promoted by some narrative legal theorists as an emancipatory function essential to storytelling could encourage empathy with the victims of witchcraft, or convince an audience that they were themselves bewitched. Responses to accounts of witch trials were as difficult to manage as were responses to the accounts of trials for other crimes, such as murder, or treason, through which the government sought to enlist print technology on behalf of social order. Criminals could become popular heroes, or prosecutions could be fueled by a sense of panic spread by the reiteration in print of isolated events. The communal interests audiences brought to stories of witch trials interacted with the narrative constructions of witches—whatever their authors' or ecclesiastical censors' intentions might have been—to create new relationships to legal institutions and understandings of crime, sin, or deviance.

Although the political effect of early legal print culture is far from direct (promoting a tolerant skepticism, for example), it certainly helped to speed the transformation of features of early modern cultures of evidence in several respects, with far-ranging consequences for gender advocacy. As Richard Green has shown, scribal culture had already placed severe pressure on the communal mechanisms of justice which prevailed under conditions in which *lex non scripta* was the norm.[45] It might be noted that, contrary to Green's celebration of folk law, the effects of *lex scripta* were at least as politically ambiguous as were the effects of print technology from the sixteenth century onward. But if there had ever been a time in which the illiterate and disenfranchised could tell their stories before the law—stories that were not pre-scripted by other narratives, even if they may have been judged in such terms by a literate elite—those conditions rapidly changed with new publication technologies. As Teresa de Lauretis's evocation of the unintelligible woman burned as a witch in Eco's *Name of the Rose* suggests, this transformation has been construed as a principal example of a discursive technology that produces deviance by rendering alterity as unintelligibility.[46] But in the case of witch trials in early modern English legal procedure, print technology can also be seen to distribute communicative competence. In short, a study of witch trial literature should purge whatever longing we may have for storytelling as a uniquely efficacious form of representation by which outsiders may secure the empathic identification of legal decision makers. Both Victorianists and legal theorists may arrive at a more judicious appreciation of literary advocacy by examining the history of witchcraft literature through which gender advocacy was shaped.

CHAPTER TWO

Witchcraft Precedents as Literary History

From *The Discoverie of Witchcraft* to Sir Matthew Hale

WITCHCRAFT WAS PERHAPS the first crime legal historians understood as having been created discursively. The Victorian legal historians Sir Frederick Pollock and Frederic William Maitland remarked that "sorcery is a crime created by the measures which are taken for its suppression."[1] The crime of witchcraft was defined as much by its modes of publication as by its modes of suppression, however. Whereas actual prosecutions arose and subsided for what appear to have been particular, discrete, and even personal causes, such as those proposed in *Lois the Witch,* literature on witchcraft prosecution has continued to flow steadily since the sixteenth century. What is more, Pollock and Maitland were compelled to address witchcraft because the founding documents of historical jurisprudence had been produced by a judge in a witchcraft trial, Sir Matthew Hale. This chapter traces the literary history of witchcraft law from the sixteenth century, notably Reginald Scot's skeptical critique, *The Discoverie of Witchcraft,* to Hale's notorious conviction of two women for witchcraft in 1662.

The prosecution of witches in England coincides with significant evolutions in print culture, which, in turn, theorists have related to epistemic crises, particularly the rise of historicism. In its decontextualizing effects, print technology produced a kind of epistemic "time warp." Elizabeth Eisenstein notes that "when 'technology went to press' so too did a vast backlog of occult lore, and few readers could discriminate between the two."[2] Witchcraft prosecution urgently pressed questions of truth simultaneously as textual and empirical problems and the dissemination of witch trials in a range of printed forms created something of a feedback loop between legal procedures and popular beliefs. Indeed, the literary history of witchcraft prosecution is not only rich, but so intertwined with the epistemic changes wrought by print technology that law and literature are difficult to separate. The significance of this intertwining for gender advocacy is at the core of my argument.

As Barbara Shapiro has argued, it was law, not science, that supplied the culture with "a respected, ready-made technology of fact finding."[3] Linked to the audiences of print culture, witchcraft prosecutions ramified their evidentiary controversies well beyond actual trials and helped to inject gender trouble throughout early modern culture. Some of that trouble arose from the fact that English legal procedure itself was ill suited to prosecuting a crime that had been constructed within quite different Continental civil law practices of bringing charges, eliciting confessions, evaluating evidence, and rendering verdicts. Keith Thomas notes that the sixteenth-century acts framed witchcraft in a way more consistent with English criminal law, as an offense against persons and property, rather than as heresy. Furthermore, whereas the clergy dominated Continental witch hunts and prosecutions, "The nature of crime and the criminal law [in England] made vigilance a communal obligation," as Cynthia Herrup has remarked.[4] In the less professionalized procedures of English law, victims of witchcraft (like victims of other crimes) were principally responsible for identifying the culprit, leveling accusations, and gathering and presenting evidence. The magistrates who were charged with evaluating that evidence and examining the accused, and the grand jurymen whose responsibility it was to decide upon the validity of indictments presented them by magistrates, as well as the juries that rendered verdicts, were themselves laymen, not lawyers. These groups had a demonstrable preference for concrete forms of proof and eyewitness testimony as reliable safeguards against malicious prosecutions, which themselves violated the common peace.[5] When presented with the anomalous crime of witchcraft, their traditional evidentiary standards were sorely tested.

If an indictment were proven, the prisoner and all witnesses would be required to appear at assizes, where the case would be tried by jury. This represented yet another significant difference between English and Continental procedure: English judges, unlike their Continental counterparts, could not engage in formal inquisitions or torture and depended on a jury for a verdict, even if they could instruct the jury as to the appropriate decision.[6] Assize trials were great dramas wherein the authority of the Crown, embodied in judges sent from Westminster, was enacted in pomp and ceremony, and as such, they could draw huge and ungovernable crowds for especially interesting cases, as when witches were tried. Trials could force a consensus witchcraft belief on the unruly diversity of extralegal opinion represented by various members of the elite and of a local populace. But public sentiment could force juries and judges to acquiesce. In turn, defenders of witchcraft prosecution anxious to maintain the authority of the Crown to manage its subjects were compelled to create rational reconstructions of legal decisions by incorporating popular belief into elite witchcraft theory. All told, witch trials brought serious ideological conflicts into representation, which were often displaced onto gender and widely disseminated through the various genres of witchcraft writing.

Witchcraft must be seen as a crime well suited to the various needs that were created by print culture, from those of the Crown to a popular audience, suggesting how print culture at once created the crime of witchcraft and disciplined it. England's original sixteenth-century witchcraft legislation was written in the context of "the flowering of a very substantial publishing industry," which F. J. Levy attributes to "the rapidly increasing number of the educated, together with the exigencies of Reformation theology."[7] The promulgation of Reformation theology depended upon an educated clergy and literate lay elite able to decipher a vernacular prayer book. Additionally, the Reformation required consolidation of religious and secular authority in the sovereign, which has been proposed as a cause of the English witch trials. Eisenstein argues that "Gutenberg's invention" not only encouraged literal fundamentalism within Christian theology, lending new force to the declaration "Thou shalt not suffer a witch to live" (Exodus 22:18), but also provided both the means and the imperative to enforce orthodox beliefs on a growing audience, for which there were other subversive competitors.

Notable among these competing publications was an explosion of "news media"—reports of domestic and foreign events circulated in manuscript and print.[8] Elizabeth I's government was peculiarly sensitive to gossip and rumor, given the vulnerability of a State led by a virgin queen. The spread of rumor, gossip, and news through cheap publications was closely related to activities attributed to witches and enchanters: prognostication, prophecy, and divination, which threatened Elizabeth I's rule. From the government's point of view, published accounts of trials and executions helpfully extended to a wider audience the political function of the public spectacles they recorded. Whereas the majority of executions were for property crimes, published accounts focused on the more sensational crimes of murder, treason, and witchcraft, suggesting as well the influence of audience demand on print.

Not only could disseminating news of trials engage a wide spectrum of the population in the legal mechanisms for establishing truth and enforcing order, its subject matter was appealingly sensational. "Ever since the popular press had been established in England," remarks James Sharpe, "much of its output had been devoted to crime, its major concern being the sensational and newsworthy case."[9] The spate of early modern dramas involving witchcraft has preoccupied scholars of early modern literature. But historians of witchcraft are ambiguously blessed with a wide variety of literary treatments of witchcraft prosecution, since their subject falls at the intersection of several topics that topped the earliest "best sellers" list of printed matter, conjoining with true crime, religion, law, and wonders of nature and adaptable for a wide range of consumers, from a learned elite to the ballad-monger's illiterate audience. A witchcraft pamphlet of 1613 succinctly demonstrates this thematic conjunction, listing "'treasons, murthers, witchcrafts, fires, flouds' as evidence that the Day of Judgement was at hand."[10] By the middle of the seventeenth century, as Henry Peacham exclaimed, "For a penny you may have all the Newes in England, of Murders, Flouds, Witches, Fires, Tempests, and what not, in one of Martin Parkers Ballads."[11]

Sandra Clark has remarked of Elizabethan pamphlets on witch trials that "the subject was of such universal appeal that it needed no further sensationalizing, and it is the very starkness of these accounts that makes them so compelling to a modern reader."[12] They contained a greater element of eyewitness reporting than most Elizabethan journalism, and, Clark continues, "it often happens that the unintentionally apt choice of detail and grimly honest writing reveal to a later age terrible cruelty and suffering of which the recorder was quite unaware."[13] Owen Davies characterizes the process by which accounts of witch trials were popularized in chapbooks and broadsides of the sixteenth and seventeenth centuries: "Simplify the story, add a woodcut to excite the imagination, print it in large, bold type on poor-quality paper, fold, cut, and stitch it into twenty-four pages, and sell it for a couple of pennies, and we have an elite form of literature transformed into popular literature."[14] Along with other cheap pamphlets on religion and crime, witch trial pamphlets were written for middling persons, "burgesses and yeomen . . . [,] tradesmen, merchants, bankers, shipowners, manufacturers, skilled craftsmen, and farmers . . . [,] literate as they would not have been in the early sixteenth century."[15]

Witchcraft publications for the elite included controversial writings, guides to grand jurymen, and legal and theological treatises. Reginald Scot, the author of *The Discoverie of Witchcraft* (1584), the first learned—*and skeptical*—treatise on witchcraft prosecution in England, was himself an educated landholder, who, as Clive Holmes notes, expected his peers to appreciate his erudition.[16] Obviously, judging from the proliferation of guides to grand juries, the gentry consumed such materials, and there is every reason to think those more popular forms, such as cheap pamphlets and printed ballads, were read by this class as well.[17] These popular texts on witchcraft were so plentiful that Henry Goodcole felt compelled to counter their effect with his own "serious" tract, *The Wonderfull Discoverie of Elizabeth Sawyer a Witch, Late of Edmonton* (1621), complaining of the "most base and false Ballets" and "ridiculous fictions" that were already circulating on the case. Frances Dolan remarks that "although Goodcole differentiates his text from *other* popular narratives, his pamphlet was itself 'popular': cheaply produced, available to many of the same kinds of readers who purchased the 'base and false Ballets,' and also the source for a play . . . *The Witch of Edmonton*."[18]

The various genres by which news of witch trials were promulgated are the very forms from which the novel emerged. As J. Paul Hunter and Michael McKeon have argued, the appetite for and cultural significance of cheap printed accounts of strange and true events, wonders, and sensational crimes and executions shaped the novel's subject matter, narrative devices, and representations of subjectivity. What is more, the dissemination and preservation of printed matter representing the witch trials and witchcraft controversy ensured that future generations would have to grapple with the subject as a historiographic problem. Significantly, the legislation of 1736, making pretenses to supernatural powers a punishable offense at the same time it repealed the felonious status of sorcery, comes by the nineteenth century to be regarded as a form of censorship when it is not seen as an embarrassing anachronism.[19] Of course, the embarrassment of anachronism depends on a highly developed historical sense, one that witchcraft legislation imposed on jurists, even after 1736, with particular force. This self-consciousness, which encourages at once the rise of legal historical scholarship in the nineteenth century as well as the repudiation of history in legal positivism, is the product of a long cultural process in which the law's entanglement with witches plays an important role.

Finally, to close the feedback loop: the proliferation of witch trial literature itself influenced legal precedent, eroding any claims to the autonomy of legal discourse. It is likely that from an early stage in the history of witch trials, the "simple men" who made up juries would also have been exposed to news of other witch trials. Arguing for the significance of pretrial publicity in witchcraft cases, Clive Holmes notes the four tracts published during the Elizabethan period (1566, 1579, 1582, 1589) giving details of Essex trials. Treatises, sermons, and editions of depositions and confessions "were seconded by writers whose works were more obviously popular, the authors of broadsides and ballads."[20] These latter examples, which could be consumed by both literate and illiterate audiences, spread beliefs and news of trials beyond localities and across socioeconomic strata. As Joy Wiltenburg notes, "Printed songs and stories formed a bridge between written and oral cultures, both in their own oral performance and in the exchange of texts."[21] As the exchange between oral and written cultures expanded in the course of the sixteenth and seventeenth centuries, it is conceivable that even illiterate accusers, witnesses, and the accused themselves became conscious of their roles in a legal discourse and social phenomenon and so were touched by the conflicting epistemic consequences of that consciousness. Like the other felons who were the subjects of trial and execution narratives, witches became the subjects of legal-literary representation.

Let me illustrate the form in which witch trials were published by examining one example in some detail. The "starkness," noted by Sandra Clark above, "that makes them so compelling to a modern reader" is evident in *The Examination and Confession of Certaine Wytches at Chensforde in the Countie of Essex before the Quenes Majesties Judges, the XXVI Daye of July Anno 1566* (1566). It was provided with a lengthy dedicatory epistle, a verse preface, and several woodcuts illustrating each of the defendants, in addition to reports of the examinations of the prisoners in a form represented as "verbatim, as near as could be gathered."[22]

Examinations and confessions of the accused, one Mother Agnes Waterhouse of Hatfield Peverel, aged sixty-four years, and her daughter, eighteen-year-old Joan Waterhouse, before Doctor Cole and Master Fortescue at assizes, concentrate on evidence of consorting with a familiar (a cat or a dog) and damage done to property and persons. In a second examination upon arraignment before Justice Southcote and Master Gerard, the queen's attorney, testimony given by Mother Agnes Waterhouse and Joan, her daughter, was described by the author as "no less wonderful than most true" (78). We find a spirited exchange among the Waterhouse women and the queen's attorney concerning evidence given by Agnes Brown, a twelve-year-old.

> Then the Queen's attorney asked of the said Agnes Waterhouse what she said to it; then she demanded what manner of knife that it was, and Agnes Brown said it was a dagger knife. "There thou liest," said Agnes Waterhouse. "Why?" quoth the Queen's attorney. "Marry, my lord," quoth she, "she saith it is a dagger knife and I have none such in my house but a great knife, and therein she lieth." "Yea, yea, my lord," quoth Joan Waterhouse, "she lieth in that she saith that it had a face like an ape, for this that come to me was like a dog."

The attorney asks Agnes when last a cat had sucked her blood. Never, she answers: "And then the jailer lifted up her kercher on her head and there was divers spots in her face and one on her nose. Then said the Queen's attorney, 'In good faith, Agnes, when did he such of thy blood last?' 'By my faith, my lord', she said, 'not this fortnight:' and so the jury went together for that matter" (81).

The pamphlet closes with Mother Waterhouse's dying confession: "And being demanded of the bystanders, she confessed that she sent her Satan to one Wardol, a neighbor of hers being a tailor (with whom she was offended) to hurt and destroy him and his goods" (81). She confesses also to praying in Latin, "And thus she yielded up her soul, trusting to be in joy with Christ her Saviour, which dearly had bought her with His most precious blood. Amen" (82).

This formulaic account, which is reproduced and elaborated on in many witch trial pamphlets—as well as those concerning other crimes—in James Sharpe's view "must have played a vital role in spreading official ideas about crime and punishment, and about the whole nature of authority and disorder, down to the lower orders." Sharpe notes that, based on the frequency of published "Last Dying Speeches," "traitors and rebels, high-born and plebeian alike, were willing to make confessions redolent of the show trials of Stalin's Russia."[23]

Sharpe's connection to the Orwellian sense of "witch hunt" reveals how we are apt to read these quasi-legal documents from a twenty-first-century perspective. But a dynamic between state-sponsored propaganda and popular tastes was from the outset a defining feature of the spread of literacy, and accounts for its ambiguous political impact. The genres became staples of print production for popular audiences and were even recycled in mass working-class journalism in the nineteenth century.[24] In his groundbreaking work, *Literacy and Popular Culture: England, 1750–1914,* David Vincent emphasized the disciplinary functions of literacy, which can now be traced back to the emergence of print culture. But, as Adrian Johns has argued, readers' responses could never be controlled.[25] Insofar as witch trial pamphlets disseminated the speech of witches, they could generate sympathy as well as condemnation—a phenomenon familiar to scholars of the trials of Oscar Wilde, which I will discuss in a later chapter. The powerful influence of both popular and learned literatures on witchcraft led controversialists to address their elite readership as textual interpreters, and to stress their readers' power as authoritative guides for the reading public and guardians of the illiterate masses. As we shall see, Reginald Scot would establish the interconnection between the powers of legal and literary interpretation, and would leverage gender against corruptions of English legal proceedings perpetrated by witchcraft prosecutions.

Scot's *Discoverie* and the Strategy of Gender Advocacy

The dangerous legal precedents set by the procedural anomalies of witchcraft prosecutions and the influence of various forms of pre-trial publicity, including popular pamphlets, translations of Continental treatises, and newsletters, were decried in the very first learned treatise on witchcraft produced by an Englishman: Reginald Scot's *Discoverie of Witchcraft* (1584). Importantly, it was this skeptical attack on witchcraft prosecution rather than any treatise advocating prosecution that shaped the course of debate in England into the eighteenth century. Every proponent of witchcraft prosecution felt obliged to answer Scot, and Scot remains a key source of information about the controversy. As James Sharpe notes, "It is one of the great peculiarities of the history of witchcraft in England that the first major theoretical work on the subject published by an English writer . . . was unrelentingly skeptical."[26] The outstanding feature of Scot's treatise for my argument is the function of gender in a historicist analysis of the legal culture of evidence prompted by the emergent print culture.

Scot's *Discoverie* employs many of the strategies we might anachronistically associate with the enlightened liberal's advocacy for the oppressed. Against a myriad of authorities supporting witchcraft prosecution (he cites more than two hundred foreign and thirty-eight English works),

Scot counterposes the victims of prosecutions, whom he characterizes as poor, aged, simple, melancholic women. Scot, a Kentish gentleman whose only previous publication had been *A Perfect Platforme of a Hoppe-Garden* (1574), justified his intervention in the witchcraft controversy on the grounds that

> they, which are commonly accused of witchcraft, are the least sufficient of all other persons to speake for themselves; as having the most base and simple education of all others; the extremitie of their age giving them leave to dote, their povertie to beg, their wrongs to chide and threaten (as being void of anie other waie of revenge) their humor melancholicall to be full of imaginations, from whence cheefelie proceedeth the vanitie of their confessions; as that they can transforme themselves and other into apes, owles, asses, dogs, cats, &c.: that they can flie in the aire, kill children with charms, hinder the comming of butter, &c.[27]

The rhetorical value of framing his attack on witchcraft prosecution in terms of gender is clear in his dedications and address to readers. Scot dedicates his *Discoverie* to Sir Roger Manwood, Lord Chief Baron of the Exchequer and "defender of poor"; Dr. Coldwell, Dean of Rochester; Dr. Readman, Archdeacon of Canterbury; and his cousin, Sir Thomas Scot. He addresses his cousin in his capacity as magistrate, writing: "Sir, I see among other malefactors manie poore old women conuented before you for working of miracles, other wise called witchcraft, and therefore I thought you also a meet person to whom I might comend my booke" (A.vi). To his readers, all men who share to some degree his dedicatees' responsibilities to maintain the peace, Scot makes this plea for mercy:

> The pity that should be in a christian heart, nor yet their simplicitie, impotencie, or age may suffice to suppress the rage or rigor wherewith they are oppressed; yet the consideration of their sex or kind outght to moove some mitigation of their punishment. For if nature (as Plinie reporteth) have taught a lion not to deale so roughlie with a woman as with a man, bicause she is in bodie the weaker vessell, and in hart more incline to pitie (which Jeremie in his lamentations seemeth to confirme) what should a man doo in this case, for whome a woman was created as an helpe and comfort unto him? . . . And therefore among all modest and honest persons it is thought a shame to offer violence or injurie to a woman. (B.iv)

This argument, drawing on biblical and classical authorities, reaffirms women's inferiority in order to solicit the mercy of their patriarchal protectors. Feminists have complained that Scot erases female agency by this strategy, and his argument undoubtedly contributed to historians' longstanding blindness to women's activities as witnesses in witch trials, to say nothing of the kind of agency a woman might have secured by believing herself to have supernatural powers. His deployment of gender may have less to do with a defense of women, however, than with his defense of the dignity of the law, its procedures, and its rules of evidence, all crucial to the law's just treatment of men.

Scot's attendance at the trial of Margaret Simons at the Rochester assizes in 1581 seems to have been the traumatic event that motivated him to write. The wife of John Simons was arraigned, according to Scot, "at the instigation and complaint of divers fond and malicious persons; and speciallie by the meanes of one John Ferrall vicar of that parish: with whom I talked about that matter, and found him both fonlie assotted in the causes, and enviouslie bent towards hir: and (which is worse) as unable to make a good account of his faith, as shee whom he accused" (5). But for the wisdom of one skeptical juror, Scot notes, Simons's neighbors would have succeeded in enlisting the law to achieve their malicious ends (6). Ferrall had accused Simons of bewitching his son for attacking her dog; he was cured by another witch, who had informed against Simons. He also accused her of bewitching his voice, but Scot's investigations revealed that parishioners believed him ill with French pox. Ferrall produced a certificate proving it was a lung ailment. "And this I knowe to be true by the relation of divers honest men of that parish," Scot concludes (6). Scot seems disgusted by this contamination of the justice system with vulgar beliefs and petty malice.

Gender ideology occupies an important position in Scot's thought about witchcraft prosecutions, but it is neither the case that he initiates an enlightened critique of women's legal disadvantages, nor that he cynically exploits the victimization of women to achieve ends ultimately oppressive of women. Rather, Scot's argument might better be understood as characteristic of the sort of epistemic crisis Eisenstein associates with the spread of print technology. And his is a fundamentally historicist critique of belief formation, of the social construction of cultures of evidence. "My greatest adversaries are yoong ignorance and old custome," he announces. Old custom encompasses ancient belief in witchcraft reiterated in learned foreign treatises and invoked in contemporary legislation and ultimately in trials, "for," as Scot cautions, "every old opinion is not sound" (B.iij). Young ignorance is the credulous acceptance of new and sensational stories about witches in the absence of any historical appreciation of the demystification of earlier legends. The remedy for both perversions is a disinterested application of rules of evidence, which Scot associates with procedures unique to English Common Law coupled with historical hindsight. "I had rather refer the reader to common fame," Scot writes, "and their owne eies and eares to be satisfied; then to send them to a Stationers shop, where manie times lies are vendible, and truth contemptible" (A.vi).

To combat the influence of marketable lies, Scot inquires into the "means [by which] the name of witches becommeth so famous, and how diverslie people be opinioned concerning them and their actions" (14). He worries a great deal about the spread of witchcraft hysteria through foreign influences on witchcraft trials, including the treatises entering the English book market with both papist theology and rules of evidence derived from Civil Law, as well as through popular publications, such as the Essex trial pamphlet (which he cites). Each exercises troubling influences on belief formation at all levels of society, leading Scot to concentrate on the causes of "credulity." He complains of the "miraculous actions [that] are imputed to witches by witchmongers, papists, and poets" (9). Stories of witchcraft will appear as incredible a hundred years hence, he tells his readers, as the old legends of Robin Goodfellow are to them (B.ij). The law should play a positive role in discrediting such fables, for "if the lawe of nations would joine with such custome, to the maintenance of ignorance, and to the suppressing of knowledge; the civilest countrie in the world would soone become barbarous, &c. For as knowledge and time discovereth errors, so dooth superstition and ignorance in time breed them" (A.vii).

The civilizing influence of the law is for Scot embodied in the enlightened and merciful monarch and her judges and magistrates, who act simultaneously as instruments of the law and authoritative, critical interpreters of witchcraft texts. They stand between the prolific advocates of witchcraft prosecution and their growing body of readers on the one hand, and their "simple," illiterate female victims, on the other. "I therefore (at this time) doo onelie desire you to consider of my report," Scot enjoins his readers, "concerning the evidence brought before you against them. See first whether the evidence be not frivolous, & whether the proofs brought against them be not incredible, consisting of ghesses, presumptions, & impossibilities contrarie to reason, scripture, and nature. See also what persons complaine upon them, whether they be not of the basest, the unwisest, & most faithles kind of people" (A.vi).

The danger of witchcraft prosecution lies in its contamination of reliable English rules of evidence with technologies of knowledge that set precedents threatening the very legitimacy of the post-Reformation monarchy. All on the grounds that witchcraft is *crimen exceptum,* Scot complains, prosecutions follow Bodin and other Continental sources, noting that corroborative evidence is not needed, that lewd women are allowed to testify, and that confessions elicited under torture and conjectures are credited. As "*Bodin* saith, . . . bicause this is an extraordinarie matter; there must heerin be extraordinarie dealing; and all maner or waies are to be used, direct and indirect" (24). But once introduced into English criminal procedure, these anomalous practices cannot be cordoned off, but serve as precedents that should worry all Englishmen who "remembreth the persecutions of Queene *Maries* time" (37). Scot can be seen to have genuine sympathy for the victims of witchcraft prosecution, especially those whose innocence is underscored by his conviction that, as poor, simple, melancholic women, they cannot be taken seriously as agents. But the pernicious influence of witchcraft literature on the judgment of legal decision makers is clearly his primary concern, and he strives to interpellate his male readers into the narratives of witchcraft trials by emphasizing their own vulnerability to capricious rules of evidence.

Scot's *Discoverie* exercised a profound influence on subsequent writers, part of a nascent jurisprudence on gender, evidence, and legal procedure. A Dutch translation appeared in 1609, dedicated to the curators of the university and the burgomasters of Leyden, and a second Dutch edition was published in 1637 at the request of the professorial boards of law and history at the University of Leyden. New English editions appeared in 1651 and 1665; significantly, neither was registered with the Stationers' Company. Nicholson, the editor of an 1883 edition, opines that the 1665 edition was occasioned by the 1662 trial of Amy Duny and Rose Cullender, presided over by Sir Matthew Hale. As we shall see, advocates of witchcraft prosecution were obliged to answer Scot's arguments and to battle him for control over the interpretation of evidence of witchcraft. Thanks to Scot, in appealing to their readers as authorized interpreters—as jurists, magistrates, and jurymen—they had also to address them as readers of gender.

Significantly, women were more involved in witchcraft prosecution in the seventeenth century than they had been in Scot's time, but not necessarily as the accused. Sharpe reports that Home Circuit assize records for witch trials between 1600 and 1702 show that of the 1,207 calls for witnesses, 576 (48 percent) were for women. The same record indicates an increase in the course of the seventeenth century from a ratio of 46 female to 80 male witnesses called during 1600–1609 to a preponderance of women witnesses in the 1660s and 1670s. "Women were over 11 times more likely to act as witnesses in witchcraft trials at the assizes than they were in all felony cases," Sharpe concludes.[28] Larner was right to dismiss the frequency of female witnesses as evidence against the claim that witch-hunting was woman-hunting. Rather, as Clive Holmes has argued, patriarchal social relations set women in conflict with one another, and women may have been inclined to seize the relatively unusual authority afforded them in witch trials.[29] As a result, legal writers on witchcraft prosecution began to develop gendered concepts of testimony, forensic evidence, and indictment.

James I, who succeeded Elizabeth in 1603, acquired his reputation for witch-hunting as much by authorship as by his actions as a monarch. His *Daemonologie in Forme of a Dialogue* (1597) was probably the most notable witchcraft treatise in English after Scot's, and it urged the adoption of continental witchcraft theory. The felony sorcery statute of 1604 (1 Jac. I, c. 12) announced itself as a stronger measure than the Elizabethan statute, and along with introducing the Continental theory of a demonic pact, it increased the severity of punishment for a second conviction from forfeiture of goods and life imprisonment to forfeiture and death. The language of the act reflects a fear of witchcraft as a threat to both property and male agency, defining the crime as dealing with spirits, divining location of lost goods, provoking to unlawful love, or destroying, wasting or impairing chattels or goods.[30] But as James Sharpe remarks, "The problem with his legendary status as a witch-hunter, as has long been known, is that despite his involvement in the [Scottish] trials of 1590–91 and his tract of 1597, James, at least as monarch of England, seems to have been more likely to intervene to save witches than to secure their convictions."[31] Whatever James I feared from witchcraft, he shared Scot's concerns about the difficulty of interpreting evidence and proving witchcraft in courts of law.

The principal dramatic treatments of witchcraft in this period indicate that there was a growing tendency to treat witchcraft as a popular spectacle, even a source of humor. *Macbeth* (1606) is merely the most celebrated of the dramas dealing with witchcraft. But other dramatic works include John Marston's *Sophonisba* (1606); Ben Jonson's *The Masque of Queens* (1609);

Thomas Dekker, Samuel Rowley, and John Ford's *The Witch of Edmonton* (performed 1621, published 1658); Thomas Middleton's *The Witch* (1778); and Thomas Heywood and Richard Brome's *The Late Lancashire Witches* (1634). As Frances Dolan notes, these plays might derive from pamphlets describing actual trials, such as the 1612 trials at Lancaster, or might be largely fanciful; they were performed before different kinds of audiences, from the court to the groundlings at London theaters.[32] In many respects, these plays, like popular pamphlets about witchcraft, do not significantly revise understandings of witches' powers or activities; that is, they would not have suggested new ways of prosecuting witches. Nor can they be characterized as a group in terms of their ideology: dramatic representations were not necessarily committed to skepticism or belief. But they did introduce an element missing from published accounts of trials, namely, overt attempts at humor. Excepting *The Witch of Edmonton,* they could be construed as subversive of witchcraft legislation because, in encouraging laughter at witches, they indirectly ridiculed the legal machinery brought to bear against such a trivial threat. Even *Macbeth*'s witches could be co-opted into this comic scheme, as Davenant did, thereby setting the production conventions for *Macbeth* into the nineteenth century.[33] In this respect, these dramas cohered with Scot's strategy of undermining the authority of witch trials by emphasizing the pathetic status of their victims. Yet, just as I have suggested the inadvisability of construing Scot's strategy in feminist terms, so too it should be recognized that the comedic elements of these plays, as Frances Dolan notes, "do not translate into compassion for or defenses of accused women."[34]

Dolan's caution is confirmed by the body of literature on evidence offering professional advice to magistrates and grand juries that followed upon the stricter Jacobean witchcraft legislation. These works have broad significance in Anglo-American legal history since, as Shapiro demonstrates, they introduced concepts of proof and evidence borrowed from continental sources.[35] Furthermore, in responding to Reginald Scot, each elaborated on a gendered theory of evidence. John Cotta's *Trial of Witchcraft* (1616), Thomas Cooper's *Mysterie of Witchcraft* (1617), Michael Dalton's *The Country Justice* (1618), and Richard Bernard's *A Guide to the Grand-Jury Men* (1627) each supported the prosecution of witches while at the same time stressing the complexity of evidence, the likelihood of fraud, and the opportunities for error. Cotta was a physician and author of a treatise denouncing medical treatment by ignorant amateurs. Bernard was a clergyman who had had his own brush with heresy when fellow Puritans among his congregation declared separatist intentions. Cooper was a minor divine, and Dalton had the Commission of Peace for Cambridgeshire. Whereas the probity of English magistrates and grand juries had traditionally rested on their local knowledge and common sense, witchcraft, these authors argued, demanded extraordinary forensic expertise and heightened suspicion of accusations based on "vulgar superstition."[36] Thus did the epistemological requirements of witchcraft legislation bring into focus the evolving political role of laymen as administrators of English law, on the front line between the elaboration of *lex scripta* in the form of nascent jurisprudential theory and a newly authorized *lex non scripta* of custom and folk belief, anxiously contained in elite discourse as "superstition."

Characteristic of these guides on witchcraft prosecution is Bernard's counsel to grand jurymen: "Better it were, till the truth appeare, to write an *Ignoramus,* then upon oath to set down *Billa vera,* and so to thrust an intricate case upon a Jury of simple men, who proceed too often upon relations of mere presumptions, and these sometimes very weake ones too, to take away mens lives" (25). Citing Scot, he offered his own explanation for the preponderance of females among the accused. Women were more "addicted" to witchcraft (91) because they were more credulous, impatient, "tongue-ripe," and "proud of their rule" than men (92–93). Men resort to witchcraft out of Faustian desire for knowledge (99). It seems as though Bernard regretted that witchcraft accusations so rarely provided worthy foes, men of learning whose immense curiosity bridled at human limitations. Instead, Bernard and his fellow writers must assist men in their dealings with the "basest sort of people" (155), by which he meant not only the accused but also their accusers. In his directions for examining witnesses, it is often difficult to gauge whether Bernard is more disgusted by witches or by the women who testify against them. He asserted that women were more than willing to testify against other women accused of witchcraft, flooding magistrates and grand juries with lewd, malicious, "tattling gossip" (82). By enabling an extraordinary number of women to speak when the subject was witchcraft, the communal procedures of criminal law provoked professionals to devise standards of evidence aimed at discrediting and excluding them.

Yet the more intent legal authorities were to convict women of witchcraft, the more they authorized female legal authority. The somatic evidence of witch trials compelled judges to overcome their disgust to seek out a peculiarly feminized expertise and constitute women as examiners and jurors, of a sort. Barred from jury service, and deemed inexpert on virtually all other matters, women were called upon at least as early as 1579 to examine female prisoners for signs of the "witch's teat."[37] Interest in the witch's teat already represented an accommodation of the learned elite to popular belief: familiars embodying the devil and suckling at a witch's teat had no counterpart in Continental witchcraft theory.[38] Women, credited because of their "good characters" rather than any professional expertise (though in the 1640s Matthew Hopkins would come to favor midwives), were deputized to carry out physical examinations for the teat and present their evidence before the court.[39] Importantly, this rival form of forensic knowledge heightened the social pressure placed on doctors in witch trials, a phenomenon, as I shall argue in later chapters, that stands near the head of a long tradition wherein legal "common sense" asserted itself against medical expertise by enlisting the arcane evidence of female bodies. In constructing the authority of female examiners along the model of the juror's local knowledge, it suggests a close call with the logic by which nineteenth-century women complained that they were not tried by a jury of their peers.

Finally, the stricter statute law, while it appears to have fueled a market in witchcraft literature, did not result in an overall increase in prosecutions or convictions. Instead, witchcraft prosecution remained a sporadic phenomenon, driven by local concerns rather than centralized legal authority. Lancashire saw two large-scale prosecutions, one in 1612, when thirty-five persons were tried and ten hanged, and another in 1633, with twenty accused, seventeen convicted, and none hanged, though many died in jail. The first trial became the subject of Thomas Potts's pamphlet *The Wonderfull Discoverie of Witches in the Countie of Lancaster* (1613), which widely publicized the confession of Elizabeth Southerns, known as "Old Demdike," accused of training her children in witchcraft, participating in witches' sabbaths, consorting with a familiar, and bewitching a man to death. Wallace Notestein construes the second Lancashire trial as the direct outcome of the legendary status of the first. The accusations were made by a young boy, and his stories were taken up by local justices of the peace. Seventeen people were convicted, three of whom died in jail before Charles I's secretary of state, Sir Edward Coke, could intervene and order examinations of the prisoners. Several women were examined by Henry Bridgeman, the bishop of Chester, and several more were transferred to London to be examined by physicians, including William Harvey. But as Notestein remarks, their skeptical conclusions were supported by the results of examinations for a witches' mark, the very test women had been conscripted to carry out in earlier cases. Whatever the Crown's desire, then—and Notestein believed that it included "break[ing] down the evidence of the female juries"—the effect was what Scot had feared: to set a new evidentiary precedent at the highest levels of English law, one that would prove significant during Interregnum trials.[40]

During the reign of Charles I, witchcraft prosecution levels remained low, but peaked during the Interregnum.[41] By that time, Crown indifference to witchcraft prosecution could be cited as evidence of impiety. Nigel Smith has discussed the "media revolution" of the 1640s and 1650s and noted that the struggles between Charles I and Parliament "began on paper."[42] Whereas the impious productions of the theaters were suppressed, the Puritan government would rely heavily on print propaganda, and a wide range of subject matter, including witchcraft, could be enlisted in this deadly earnest cause. Lay religious authorship expanded on an unprecedented scale. Women printers were also thriving under these conditions.[43] Adrian Johns has argued that the prominence of women in the print industry "was but one sense in which the domains of print were riven by representations of gender."[44] What is more, Johns emphasizes the role of Puritan scriptural reading habits in unleashing female readers, some of whom became published prophets in the 1640s.[45] Puritan ideology helped to dismantle what J. Paul Hunter has called "the old sacramental world available to priests and specially designated decoders (but only to others through them) . . . translat[ing it in]to a dynamic world with emblems spatial and temporal that anyone with determination and patience could read. The democraticization of empiricism meant that texts were constantly evolving and crying out to be read; 'readers' did not even have to be literate."[46]

At the same time, the court system was in disarray, creating a situation ripe for enterprising witch-hunters, such as Matthew Hopkins and his associate, John Stearne. Hopkins, who professionalized detection and prosecution, achieved a record-high 42 percent conviction rate in the period 1645–47.[47] Along with John Stearne, Hopkins was involved in trials leading to the execution of two hundred people. The majority of prosecutions involving Hopkins were against women. He succeeded because he was adept at managing the disparate components of witch trials as they had developed over the course of more than forty years and came to play under the peculiar political conditions of the Interregnum. As such, he would become a convenient scapegoat for later skeptics who could avoid condemning either judiciary or populace for the witch trials by foisting all their scorn on this parvenu. Still, insofar as witch-hunting could be woman-hunting, it would seem that women were better off when conventions of legal procedure were authoritatively enforced.

Nevertheless, Hopkins employed women as expert witnesses in his law-and-order crusade. In his *Discovery of Witches* (1647), Hopkins urged the use of "ancient skillful matrons and midwives" in detecting physical signs identifying witches.[48] Through her role as Hopkins's examiner in the Essex trials of 1645, Mary Philips gained a reputation as an expert on the witch's teat and was paid as an expert by local authorities in subsequent trials.[49] Hopkins managed public opinion as well, drawing on the testimony of local people to condemn witches. Finally, he satisfied the long-standing desires of the clergy to define witchcraft not in terms of damage to persons and property, but as a compact with the devil, wherein their expertise rather than vulgar knowledge was required for conviction. But Hopkins himself would be discredited after a relatively brief, if destructive, career. In fact, his notoriety might be credited with provoking a backlash of skeptical writing in the 1650s.

The constitutional crises provoked by the Civil War, the Restoration, and the Glorious Revolution placed pressures on the Common Law as the repository of political legitimacy, as the Reformation had done in the sixteenth century. As the conditions of judicial and political legitimacy shifted, witchcraft prosecutions provided leverage in political battles unimagined in 1604. Radical shifts in the constitution of state authority produced a lot of political heretics out of one-time insiders. First, during the Interregnum, Royalists' objections to parliamentary authority could be raised indirectly through an attack on witchcraft prosecutions as examples of the incoherence of covenantal political theory. Then, after the Restoration, defense of witchcraft prosecution was part of a Royalist attack on the philosophical materialism of Hobbes. After 1688, witchcraft prosecution would enter Whig ideology as a sign of the abuses of monarchal authority corrupted by vulgar superstition against the judicious wisdom embodied in English law. In this way it would come down to the philosophical radicals of the late eighteenth century. Throughout, debate was framed in terms of the politics of print culture, with authors seeking to regain control of a medium wherein the truth had been contaminated by enthusiasts, factionalists, and women.

Robert Filmer, best known to feminist and political historians for his *Patriarcha; or, The Natural Power of Kings* (1680), was also the author of a skeptical treatise on witchcraft prosecution, *An Advertisement to the Jury-Men of England, Touching Witches* (1653). Filmer had earlier expressed belief in the reality of witches, but in this work his attack on witchcraft prosecution is consistent with *Patriarcha* in denouncing the Calvinist underpinnings of the current government and its courts. The stated occasions of Filmer's tract were the execution of witches at the summer assizes, Kent, July 30, 1652, before Peter Warburton, Maidstone, and the republication of William Perkins's *A Discourse of the Damned Art of Witchcraft,* a guide for detecting witchcraft, originally published in 1608. Ian Bostridge notes that Filmer's "imprisonment and intimidation at the hands of Parliament men" might have spurred this response to the ruling party's witch-hunting activities in his county. But above all, as Bostridge sees it, "Filmer's interest in covenant is most plausibly a reaction to the religious and political events of the 1640s, and a thoroughgoing reaction at that, one which touched his demonology as much as his theology or his ideas on government."[50]

The only use Filmer makes of gender is to deny the witch's agency in acts of *maleficium.* If the witch acts by virtue of her compact with the devil, then she is not the agent of evil, but the devil, and she is innocent under Common Law. If she is indeed the agent, "principall her selfe," then it must be by natural means that she has effected harm and is, therefore, no witch.[51] Filmer is more concerned with countering the abuse of legal procedure he detects in Perkins's use of presumptions, in fact, attacking the whole theory of probabilistic reasoning and circumstantial evidence elaborated in earlier legal treatises on evidence in witchcraft accusations. Here we see the witch trial described in terms resembling Orwell's.

Thomas Ady, in *A Candle in the Dark: or, A Treatise Concerning the Nature of Witches and Witchcraft* (1656), extended Filmer's critique. Addressing himself principally to "Judges, Sheriffs, Justices of the Peace, and Grand-Jury-Men,"[52] he presents witchcraft doctrine as a threat to their constituted legal roles, and their responsibility to protect men of property:

> The Doctrine of Witches power is the main strength of Antichristian policy; for whereas that *Romish* Whore knoweth, that in all Nations the Civil Magistrate will hold power, and not resign it to her, to have absolute power to kill for Religion, she maintaineth this damnable Doctrine to the end, that under the name of Witches she may melt away those whom she feareth, or suspecteth will be opposers of her Antichristian pride, and herein engageth the Civil Magistrate, by her subtill

> Doctrine, to cut off whom she pleaseth; and how can this be said to be a Government for the defence of peoples Lives and Estates? (138)

As Ady goes on in this remarkable passage, he comes close to implicating a credulous magistracy in a political conspiracy contrary to the word of God:

> And these poor accused people have no redress, or help at the hands of the Magistrate; but he who ought to be their Defender is bewitched, and engaged against them; he is taught who, and what are Witches; and that many times they that engage him by their lying Doctrine, are the very Witches themselves, aimed at in the Scriptures, that ought not to be suffered to live. (138)

This is the witch trial rewritten as a parliamentary conspiracy against the protections that the law should hold out to Royalists against the confiscation of their lands. There is no mention of advocacy on behalf of poor, silly, old women; instead Ady employs Scot to demonstrate that skepticism regarding the procedures of witch trials does not imply a denial of the reality of witches (sig. A3). In Ady's work, witches are abstracted from documentary evidence of actual witch trials, wherein the accused are overwhelmingly likely to be female, and reconstituted as the silenced, helpless, *male* victims of an elite conspiracy to deprive them of their lives and estates.

The evolution of legal writings on witchcraft over the course of the seventeenth century illustrates how Reginald Scot's *Discoverie* wrote gender into the precedents of English jurisprudence, but less as a strategy of feminist advocacy than as a sympathetic subject position occupied by men who might, for political reasons, be victimized by the anomalous forms of evidence and procedure allowed in witchcraft trials. This is a strategy we will see at work in subsequent chapters on gender advocacy as a form of resistance against lunacy incarcerations and even sodomy prosecutions. Nevertheless, the literary tradition that kept witchcraft prosecution alive would produce a legal precedent of extraordinary salience, one in which the victimization of women had a traumatic effect on the founding of English historical jurisprudence. The conviction of two women for witchcraft in a 1662 trial presided over by Sir Matthew Hale (1609–76) would plague subsequent legal historians who sought to trace the rational progress of the English law back to Hale as the father of English jurisprudence. There is no better example of how thoroughly witchcraft prosecution had permeated early modern cultures of evidence and with what contradictory effects than is afforded by the career of Sir Matthew Hale.

Witchcraft Precedent and the Traumatic Foundations of Historical Jurisprudence

Sir Matthew Hale (1609–76) was highly regarded as a jurist in his own time by Royalists and Roundheads alike, who respected his reputation for fairness, knowledge of the law, and ability to rise above sectarian politics. He served as a Justice of Common Pleas and Member of Parliament during the Protectorate, and became Lord Chief Baron of the Exchequer under Charles II and Chief Justice of the King's Bench in 1671. By virtue of the posthumous publication of his legal manuscripts, which continued over the course of the eighteenth century, Hale also exerted a lasting influence on English jurisprudence. His writings were celebrated after his death in biographies by his friend Richard Baxter, author of *The Certainty of the World of Spirits* (1691), and Bishop Burnet. Hale, in his *History and Analysis of the Common Law* (1713), *The Jurisdiction of the Lords' House* (1796), and *The History of the Pleas of the Crown* (1736), founded a genuinely historical tradition of legal writing. The great twentieth-century historian of English law, W. S. Holdsworth, asserts that Hale's contribution was unequalled until Maitland, in the 1880s.[53] Much of his reputation depends not merely on his ability to make sense of legal history but also on his "scientific method," learned from his teacher, the eminent legal scholar John Selden. Like Selden, Hale worked from original documents, and therefore became a reliable guide for subsequent scholars.

Ironically, Hale's status as the founder of English jurisprudence guaranteed that the very project he initiated—a theory of law's rationality based on its historical development—would be called into question by the anomaly of witchcraft prosecutions and their peculiar susceptibility to literary influence. In 1662, when he was Chief Baron of the Exchequer, Hale was called upon to preside at the trial of Rose Cullender and Amy Duny at Bury St. Edmunds. These women were accused of bewitching children over a period of years, and their trial was marked by all the evidentiary irregularities that had been made notorious by witchcraft literature: children's spectacular courtroom displays of possession, testimony by interested parties, scratching, claims of a witch's mark, and so forth.

Two other features of Hale's procedures in this trial have demanded apology by his champions. Near the end of the trial, he allowed testimony by the author of *Religio Medici* (1642), Thomas Browne, regarding the reality of witchcraft based on his recent experiences of trials on the Continent. Hale consulted Browne in his capacity as a medical man, but later writers were hard pressed to account for the undue influence exercised by a literary author who had already distinguished himself as a partisan in the witchcraft controversy in *Religio Medici.* Historians have also disagreed over the significance of Hale's failure to sum up evidence in the Cullender-Duny trial. Opinion as to his motives has ranged from guilty conscience to conviction as to the overwhelming evidence against the women. The jury found against the prisoners, and they were hanged.

With this decision, historians and legal writers committed to the steady progress from superstition to enlightenment as the guarantor of justice through the law were saddled with a powerful counterexample. How could Hale, defender of both Royalists and dissenters against arbitrary laws and the founder of a tradition of Enlightenment jurisprudence, have been susceptible to the superstitions of his contemporaries and complicit in the execution of two simple women? As Matilda Gage would put it in 1893, Hale "was spoken of by his contemporaries as one of the most eminent jurists of the world, whose integrity, learning and knowledge of law were scarcely to be paralleled in any age, and yet he became entirely convinced of the diabolism of two women as to condemn them to death while sitting at Bury St. Edmunds, without even summing up the evidence."[54]

Hale's own reflections on the trial, published after his death as the preface to *A Collection of Modern Relations of Matter of Fact, Concerning Witches and Witchcraft upon the Persons of People* (1693), show Hale defending a belief in the reality of witchcraft as necessary to social order. But it has been read as evidence of Hale's uncertainty over the case. Hale would not have been alone in arguing that the social order would be threatened by any erosion in witchcraft belief, however, as seen in the Restoration treatises discussed above. It was Hobbes's attack on metaphysics and clerics in *Leviathan* (1651) that provoked the major Restoration defenses of witchcraft belief, including Meric Casaubon's *Of Credulity and Incredulity in Things Natural, Civil, and Divine* (1668), Joseph Glanvill's *A Blow at Modern Sadducism* (1668), and Richard Baxter's *The Certainty of the World of Spirits.* As Ian Bostridge remarks, "A proper degree of credulity, and a belief in the operation of the supernatural and the marvellous, were essential to the continued security of the Royal state."[55]

Disciplining women per se seems far from the minds of any of these controversialists, yet given the centrality of gender in the tradition of skeptical witchcraft treatises since Scot, each of Hobbes's critics writes gender into a new political dynamic each time he insists upon the necessity of witchcraft belief to the success of the newly reconstituted monarchy. Adrian Johns argues that the Protestant prophets "John Rogers, Rebeckah Travers, Mary Cary, Elizabeth Poole . . . were precisely the people whom Samuel Parker, Henry More, Meric Casaubon, and others had in mind when they condemned 'enthusiasts.'"[56] Indeed, judges who were lenient in witchcraft could find themselves accused of atheism and disloyalty to the Crown. As Lord Chief Justice North complained to the secretary of state in 1682: "We cannot reprieve them without appearing to deny the very being of witches, which . . . is contrary to law."[57] When Justice Powell ignored the guilty verdict against Jane Wenham in 1712, concealing her at the home of a friend, he became the target of a virulent pamphlet campaign accusing him of undermining religion and the law. It was this newly politicized understanding of witchcraft connecting sympathy for the accused with hostility to the Crown that was passed on to the eighteenth century with the legacy of Hale's jurisprudence. As we shall see, proponents of abolishing felony sorcery legislation could be denounced, in the words of Royal Society member Henry More, as "Hag-Advocates." In this context, historical writing as an instrument of enlightened reform and as an instrument of advocacy on behalf of women would be intimately conjoined.

CHAPTER THREE

The Historical Turn in Witchcraft Literature

From Enlightenment Historiography to Historical Realism

FRANCIS HUTCHINSON'S *An Historical Essay Concerning Witchcraft* (1718) was the first skeptical treatment of the witch trials styled a "history." It aligned the skeptical tradition with advocacy on behalf of women and demonstrates the interconnections between historical interpretation and legal reform that remain a significant strain in witchcraft studies. Hutchinson worried that the "legends" being promulgated through the popular press would overwhelm sober historical analyses and spread the superstitions that might provoke new waves of prosecution. Hutchinson had met the last woman to have been convicted of witchcraft, Jane Wenham, whom Lord Chief Justice Holt had spared after her 1712 conviction, and Hutchinson considered witchcraft prosecution a live threat. Not least among the reasons Hutchinson worried about the revival of witch trials was the way in which they were entering into history. Of Richard Baxter's *The Certainty of the World of Spirits* (1691), Hutchinson wrote:

> by Mr. *Baxter's* Method of writing Histories, I see one of the Ways, how lying legends come to get Belief in the World. In the beginning there is something true for a Foundation. Forty or Fifty Years after, when the Parties concerned are dead, Men of too easy a Belief venture to publish hearsay stories. None trouble themselves to confute them, or if they do, many Times the Confutation is seen but by a few, and many soon may be lost, when the History may continue: As very likely Mr. *Baxter's* Book upon such an acceptable Subject, may have a Tenth impression, when this obscure Dialogue will be forgotten. Thus fabulous Histories get Credit, and poison the Generation after them.[1]

No historian of print culture could have described the effects of disseminating and preserving printed matter more vividly, or hoped for a better statement of how print culture shapes historical consciousness.

Citing the pro–witchcraft prosecution writings of Joseph Glanvill, Meric Casaubon, and Cotton Mather, as well as pamphlets chastising Justice Powell for failing to hang Jane Wenham after a jury convicted her of witchcraft in 1712, Hutchinson complained that "these Books and Narratives are in Tradesman's shops, and Farmers' Houses, and are read with great Eagerness, and are continually levening the Minds of the Youth, who delight in such subjects; and considering what sore Evils these Notions bring where they prevail, I hope no Man will think but that they must still be combatted, oppos'd and kept down" (xiv). Hutchinson's own history relied not on court records, but on unofficial published accounts of trials, controversial literature, biographies, and legal treatises, without much concern for their status as published materials shaped by many of the same market and political forces that he thought should discredit "legends." Nevertheless, right down to Pollock and Maitland's *History of English Law* (1895), Hutchinson was cited as the authoritative source on English witch trials.

Hutchinson's prediction proved true insofar as printed evidence of witchcraft prosecutions did drive historical study in the absence of official court records. The most copious and best-preserved printed materials on witch trials come from the seventeenth century, especially the period after 1641, when cheap publication flourished after Parliament abolished ecclesiastical censorship. The history of witch trials dependent on this literary evidence could lay blame for the prosecutions on James I, who, after all, had made his own influential contribution to the literature with his *Daemonologie*. In her introduction to an 1861 volume of witch stories she had collected at the British Museum, Eliza Lynn Linton condemned James I as England's most blood-thirsty English witch prosecutor while Pollock and Maitland reserved that distinction for the Commonwealth.[2] Thomas Potts's pamphlet *The Wonderfull Discoverie of Witches in the Countie of Lancaster* (1613) not only widely publicized the 1612 trial of thirty-five persons, ten of whom were hanged as witches, but also founded an important literary tradition. Potts, a clerk for the Lancaster Assizes, produced an account filled with sensational, hyperbolic, and colorful language—including efforts to reproduce Lancaster dialect—and this account was reprinted numerous times in the seventeenth century, and again in the

Somers Tracts (1810) by the Chetham Society (1845). This is but one example of the endurance of witchcraft literature in print culture.

The vast body of witchcraft literature in all its forms that I sketched in the preceding chapter became the objects of collectors, antiquarians, and folklorists in the course of the eighteenth and nineteenth centuries. That these documents have survived into our own time as sources for historians of witchcraft is owing to the activities of these individuals. Similarly, the arguments of literary historians that trace the origins of the novel to popular crime literature, pamphlets describing supernatural events, almanacs, broadsides, and the like, derive their evidence from such collections as those of Samuel Pepys and Anthony Wood. What is more, neither the repeal of the statute enabling the prosecution of witches, nor the rise of more elite forms of narrative, such as the novel, put an end to traditional popular print forms with their conventional subject matters. On the contrary, growing literacy and the expanding production of printed matter reinforced one another, adding substantially to the body of popular literature concerning crime and supernatural wonders. Well into the nineteenth century, witchcraft narratives were reprinted for a popular audience, creating, in Owen Davies' view, another "time warp," similar to the one Elizabeth Eisenstein associated with the origins of print culture.

The persistence of witchcraft literature well after the repeal of felony sorcery laws in 1736 placed burdens on elite interpreters of witchcraft history, especially those who were themselves engaged in literary pursuits. Later in this chapter I will discuss two: Sir Walter Scott, author of *Letters on Demonology and Witchcraft* (1830), and William Godwin, author of *Lives of the Necromancers* (1834). Despite their political differences—Scott was a Tory, and Godwin, a philosophical radical—each was invested in a history that celebrated the progress of enlightened thought. No longer would they address themselves to potential judges and jurymen in witchcraft trials. Rather, they engaged with the history of witchcraft in order to secure the proper relationship between print culture and their respective views of a legitimate state. The key difference between them, then, would come on the question of aesthetics in relation to historical analysis and political argument. In this way, the debate over witchcraft entered into the politics of literature in the Romantic period. At the head of this historical tradition stood Francis Hutchinson.

Hutchinson, a Chaplain in Ordinary, took up the subject of witchcraft while serving as minister of St. James in Bury St. Edmunds, where Hale had condemned Amy Dury and Rose Cullender. Hutchinson's goal as a historian was to shame his contemporaries into condemning once and for all the persecution of witches by demonstrating the superstition, cowardice, and perversions of justice on the part of the clerical and judicial elite that had brought about the executions of, by his count, one hundred and forty innocent people. Echoing Reginald Scot, Hutchinson saw that the historian's duty was to speak "on the Behalf of those that were drawn to Death, and were not able to plead their own Cause against *Hebrew Criticisms,* and fallacious, tho' deep Reasonings" (xv). Along with this retroactive advocacy, Hutchinson proposed a prophylactic value for his history as well, offering *An Historical Essay* "as an Argument on Behalf of all such miserable People, who may ever in Time to come be drawn into the same Danger in our Nation" (xv). Historical narrative that met proper standards of proof was required to counter the legends that themselves operated according to the same depraved evidentiary standards that had characterized the witchcraft convictions and could abet future prosecutions by corrupting true judgment.

For his pains, Hutchinson anticipated that he would be reproached as a "Hag-Advocate." That epithet, with which Henry More had branded all witchcraft skeptics, signals the gender of the silenced and defenseless victims Hutchinson undertook to represent. For Hutchinson, witch-hunting was woman-hunting in terms of its victims, if not the motives of the persecutors; while he does not see the persecution as motivated by misogyny, he nevertheless represents its victims as having been principally poor, silly, vulgar, loose, old women, as Reginald Scot had done in 1584. Hutchinson ignores cases in which males were convicted of witchcraft and cites almost exclusively cases involving female defendants. But he argues that this legalized abuse of women may have set evidentiary precedents that could threaten men in the future. Where Hutchinson imagines male victims, they are abstract, the casualties of evidentiary precedents set by witch trials: since judges had permitted unanswerable evidence to be admitted against women accused of witchcraft, how can the innocent man defend his life? As he warns, "If the same Notions were to prevail again, (and Superstition is never far off) no Man's life would be safe in his House; for the fantastic Doctrines that support the Vulgar Opinions of Witchcraft, rob us all of the Defense that God and nature have plac'd for our Security against false Accusations" (vi). To protect themselves, men must repudiate this historical injustice against women.

Framing his advocacy as a history allows Hutchinson to identify sympathetic victims of a practice, but also distinguish blameworthy agents from those to whom he addresses his appeal. He dedicates *An Historical Essay,* wherein he will condemn earlier judges and clerics, to the Lord Chief Justice, Thomas Parker; Sir Thomas Bury, the Lord Chief Baron of the Exchequer; and Sir Peter King, the Lord Chief Justice in Common Pleas. Significantly, Hutchinson does not ignore female agency in the witch trials. Rather, he apportions responsibility according to the actors' power, producing a more nuanced distribution of culpability and agency than would a simple gender opposition. His dedicatory preface encapsulates this strategy:

> But in Prosecutions for Witchcraft, that most natural and just Defence is a meer [*sic*] Jest; for if any wicked Person affirms, or any crack'd brain Girl imagines, or any lying spirit makes her believe, that she sees any old Woman, or other Person pursuing her in Visions, the Defenders of the Vulgar Witchcraft tack an imaginary improv'd *Compact* to the *Deposition,* and hang the accus'd Parties for things that they were doing, when they were, perhaps, asleep upon their Beds, or saying Prayers; or, perhaps, in the Accusers own Possession, with double Irons upon them. But as such fantastick Notions are so far from raising sickly Visions into legal Evidence, that they are grounded upon the very Dregs of Pagan and Popish Superstitions, and Leave the Lives of innocent Men naked, without Defence against them: To whom should I dedicate their Confution, but to your Lordships, whom, with your learned Brethren, the *Best of Kings* hath appointed Guardians of his Subjects Rights and Lives; and whom universal Knowledge and great Experience have qualify'd for the true Judgment of such dark Cases. (vii)

Hutchinson allows for a range of actors both male and female in witchcraft prosecutions, though his particularized examples are of a "crack'd brain Girl" as accuser and an "old Woman" as victim. But the apparatus of the state—from the formulation of an indictment of witchcraft that improves upon an unofficial accusation according to the legal requirement of a compact with the devil, to the "double Irons" of imprisonment, to rules on the legal status of evidence, to law making and royal prerogative—makes evident the correlation between power and responsibility that identifies magistrates, prosecutors, judges, members of Parliament, and, ultimately, the king, the "Guardians of . . . Subjects Rights and Lives," as the parties Hutchinson indicts.

It is difficult to fault Hutchinson merely for reducing female accusers to demented or impressionable children when he vilifies the clerics and legal officials who alone had the power to prosecute and pass sentence. Along with the authors of defenses of witchcraft prosecutions, Hutchinson indicts the clergy who lent their authority to prosecutions and, above all, the judges who were responsible for convictions. He bemoans the fact that as recently as the Wenham case, some clergymen were "so weak as to try Charms, and give way to scratching, and promote the Prosecution" (viii). Judges are to be blamed for "unpardonable Partiality and perfect Humour in judging what are Acts of Sorcery and what are not," and "for discovering a suppos'd Witch . . . allow[ing] any that call themselves Accusers, to use barbarous and unnatural Charms, which must have their Force, if they have any at all, from the same Diabolical Power, because they are no natural Causes of such Effects" (48). Hutchinson turns the tables on witch prosecutors, representing them as the agents of the devil who have failed the test God has set to prove their temporal authority. "And when they [judges], or Kings are ignorant, wicked, or superstitious," Hutchinson concludes, "how many thousand innocent Lives doth he [God] suffer to fall by their Hands in all Ages?" (54).

Nor does Hutchinson fail to name names. Of all those who abused their temporal power, Matthew Hale causes Hutchinson the greatest distress, and he discusses at some length Hale's role in the conviction of Duny and Cullender. Hale's reputation as a jurist and statesman was well established by 1718 and he was on his way to joining Coke as a leading voice in English jurisprudence. Hale's acquiescence in a witchcraft prosecution, therefore, tested Hutchinson's faith in enlightened judgment to safeguard against perversions of justice. "That one Case weighs more with me than all the rest," Hutchinson confesses (109). He describes Hale as a "great and good Man" for whom he has "Honour and Reverence" (109), and is at some pain to explain Hale's admission of forms of evidence against Duny and Cullender that, he alleges, would never have been "used against their [the prosecutors'] own Relatives, or Persons of the better Rank, whom they knew to be Innocent" (120). Rather than attribute such venal motives to Hale, however, Hutchinson stresses "the common Frailty of our human Nature" that led "a great man to be in one Error" (109). Hale is guilty of abdicating his power to render just judgment to an expert witness, Sir Thomas Browne. Browne's testimony as to the reality of witchcraft raised doubts in Hale's mind and put him in "such Fears" that he "proceeded with such Caution, that he would not so much as sum up the Evidence, but left it to the *Jury*, with Prayers, *That the great* God of Heaven would direct their Hearts in that weighty matter" (120). "After this [the jury's verdict] my Lord Chief Baron gave the Law its Course, and they were condemn'd, and died, declaring their Innocence" (120).

The centrality of Hale in *An Historical Essay* and Hutchinson's difficulties in explaining Hale's behavior in this witch trial points up the principal weakness in Hutchinson's argument, stemming from the incompatible historical paradigms that underpin his analysis. If he wishes to argue that witchcraft prosecutions must be condemned as dangerous anomalies in a tradition of English law legitimated as the manifestation of timeless natural law principles of justice, he cannot appeal to the law as a safeguard against just such violations of justice, at least not if he wishes to withhold condemnation from all parties to such prosecutions. Hale, in Hutchinson's estimation, was neither "vulgar" nor evil. To say he was "mistaken" implies a historicized notion of truth that threatens the continuity of English law with a relativism that would discredit his grounds for retroactive blame. With that, the value of his history as "hag-advocacy" would be seriously compromised.

Whereas Hutchinson attempted to shame England's elite by confronting them with the judgment of history on such notable figures as Hale, an alternative tradition of historical argument was well under way. As early as 1676, witchcraft skeptics celebrated the English judiciary for exercising mercy and discretion in witchcraft prosecutions. The author of the *Doctrine of Devils* (1676) wrote that "the reverend judges, especially of England are now much wiser, not only than the proletarian rabble, but than they too who profess themselves to be the great philosophers . . . and give small or no encouragement to such accusations."[3] Skeptical judges, especially Chief Justice Holt and Chief Justice Powell, would become heroes in a narrative of the steady decline of witchcraft prosecution and the eventual repeal of the Jacobean Act, initiating a tradition of looking toward highest legal authority to protect the interests of the weak, a position that would be adapted by both radicalism and feminism. But the repeal of witchcraft legislation and the drafting of new laws criminalizing false accusations of witchcraft and witchcraft imposture (9 Geo. II, c. 5) bear no sign of interest in women's legal disabilities.

Ian Bostridge notes that the 1736 parliamentary repeal seems to have come out of nowhere. Lacking any official records of the parliamentary debate beyond the bare outline provided by the journals of the houses,

Bostridge can only opine that the bill's sponsors—John Crosse, friend of Robert Walpole; John Conduitt, master of the Mint and nephew by marriage of Sir Isaac Newton; and Alderman George Heathcote, a republican Whig—may have been designed to "enhance the identification of Newtonianism as the ideology of a sound and rational Whig settlement which purged the nation of antique superstition" (182). With the consolidation of Whig power, witchcraft controversy was no longer needed as political strategy.

Nevertheless, long after the repeal of the felony sorcery legislation in 1736, historians would reiterate Hutchinson's strategies in defending the enlightened progress of the law. Their goals would do much to establish "the great condescension" toward the past, which E. P. Thompson bemoaned, and which so many ethnographic works by twentieth-century historians have sought to correct. The implications for a history of women and the law would be complex.

After Witch Trials: Aesthetics, Politics, and Gender

Belief in the supernatural could itself become an object of aesthetic pleasure rather than a prerequisite for social order. E. J. Clery has discussed the commodification of the supernatural in events ranging from the Ghost of Cock Lane, which preoccupied fashionable society, including Dr. Johnson, in 1762, to the rise of the Gothic novel.[4] But Owen Davies notes that the two most sensational instances of popular credulity, the Tring witch-ducking of 1751 and the Cock Lane Ghost, provoked another spate of skeptical witchcraft pamphlet literature.[5] Davies maintains that witchcraft continued to have a role in political controversy after 1736, and in the development of historical self-consciousness as well. William Blackstone, heir to Hale's jurisprudential project, was a Tory, and argued in his *Commentaries* that the very historical precedent of witchcraft, its ubiquity in the records of past civilizations, and its enshrinement in Scripture demanded that the reality of witchcraft could not be denied.[6] As Davies remarks, "For some Tories the denial of witchcraft was associated with noxious, free-thinking, skeptical Whiggery."[7] Dr. Johnson took a similar line, arguing that "wise and great men have condemned witches to die."[8] For eighteenth-century Tories, the authority of history itself joined witchcraft belief on the list of traditional values threatened by Whiggish rationalism. One wonders if that thoroughgoing Whig, Joseph Addison, would have stood by his conviction, articulated in the *Spectator* for July 14, 1711, that witchcraft was a historical reality, even if contemporary allegations remained unconvincing, in the context of mid-century Whig hegemony.

In the latter half of the eighteenth century, historical jurisprudence would become politicized, first through the rationalist critique of Bentham and his fellow Utilitarians, who associated historicism with the mystification of entrenched power in precedents located "time out of mind," and then, when the threat of the French Revolution provoked English thinkers, notably Edmund Burke, to a more passionate defense of tradition as a safeguard against regicide and the breakdown of social order. Nevertheless, while political radicals might have preferred to forget the past, their very commitment to the steady progress of reason over superstition compelled attention to the uneven history of witchcraft prosecution, with significant consequences for the politics of early feminist historiography. This problematic is evident in William Godwin's *Lives of the Necromancers* (1834).

For Godwin, who had long resisted historical writing in favor of radical philosophical treatises on political reform and a novel denouncing a legal system managed by an unscrupulous elite, the history of witchcraft prosecution presented a disturbing historical precedent.[9] Godwin found necromancy a distasteful topic, justified insofar as it offered instruction regarding present practice. "The main purpose of this book," Godwin wrote in the preface to *The Lives of the Necromancers,* "is to exhibit a fair delineation of the credulity of the human mind. Such an exhibition cannot fail to be productive of the most salutary lessons."[10] *The Lives of the Necromancers* deals with magic and credulity broadly, but when Godwin turns to the English prosecutions, he describes them as "the most painful part of my subject, but which does not the less constitute one of its integral members, and which, though painful, is deeply instructive, and constitutes a most essential branch in the science of human nature" (299). For this consummate rationalist, evidence of the abuses of reason are a check on pride: "But, if a recollection of the examples of the credulity of the human mind may in one view supply nourishment to our pride, it still more obviously tends to teach us sobriety and humiliation" (vii).

History also enables Godwin to reiterate a critique of contemporary social relations, familiar to anyone who recalls the critique of the corruption engendered by hierarchy in the major philosophical work of his wife, Mary Wollstonecraft, *A Vindication of the Rights of Woman.* Remarkably, Godwin begins his history with *male* witches, to whose agency he attributes the delusion of the simple. "Mankind, particularly in the dark and ignorant ages, were divided into the strong and the weak," Godwin writes of the era of witchcraft beliefs, "the strong and weak of animal frame, when corporeal strength more decidedly bore sway than in a period of greater cultivation; and the strong and weak in reference to intellect; those who were bold, audacious and enterprising in acquiring an ascendancy over their fellow-men, and those who truckled, submitted, and were acted upon, from an innate consciousness of inferiority, and a superstitious looking up to such as were of greater natural or acquired endowments than themselves" (2–3).

Furthermore, Godwin, like Hutchinson before him, focuses on the inexplicable complicity of Matthew Hale in the conviction of women as witches. Hale challenges Godwin's own faith in the sure progress of reason, and imposes upon him a mild form of historical relativism. Of Hale and Thomas Browne, Godwin writes, "Sir Matthew Hale and Sir Thomas Browne are eminent authors; and there is something in such men, that in a manner renders them the contemporaries of all times, the living acquaintance of successive ages of the world. Names generally stand on the page of history as mere abstract idealities; but in the case of these men we are familiar with their tempers and prejudices, their virtues and vices, their strength and their weakness" (446). Refusing either to relegate these figures to a distant and undemanding past or to indulge in a bout of "the great condescension," Godwin feels obliged to understand their motives. In this respect, the radical Godwin seems more constrained by the burden of the past than does his Tory contemporary, Walter Scott, as we shall see.

Working from the *Trial of the Witches executed at Bury St. Edmund's* (1644), Godwin emphasizes Hale's careful consideration of the evidence, and construes his failure to sum up as his unwillingness to unduly influence the jury. Still, he is compelled to conclude:

> What right we have in any case to take away the life of a human being already in our power, and under the forms of justice, is a problem, one of the hardest that can be purposed for the wit of man to solve. But to see some of the wisest of men, sitting in judgment upon the lives of two human creatures in consequence of the forgery and tricks of a set of malicious children, as in this case undoubtedly it was, is beyond conception deplorable. Let us think for a moment of the inexpressible evils which a man encounters when dragged from his peaceful home under a capital accusation, of his arraignment in open court, of the orderly course of the evidence, and of the sentence awarded against him, of the

> damned minutes and days he counts over; from that time to his execution, of his being finally brought forth before a multitude exasperated by his supposed crimes, and his being cast out from off the earth as unworthy so much as to exist among men, and at this being wholly innocent. The consciousness of innocence a hundred fold embitters the pang. And, if these poor women were too obtuse of soul entirely to feel the pang, did that give their superiors a right to overwhelm and crush them? (448)

Importantly, Godwin does not render Duny and Cullender as agentless victims, emphasizing instead their querulous behavior; yet while this may explain their persecutors' motives, it does not wholly exculpate their judges. But what is most striking is Godwin's effort to make male readers identify with the victims of witchcraft prosecution, a move made credible by the precedents of evidence set by witchcraft trials, which threatened the rights of male property holders. This is the consequence of witchcraft prosecution that had troubled so many early modern critics, and that would be repeated by nineteenth-century critics of the wrongful incarceration of women as lunatics, as we will see in part 3.

Godwin has recourse to a historicized vision of political and epistemic crises to explain the prosecutions, from the sixteenth century onward. His account evokes the seditious libel and treason trials in England following on the French Revolution.

> In the dawn of good sense, and when historical evidence at length began to be weighed in the scales of judgment, men became less careless of truth, and regarded prodigies and miracles with a different temper. And, as it often happens, the crisis, the precise passage from ill to better, shewed itself more calamitous, and more full of enormities and atrocity, than the period when the understanding was completely hood-winked, and men digested absurdities and impossibility with as much ease as their every day food. They would not now forgive the tampering with the axioms of eternal truth; they regarded cheat and imposture with a very different eye; and they had recourse to the stake and the faggot, for the purpose of proving that they would no longer be trifled with. They treated the offenders as the most atrocious criminals, and thus, though by a very indirect and circuitous method, led the way to the total dispersion of those clouds, which hung, with most uneasy operation, on the human understanding. (300)

Yet, having recounted a wide range of Continental, English, and New World persecutions, Godwin can do little more than resort to his faith in the progress of reason to explain their subsidence in the present. "The improvements that have been effected in natural philosophy," writes Godwin, "have by degrees convinced the enlightened part of mankind that the material universe is every where subject to laws, fixed in their weight, measure and duration, capable of the most exact calculation, and which in no case admit of variation and exception. . . . Such is the creed which science has universally prescribed to the judicious and reflecting among us" (1). This palliative, offered at the opening of *The Lives of the Necromancers,* seems grossly inadequate by its close, and seems once again to be a dodge, a way of avoiding, rather than facing the past.

Undeniably, the witchcraft prosecutions posed difficult problems for rationalist historians. Not only are their causes resistant to rational explanations, but the recurrences after years of quiescence challenge faith in the sure and steady advance of reason against superstition. The trends illustrated by Godwin's *Lives of the Necromancers* were continued into the Victorian period by such writers as the Unitarian William Howitt, who in his *Popular History of Priestcraft* (1833), attributed the irreversible decline of priestcraft to Cromwell.[11] In the same year Elizabeth Gaskell published *Lois the Witch,* her close friend Mary Howitt published her *Popular History of the United States of America,* wherein she wrote of the Salem witch trials that they were "a chapter out of the history of the middle ages."[12] Eliza Lynn Linton, in her 1861 collection of witchcraft cases, could "thank God, [that] the march of humanity has been steadily, if slowly, towards the daylight."[13] And even Elizabeth Cady Stanton, who in her 1885 London sermon "Has Christianity Benefited Woman?" could still insist on the witchcraft trials' traumatic legacy, nevertheless ended with a statement of faith in rational progress. Out of the Christian doctrine associating women with original sin, Stanton wrote, "grew the terrible persecutions of witchcraft, which raged for centuries, women tortured, burned, drowned, dragged into the courts, tried, and condemned, for crimes that never existed but in the minds of religious devotees. The clergy sustained witchcraft as Bible doctrine, far into the eighteenth century, until the spirit of rationalism laughed the whole thing to scorn and gave mankind a more cheerful view of life."[14]

That "more cheerful view," it could be argued, relied as much on literary aestheticization of the history of witchcraft prosecution as it did on enlightened rationalism. This can be seen in the work of Sir Walter Scott.

Witchcraft and demonology played significant roles in Scott's novels, which substantially defined the genre of historical fiction in the nineteenth century, a tradition inherited by Gaskell. As sheriff of Selkirkshire, Scott was brought a charge of witchcraft and had to calm his fears by explaining to the complainant that there was no legal basis for a charge.[15] Despite this personal experience, Scott's interest in witchcraft stemmed primarily from his antiquarian studies and efforts to make sense of the past. Coleman O. Parsons describes Scott's enthusiasm for collecting historical documents and oral tales and ballads dealing with witchcraft and demonology. As Parsons notes, Scott's depiction of witchcraft in his novels divides into two categories: one in which he focuses on the problems of mob psychology (e.g., *Heart of Mid-lothian*), and another in which he treats the disruptive behavior of women, in particular, who brought persecution on themselves (e.g., *The Bride of Lammermoor*).[16] In general, Scott's evocations of the supernatural waver between belief and disbelief, James Kerr has argued, "allow[ing] the exploitation of the supernatural sense of fatality in the service of historical analysis."[17]

Scott's sources include Pitcairn's *Criminal Trials in Scotland,* Thomas Potts's "curious rare book," and several pamphlet accounts. He emphasizes the importance of legal documents over literary sources, though, not surprisingly, he does not confine himself to such documents. Contrasting the triviality of other superstitions with witchcraft, Scott writes:

> When witchcraft arises, Superstition dips her hand in the blood of the persons accused, and records in the annals of jurisprudence their trials, and the causes alleged in vindication of their execution. Respecting other fantastic allegations, the proof is necessarily transient and doubtful, depending upon the inaccurate testimony of vague report, and of doting tradition. But in cases of witchcraft, we have before us the recorded evidence upon which judge and jury acted, and can form an opinion with some degree of certainty of the grounds, real or fanciful, on which they acquitted or condemned. It is, therefore, in tracing this part of Demonology, with its accompanying circumstances, that we have the best chance of obtaining an accurate view of our subject.[18]

Scott imagines his audience as being made up of polite readers, with an amateur literary curiosity in his subject. With that in mind, he announces that his "information is only miscellaneous,"

> and I make no pretensions, either to combat the systems of those by who I am anticipated in consideration of the subject, or to erect any new one of my own, my purpose is, after a general account of Demonology and Witchcraft, to confine myself to narratives of remarkable cases, and to the observations which naturally and easily arise out of them;—in the confidence that such a plan is, at the present time of day, more likely to suit the pages of popular miscellany, than an attempt to reduce the contents of many hundred tomes, from the largest to the smallest size, into an abridgement, which, however compressed, must remain greatly too large for the reader's powers of patience. (3)

He declares his abhorrence of "that odious law, so long the object of horror to all ancient and poverty-stricken females in the kingdom" (273), though he does his best to render their stories aesthetically pleasing to his readers.

Glossing cases drawn from Pitcairn, Scott remarks on the case of Bessy Dunlop, tried on November 8, 1576, that "the sad words on the margin of the record, 'convict and burnt,' sufficiently express the tragic conclusion of a curious tale" (153). He refers to Alison Pearson, tried for invocation of spirits in Byrehill, May 28, 1588, as an "elegant Titania embodied by this humble woman." Pearson was convicted and executed (153–55). Scott concludes, "The two poor women last mentioned are the more to be pitied, as, whether enthusiast or impostors, they practised their supposed art exclusively for the advantage of mankind" (155).

Turning from Scottish to English trials, judge and jury in the notorious Witches of Warbois case come in for Scott's condemnation. "One is ashamed of an English judge and jury," Scott writes, "when it must be repeated, that the evidence of these enthusiastic and giddy-pated girls was deemed sufficient to the condemnation of three innocent persons" (241). Their case turns into an archetypal tale of the poor abused by their betters.

> Indeed, their story is a matter of solemn enough record; for Sir Samuel Cromwell, having received the sum of forty pounds as lord of the manor, out of the estate of the poor persons who suffered, turned it into a rent charge of forty shillings yearly, for the endowment of an annual lecture on the subject of witchcraft, to be preached by a doctor or bachelor of divinity of Queen's College, Cambridge. The accused,

> one Samuel and his wife, were old, and very poor persons, and their daughter, a young woman. The daughter of a Mr. Throgmorton, seeing the poor old woman in a black knitted cap, at a time when she was not very well, took a whim that she had bewitched her, and was ever after exclaiming against her. The other children of this fanciful family caught up the same cry, and the eldest of them at last got up a vastly pretty drama, in which she herself furnished all the scenes, and played all the parts. Such imaginary scenes, *or make-believe stories,* are common amusement of lively children; and most readers may remember having had some Utopia of their own. But the nursery drama of Miss Throgmorton had a horrible conclusion. (238)

Of the conviction of a whole family for witchcraft, Scott asserts, "The purposes of Justice were never so perverted, nor her sword turned to a more flagrant murder" (242).

Yet, with all of Scott's indignation, it is hard to imagine how he expected his readers to respond, except with a sensation of horrified interest. Scott does not attempt a coherent explanation for witchcraft beliefs, nor an investigation of the motives for prosecution. He variously blames vulgar superstition, papist influences, and corrupt witch-hunters—notably Matthew Hopkins. He is, however, consistent in his sympathy for the victims of witchcraft prosecution as poor, simple, old women. Of course, Scott had created his own witchcraft persecution out of Pitcairn's records in *The Heart of Mid-lothian,* where Madge Wildfire, whose mother fell victim to attack by a mob enflamed by witchcraft hysteria, herself goes mad, stealing the infant whose alleged murder forms the crux of the plot. In that novel, a romanticized account of female sympathy—ranging from the accused Effie Dean's sister Jeanie, up to Queen Caroline, from whom the intrepid Jeanie gains a reprieve for Effie, condemned for concealing a birth—triumphs over the law in a magical fashion.

Scott clearly finds this aesthetic solution to the trauma of witchcraft prosecution satisfactory. As he concludes his letter dealing with the vicious persecutions by Hopkins,

> We then take leave of this fascinating article of the popular creed, having in it so such of interest to the imagination, that we almost envy the credulity of those who, in the gently moonlight of a summer night in England, amid the tangled glades of a deep forest, or the turfy swell of her romantic commons, could fancy they saw the fairies tracing their

> sportive ring. But it is in vain to regret illusions which, however engaging, must of necessity yield their place before the increase of knowledge, like shadows at the advance of morn. These superstitions have already served their best and most useful purpose, having been embalmed in the poetry of Milton and of Shakespeare, as well as writers only inferior to these great names. (184)

The aestheticization of witchcraft prosecution in the collected artifacts of earlier ages seems sufficient safeguard against future abuses of legal power. Its possible implications for the poor, simple, or females of Scott's own time are never considered.

Admittedly, Scott's treatment of witchcraft is not meant to be a critical analysis of witchcraft for an audience of historians or legal professionals. Still, he addresses a readership with some influence on legal decision making, and his capacity for aestheticizing the victims of witchcraft deserves some attention. While his depiction of the victims of witchcraft are in many respects similar to those of Reginald Scot, who was arguing against the rise in prosecutions, Walter Scott appears content to relegate the horrors of the past—and he does see them as horrors—to the realm of historical fiction: tragic tales, with no purchase on the present.

The precedent of witchcraft prosecution was not to be excised from nineteenth-century legal histories, however, any more than it could be excluded from literary history. Nor would this precedent cease to have purchase on theories of evidence, notably on the rising field of medical jurisprudence, where gender posed special challenges. For example, lives of eminent judges emerged as a hagiographic form of English legal history, charting the progress of the law handed down from one great man to another. Hale was a crucial founding figure in this litany of juridical wise men, and each biographer who celebrated his contributions to jurisprudence was obliged to account for his role in the Duny-Cullender conviction. Edward Foss, in *The Judges of England* (1864), applauded Hale as "one of the brightest luminaries of the law," who, "despite monarchal principles," did not "engage in any faction."[19] Yet he had to admit that

> the best men cannot hope wholly to escape vituperation, and the blot which cavilers have discovered in Hale's reputation has been that he presided at the trial of two women charged with witchcraft, and that, the jury having found them guilty, he left them for execution. But the censurers forget that as a judge he was bound by his oath to adminis-

> ter the law as it stood, without regard either to its severity of even its absurdity; that the evidence, tough in these enlightened days it might be deemed puerile and unconvincing, being cumulatively circumstantial and entirely uncontradicted, fully satisfied the jury, whose verdict left the judge no choice but to pronounce the sentence enjoined by the statute; and that they might as justly condemn every judge who, contrary to his own private feeling, has doomed a prisoner to capital punishment under an act that has since been repealed. In censuring him for his belief in witchcraft, they should remember that it was the almost universal persuasion of the time, in which he had for his associates some of the most eminent men of all ages, and which even now is not wholly abandoned; and they should hesitate to select such a man, whose excellence in other respects they are obliged to acknowledge, for the blame that should at all events be shared by his contemporaries. (114–15)

Foss's historical relativism is exemplary of one strategy employed in legal biographies to construct a progressive historical jurispudence.[20]

Yet other writers in this genre were eager to identify judges who bucked public opinion and led the fight against witchcraft prosecutions. For example, John Campbell, in his *Lives of the Chief Justices* (1858) extolled Chief Justice Sir John Holt (1642–1710), whose eleven successive acquittals in witchcraft cases tried in his court earned him "the merit of effectually repealing the acts against witchcraft, although they nominally continued on the statute book to a succeeding reign." Thus he was distinguished from Hale:

> Eleven poor creatures were successively tried before him for this supposed crime, and the prosecutions were supported by the accustomed evidence of long fasting, vomiting pins and tenpenny nails, secret teats sucked by imps, devil's marks, and cures by the sign of the cross or drawing blood from the sorceress—which had misled Sir Matthew Hale: but in every instance, by Holt's good sense and tact, the imposture was detected to the satisfaction of the jury, and there was an acquittal.[21]

W. N. Welsby asserted that Holt was representative of the majority of English judges, in an effort to purge the embarrassment of Hale's behavior from a history of enlightened English jurisprudence. "Although Holt was the first who ventured to direct juries to acquit in charges of witchcraft on the ground of their absurdity," Welsby wrote in his *Lives of the Eminent English Judges* (1846),

> yet there is every reason to suppose that long before this time they were discouraged by enlightened judges: although some might give way from weakness, others from a sense of the importance of upholding even erroneous law, and others . . . from feeling that in summing up in favour of a prisoner, they frequently caused him to run a greater risk, by running counter to the obstinate prejudices of juries. But Hale reflected with perfect satisfaction on the judgment he had pronounced, which speaks ill for his enlightenment, although well for his honesty.[22]

Witch trial precedents were not confined to works of legal history, however, but made their way into a historically self-conscious nineteenth-century jurisprudence on evidence as well. In *An Introduction to the Science of the Law* (1815), Frederick Ritso quoted Blackstone's position that the ubiquity and antiquity of witchcraft laws counseled continuing belief in the reality of witchcraft. Ritso's riposte is characteristic of the growing utilitarian critique of law:

> It only proves that the nations and the sects of the Roman world were under the dominion of the same blind and barbarous delusion, were the dupes of the same odious and cruel prejudice, without at all proving the actual existence, no, nor even the possibility of the supposed offenses, One might just as well assert that there were wizards and sorcerers in England, as far down as the ninth of George the second, because, forsooth, the law against witchcraft and sorcery remained till that period upon our statute book, a disgrace to our penal code.[23]

No less a utilitarian than John Stuart Mill similarly felt compelled to address the evidence of witchcraft prosecutions in "Jeremy Bentham's Rationale of Judicial Evidence" (1827), where he wrote that "no evidence can *prove* witchcraft; since there *can never be* any evidence of it, good or bad, trustworthy or the reverse."[24]

One of the nineteenth century's leading theorists of evidence, John George Phillimore, was particularly indignant in his attack on judges who had condemned witches. In his authoritative *History and Principles of the*

Law of Evidence (1850), Phillimore drew a broad lesson for contemporary judges inclined to overstep their legal authority from Hale's conviction of Rose Cullender and Amy Duny "for that imaginary offence."

> When men of respectable abilities, (but far inferior morally and intellectual to the excellent man who fell into the grievous error), elated with the technical knowledge which they have sacrificed the noblest opportunities of study, and the highest qualities if their nature to attain, and full of that presumptuous arrogance which is the infallible mark of contracted studies and narrow (though it may be an acute) intellect; when such men, on or off the Bench of Justice, feel themselves disposed to talk of legislation, as if their opinions were the dictates of inspired wisdom . . . [,] let them reflect on this sad event in the life of their illustrious predecessor, and if the thought chastens their presumption, and teaches them to suspect their prejudices; if it induces them, for one moment, to look elsewhere than to the little knot of flatterers which every man rich or in office can among *us* command, for a true estimate of their abilities, and to pause before they lend their sanction to oppression and chicanery, aggravating the inequalities of society, increasing the advantages of wealth, and adding to the burdens of poverty—the death of these unhappy women will contribute, and that in no inconsiderable degree, to the progress and lasting welfare of this community.[25]

Phillimore's attack on the arrogance encouraged by narrow legal knowledge as a particular threat to justice for outsiders, informed by his engagement witchcraft precedents, strikingly resembles the arguments made on behalf of literary legal education for outsider jurisprudence.

The fledgling field of medical jurisprudence lent particular urgency to concerns about the history of evidence in witchcraft trials, both because medical men had been called to give evidence and because modern scientific practitioners could establish their own authority at the expense of the mistaken beliefs of earlier generations. Whereas we might expect these writers to concentrate their efforts on medicalizing female deviance, instead they focus their attention on legal decision makers, and condemn the credulity of judges. Michael Ryan argued in *A Manual of Medical Jurisprudence* (1831) that earlier ages had naïvely posited supernatural agency in witchcraft prosecutions, whereas modern medical men understand individual agency under the influence of delusions.[26] John Gordon Smith, in his *Analysis of Medical Evidence: Comprising Directions for Practitioners in the View of Becoming Witnesses in Courts of Justice* (1825), found the examination techniques of Chief Justice Holt so compelling that he quoted at length from his skeptical questioning in the case of Richard Hathaway, tried for being a cheat and impostor. Smith cautioned "that in too many cases of vital importance, a reliance has been placed upon the judgment of professional men, which has contributed to verdicts and decrees that have proved woeful warnings to succeeding jurors and judges."[27]

Still, the various reassurances of rational progress by historians, legal writers, and medical men seem designed to allay fears about mob psychology for writers experiencing the simultaneous emergence of mass culture and democratic political institutions. Laws against "combination" in trades unions, new censorship and heresy cases, hysterical backlashes against the first Reform Bill and Catholic Emancipation, and above all, such spectacles of violent repression as the Peterborough massacre all betray an anxiety that rendered the witchcraft trials a peculiarly resonant topic for Victorians. Within the context of rationalism, belief in witchcraft could be understood only in terms of madness or delusion, its spread medicalized as "contagion," its sporadic occurrences as "outbreaks" and "recoveries." But this vocabulary merely provided metaphors by which writers groped toward an understanding of what we might now label ideology and hegemony.

Charles Mackay devoted a chapter to witchcraft persecution in his 1841 *Memoirs of Extraordinary Popular Delusions and the Madness of Crowds,* where he classified it with other "moral epidemics," including the Mississippi delusion and South Sea Bubble mania. This curious collection, reprinted in 1852, brings to the fore worries about how ideologies are formed and spread, and appeals to a distinctly psychological vocabulary that at once constructs and trivializes witchcraft prosecutions as trauma.

> In reading the history of nations, we find that, like individuals, they have their whims and their peculiarities; their seasons of excitement and recklessness, when they care not what they do. We find that whole communities suddenly fix their minds upon one object, and go mad in its pursuit; that millions of people become simultaneously impressed with one delusion, and run after it, till their attention is caught by some new folly more captivating than the first. We see one nation suddenly seized, from its highest to its lowest members, with a fierce desire for military glory . . . Another age went mad for fear of the devil,

and offered up hundreds of thousands of victims to the delusion of witchcraft.[28]

To explain this phenomenon, Mackay has no resort beyond the crude assertion that "men . . . think in herds; it will be seen that they go mad in herds, while they only recover their senses slowly, and one by one."[29] So anemic an analysis would do little to reassure groups subjected to past persecutions that enlightened men would preserve them in future.

In the face of the explanatory difficulties posed by the precedent of witchcraft prosecution, preserved and obsessively reiterated in a host of witchcraft literature genres, it is hardly surprising that traumatic narratives emerged. But literary realism evolved to address the very pressures so strikingly manifest in the witchcraft trials and their legacy, namely, conflicts among cultures of evidence—revelatory, empirical, deductive—arising under correlative conditions of social tension and the need to negotiate among these methods of legitimation. Its formal qualities—such as the probable and coherent plotting, concrete detail, and psychologically complex characterization extolled by Law and Literature scholars for their forensic force—were designed by authors anxious to place their defense of metaphysical beliefs on a firmer footing than that eroding under romance. In this respect, realist fiction, as Alexander Welsh has argued, fulfilled an evidentiary demand similar to that fulfilled by its contemporary in law, circumstantial evidence, which drew upon similar narrative techniques to persuade jurors in the absence of eyewitness testimony. At the same time, realists defended the authority of their representations by contrast with the audacious improbabilities of romance in a manner analogous to the discrediting of spectral evidence. In this manner, the probabilistic plotting conventions of realist fiction served much the same goals Enlightenment liberal political theorists sought to achieve through proceduralism. That is, both offered formal guarantees of legitimacy—techniques such as disinterested objectivity, predictability, "fair play"—in lieu of the techniques of divine revelation, mystery, and authoritative tradition ("time out of mind") favored by divine right theorists.

For these reasons, realism provided means for representing the trauma of witchcraft trials that were not only psychologically therapeutic but also historiographically salient. Specifically, realist techniques afforded the historical novelist Elizabeth Gaskell with the tools for interpreting the vast literary legacy of witchcraft prosecution that had come down to the nineteenth century at the same time legislation was emerging as the principal means by which to achieve not only bourgeois hegemony but also democratic legal recognition. Moreover, the features of realism that enabled this breakthrough on a conundrum perplexing legal historians are precisely those which continue to afford viable techniques for imagining equity and achieving political recognition.

Realist novelists, though they often aspired to the probative force of legal evidence (when they were not claiming superior knowledge), could employ narrative innovations not readily available to legal advocates. Most notable among these are the devices of omniscient narration and dialogism. The former allowed for a wholly imaginary access to the motives of complex subjectivities that relied for its authenticity on coherence and probability. Translated into legal terms, this meant that novelists could construct the *mens rea*—literally, the "mind thing," or motive—that lawyers could only infer from observable evidence. But they could also construct the tacit motives for legal decision making on the part of judges, lawyers, and jurors, a power obviously lacking in nonfictional critiques of legal decision making, from Hutchinson's, through Bentham's and down to twentieth-century legal realists, where "sinister motives" could only be alleged. The dialogic quality of realism is the feature of literary narrative Nussbaum credits with educating readers as "judicious spectators," capable of entertaining multiple and mutually exclusive ideological perspectives on the same evidence. Verdicts and rulings, by contrast, demand the imposition of a monological interpretation on evidence, which postmodernist legal theorists have argued can be achieved only by suppressing the conflicts inherent in any human decision-making process. For Gaskell, dialogism enabled a negotiation not only between past and present cultures of evidence necessary to adjudicate the question of historical justice, but also among the various cultures of evidence required for feminist advocacy, including between sentimental aestheticism and empiricism. Together, these devices of realist narrative made it possible to imagine one's way into a historical legal problem in order to investigate mixed motives and to arrive at an understanding of precedent within a dynamic cultural process.

This chapter and the two preceding it have contextualized one example of Victorian fiction, Elizabeth Gaskell's *Lois the Witch,* in both contemporary theory and the historical texts it aims to interpret. In so doing, these chapters have sketched out what the project of a historical narrative jurisprudence for gender advocacy might entail. As I indicated in the preliminary conclusions for narrative jurisprudence that I drew from *Lois the Witch* in chapter 1, my intention is not to claim that Gaskell's story is a comprehensive synthesis of its many precursors, nor a final antidote to the traumatic role of witchcraft prosecution in contemporary theory. Gaskell's realist practice, however, goes some way toward explaining why narrative jurisprudence has been preoccupied with Victorian texts. I hope it has also provided incentive to Victorianists to open up new lines of inquiry into the pretexts of Victorian writing to engage more robustly with narrative jurisprudence.

Three key topics emerge from the historical narrative jurisprudence of witchcraft prosecution I have constructed: agency, evidence, and motive. Each of these topics is fundamental to any jurisprudential theory and, in the context of witchcraft prosecution, each has been shown to be problematized by gender. As I have demonstrated, they are problematized not by a transhistorical structure of difference, but by gender operating within a dynamic of literary, political, and social forces that demand careful attention to historical specificity and the construction of historiographic consciousness within print culture. Indeed, the jurisprudential concepts of agency, evidence, and motive have been significantly shaped by the particular precedents of witchcraft prosecution, as will be evident in parts 3, 4, and 5, which take up each of these concepts in turn. Whereas part 1 has proceeded diachronically, the remaining sections of my argument work synchronically, focusing in greater detail on gender advocacy in nineteenth-century law and literature. As in part 1, I will introduce the theoretical responses in legal and literary scholarship to the problems gender poses for each of these three jurisprudential concepts. I will then consider nineteenth-century literary interventions in the construction of gender advocacy, examining their diverse political investments and implications. This strategy is intended as a sympathetic critique of narrative legal theorists' claims for the emancipatory features of nineteenth-century literature. I aim as well to draw attention to neglected examples of nineteenth-century literature that more robustly model strategies of gender advocacy for contemporary narrative jurisprudence. Finally, with respect to agency, evidence, and motive, I will suggest the benefits of a dialogue between literary and legal scholars that privileges neither discipline, but draws critically upon each to forge a more genuinely dialectical practice for teaching and theorizing literature and law.

PART TWO

Agency

CHAPTER FOUR

Theories and Histories of Agency

Mary Wollstonecraft's Narrative of the Reasonable Woman

REASONABLE PERSONS did not exist in nineteenth-century Britain, though the Reasonable Man surely did. The Reasonable Person is a legal fiction of late-twentieth-century American jurisprudence, a standard of proof created in response to the perceived inadequacy of the Reasonable Man as a norm by which to judge evidence in sexual harassment suits, or where self-defense is pleaded by a woman accused of murdering her abusive husband, or other such cases in which the courts have understood gender to hold peculiar evidentiary significance.[1] That critique holds that the Reasonable Man standard, by excluding relevant evidence, denies equal treatment under the law.[2] In the manner of nineteenth-century liberalism, the Reasonable Person is a procedural attempt to expand liberal ideals of judicial impartiality and equality before the law to accommodate sexual difference. It grants the gendered nature of some kinds of evidence and of what constitutes reasonable inferences therefrom, and seeks to remedy resulting inequities by improving the rules.

This remedy is not without its own problems. For one, its radical critics allege the incoherency of conceding the gender bias of rules of evidence only to posit an evidentiary standard that purports to transcend gender altogether.[3] A Reasonable Woman standard would seem to answer this objection, but its logic undermines the principle of generalizability, normative rules of evidence, and the conception of justice they are designed to serve.[4] And gender represents only one of the challenges brought against liberal ideals of impartiality and objectivity in legal decision making. This debate goes to the heart of the conflicts between objective and subjective forms of evidence that characterize struggles for legal recognition by persons whose group identifications historically have been construed as deviant or, indeed, criminal. It is a familiar and dramatic instance of the inherent difficulty of achieving *de facto* legal recognition for diverse populations within liberal theories of justice.

Jürgen Habermas has proposed that the history of feminism since the late eighteenth century offers a paradigmatic demonstration that the realization of equal rights requires a "politics of recognition that protects the integrity of the individual in the life contexts in which his or her identity is formed." "Like the development of law in Western societies in general," Habermas writes, "the feminist politics of equality during the past hundred years follows a pattern that can be described as a dialectic of *de jure* and *de facto* equality."[5] In the nineteenth century, "classical feminism," as he terms it, sought to achieve political equality by means of equal access to social institutions, whereupon gender difference would drop away.[6] In a pattern adapted by other Enlightenment emancipatory movements, feminism first challenged patriarchy by elaborating a liberal conception of the self that included women as meriting *de jure* equality on the basis of universal rationality, which could be demonstrated by the discursive performances of disenfranchised speakers. "But the formal equality that was partially achieved thereby," Habermas would respond, "only made the *de facto* unequal treatment of women all the more obvious."[7] The challenge, then, as the problem of the Reasonable Person standard of proof illustrates, is to find an effective means of representing to the law the *de facto* inequality that proceeds from "individual life contexts" and devising legal mechanisms that achieve equal treatment in light of diverse contexts without succumbing to the ungeneralizability of difference in cultural feminism. "As long as policies are focused on safeguarding private autonomy, while the internal connection between the individual rights of private persons and the public autonomy of citizens who participate in making the laws is obscured from view," asserts Habermas, "the politics of rights will oscillate helplessly between the poles of a liberal paradigm in the Lockean sense and an equally shortsighted social-welfare paradigm."[8]

Narrative jurisprudence, as I noted in the introduction, makes claims for the efficacy of storytelling for validating non-normative, or alternative, realities and plotting the reasonable chains of inference that proceed from their premises. I seek to test those claims in this chapter by considering Robin West's feminist theory of Enlightenment narrativity and Jürgen Habermas's communication theory of legal recognition in light of legal and literary histories of *compos mentis*. I will argue in this chapter and the next that jurisprudential problems such as the Reasonable Person standard of proof, and other procedural mechanisms for extending the boundaries of rational inference in legal argument, are lodged within the history of legal procedures and literary practices wherein *compos mentis* was established, from Chancery lunacy inquiries beginning in the early modern period through fictional and journalistic exposés of wrongful confinement in the eighteenth and nineteenth centuries and Victorian efforts to reform lunacy law by evaluating the stories of asylum inmates for evidence of rationality. My emphasis is not on the production of deviance, but rather on the positive arguments by which the privileged and outsiders alike sought to establish their agency by demonstrating that they were reasonable persons, the evolving standards by which those discursive demonstrations of rationality were judged, and the print culture conditions under which they were disseminated as paradigms of legal competency. As with the dynamics of gender in witchcraft literature, gender will feature in this discussion not only as a determinant of legal competency but also as a product of the narratives of *compos mentis* dictated by legal procedures and by literary genres and publication conditions.

From the perspective of literary criticism, standards of proof, be they reasonable man, woman, or person, are attempts to construct the subject position of the *reader* in order to judge the credibility of an *author*. As such, they presuppose the ability of readers to transcend their subject positions or, in the terms of Habermasian communication ethics, to negotiate between divergent "life worlds" via intersubjective linguistic exchanges, so that they might recognize the legitimate agency of a plaintiff or defendant. In this chapter and the next, I will analyze two novels, both exposés of wrongful incarceration for lunacy as a mechanism for denying legal agency: in chapter 4, Mary Wollstonecraft's *Maria; or, The Wrongs of Woman* (1798), and in chapter 5, Charles Reade's *Hard Cash* (1863). These stories of agency are communicative negotiations between legally nullified speakers and privileged audiences. They succeed, or fail, neither by virtue of ahistorical formal qualities, nor because of a *de jure* speech right. Rather, they work toward their goal in dialectic with the historical conditions—legal and literary—under which speakers address themselves to a privileged audience. For this reason, transformative reading, or *listening*, is as crucial an element in the process of legal recognition as is the right to self-representation, or authorship, and I will draw attention to how narratives asserting legal competency thematize their readers', or judges', interpretive practices. Recognition of agency, I will argue, depends upon multiple dialectics, between law and literature, privileged agents and disenfranchised speakers, readers and authors.

This chapter begins by laying the theoretical groundwork for a discussion of Wollstonecraft's and Reade's novels. I begin by discussing two accounts of how legal recognition was achieved within early democratic formations. The first is Robin West's theory of "Enlightenment narrativity," a jurisprudential response to cruxes in feminist literary theory and historical scholarship of agency. The second is Jürgen Habermas's theory of communicative action. I then turn to *The Wrongs of Woman* to examine Wollstonecraft's attempt to transform privileged readers into informed judges of the rationality of alternative "life worlds" by means of narrative techniques unavailable to her in her *A Vindication of the Rights of Woman.*

In chapter 5, I will analyze the limitations of Wollstonecraft's narrative techniques by setting them in the context of legal and literary histories of *non compos mentis* (the legal nullification of agency) wherein standards of rationality were defined. Lunacy inquiries, the legal procedure by which the Court of Chancery determined *non compos mentis,* shared many of the evidentiary difficulties of witchcraft prosecution, including contested expert testimony and the disability of the subject of the inquiry to counter charges. Just as these problems produced a "feminized" prisoner in witchcraft prosecution, so too did they render the plaintiff in lunacy inquiries "feminized," stripped of the rights of a property-holding male, and constituted a *de facto* presumption of guilt. And, as with witchcraft prosecution, they gave rise to an extensive body of articles, pamphlets, and treatises aimed at exposing legal abuses, including sensational works of fiction, from Wollstonecraft's novel *Maria; or The Wrongs of Woman* to Charles Reade's *Hard Cash.* This history, and the theoretical models for interpreting it, are of special relevance to feminist criticism of nineteenth-century literature, where madness has been linked to female authorship. Significantly, as I will argue in chapter 5, it was a change in the law respecting women as property holders—the Married Women's Property Act (1882)—that granted women the power to author their agency in courts of law.

Narrative Theories of Recognition

Robin West's theory of "Enlightenment narrativity" goes a long way toward creating a multidisciplinary account of legal recognition, engaging storytelling, property rights, and the history of rationality. As a means of securing legal recognition for women (and, by implication, everyone who deviates from the dominant norm of rationality), West argues for a return to a property-rights model of self-narration. In this model, authorship is the discursive performance of agency, construed as the exercise of a property right, not evidence of a quality like rationality, by which a judge decides whether or not to recognize the speaker's legitimacy based on her conformity to a norm. If West is right, that agency consists in owning one's own stories, then her theory of narrativity would answer the challenge Jürgen Habermas says faces feminism, namely how to find discursive means to achieve not merely *de jure*, but *de facto* equality. *De facto* equality depends upon the recognition of diverse forms of rationality, or "life worlds," which West believes ownership of one's stories would entail. But West's model of narrative agency fails to explain just how a property right possessed by a speaker necessarily overcomes resistance in an interpreter.

West's argument is intriguing to feminist literary historians, but it also raises many problems. Among its appeals is that, unlike feminist critiques of liberal political theory, West's model is amenable to a historicist view of authorship and authenticating narrative strategies as products of the conditions of writing, reading, and publication inseparable from bourgeois social and economic formations. That is, what we understand to be our own stories cannot be detached from what our culture tells us constitutes a self, and readers recognize as a self: namely, an individual, with a meaningful degree of agency, however mediated. This helps us to qualify the narrative jurisprude's preference for autobiography as a transparent form of self-representation in narrative jurisprudence. Nevertheless, West is too readily dismissive of the deconstruction of authorship as a freak of literary theory that should be rejected by feminist narrative jurisprudence. Furthermore, feminist literary criticism has long been engaged in the deconstruction of rationality and the celebration of deviance and irrationality as subversive features of women's writing. Recently, however, feminist literary historians have begun to move away from these commitments and identified the more capacious understanding of rationality constructed in women's writing, particularly through their contributions to the development of novelistic narrative techniques. This tack offers a point of negotiation between West's view of literary history and that of feminist literary critics. Like West's theory, however, claims for the historical success of women writers in transforming norms of rational agency fail to explain how readers were persuaded to accept such changes. Before we would embrace even a modified version of Enlightenment narrativity, therefore, it would be necessary to address the cultural and economic conditions of authorship that arose in the nineteenth century and persist into our own. These include not only the commodification of literature, a phenomenon Habermas argues ultimately disqualified literature as a site of critical debate, but also the profound changes in property rights themselves, which seem to be the preconditions for, rather than the products of, authorship.[9] As Pierre Bourdieu remarks in *Language and Symbolic Power*, insisting on the dialectical nature of recognition, "A performative utterance is destined to fail each time that it is not pronounced by a person who has the 'power' to pronounce it, or, more generally, each time that the 'particular persons and circumstances in a given case' are not 'appropriate for the invocation of the particular procedure invoked'; in short, each time that the speaker does not have the authority to emit the words that he utters."[10]

Feminist narrative legal theory addresses the problem of equal treatment by two related methods. One entails a critique of the objectivist claims of legal reasoners that unmasks their arguments as coercive narratives that emplot their interests as normative standards. The other seeks to gain recognition for alternative realities through stories narrated from outsiders' points of view, granting probative force to subjective experience. As Robin West graphically states the problem, "We must be able to say . . . 'Don't do that—you're hurting me,' and we must be able to hear that utterance as an ethical mandate to change course."[11] The shift in pronoun reference—from the "we" who testify to the experience of pain, to the "we" who, as legal decision makers, take responsibility for that pain and for providing a remedy—registers the intersubjective quality of this legal communication problem. Somehow, the legal decision maker who receives the autobiographical narrative must not only recognize another's pain but also learn what action would stop a harm unjustly caused by the law without inflicting a new harm on the original complainant or others. This is not only an ethical problem but also one of historical epistemology.

Significantly, West would return feminist jurisprudence to its Enlightenment origins to solve the problem posed by Habermas. West's illustration—"Don't do that, you're hurting me"—concerns the ability and authority to tell one's own story, to testify to subjective experience, in a public context. Despite the long history of the bar against defendants testifying under oath, the opportunity to be bodily present to present one's case and answer accusers is a value enshrined in Anglo-American law by rights so fundamental as *habeas corpus* and trial by jury. If the protocols of legal storytelling, the rules of evidence and standards of proof, such as the Reasonable Man, interfere with the ability of some persons to enjoy the full benefit of these rights by excluding the experience of otherwise competent witnesses as irrational, then they are violations of equal treatment and must be changed, by, for example, adopting a more capacious, literary conception of narrative plausibility. What interests me about such a claim is the history of literature within larger cultural processes that had led some advocates of inclusive legal, political, and social structures to fix upon self-narration and literary reading as the forms of evidence and judgment most likely to bring about their goals. It might be claimed that establishing presence through storytelling is ubiquitous, a component of what it is to be human. But surely the claims of narrative legal theorists have their origins in a more discrete historical moment, as West herself maintains. Critiques of objectivism are not simply philosophical disputes but historical ones, according to West. "We should look to the practice of objectivist evaluative inquiry, not its asserted nature," she argues, "to determine whether a non-authoritarian type of objectivism is now or has ever been possible."[12] In *Narrative, Authority, and Law,* West warns that the relativist critique of rationality as a universal norm can itself become an authoritarian doctrine that discounts testimony of a felt harm by deconstructing the storyteller's privileged relationship to her own narrative. Defending narrative jurisprudence against the indeterminacy thesis of Stanley Fish, West posits a conception of narrativity and authorship that depends upon the historical success of liberal political thought. She asserts that "the sense of self-possession on which the use of narrativity rests—that my experience is my own, that it ought count as my own, that for reasons of both compassion and justice it should matter whether the quality of that experience is good or bad—is socially constructed: its felt force depends not on the authenticity of the experience, or the degree of self-delusion or enlightenment of the subject, but rather on a liberal conception of the self."[13]

West's solution is to recover "enlightenment, traditional understandings of meaningfulness of literary and legal texts, social criticism, moral change, subjectivity, experience, and selfhood."[14] Conferring rights on the basis of demonstrated rationality and the theoretical—if not actual—commitment to reasoned discourse as evidence of rationality are obvious hallmarks of Enlightenment political thought. In exhorting narrative legal theorists to investigate this particular politico-aesthetic history, West insists upon the continuing importance of liberal conceptions of selfhood that assert rights to ownership, including the ownership of one's experiences and stories, as foundational to the reading practices that secure an audience for outsiders' stories and gives those stories moral force. But in light of the vigorous attacks on Enlightenment politics and values, from Carole Pateman's feminist critique of contract theory to Horkheimer and Adorno's thoroughgoing assault on the instrumentality of Enlightenment reason, West is looking at a hard sell.[15]

A related set of historical and philosophical claims is made by Habermas in developing his discourse theory of law and democracy, one that figures political recognition in terms of communicative action and deliberation. Although Habermas does not directly address the literary domain in his recent work, his commitment to a model of deliberative democracy owes much to his historical investigation in *The Structural Transformation of the Public Sphere,* wherein he argued that literary exercises of rationality by politically excluded authors exerted pressure for a more inclusive political sphere. Since the legitimacy of the bourgeois state depended not upon tradition, but upon the exercise of "critical-rational debate," rationality itself became the condition for legal recognition. Like West, Habermas emphasizes the outstanding claims of struggles for recognition and insists upon the continuing importance of—if not the liberal self, precisely—a theory of individual self-determination to realizing these goals. But Habermas has analyzed the commodification of the literary, coming hard on the heels of the emergence of a literary public sphere, as rendering literary discourse "apolitical." "The web of public communication" under these conditions, he argues, "unraveled into acts of individuated reception, however uniform in mode."[16] How other forms of discourse or communicative action, including his own, escape that fate remains a difficult point in Habermas's theory. Looking at the same historical phenomenon—the effort of Enlightenment-era women to gain legal recognition through literary discourse—Habermas sees a failure where West sees a vital model for contemporary advocacy, one that would supply Habermas's project with the very discursive practice it now lacks.

What lesson ought narrative legal theory draw from the history of Enlightenment literary advocacy? Has the narrative construction of rational subjectivity proven useless—or, indeed, counterproductive—in the quest for meaningfully equal treatment, or is it an experiment that has never been fully implemented? If we take as a fundamental goal of narrative legal theory the use of narrative to expand understandings of rationality to include what Habermas calls "life contexts" in order to achieve *de facto* justice for women, as well as for others disadvantaged by Reasonable Man standards of proof, then a preliminary effort to assess the continuing import of Enlightenment narrativity should focus on the narrative methods by which possession of rational subjectivity was asserted, and how those methods evolved under the changing political conditions, including that of liberal legislative reforms.

The Limitations of Enlightenment Narrativity: *Maria; or, The Wrongs of Woman*

Mary Wollstonecraft's *Vindication of the Rights of Woman* (1792) is surely one of the most famous documents in the history of advocacy for women's legal recognition on the basis of their rationality. But her lesser-known, unfinished, posthumously published novel, *Maria; or, The Wrongs of Woman* (1798), has generated controversy among literary critics for its recourse to sentimental narrative conventions that should make it a centerpiece of debate within feminist jurisprudence regarding the politics of literary advocacy. Wollstonecraft's novelistic critique of the unequal treatment of women in the law, or "partial law," has been read as problematizing, if not refuting, the claims she made in these earlier writings for universal reason as the foundation for equal rights. Interpreting the politics of Wollstonecraft's novel is a problem of literary history, one that calls for an investigation of gender, genre, rhetoric, and reading practices in the context of late-eighteenth- and early-nineteenth-century culture. At the same time, it is a problem in legal history, its representation of female rationality participating at once in a male-centered debate over civil rights in the wake of the French Revolution and the erosion of married women's rights in the same period. *The Wrongs of Woman* is a crucial test of Robin West's thesis that narrative jurisprudence must embrace a conception of the liberal self as *storyteller* in order for narrative to succeed as a form of intersubjective communication within the law.

The plot of *The Wrongs of Woman*, beginning with the protagonist Maria Venables being wrongfully incarcerated in a private lunatic asylum by her debauched husband when she refuses to sign over control of her inheritance, and culminating in a deposition Maria writes in the action her husband brings for seduction and adultery against Darnford, another asylum inmate with whom she has an affair, demonstrates the systematic legal, economic, social, and sexual disabilities of women, which render them "outlaws of the world" in Wollstonecraft's phrase. That is, *The Wrongs of Woman* locates the barrier to the recognition of female legal agency at the intersection of marriage and lunacy laws, each of which denied speakers ownership in their own stories. Wollstonecraft fastens on wrongful incarceration, however, not only because it posed a real threat to married women in the absence of meaningful legal provisions for divorce, but also because it interpellated propertied male readers into a plot of legal nullification. Wollstonecraft's novel would seem to make its appeal on the basis of the connection between legal rights and authorship that West locates in the Enlightenment conception of the self. And, in its emplotment of the individual life contexts that shape female subjectivity, it might also respond to Habermas's requirements for a politics of recognition that uncovers the "internal connection between the individual rights of private persons and the public autonomy of citizens who participate in making the laws."

The very literary qualities of *The Wrongs of Woman* that might be seen to address both West's and Habermas's demands have posed problems for some feminist literary critics, however, leading them to reproduce many of the same philosophical cruxes regarding the relationship between objective and subjective modes of argument that plague narrative legal theory. *The Wrongs of Woman* is classified as a sentimental novel, a genre with a very dubious political past. As Ann Cvetkovich remarks, "The association of femininity with emotional excess [characteristic of sentimental fiction] underwrites, for example, the nineteenth-century production of ideologies of domesticity which depended on the construction of the middle-class woman as responsible for and ideally suited to the affective labors to be performed at home."[17] *The Wrongs of Woman* has been seen as opposing reason to emotion, sensibility, and sexuality, with critics generally divided into two camps: those who argue that Wollstonecraft had come to recognize the delusory nature of Enlightenment reason and therefore rejected a rationalistic model of political reform, and those who fault Wollstonecraft for undermining her defense of female rationality with the very sentimental delusions she attacked in her *Vindication of the Rights of Woman* in 1792. Both positions treat the novel's theme of lunacy as related exclusively to women, whether it is construed as a difference to be celebrated or as a disability to be overcome by attacking patriarchal norms of rationality. In either event, Wollstonecraft is read as departing from what G. J. Barker-Benfield has construed as her greatest achievement: "to extend the Commonwealth analysis of male corruption and program of male reform to women."[18]

One explanation of Wollstonecraft's decision to return to fiction writing with *The Wrongs of Woman* is that she wished to popularize the arguments of *The Rights of Woman,* and to reach a larger female audience through a sentimental novel.[19] In her *Female Reader* (1789), Wollstonecraft had argued "that those whose 'passions have never led them to reason' cannot be affected by abstract, theoretical arguments but require 'amusing tales' and 'allegories . . .'"[20] Syndy Conger asserts that *The Wrongs of Woman* "transforms implausible polemic into a plausible and moving narrative."[21] Still, Conger predicates her approval on the compatibility of a subversive sensibility with radical reform, construing Wollstonecraft as a defender of the power of sensibility to "extricate [women] from any psychological oppression perpetuated by misogyny."[22] Framing the problem in terms of an opposition between rational discourse and sentimental discourse, has led, however, to readings of *The Wrongs of Woman* as incoherent, as sabotaging its critique of aristocratic social structures with the delusional "romantic expectations" inherent in the sentimental novel's form. Mary Poovey takes a hard line on the failings of *The Wrongs of Woman,* claiming that "the fiction that Wollstonecraft believed 'capable of producing an important effect' repeatedly threatens to lose sight of its political purpose and become just another sentimental novel."[23] For Poovey, the novel's narrator is seduced by the very longings for romantic fulfillment Wollstonecraft had so strenuously condemned as enfeebling, deranging, and corrupting women in *The Rights of Woman.*

These arguments, I believe, misconstrue the relationship of reason and emotion in the context of late-eighteenth-century political discourse. By contrast, Claudia Johnson maintains not only that the fragmentary nature of the unfinished *Wrongs of Woman* spells neither authorial ambivalence, nor fundamental philosophical contradiction, but also that the novel offers a view of female rationality consistent with Wollstonecraft's position in *The Rights of Woman.*[24] Rather than cast her analysis in terms of an opposition between rationality and sensibility, Johnson focuses on the embodied quality of rationality in *The Wrongs of Woman.* Briefly put, sex and reason need not be understood as antagonistic, or even incompatible. Arguments such as Johnson's avoid imposing a postmodern critique of rationality on Wollstonecraft's fiction and help us to see how Robin West's ideal of the liberal author and reader relied upon the historically specific conditions of literary culture for their creation.

In the *Vindication of the Rights of Woman,* Wollstonecraft had objected to men's exclusive power to judge and legislate on the grounds that it led to tyranny and, in turn, to immorality. In so doing, Wollstonecraft came close to undermining the premise of her principal argument in *The Rights of Woman,* that a universal standard of reason must be applied to, and demanded of, men and women impartially. Addressing herself to her dedicatee, the French legislator Charles Maurice de Talleyrand-Périgord, Wollstonecraft urged that "truth must be common to all, or it will be inefficacious with respect to its influence on general practice." But whereas her critique led to hopeful calls for reform in *The Rights of Woman,* the climax of *The Wrongs of Woman* stages the futility of rational critique of patriarchy in a society governed not by a Reasonable Person—but a Reasonable Man—standard of evidence.[25] To put the problem in contemporary theoretical terms, partial law insulates male legal decision-makers from recognizing the intersubjective nature of their decisions, that their alleged autonomy is a fiction and their standard of rationality fatally dependent upon the exclusion of alterity. As such, the Reasonable Man standard of proof could have dire consequences for men, rendering them "outlaws" as it did women.

First, Wollstonecraft's choice of genre should not be seen as limiting her audience to female novel readers, but as intervening in debates about rationality, representation, and gender, which had evolved significantly even in the brief time since she had published *The Rights of Woman.* David Simpson refers to the "trials of reason" in the 1790s, wherein the pressures exerted on English political thought in the wake of the French Revolution and the rise of a literature of English radicalism tested the generic and rhetorical resources of writers across the political spectrum. Simpson locates his argument in the history of rationality in print culture, and his analysis resonates with my discussion of witchcraft trials in the previous chapter. Female literacy and the dissemination of printed texts occasioned displays of women's reasoning powers threatening to the gender ideology that underpinned the Whig social order. Simpson reports that "after the printing of Descartes' works at least one observer noticed that 'ladies reasoned much more sensibly in metaphysics than three-fourths of the nation's theologians.'"[26]

Women's reasoning was merely the most dramatic challenge to traditional political ideology, however, and as such, presented a powerful strategy by which to attack radical appeals to reason. Women who reasoned were vilified as masculine, while radical reason, such as that displayed by Wollstonecraft's husband, William Godwin, was denounced as feminine and irrational. Good, reliable *masculine* common sense and tradition were the prescribed remedies. As Sir James MacKintosh put it in an address delivered at Lincoln's Inn in 1799, the "politician, like the poet, should address himself to 'general feelings and sympathies of mankind' . . . neither warped by system, nor perverted by sophistry."[27] In Simpson's account this is an authority that English and American Romanticism embraced, a politicization of literature and sensibility that appears to Guyora Binder and Robert Weisberg as the moment when literature removed itself from the public, practical sphere. Indeed, it did anything but. Wollstonecraft and Catherine Macaulay may have countered criticism by accusing their enemy, Edmund Burke, of failures of close reasoning and manipulative melodramatic excesses in his *Reflections on the French Revolution,* but political writers defending entrenched political interests had captured the aesthetics of feeling for their own ends.[28] Simpson concludes that the conservative politics of Romantic poetics effectively ruled out a radical literature, and this accounts for radicals', particularly Bentham's, hostility to literature.

This dialectic, which has proven so crucial to the history of literature and law, gave rise to important examples of radical fiction, however, including Godwin's *Things as They Are; or, The Adventures of Caleb Williams* (1794). Godwin contrasted his efforts in *Caleb Williams* with those of his philosophical treatise *Enquiry Concerning Political Justice, and Its Influence on General Virtue and Happiness* (1793) as "no refined and abstract speculation," but "a study and delineation of things passing in the moral world." A novel would reach a wider audience, he avowed, but it would also contribute "a general review of the modes of domestic and unrecorded despotism" to an increasingly polarized political debate wherein "one party pleads for reformation and change, [while] the other extols in warmest terms the existing constitution of society."[29] Like Godwin's, Wollstonecraft's choice of genre in *The Wrongs of Woman* can be seen as resisting this polarization in order both to assert a more capacious understanding of rationality and to engage male as well as female readers in an experience of intersubjective communication that would undermine efforts to exclude evidence of "unrecorded despotism" from rational-critical debate.

These arguments regarding the historical dialectic of reason and emotion in late-eighteenth- and early-nineteenth-century political discourse have returned critics to Wollstonecraft's narrative methods in both *The Rights of Woman* and *The Wrongs of Woman.* For example, Orrin N. C. Wang has credited Wollstonecraft in the *Vindication of the Rights of Woman* with disrupting the reason versus imagination opposition and its concomitant opposition of male versus female by presenting a host of female characters whose very diversity defies easy classification. "The moral," as Wang sees it, "is the dialectical limit reason and passion impose on each other's perceptual powers."[30] This epistemological dialectic is related to Wollstonecraft's understanding of historical change, displayed in an "irreducible tension in *The Rights of Woman* between a diachronic longing for an unambiguous political progress from passion to reason and a synchronic apprehension of the shifting epistemological boundaries between passion and reason, wherein reason functions not as a final goal but as a constant imperative toward critique, toward even the unmasking if its own dependency on the shadowed 'wisdom' of passion."[31] If Wang is correct, then Wollstonecraft had already interjected the alterity of female sexuality into the concept of universal reason, thus enabling, as Ernesto Laclau and Chantal Mouffe claim, "the birth of feminism through the use made of it in the democratic discourse, which was thus displaced from the field of political equality to the field of equality between the sexes."[32]

Rather than abandoning common sense to her opponents, however, Wollstonecraft would attempt to enact it through novelistic discourse. Feminist negotiations with Enlightenment theories of universal reason and common sense led to important developments in narrative technique. Julie Choi has drawn connections between Wollstonecraft's own appeals to common sense in *The Rights of Woman,* like those of Tom Paine in *Common Sense,* and the feminist uses of omniscient narration and free indirect discourse in the novel. She characterizes the narrator of feminist novels not as omniscient but as "common," that is, one sharing in the general sympathies of humankind.[33] In this manner, women writers contributed to the "view from Nowhere" we associate with nineteenth-century realism. Along with her analysis of free indirect discourse as sympathetic rather than intrusive, she is able to make a broad claim about literary history: "In a period celebrated for the male flights of lonely genius . . . [,] novels, mere novels, written on the whole by women, exemplify the narrative workings-out of infinitely knowable subjectivities in the fluidity of boundaries between self and other. Common sense is an especially fortuitous terrain, because it covers both the empathy as well as the ironic distance that are simultaneously held by the third-person narrator vis-à-vis her literary heroine."[34] These narrative innovations ought to have bridged the gap between West's "Enlightenment narrativity" and Habermas's vision of communicative action to produce an intersubjective agency, one that could achieve *de facto* recognition. Why did Wollstonecraft's novel end with an admission of failure?

One simplistic answer is that Wollstonecraft was not an especially skillful novelist. Yet there is considerable evidence in the narrative techniques of *The Wrongs of Woman* that support Choi's assessment of the politics of form. As Wollstonecraft explained her purpose in a letter to George Dyson, *The Wrongs of Woman* would "show the wrongs of different classes of women, equally oppressive, though, from the difference of education, necessarily various."[35] Whereas a defter stylist, such as Austen or Burney, might have managed this aim entirely by means of free indirect discourse, representing through one center of consciousness the diverse interiorities of characters by adopting their various speech patterns and discursive registers, Wollstonecraft depends heavily on the introduction of first-person narratives into her plot to convey alternate "life worlds." Maria elicits life stories from both Darnford, the radical gentleman incarcerated along with Maria in a lunatic asylum, and Jemima, their working-class keeper. In the context of journalistic reporting on wrongful incarceration, Darnford's tale would lend the authenticity of factual discourse to the entire novel. Jemima's story, on the other hand, an almost relentless "progress" from abused child, to seduced servant, to outcast and grieving mother, to exploited mad-house keeper, gains significance from the fact that Jemima speaks it out loud, as if giving testimony. By telling her story, and understanding its significance, Jemima becomes a reliable witness to her own wrongs and a forceful accuser of the persons who, and systems which, have maltreated her. The novelist functions like a judge issuing a writ of *habeas corpus* to bring the victims of unreported despotism before a jury of readers.

Well into the novel, Wollstonecraft abandons third-person narration, and the novel continues as a memoir Maria writes for her daughter, in the event that she and the child George Venables has separated from her are never reunited.[36] Still, whatever the limitations Wollstonecraft felt third-person narration had imposed upon her, that narrator does manage the kinds of sympathetic judgments of her heroine that Choi finds in other female novelists of the period. What Choi describes as a balance between empathy and irony, and Wang as reason's critique, is evident, particularly in the narrator's remarks on the power of even the most rational of discourses to act seductively. Before she meets Darnford, Maria begins to fantasize about her fellow inmate when she reads his marginal comments in a book on government. Maria's "fancy, treacherous fancy," the narrator tells us, "began to sketch a character, congenial with her own, from these shadowy outlines. . . . What a creative power has an affectionate heart!" (86). Indeed, the narrator is always most distant from Maria when describing her passion, though she is also careful to underscore its comprehensibility. This judicious narrative quality has been overlooked by critics focusing on Maria's own melancholy reveries.

When we turn to Maria's first-person narrative, Wollstonecraft presents us with visceral evidence of the brutality inflicted on even middle-class women by violent, drunken, and sadistic husbands. Such a graphic account of domestic and sexual abuse would not appear outside pornography until Anne Brontë's *Tenant of Wildfell Hall* (1848). Once again, there is a point in representing a woman as telling her own story. As we shall see in chapter 6, rape victims would not be so lucky in criminal cases. Finally, in the deposition Maria writes to be read at Darnford's trial, we see not only full-blown forensic eloquence joined with careful reasoning, but the sorts of appeals to jurymen that are the legal equivalent of addresses to the reader. Wollstonecraft's male audience, if not her female readers, would have been familiar with the extensive and quasi-pornographic genre of published criminal conversation and divorce cases. The *Trials for Adultery* volumes were probably Wollstonecraft's own source for legal procedure.[37] While these publications drew their enormous popularity from the salacious testimony that characterized these proceedings, including that from female servants with intimate knowledge of their mistresses' bodies, clothing, and linens, wholly absent from the trials was any testimony from the wives whose bodies were being contested. Wollstonecraft inserts into the public—and published—drama of criminal conversation and divorce trials the reasoned and impassioned advocacy of a woman on her own behalf. That advocacy is addressed to judge and jurymen in their equitable capacity, to look beyond the letter of the law to a standard of universal justice that should be rendered to all reasonable persons.

Finally, in *The Wrongs of Woman*, Wollstonecraft changed her discursive tactics—though not her politics—in order to exploit the fear of propertied males that they, too, could suffer legal erasure and be robbed of their rights as rational agents. William Belcher, the grammarian and self-styled "Rational Mystic," was confined in a madhouse for seventeen years. In his *Address to Humanity*, published a year before Wollstonecraft's death, he complained:

> Should my injuries, of the most crying kind imaginable, of which the following pages are a sketch, be the means of turning the thoughts of men in power to atrocities far beyond words to express (which, through the practices of the law, are not yet at an end respecting me), I shall have the consolation that my sufferings have not been in vain. At all events, sacrificing my feelings to a faint hope of public good I hope that, without impiety, I may say with Sir John Scott, who has my thanks, *Liberavi animan meam;* or rather, that it has always been free, and sometimes smiled, even in the bosom of horror.[38]

What made such cases particularly disturbing was the presumptive loss of credibility that robbed a sane man not only of his civil rights but also of the power to assert his rationality. In such circumstances, stripped of civil rights and of the authority to assert one's rationality, privileged males could experience the legal condition suffered by married women as *femes coverts,* whose protests would be dismissed as delusional ravings. That status, which in the case of women rendered them "outlaws of the world," should have generated some sympathetic allegiance between bourgeois male critics of lunacy law and married women. The point made in this, and similar complaints against lunacy law, is its peculiar rules of evidence, which appear to exclude a priori the right of the accused to offer a reasoned defense. Surely this has important implications for Wollstonecraft's choice of genre. The novel had developed, as much in the practices of rational realists like Fielding as in those of sentimental novelists like Richardson, as a mode of representing "private history," to use Fielding's term in *Tom Jones.* Novels offered a supplement to public history, credible, according to Fielding, insofar as they followed comparable rules of evidence, such as Alexander Welsh has analyzed in his study of realistic narrative and the rise of circumstantial evidence. In *The Wrongs of Woman,* Wollstonecraft stages the contest between public modes of representing subjectivity and private subjective experience to demonstrate the logical difficulties produced by medical and legal definitions of insanity and to expose their mercenary interests.

Little critical attention has been paid to the reasons for Darnford's incarceration, which are key to appreciating precisely what significance Wollstonecraft would have her readers attach to lunacy and imprisonment and its place in her account of the rights of men and women. Darnford's family has incarcerated him for his democratic political views, hoping thereby to preserve their estate and reputation. Darnford, whom Wollstonecraft describes as sexually exploitative and irresponsible, is, nevertheless, not insane; rather, he is an example of the corruption of male civic virtue in an aristocratic culture. Yet, once he is incarcerated, he is no better able to establish his right to act as a rational agent than is Maria. Further, the particular grounds for his incarceration—political beliefs deviating from those of his family—become irrelevant to establishing or refuting a charge of lunacy.

Similarly, Maria's ravings against the injustice of imprisonment and appeals to the judgment of the madhouse proprietor are met with his "malignant smile" (77). He, in turn, has prejudiced Maria's keeper, Jemima, against her. Jemima approaches her charge with the Alice in Wonderland logic that Maria must be insane because she is in a madhouse. Furthermore, the madhouse proprietor has warned her that medical experts know that the insane are capable of lucid intervals—hence, any signs of rationality on Maria's part can be subsumed into an expert definition of lunacy. Medical theories about hereditary insanity are also brought to bear against Maria, whose own mother had failed to thrive in her domestic duties. Only when Jemima learns that Maria has been separated from her child does she begin to credit her claims, a belief that depends wholly on her own position as an exploited woman and grieving mother. It is unlikely that Maria would find another jury of her peers, particularly one with the legal power to redress the injustices perpetrated against her. That Jemima's positionality enables her to assess evidence empathetically and accurately indicates that Wollstonecraft's choice of genre and audience is not at odds with her political goals, but rather is dictated by her critique. Narrative legal scholars argue that the stories of the disenfranchised constitute evidence necessary to a determination of an individual's reasonable expectations of danger, or harassment. Wollstonecraft constructs a jury of readers able to understand the inadequacies and prejudices of a standard of rationality that excludes such stories. She does so by contextualizing Maria's deposition in stories of her experiences as a wife, mother, and lover, and in Jemima's unsentimental account of her own history of abuse, poverty, prostitution, and imprisonment.

Wollstonecraft's unfinished novel culminates in a trial scene. Maria and Darnford have escaped the asylum with the assistance of Jemima. Venables tracks Maria down and sues his wife for divorce on the grounds of adultery and Darnford for seduction. There is some confusion in the novel about these legal proceedings, but the salient point is Wollstonecraft's handling of the case against Darnford. Some of the criticism of the novel's legal inaccuracies might be answered if we understand Wollstonecraft to have modeled her trial on a Chancery lunacy proceeding rather than a divorce suit. What is crucially at stake is not Darnford's actions, but Maria's mental competence—her right to legal agency as a rational actor. Her deposition, out of place in a divorce case, would be heard by Chancery in determining her status as *compos mentis.* Maria undertakes Darnford's defense by insisting on her own power to act as a rational agent, competent to make decisions regarding not only her obligations to her marriage contract but also the disposition of her body as a sexual partner. She directs Darnford's counsel to plead guilty to adultery, but innocent to seduction, thereby refuting the very charges critics have frequently aimed at the novel as giving way to romantic delusions. This combination of pleas emphasizes Maria's status as a rational agent: she does not deny that adultery took place and she insists that it was the result of rational choice on the part of both parties, not the act of a weak-minded woman succumbing to the blandishments of a seducer. Maria's deposition for Darnford's trial is written in the rational language of *The Rights of Woman,* not the language of sensibility. Its effect is not, as Syndy Conger argues, to elevate sensibility to the status of political critique, but rather to demonstrate that although both men and women may be susceptible to intervals of romantic delusion—as when Maria married Venables—or be driven to distraction by impossible demands, they must not be denied the power of rational decision making and self-representation by partial and logically incoherent rules of evidence.

The deposition, carefully detailing the logical contradictions and injustices in the laws governing women, is dismissed by a judge, who "allude[s] to 'the fallacy of letting women plead their feelings.'"[39] "Women, thus sentimentalized," Susan Staves remarks, "were seen to lack not only the rationality required for citizenship but also the rationality required for the active management of property."[40] Worse still, the judge remarks on Maria's sojourn in an asylum and the "hereditary insanity" in her family to discredit her. While her contemporaries Jeremy Bentham and James Mill would debate the competency and credibility of witnesses, Wollstonecraft charged that her entire sex was rendered incompetent a priori in matters of self-representation and self-government.

As early as *The Rights of Woman,* Wollstonecraft had confronted a dilemma of the liberal account of rational subjectivity, one that continues to plague modern jurisprudence. On the one hand, Wollstonecraft made a plea for female liberty and agency on the grounds that women possess reason of the same order as men's; on the other, she critiqued reason (institutionalized in law) as itself partial, constructed according to male interests and experience, defined against peculiarly female interests and experience. If the second proposition is true, then there is little hope that the reasonable men who act as judges and legislators will credit the first. Rather, any claim to rationality on the part of a critic of patriarchy can be dismissed as delusion. As a female speaker, Wollstonecraft lacks the authority to make her argument, regardless of its adherence to standards of rational argument and evidence. She cannot manage the property of her own story.

Wollstonecraft's novel points to an impasse in the history of feminist appeals to liberal conceptions of the self. Narratives in which women perform their rationality in order to demand equal treatment under the law are constructed by patriarchal authority as evidence of irrationality because their authors lack legal status to act as rational agents. As we shall see, only under reformed legal conditions, notably the passage of the Married Women's Property Act in 1882, would women acquire the right to do what Wollstonecraft imagines her heroine doing. Corollary to the right to act as an independent agent with respect to her property was a wife's right to bring a suit on her own behalf against her husband, granting legal recognition to her narrative as a plea. What role, if any, could the liberal conception of narrativity espoused by Robin West play in achieving this new legal status for women? Were narratives like Wollstonecraft's merely epiphenomena of a process that was governed by economic and political interests that had, as an unintended consequence, the extension of new, albeit limited, legal recognition for women?

Perhaps the key difference between Wollstonecraft's argument in *The Rights of Woman* and her strategy in *The Wrongs of Woman* stems from her despair at receiving comparable justice for men and women. But it should be remembered that it is the judge's dismissal that we hear. As always, the jurymen's reasoning processes remain opaque. The novel was unfinished at Wollstonecraft's death, and Godwin appended to this final courtroom scene sketches she had left for the remainder of the narrative. In those sketches she summarized the trial, a partial guilty verdict leading to further legal entanglements, consultations with lawyers, and so forth. This sketchy ending fittingly describes the uncertain future of women's efforts to gain equal treatment under the law. Wollstonecraft did not have time to project the law's future. Instead, she wrote out two endings of which she could be sure: one in which Maria commits suicide; another in which she is reunited with her daughter.

Wollstonecraft had every reason to take a pessimistic view of the future of women's equal rights in a state in which a reactionary government was asserting patriarchal norms with increasing force. The whole radical movement came under assault, condemning their published performances of rationality in a series of trials for seditious libel in the 1790s and early 1800s.[41] Yet the fundamental claim to rationality construed as ownership of one's stories would remain a key element of conceptions of the Englishman's civil rights, and one that would be influenced by the literary forms of evidence developed in novels such as *The Wrongs of Woman.*

It would be hard to argue for a direct impact of *The Wrongs of Woman* on legal conceptions of rational personhood. Not only the government suppression of radical critique through the seditious libel trials and suspension of *habeas corpus* soon after Wollstonecraft's death, but also the blow to her own reputation that followed on Godwin's publication of a memoir misrepresenting her as an atheist and publicizing her affairs and suicide attempt, ensured that years would pass before the rights West claims are conferred by narrativity were restored to Wollstonecraft. But in a more general sense, as a key example of women's unprecedented participation through literary means in the rational discourse of public sphere, *The Wrongs of Woman* contributes to a feminist-aesthetic revision of the legal agent as man of property. From Hannah More to Mary Shelley, women writers insisted that rational behavior take cognizance of relations and obligations, and in this sense were the forerunners of the dialectic between care and justice advocated by Robin West and between individual self-determination and life context, necessary for Habermasian recognition. What is more, women writers of this period promulgated an aesthetic corollary with their view of rationality, a "third way" avoiding both the heroism of traditional masculine tragedy and epic and the genius celebrated by their male Romantic contemporaries.

A powerful strain in feminist literary criticism has contributed to the belief, influential among some narrative legal theorists, that narrative is emancipatory insofar as it critiques normativity, or functions in effect as an antidote to rational discourse and rule-based legal reasoning. Recently, Anne K. Mellor has offered an alternative account of the historical relationship between feminist advocacy, literary practice, and rationality. Through their historically unprecedented participation in the discursive public sphere, Mellor argues, women writers of novels, dramas, poetry, and philosophical treatises during the late eighteenth and nineteenth centuries produced a new understanding of rationality, one that revised the

Lockean model based on the propertied male by insisting upon an "ethics of care" as the foundation for a rational distribution of social goods. This ethic required an aesthetic distinct both from the mimesis of neoclassicism and the Romantic cult of individual genius, one that "sustain[ed] the earlier Enlightenment image of literature popularized by Addison and Cowper, the trope of literature as a balance or scale that weighs equally the demands of the head and the heart, of reason and emotion."[42] That scale, as Mellor remarks, was held by a woman, whose powers of rationality involved imaginative engagement with others as well as critical judgment. Contrary to the view of literary history offered by Binder and Weisberg, this was the aesthetic—particularly the version of realism—that would prevail in the course of the nineteenth century.

Mellor notes that Wollstonecraft, like Mary Hays, Joanna Baillie, Charlotte Smith, and many other turn-of-the-century women writers, may have encountered hostility, whereas conservative writers such as Hannah More or Jane Porter, themselves contributed to the attack on feminism. Nevertheless, the understanding of rationality that they shared and the aesthetic means of representing it eventually prevailed. The characteristics Mellor ascribes to women writers of this period certainly pertain to Wollstonecraft's reasons for casting her argument in novelistic form:

> They insisted that the cultural role of literature is to educate even more than to delight, to educate by teaching readers how to take pleasure in the triumph of moral benevolence, sexual self-control, and rational intelligence. To inculcate such values and practices, literature must be both vivid and realistic, depicting events and characters rendered in sufficiently accurate and telling detail to be convincing. Generically, the novel provides the largest scope and most finely woven texture for such realistic portrayals . . . devoted to the quotidian, that 'occasional verse' which records individual responses to daily events. . . . Theirs were the critical positions that historically have triumphed: the novel (inextricably bound up with the formal conventions of realism) is now indisputably the dominant literary genre in Western culture.[43]

The triumph of a female aesthetic by which a female-authored conception of rationality is represented and promulgated would constitute a major supplement to West's Enlightenment narrativity, one that explains more comprehensively and with greater historical accuracy the appeal of literary narrative, particularly the novel, for feminist jurisprudence. As the form shaped by women to contribute reasoned argument in the public sphere and thereby to revise the definition of rational action, the novel already addresses the gender bias of Lockean conceptions of individuality based on contract theory while maintaining the significance of the individual subject and her capacity for meaningful agency. If this were the case, then narrative legal theory would be engaged in a recovery of a peculiarly female politico-aesthetic tradition. As I will argue in chapter 5, nothing so straightforward was the case.

Nevertheless, in the formulation cited above—"Don't do that, you're hurting me"—West illustrates the moral obligation imposed by stories of pain in terms of a mother-child relationship, one that should be located within a history of Enlightenment rationality indebted to women writers. Recovering this history provides the link between West's claims for narrativity as a construct of liberal selfhood, and Habermas's demand for a form of recognition that uncovers the relationship between an autonomous political self and the life contexts in which that subjectivity is formed. But it also affords the grounds for a critique of the interconnected phenomena of an ethics of care and an aesthetics of sympathy. Indeed, in *Caring for Justice,* West herself tries to integrate a "relational-feminist . . . ethic of care" into traditional paradigms of impartial justice, represented by the blindfolded judge, an activity that calls on both sides to abandon claims that "care and justice are oppositional virtues."[44] Both feminist jurisprudence and the Law and Literature Movement contribute to this goal, according to West, insofar as each seeks a "thorough reconstruction of the flawed theory of justice we have inherited, and which of necessity guides the effort."[45] For these reasons, a discursive history of rationality within the context of struggles to extend liberal forms of legal recognition are of utmost importance to narrative legal theory. How was narrative self-possession created and how did it contribute to political recognition, or "care"? As we shall see, it is the case not only that a conception of narrativity rests on liberal conceptions of the self, but that liberal self-hood depends upon the historical development of legal procedures, narrative techniques, and the category of the literary itself.

The realist novel did indeed triumph over the aesthetics of the epic and of Romantic poetry, of course. In the context of my argument here, that triumph is significant primarily in that the novel, which afforded to persons excluded from legal agency a means of representing their rational subjectivity in the public sphere, also became an authoritative mode for representing rationality. Furthermore, it conferred on literary authors an expertise that enabled them to critique the competing judges of *compos mentis* that arose in the nineteenth century: the men of law and medicine. In other words, whereas one strain of literary history has stressed the retreat of the literary from the rational, instrumental, and normative and/or its exile from a public sphere governed by rational choice, another has emphasized its role (or complicity) in the production of the rational, enlightenment, bourgeois subject. What if the very success of female writers to revise rationality through novelistic means resulted not in their legal recognition, but rather in the privileging of narrative as the appropriate form in which to represent rationality and, by extension, the privileging of novelists as authoritative judges of rationality? Women may have created new stories of agency, but they didn't necessarily own them.

As I shall argue in chapter 5, the consequences of this phenomenon complicate feminist appeals to narrative legal theory and may in fact counsel a strategic legalism. Although lunacy law reformers embraced Enlightenment narrativity as a safeguard of legal agency, instituting a bureaucracy engaged in gathering and bringing to public notice the narratives of lunatic asylum inmates, the relative failure of this activity to restore agency to alleged lunatics, especially to women whose agency was already circumscribed by law, justified novelists in their appropriation of representational authority on behalf of the disenfranchised. To demonstrate these points, I will turn next to nineteenth-century lunacy law reform and the narratives of alleged lunatics preserved in the Minute Books of the Commissioners in Lunacy, and then discuss *Hard Cash,* a novelistic exposé of lunacy law by one of the most extraordinary literary activists of the Victorian period, Charles Reade.

As a venerable source of precedents regarding *compos mentis,* the procedures of Chancery lunacy inquiries exerted a strong influence on these reforms, and both the inquiries and statute reforms existed in a dialectical relationship with narrative performances of rationality in the culture, generally. The implications for women were both literal and metaphorical. Not only were female property owners held to androcentric norms of behavior, but women more generally came to represent their legal disabilities in terms of the "civil death" suffered by lunatics, as Frances Power Cobbe so vividly illustrated by titling her 1869 indictment of married women's property law *Criminals, Idiots, Women, and Minors: Is the Classification Sound?*[46] As Susan Staves concluded in her landmark study of married women's property law reform, "One defect of the liberal history of married women's separate property is that the legal changes allowing married women to become 'autonomous' owners of property did not—as liberal theory would predict—notably empower married women."[47] Yet it was the cases determining mental competency to manage property that overwhelmingly set the terms by which women's legal recognition was advocated throughout the nineteenth century. By placing Enlightenment narrativity in the context of legal procedures to nullify the agency of persons determined to be *non compos mentis,* we can more clearly understand the failure of Wollstonecraft's failure to achieve recognition for women as rational agents.

CHAPTER FIVE

Agency, Equity, Publicity

Compos Mentis in Charles Reade's *Hard Cash* and Lunacy Commission Reports

THE HISTORY OF agency in the law is embedded in a complex matrix of issues, including culpability, contract, and property ownership. Rationality as a qualification for legal judgment is itself a product of Enlightenment liberalism: the Reasonable Man emerges to replace the aristocratic man as the repository of decision-making power. Robert Unikel remarks that "it is difficult to pinpoint the precise origin of the legal concept of 'reasonableness.'"[1] However, he notes its early use in a treatise on property, *An Essay on the Law of Bailments* (1781), by Sir William Jones, who wrote that "the omission of care, *which every prudent man takes of his own property,* is the determinate point of negligence."[2] The inherent gender bias of construction of agency that presupposes a condition of property ownership denied to virtually all women is reproduced in the Lockean contract theory of rights, a bias that has been the target of feminist critique from Mary Wollstonecraft to Carole Pateman. This conjunction was not created by John Locke, however, but inherited from legal proceedings determining *compos mentis* wherein the procedural and discursive practices for establishing agency in democratic political theory were produced. These concepts predate and shape agitation for wider political representation, exerting a strong influence on how self-determination was understood and why it was valued. They are powerful sources of the social construction of the liberal self Robin West characterizes as one who owns his/her own stories, instantiated in contracts, surely, but also more broadly in the legal capacity to bring suits and to give testimony, and ultimately in rights of *habeas corpus* and trial by jury.

Although much attention has been focused on the emergence of the insanity plea in criminal law as a barometer of legal thought regarding agency, disputes over *mens rea* (particularly given the fact that defendants in criminal cases were forbidden to testify under oath until 1898) obscure the positive articulation of rationality in lunacy inquiries as the grounds for agency. In chapter 10 I will discuss Lisa Rodensky's analysis of the fundamentally literary quality of *mens rea,* realized most fully in nineteenth-century realist novels while criminal law continued to resist medical evidence of states of mind.[3] Here I would note that, well before the landmark insanity plea of James Hadfield had prompted the Criminal Lunatics Act of 1800, a substantial body of case law on agency had been built up in Chancery lunacy inquiries, which determined competency to manage property. Under Henry VIII, the Crown assumed responsibility for managing the property of persons found to be *non compos mentis* in Chancery lunacy inquiries (a practice that was not made statutory until 1833). As Roger Smith has argued, "There was . . . historical continuity between the law's concern with the rights of 'freeborn Englishmen' (such as the right to disposal of property and to *habeas corpus*) and the legal form of the new powers to certify [lunacy]."[4]

Wrongful incarceration for lunacy provoked passionate outcries from propertied males because it robbed them of agency, understood most basically as ownership of their own stories, and Chancery lunacy proceedings offered a paradigm for the legal protection of this civil right, a paradigm women might apply to their own condition of legal nullity. In the eighteenth- and nineteenth-century journalistic scandals regarding wrongful incarceration, we can trace a Benthamite principle of reform: that publicity secures justice. At the same time courts imposed strict sanctions against commentary on the guilt or innocence of the accused, or the validity of testimony in criminal cases that were *sub judice,* the literary or journalistic exposé functioned as a popular discursive writ of *habeas corpus,* bringing before the court of public opinion a previously concealed, or "imprisoned," body of evidence.[5] Print media exposés followed the form of Chancery lunacy proceedings, which brought the alleged lunatic before the court to demonstrate his legal competency through rational discourse, and sought to disseminate narrative agency.

Between Wollstonecraft's *Maria; or, The Wrongs of Woman* (1798) and Reade's sensation novel *Hard Cash* (1863), a series of lunacy law reforms were enacted, driven in large part by literary advocacy in both novelistic and journalistic exposés. Along with concerns for the rights of property-owning men, these reforms created inspection schemes that afforded ownership of their stories to alleged lunatics. Whereas Foucauldian critiques of Benthamite reforms, especially regarding madness, have focused on surveillance, I wish to stress the significance of listening. The communicative conditions created by the requirement that government-appointed visitors attend to inmates' stories provided an unprecedented opportunity for one-on-one exchanges between dispossessed speakers and privileged auditors. The discursive features of visitors' reports display what Krista Ratcliffe terms a "rhetoric of listening."[6] Or, in Habermasian terms, they record a negotiation with a different "life world" necessary for legal recognition. Importantly, the result of successful advocacy by a lunacy commission visitor on behalf of someone wrongfully incarcerated for lunacy was a writ of *habeas corpus,* bringing the alleged lunatic and her story before the Court of Chancery. Yet, as we shall see, this system regularly failed, especially for women already denied agency as *femes coverts.* Furthermore, it remains unclear how literary narratives might recreate these transformative negotiations under the radically different communication conditions of mass publication and mass readership, which governed the exposé from the mid-nineteenth century.

Such a transformative negotiation with his audience was clearly the intent of the muck-raking Victorian novelist and playwright Charles Reade, who took up the cause of victims of wrongful lunacy incarcerations as one of his many literary campaigns. In the context of a burgeoning sensation-mongering popular press, however, Reade's publications could be subsumed into the mass of commercially motivated reports on a variety of sensational topics. As witchcraft prosecutions had jostled with reports of monsters, storms, and true crime in early modern print culture, lunacy incarceration panics vied with panics regarding infanticide (which I discuss in part 5), media juggernauts such as the Tichborne Claimant trials, and salacious reporting of adultery trials and sex scandals in the nineteenth century.[7] Importantly, nineteenth-century consumers of print culture included a growing number of female readers, provoking threats of censorship. Indeed, as Barbara Leckie sees it, the very hallmark of literary modernism—the assertion of an autonomous aesthetic realm—can be understood as a defensive reaction against such threats. Leckie's account offers a stark contrast with Binder and Weisberg's claims about the Kantian origins of an apolitical literary sphere, reinserting literature into the politics, economics, technology, and gendering of print culture. Within this dynamic, it would require a change in property law—the Married Women's Property Act (1883)—to produce a meaningful example of what Robin West means by narrative agency.

In part 3, I will treat the status of women witnesses in Victorian literature and law, culminating in the *pro se* representation of Georgina Weldon against those who had wrongfully incarcerated her in a lunatic asylum, a phenomenon made possible only by the passage of the Married Women's Property Act. In this chapter, I will consider the limitations of literary and legal narrative advocacy on behalf of agency for women who remained *femes coverts.* I will begin with two strains of legal narratives. The first are the narratives of agency developed in Chancery lunacy inquiries. As was the case with witchcraft prosecutions, these proceedings did not exist in an autonomous legal realm, but interacted with developments in print culture, notably the rise of a popular press. I will describe the role of Chancery lunacy inquiries in creating a space for alternative rationalities and argue that this practice would ultimately contribute to changes in women's property rights, necessary for the realization of Enlightenment narrativity. The second form of legal narratives I discuss are the reports of lunatic asylum "visitors" charged to protect the interests of inmates and uncover cases of wrongful confinement. Visitors' reports in the Minute Books of the Commissioners in Lunacy offer stark evidence of the failure of narrative advocacy to negotiate with a legal system predicated on a theory of agency tied to property ownership. Last, I discuss Charles Reade's literary advocacy on behalf of alleged lunatics, particularly *Hard Cash* as it relates to actual cases of wrongful incarceration, including that of the author Rosina Bulwer Lytton. Reade sets Chancery and Common Law in opposition to statute law, crediting the first with defending the ancient rights of English subjects against laws that conspire with venal financial interests and parvenu medical experts to rob victims of property and agency. Like Reginald Scot in his critique of witchcraft prosecution, Reade appeals to the conscience of his readers as well as their self-interest, inviting them to empathize with the victims of wrongful incarceration. Like Scot, he firmly identifies his literary advocacy with a defense of English Common Law and common sense. Yet, though women have access to print culture in Reade's time as they did not in Scot's, they remain outside a common legal tradition, barred from owning their stories.

Restoring the Properties of Lunatics: Agency and Equity

Only in England was the modification of strict law by moral considerations or extralegal notions of justice institutionalized in a distinct set of rules administered by a separate court. Chancery had repeatedly been a source of scandal from its inception in 1238, in part because its decisions were not bound by *stare decisis,* or legal precedent. The equitable powers of the Court of Chancery had broad implications, as I will show, but for persons wrongfully incarcerated for lunacy, and their advocates, Chancery afforded a unique remedy. The competency of persons to manage property was determined in Chancery upon the evidence of lawyers, medical men, laypersons, and the alleged lunatic. Deemed incompetent, the subject of a lunacy inquiry would become a ward of Chancery, and a guardian would be appointed to manage the ward's affairs. As Kathleen Jones has noted, until the eighteenth century when widespread publicity drew public and parliamentary attention to the plight of persons wrongfully incarcerated as lunatics, it had been relatively easy to have someone confined privately, without invoking the cumbersome and expensive mechanisms of a Chancery lunacy hearing. When such cases came to light, however, Chancery could issue a writ of *habeas corpus,* setting in motion a proceeding that would bring the inmate before a jury. Thus, Chancery was identified as extending the fundamental rights of a freeborn Englishman, granting him the right to defend his status as a rational agent before the law.[8]

Equity, as the Court of Chancery was also known, has been theorized by Dieter Paul Polloczek as functioning in a decidedly literary manner with respect to the normative, rule-based features of law. Both Equity and literature can introduce considerations of conscience into the processes that bring about political recognition. "To value claims to recognition is . . . to go beyond measuring injustices distributively in terms of physical injury and reputational harm," Polloczek notes. "Appeals that encourage, or are encouraged by, a call of conscience suggest at the least a possibility of withdrawal—at the interface of conflicting normative, cognitive, and affective orientations—from those processes of revaluation which external supervisory institutions hold out as promises."[9] In the narratives of Chancery, with its motley jurisdiction, we find interwoven the subjects of marriage, divorce, property, and lunacy, suggesting a site where norms of female subjectivity were constructed and where women might imagine contesting them. Proceeding from the traditional interest of the Crown in protecting estates, these cases yielded powerful normative standards governing the behavior of propertied individuals.[10] However, Chancery seemed uniquely empowered to recognize alternative rationalities.

It is certainly the case that Chancery, so pilloried by Dickens in *Bleak House,* afforded to women a kind of recognition denied elsewhere in law. Lee Holcombe has argued that "diametrically opposed to [the] common-law views [of women's rights] were the principles and practices of equity, which had developed over the centuries to correct the injustices and omissions of the common law and which by the nineteenth century had come to recognize a wife's existence and right to property separate from her husband."[11] We can look to none other than A.V. Dicey for confirmation of Holcombe's account of the historical workings of Chancery regarding women's rights. In his *Lectures on the Law and Public Opinion in England,* Dicey pointed out:

> In 1800 the Court of Chancery had been engaged for centuries in the endeavor to make it possible for a married woman to hold property independently of her husband, and to exert over this property the rights which could be exercised by a man or an unmarried woman. . . . By the early part of the nineteenth century, and certainly before any of the Married Women's Property Acts, 1870–1893, came into operation, the Court of Chancery had completely achieved its object. . . . This success was achieved, after the manner of the best judge-made law, by the systematic and ingenious development of one simple principle—namely, the principle that, even though a person might not be able to hold property of his own, it might be held for his benefit by a trustee whose sole duty it was to carry out the terms of the trust.[12]

Dicey is clear about the Court's motives: to protect the rights of men who wished their married female heirs and relatives to have control over bequests and trusts without interference from their husbands. This is precisely the circumstance of Wollstonecraft's character Maria.

As early as 1706, Daniel Defoe had brought public attention to the practice of confining wives in asylums as an easy option for husbands unwilling or unable to undertake the onerous proceedings for divorce under eighteenth-century statutes.[13] By the mid-eighteenth century, pamphlet writers had widely publicized the abuses of civil rights encouraged by private madhouses run for profit.[14] Several allegations of wrongful confinement in asylums in the 1760s, which came to light only because they became the object of suits in Chancery, drew both public and parliamentary attention to legal definitions of insanity. In *R. v. Turlington* (1761), the relatives of Mrs. Deborah D'Vebre sought a writ of *habeas corpus* directed to the keeper of the madhouse where she had been incarcerated by her husband. In a Chancery lunacy inquiry, a physician's report declared her sane. The writ of *habeas corpus* directed in *R. v. Clarke* (1762), on the other hand, was countered by an affidavit from the physician declaring the subject, Mrs. Anne Hunt, to be insane. In January of 1763, the *Gentleman's Magazine* published "A Case Humbly offered to the Consideration of Parliament," detailing the experience of men wrongfully incarcerated for lunacy. Once confined, the article reported, "if the revolted victim offers to argue against it by alleging any proofs of sanity, a motion is made by the waiter for the doctor to withdraw, and if the patient, or rather the prisoner, persists in vindicating his reason or refuses to take the dose, he is then deemed raving mad."[15] The ensuing scandal helped to force a parliamentary select committee investigation, leading to the Lunacy Act of 1744.

Despite the fact that several of these causes célèbre involved women, the public debate on lunacy law would be framed as a civil rights issue affecting men. The bulk of Chancery cases, not surprisingly, dealt with men. The majority of women who became the subjects of writs of *de lunatico inquirendo* were spinsters and widows; married women, as *femes coverts,* were largely barred from property ownership and were already in effect the wards of their husbands. The parliamentary select committee formed in 1763 to investigate wrongful incarcerations in private asylums had to proceed carefully, since these institutions housed so many prominent male inmates.[16] Indeed, medical men of the mid-eighteenth century had theorized an "English Malady" besetting the aristocracy—and even the royal family—well before George III was subjected to the moral management of Dr. Willis. By 1788 the open secret of George III's bouts of insanity had become a cause for political concern, and knowledge of the king's condition did much to elicit public sympathy for lunatics.[17] These events presented an urgent need for legal safeguards on the fundamental right of self-possession, necessary for the agency of propertied men, and set in motion a long process of investigations leading to a series of legislative reforms, each of which put in place more stringent evidentiary rules for determining *compos mentis.*

Around the nineteenth-century movement for lunacy law reform coalesced a range of issues, including property and civil rights, marriage and divorce law, state versus private interests, and legal versus medical expertise. Implicit in the reform of statute law on lunacy was a contest between Parliament and Chancery for authority to "safeguard" or, more accurately, to confer agency. Lunacy law reform was highly politicized because the rights fundamental to legal agency were at stake. Kathleen Jones notes that high Tories, such as Eldon, the Lord Chancellor, resisted any improvement in the condition of lunatics "as but one more aspect of the social unrest and the growth of liberal sentiments which they so greatly deplored."[18] As Mill's defense of eccentricity in *On Liberty* suggests, supporters of democratic political reforms expressed the view that lunacy should not be applied to individuals of the middling or upper ranks whose behavior was merely unorthodox, causing harm to estates perhaps, but not to the bodies of persons.

The Madhouse and Lunacy Acts of 1816, 1828, and 1845 were passed thanks to the same combination of exposé and scandal-mongering that had provided Wollstonecraft with her sources. Each act was the result of parliamentary select committee hearings in which legal and medical experts, humanitarian reformers, and even the subjects of wrongful incarcerations produced reams of testimony, all contributing to—and shaped by—narratives of rational agency. As Peter McCandless has shown, the growing power of the press provoked parliamentary action and investigation by rousing public outrage through periodic exposés of wrongful lunacy incarcerations. For example, in 1839 the *Spectator* complained that

> a lunatic, in law language, is *civilitus mortuus*. . . . If committed unduly, he receives in his single person nearly all the civil injuries that can be inflicted; for not only is his liberty thereby taken away and his property removed from his control but he suffers an imputation which operated with all the force of a libel. . . . A party detained on a charge of insanity may be acquitted and restored to liberty; but we all know that this is a question of such a nature that it cannot even be raised without attaching suspicion ever after to the individual to whom it relates.[19]

Around such scandals, resistance could form. McCandless remarks on "the number of those who fought against [the] tendency [to enlarge the boundaries of insanity]. Whether these people demurred out of simple concern for individual liberty, or because they themselves felt stifled by the rigidities of Victorianism, is difficult to say. The latter possibility, if correct, would indicate a widespread, if oblique, attack on the accepted code of behavior."[20]

Significantly, the most effective organized movement calling for legal protection for asylum inmates, the Alleged Lunatic's Friend Society, was founded in 1845 by Louisa Lowe, who, like Wollstonecraft's character Maria, had herself been incarcerated in an asylum by her husband. Lowe's movement was not explicitly feminist; her advocacy on behalf of alleged lunatics was gender neutral and her primary targets were the "Mad Doctors" who made their livings off of the incarceration of lunatics. Nevertheless, to advocate on behalf of female alleged lunatics was necessarily—if covertly—to challenge the marriage and property laws that made them peculiarly vulnerable to wrongful incarceration and a rising class of complicitous male professionals.

At least since Elaine Showalter's *The Female Malady,* we have tended to see the medicalization of lunacy as uniquely hostile to women. However, in focusing on "Mad Doctors," Louisa Lowe sought to enlist the hostility the medicalization of lunacy provoked in men. A measure ostensibly enacted to protect lunatics, the requirement that physicians certify lunacy was interpreted as a statutory challenge to the alleged lunatic's right to self-representation. The correlation between Lowe's strategy and the legal model provided by Chancery proceedings is evident in a treatise on medical evidence by Dr. Forbes Winslow, who complained of the hostile treatment medical witnesses received in Chancery:

> The legal profession is too disposed to regard all judicial investigations involving the question of mental capacity, as they do proceedings at *nisi prius;* and under, I have no doubt, a conscientious appreciation of their functions as advocates, often strive their utmost to destroy, if possible, the opposing medical testimony. Knowing the obscurity of the subject, and the difficulties with which the medical witness has to contend, in giving an accurate definition of insanity, the counsel most unfairly endeavours to pin him down to one; and the, by demonstrating its fallacy, overthrow the whole moral effect of his testimony.[21]

He counseled his fellow doctors to maintain a "manly bearing": "It will often be his duty, when under examination, to exercise great self-command, amidst extreme irritation."[22] Winslow deeply resented his feminized position as the object of inquiry, accustomed as he was to acting as judge of other's competency.

If the problem of wrongful lunacy incarceration, characterized by private arrangements and secrecy, was brought to light by writs of *habeas corpus* leading to Chancery proceedings reported by the press, then the solution was to implement mechanisms of observation and reporting. Chancery lunacy inquiries had brought wrongful incarceration to light in the eighteenth century.[23] Parliamentary efforts at lunacy law reform in the nineteenth century responded to press scandals with schemes for licensing and inspection of madhouses and an elaborate system of visitations by lunacy commissioners and certification of insanity by physicians' evaluations that bureaucratized many of the features of the Chancery lunacy inquiry. These mechanisms brought to light many instances of wrongful incarceration, leading to more writs *de lunatico inquirendo* and more Chancery cases, which were reported in the *Times* legal columns, thereby leading to a even greater sense of scandal.[24] When sufficient evidence of the failure of the inspections to prevent abuses came to light, the only remedy appeared to be to expand the system of inspection.[25] Especially after 1845, the mandated visitors' reports on individuals incarcerated in private and public asylums would bring into representation not only the stories of propertied men, whose interests had largely generated the public outcry for legislative reforms, but also those of women, paupers, and children, who were, by extension, gathered into the class of individuals whose right to self-representation deserved legal protection. It is pertinent, then, to consider what these statutory mechanisms brought to light, and what—intentionally or inadvertently—they concealed.

The opportunity for alleged lunatics to speak for themselves became an imperative of lunacy law reform in the nineteenth century. What was once the polite recreation of visiting Bedlam—the very practice through which Wollstonecraft had gained the knowledge of the asylum depicted and metaphorized in *The Wrongs of Woman*—became the favored method for devising and implementing lunacy law reform.[26] However, the bureaucratic structures and investigative practices consequent on reforms of lunacy law aimed preeminently at protecting the civil rights of property owners called for a different form of narrative representation than did Chancery proceedings. Unquestionably influenced by the exposés of wrongful lunacy incarceration that continued throughout the nineteenth century, the reports of asylum inspectors nevertheless demonstrate their authors' anxieties brought about by face-to-face encounters with inmates asserting their rationality and narrating the circumstances leading to their incarcerations. Out of the glare of publicity and exempt from legal rules of evidence, inspectors attempted within the confines of bureaucratic procedures to articulate a narrative form by which to recognize rationality and advocate on behalf of the wrongfully incarcerated, many of whom were women. Consistent with the expectations that Foucauldian-inspired analyses of the bureaucratization of insanity might raise, these reports reveal an effort to rationalize lunacy laws, but they also record conflicts over the meaning and representation of rationality experienced by inspectors unprepared for the advocacy roles into which their duties drew them. I certainly do not mean to suggest that these reports are more authentic because unmediated narratives of persons incarcerated for lunacy or, for that matter, of the reactions of inspectors themselves. They are obviously shaped by the circumstances of the interviews—most notably their setting in asylums—as well as by the official status of the inspectors. Still, unlike the published autobiographies of persons released from asylums, journalistic exposés, or select committee testimony, they are unusual in representing a remarkably intimate encounter between individuals deputed to represent rational legal actors and those whose status as legal actors had been denied by the law. They allow us a glimpse into the divided loyalties of legal actors—the inspectors—when confronted with procedures and bureaucracies instituted by law that appear less rational than the persons they are meant to regulate.

Listening to Lunatics

The Victorian minute books of the Commissioners in Lunacy preserved in the Public Record Office (PRO MH 50, 51, and 85) offer some insight into the discursive methods of advocacy for asylum inmates in the wake of lunacy law reforms and provide an important perspective from which to gauge the status of West's Enlightenment narrativity as a method of securing legal recognition within changing conditions for literary production. These Minute Books include reports of lunacy commission visitors required by the 1845 statute to interview inmates as well as correspondence from interested parties and commissioners' responses. They were not meant for publication, but they were written in the context of public scandals over wrongful confinement and their raison d'être was the principle that publicity in the form of governmental inspection would guarantee justice.

The inspectors' reports that are preserved are recorded in the Minute Book of the weekly meetings of the Commissioners in Lunacy (PRO MH 50, 51, and 85). Beginning with their second meeting, August 20, 1846, the secretary was instructed to keep a book in which were entered reports on cases requiring special attention from the commissioners. These cases concerned such matters as inspectors' observations of signs of cruel treatment (bruising, marks left by restraints, and so on), incidents of escape, and updates on inmates who were awaiting release after having been deemed cured. Many, at least in the first few months of the commissioners' meetings, were fairly terse, and the action taken sometimes difficult or impossible to determine. But as time goes on, there are several cases in which inspectors appear to have taken a special interest in the plight of an inmate, and the series of reports develop into personal sagas of the inmate's suffering as well as the inspector's struggles on his/her behalf. Reported in the dispassionate language of a bureaucratic record, they take on a Kafkaesque quality, especially when the very legal mechanisms by which the commissioners were meant to exercise their power on behalf of inmates prove not merely impotent, but obstructive.

Among the most extensively reported cases involved Mrs. Martha Elizabeth Rhodes, alias Shuttleworth (a relative of James Kay-Shuttleworth), who had been certified insane by Mr. Willmott, a surgeon, and Mr. William Griffith, and for whom an order of admission into York House Battersea had been signed by the Reverend J. C. Rowlatt, assistant minister of St. Peter's Pimilico. Rhodes had resisted removal from no. 10 Upper Eaton Street Pimlico, where she resided with Dr. Quail, and Willmott was seeking the commissioners' aid. Between Willmott's application on August 6, 1845, and her death on January 13, 1846, Rhodes would be the subject of weekly reports chronicling disputes among doctors and family members, Rhodes's incarceration, legal actions to free her (including a writ of *habeas corpus* issued at Queen's bench and a hearing in the Court of Common Pleas), involvement by Lord Palmerston and Kay-Shuttleworth, and interviews with Rhodes in which she related the abuse she had suffered at the hands of Dr. Quail, as well as her admission that she behaved violently in the asylum and had threatened to break its windows. Caught between a doctor who abused Rhodes in his private care and the medical experts whose determination of her insanity was upheld by the court, Rhode had but one ally: her sister Sarah, who besieged the commissioners with assertions of Rhodes's sanity and demands to see the particulars of her sister's statement to the examining physicians in the commissioners' memorandum book. Grotesquely appropriate is the final entry, a letter from Mrs. Rhodes's sister requesting permission to bury her, to which the commissioners replied that they had no jurisdiction or authority to interfere in the matter. An inquest followed on the order of the coroner, Dr. Thomas Wakley, the results of which, the Minute Book notes, were published in the *Sun*.

Faced with a narrative such as Rhodes's in so bland a source as the Commissioners' Minute Book, it is hard to imagine how a sensation novelist might improve upon its plot. Nevertheless, not all appeals to the commissioners were so futile, even when they were hideously complicated and sensational. I quote from this document at length to illustrate the style and content of visitors' reports. On May 11, 1848, statements were entered regarding a Miss Louisa Jane Nottidge by her mother and sister:

> My object in coming is to prevent my daughter's being liberated, she is under the same awful delusions as when first placed at Moorcroft House. She worships a false God. If discharged she would return to Mr. Prince, and be absolutely under his influence as before. If she could be persuaded to return home in a proper state of mind, that is, if she gave up her delusions, I have expressed by willingness to receive her. My real apprehensions are that she would go to Mr. Prince. Mrs. Thomas: If my sister were discharged, she would return to Mr. Prince. He is far from a moral man. He had unlimited influence over me. He induced me to marry Mr. Thomas having made me promise to carry out the will of God. He assured me that it would be only a spiritual marriage, and that I was not likely to have a family. I wished for a settlement upon my marriage. There was none. My property was vested in the joint names of my Husband and myself. I now receive the Dividences. Eight weeks after my confinement and the birth of my child, Mr. Williams came to me at Weymouth with a message from Mr. Prince saying that the curse of God was upon me. I wrote to Mr. Prince to know the mind of God, his answer was that I did well to acknowledge him as the servant of God, but that I should no longer know him as such. I told him that I could not acknowledge him as God, he then said that I was cast out. I have seen in my sister's accounts sums of £20, £30, etc. entered "given to Mr. Prince as for the Lord" think that she would not hesitate to give up all her fortune to Mr. Prince if he said the Lord had need of it. All Mr. P's followers are in bondage to him and under similar influence. I am persuaded that Mr. Prince would induce my Sister to marry neither she nor my two other sisters who are with Mr. Prince, have every written or taken any notice of me since I left them. I believe that when I was one of Mr. Prince's followers I was not in my right mind, and I think that my family would have been justified in taking me away from my husband and confining me. I would have done anything he told me and would even have given up my child to him. . . . My Sister has always threatened us with punishment sooner or later for confining her.

Having heard this testimony, the chairman expressed his opinion that Miss Nottidge ought to be forthwith liberated. The commissioners came to the following resolutions: "1) that Miss Louisa Jane Nottidge is now detained at Moorcroft House without sufficient cause. 2) that a letter be written by the secretary to Mrs. Nottidge informing her of the decision of the Board and stating that unless her daughter be liberated within one week the Commissioners would feel it their duty to make a preemptory order with that view pursuant to the 76th Section of the Act 8 & 9 Vict.c.100."

Pursuant to this order, Miss Nottidge was examined and it was concluded "that excepting these delusions, Miss Nottidge has not exhibited, so far as Dr Stilwell or the Visiting Commissioners can discover, any indication of mental insanity and has not shewn any incompetency to manage her property, or any tendency to maniacal excitement or violence, while her general behaviour, conversation, and manners, have in all other respects been calm and rational . . . [, and] that the delusions of Miss Nottidge are not likely, in the judgment of the Visiting Commissioners (who are confirmed in their conclusion by the opinion of Dr. Stilwell) to be removed or diminished by further treatment in a Lunatic Asylum and do not appear to be of such a nature as to render her dangerous to herself or others or incapable of taking care of herself and her affairs" (PRO MH 50/1). We must presume, since no further record was made, that Louisa Jane Nottidge was released.

One additional case deserves extended attention here, both because it deals with a pauper lunatic and because, despite the energetic and remarkably sensitive efforts of the commissioners, there is no record of the final disposition of the patient. This is the "Report on the Case of Margaret Walsh a pauper in the workhouse of St. George the Martyr, Southwark" (PRO MH 51/28), which begins with notes from visits of October 20 and 23, 1846, by Commissioners Procter and Turner. Walsh's appearance before a magistrate on the sixteenth of October had been reported in the *Standard* newspaper on the seventeenth, prompting the commissioners to order an examination. Her age was given as forty-six, and she was described as coherent and sane, despite the matron's contention that she was "violent and not fit to be at large."

The visiting commissioners examined Walsh "upon the various points upon which she was supposed to be deluded. We found her very unwilling to return answers to our questions, under the apprehension that we had come there at the instigation of W [undecipherable] (the master of the Workhouse) in order to entrap her into a confession of insanity." It is determined that she is not a spinster, but that her husband, children, and father are now dead. She had come from Ireland and, when not in workhouse, stayed with her sister. She maintained "that she is perfectly sane. . . . Never was insane." She had been incarcerated for nine months at Springfield Asylum, on the Surrey County Asylum. "Mr. Hill and Mrs. Whiskean[?] will say that the people who sent her there were more mad than she was," the report quoted Walsh as saying. They continued:

> That she worked all the time she was at Springfield—and when she came away she had presents given her—that the Justices gave her 5 shillings. That she was never fond of drinking. That she has earned her living . . . the last situation she had was as Nurse in Guy's Hospital . . . 4 years . . . this was before her father's death which was 7 years ago. Never accused anybody in the house of poisoning her. That it was impossible that she could make such an accusation as they all had food out of the same pot—the same gruel-the same soup—the same potatoes—Is quite satisfied with her food—It is very good and there is sufficient of it. That Mr. Robinson accused her of bringing in poison—to poison himself and his family after she had been in the house a fortnight. Other false accusations were made against her—Robinson said that she put knives and forks into her pillow—which was not the case. There was a girl in the house who teases her, but she is removed to another ward. Does not know her name but the Nurse does. She (Walsh) sleeps in a room with several other persons does not know how many. There is a child in the room. If she was mad she might as well kill the innocent as them—but she is not now—never was so.

The visiting commissioners concluded that "the manner of Margaret Walsh does not indicate insanity. She appeared to be a very clever woman. Speaks fluently and coherently. We could not detect insanity in anything that we observed in her manner or conversation. This stated, however, but she is sometimes violent—under delusions—that danger is to be apprehended from her, when excited or angry." They pursued their investigations, interviewing the workhouse physician and other staff, all of whom give testimony of Walsh's violence and coarse behavior. Still, the visiting commissioners appear willing to believe Walsh, and they interview her sister, who vouches for Walsh's character and behavior. After the unusual level of interest taken in a pauper woman, prompted by newspaper publicity, Walsh disappears from the commissioners' minutes.

These are just three cases investigated by the commissioners deputed to regulate the incarceration of lunatics in order to prevent wrongful confinement and ensure humane treatment through the legislative reforms of the mid-century. If the very activity of inspection was meant to reassure the public that their civil rights would be protected, the scattershot quality of the commissioners' actions—and the very practice of investigation that was the cornerstone of their regulatory powers—helped to fuel the periodic panics over lunacy law analyzed by Peter McCandless and others. As I have noted, the stories told in these reports, reports that were produced in fulfillment of bureaucratic procedures instantiated in the law and for an audience of government-appointed bureaucrats, require little embellishment in order to form the stuff of sentimental or sensational fiction. Yet they are eloquent in their simplicity and directness. Like the poignantly blunt "Wragg is in custody," quoted from a newspaper police report in Matthew Arnold's "Function of Criticism at the Present Time" (1865), these documents derive their power from the absence of hyperbole or, indeed, eloquence. The story—its "hard facts," in Gaskell's phrase—speaks for itself.

Beyond the detachment, objectivity, and terseness required of bureaucratic language, however, one must wonder about the degree to which the lack of rhetorical flourish belies overt censorship, inability to hear, or unwillingness to broach subjects touching on the legal handicaps of women. The women on whose behalf the lunacy commission visitors were advocating lacked fundamental rights of self-possession, which were merely exaggerated in the asylum. It is impossible to determine whether these female inmates understood their own circumstances in terms of gender. Indeed, as Roy Porter points out, even in autobiographies of nineteenth-century women wrongfully incarcerated as lunatics, the victim of the asylum was often figured as "the *patient,* male or female, rather than specifically the woman."[27] Instead of focusing on the effects this bureaucratic conferral of ownership in their stories had on the inmates, I would wish to speculate on the experience of the visitors.

Remember that West's example of story ownership stresses not only that we should be able to say "you're hurting me" but also that we should be *heard.* The moral imperative implicit in that formulation is that a report of unjust suffering should not only be understood but be acted upon.

It would seem that an unintended consequence of the lunacy law visitation scheme was to expose privileged males to the stories of dispossessed women. The communicative nature of recognition (of a property right, as much as of self-representation) is demonstrated by the action that lunacy commission visitors took on behalf of women they believed to be wrongfully incarcerated. Whether or not they fully recognized the peculiar legal injustices that contributed to women's incarceration, they had come some way toward recognizing a "life world" quite different from their own, discovered a shared basis of rationality, and acted as advocates. This would suggest that an important element of West's model must be a rhetoric of *listening*. Or, to shift to Anne Mellor's historical account of women writers' expanded notion of rationality, it would foreground the importance of careful readers whose own standards of proof are susceptible to modification through reading.

Importantly, that crucial act of listening is dependent upon the intimate relationship of conversation, questioning and storytelling. As an advocate for persons wrongly incarcerated for lunacy, Charles Reade would form such personal relationships. On the basis of his novelistic attack on lunacy laws, *Hard Cash,* Rosina Bulwer Lytton would entrust her story to Reade and solicit his help. Under the conditions of mass democracy and mass culture, she put faith in the political efficacy of literary advocacy, both Reade's and her own. But while Reade succeeded in his advocacy on behalf of men, he, like the Commissioners in Lunacy, were bound in a dialectical relationship with the law, which circumscribed their authority to advocate for women's agency.

Chancery and the Court of Public Opinion: Charles Reade's Sensational *Hard Cash*

The rise in Chancery lunacy proceedings consequent on lunacy law reforms and their reporting in mass-circulation newspapers occur within a new dynamic between authors and readers of stories of agency. Changing conditions of authorship and publication, particularly the growing political influence of the novel, resulted in the arrogation to novelists of the power to gain recognition for the dispossessed. The very success of the sensational exposé to mobilize the newly constituted force of public opinion overwhelmed the mundane stories of dispossessed speakers, and obscured the critique of women's legal disabilities that were inextricable from their vulnerability to wrongful incarceration. Reade construed the popular success of novelists (himself, Dickens, Bulwer-Lytton, Thackeray) as evidence that they were best able to know and represent the conditions of the dispossessed and therefore to act as advocates. As studies of nineteenth-century autobiography have shown, dispossessed persons had to conform to privileged readers' tastes for sentimental and sensational *fiction* if they wished to have their stories credited.[28] Female novelists may have created a readership ready to accept a construction of agency that included subjective emotions, relational identity, and multiple perspectives, but the very literary techniques by which these qualities were represented—complex character motives, domestic romance, and free indirect discourse—could also be cited as reasons why novelists per se were privileged advocates and the "owners" of stories of agency.

Charles Reade, best remembered today as the author of the historical novel *The Cloister and the Hearth* (1861), had a reputation among his contemporaries as a controversialist and social crusader. Choosing his subject matter from newspaper accounts of scandals, trials, and other causes célèbre, he produced muck-raking plays and novels combining graphic depictions of suffering with melodramatic plots. These works engaged with the fiery debates carried on by letter writers to the *Times, Daily Telegraph,* and other newspapers, debates which Reade helped to fuel with his own compulsive letter writing on numerous topics. Reade's most influential productions prior to *Hard Cash* were his exposés of prison conditions, including the novel *It Is Never Too Late to Mend* (1856). This work caused Sir James Fitzjames Stephen, the legal theorist and critic, to include Reade among the novelists of whom he complained in the pages of the *Saturday Review,* charging that their sensationalistic and polemical renderings of contemporary issues rendered productive political discussion impossible. Still, while Stephen appears never to have changed his mind regarding Dickens (he wrote a series of diatribes against the novelist), he recommended *Hard Cash* to his wife for its "realism."[29]

Lunacy laws, mad doctors, private asylums, were all frequently addressed in the press at the time of the composition of *Hard Cash.* As John Sutherland points out, Charles Dickens (who solicited *Hard Cash* for *All the Year Round*), Edward Bulwer Lytton, and William Makepeace Thackeray were each involved in lunacy scandals at the time. Bulwer Lytton's case was the most notorious: he had had his wife, Rosina Bulwer Lytton, certified insane and placed in an asylum after she had denounced him at one of his parliamentary campaign rallies for failing to support her according to their separation agreement. The outcry on behalf of Rosina in the newspapers was such that the queen was forced to intervene, demanding that Bulwer Lytton release his wife or resign his government post. Rosina and her friends managed to secure her release, though Bulwer Lytton continued to abuse her in other ways. Thackeray, who confined his wife Isabella for her depression, never attracted quite the attention Bulwer Lytton had, but became the subject of more subtle criticism. For example, through her depiction of the fate of Bertha Mason in *Jane Eyre,* Charlotte Brontë commented obliquely on her friend's behavior. And although Dickens merely threatened to have his wife incarcerated, he was allied with several of the doctors and lawyers involved in the Bulwer Lytton and Thackeray cases. As Sutherland summarizes the situation, "By the end of 1858, the three leading novelists of the age, Thackeray, Dickens, and Lytton (authors of such celebrations of domesticity as *Our Mutual Friend, The Newcomes,* and *My Novel*)[,] all had put their wives away."[30] Sutherland's discussion highlights gender, but even here, money is a key motive in choosing confinement in a lunatic asylum over other means of disposing of an unwanted relative. And indeed, money—not gender—appears to be the consistent element in lunacy incarcerations.

The two specific cases that prompted Reade to provide Dickens with a novel about the lunacy laws for *All the Year Round* were those of the Reverend Mr. Leech, reported in the *Times* of May 21, 1858, and of a Mr. Fletcher, which came to Reade's attention through an unknown source. Leech had inherited £30,000, and when he announced his intention to marry his housekeeper, his relatives had him incarcerated in a private madhouse.[31] Leech's case was consistent with many that had roused the indignation of free born Englishmen against the lunacy laws, wherein eccentricity in financial matters was punished by greedy relatives and the mercenary doctors in their pay.

The Fletcher case supplied the outline of the lunacy plot in *Hard Cash.* In August of 1858, the young man had escaped from a private madhouse, where he had been confined by relatives. Reade, who had been trained as a barrister, took up Fletcher's cause in an informal way, researching his suspicion that "certain of his relatives [were] keeping money from him that [was] his due."[32] As Reade wrote in "Our Dark Places," a nonfiction account of the Fletcher case and its implications for legal reform, he discovered in Doctors Commons the will of Fletcher's father, which named an uncle residuary legatee should his son die intestate. Fletcher's "'delusion' cannot be a hallucination," Reade concluded, "since it is simply good logic founded on attested facts. For on which side lies the balance of credibility?" (114). The uncle's motive for incarcerating his nephew was transparently financial. Reade addressed himself to the newspapers, complaining "the law is too silly, and *one-sided,* and *slow* to protect him [Fletcher] against the prompt and daring men who are even now hunting him. . . . You [the press] can aid justice by letting daylight in" (116). The desired end of press publicity of the Fletcher case would be a public trial, in which Reade is confident that Fletcher's rights and property would be restored.

It would seem contradictory for Reade to denounce in one breath the law by which Fletcher had been incarcerated only to demand in the next that his case be brought to the attention of judges in a court of law. But in the distinction between the two forms of law Reade had in mind lies a key element in the lunacy debate in Victorian England and literary advocacy. The law enabling Fletcher's family to have him declared insane and locked in a madhouse was statute law. For many reasons, this system was open to abuse for pecuniary motives, not the least of which was the fact that many of the so-called mad doctors required by law to certify lunacy were on the payrolls of private asylums. As Reade complained, by paying off the right doctors, anyone "can clap in a madhouse any rich old fellow that is spending his money absurdly on himself, instead of keeping it like a wise man for his heirs; or he can lock up any eccentric, bodily-afflicted, troublesome, account-shifting young fellow" (117).

In sum, the lunacy laws enacted by statute rules of evidence that contravened principles of trial procedure in Common Law revered as guarantors of civil rights, most important, *habeas corpus,* the rights of the accused to face his accusers and to mount his own defense. They substituted the authority of expert medical witnesses for judicial discretion and, moreover, for the judgment of twelve men, good and true. Reade turns to the procedures of Common Law to rescue Fletcher from unjust statute law.

This is precisely what happened. In July 1859, *Fletcher v. Fletcher* went to trial; the young man was examined in the witness box for eight hours; and not only did the jury find him sane but it also awarded him damages against his uncle as well. A summary of the trial and verdict were reported in the *Times* on July 8, 1859. Reade wrote of the case, "This particular Englishman sues not merely for damages, but to recover lost rights dearer far than money, of which rights he says he is unjustly robbed; his right to walk in daylight on the soil of his native land, without being seized and chained up for life like a nigger or a dog; his footing in society, his means of earning bread, and his place among mankind. For a lunatic is a beast in the law's eye and society's; and an alleged lunatic is a lunatic until a jury pronounces him sane" (125).

It is clear from Reade's characterization of the Fletcher case that his abhorrence of the lunacy laws was a distinctively masculine one. The rights and powers they removed were those enjoyed exclusively by males, and principally by propertied males: legal agency to manage one's property and earn an income, and an autonomous legal identity in society. The loss of these rights and powers renders the man of property a slave or beast, but they are among the rights the law denied to women, especially married women. Significantly, Fletcher—a propertied male—was able to assert his agency in a civil case in *nisi prius,* an option not available to wives in 1859. Rather, it was the Chancery writ *de lunatico inquirendo,* through which Fletcher had secured his release before suing his father, that became a powerful tool to bring the law to bear on behalf of those wrongfully incarcerated by wresting control of representation away from expert witnesses and returning to them the right to "own their own stories." This would be the legal model for Reade's literary advocacy in *Hard Cash.*

Hard Cash involves two families, the Dodds and the Hardies. Each family has two teenage children, a boy and a girl. Mrs. Dodd manages the household with her daughter, Julia, while her husband, Captain Dodd, is at sea. Her son, Edward, is at Oxford with Alfred Hardie. Alfred's mother is dead, and his sister, Jane, lives with their father, Richard Hardie, a banker. Richard Hardie, desperate to cover his losses in stock speculations, resorts to thievery. When Captain Dodd returns from his voyage, he goes directly to Hardie's bank to deposit his fortune of £14,000. Before announcing his arrival to his family, he reconsiders the deposit and returns to the bank for his money. Hardie denies receiving it; Dodd collapses in an apoplectic fit and is carried home. When he finally regains consciousness, he is declared insane because of his delusion that Hardie is in possession of his £14,000, about which only he, Hardie, and Hardie's clerk know, and he is placed in a private asylum.

Soon, Hardie is in financial trouble again, and he begins to pilfer his son's inheritance from his mother. When Alfred announces his plans to marry Julia Dodd, Richard Hardie forbids the marriage. Alfred discovers his father's theft of Dodd's money and, fearing that his son will discover he has been robbing him as well, Richard Hardie arranges to have Alfred incarcerated as a lunatic. He is aided in this scheme by a madhouse proprietor, Dr. Wycherly, modeled on Dr. Forbes Winslow and Dr. John Conolly, who enjoyed Dickens's public support. Wycherly is a minor villain, continually shown up as a fool by Alfred, and dangerous principally for the crucial—if unwitting—legal assistance he lends to greedy and dishonest men such as Richard Hardie. Nevertheless, once Wycherly authorizes Alfred's incarceration, Reade shows the powerlessness of the lunacy law's regulatory system to aid him. A government visitor, convinced of Alfred's sanity, starts the lengthy process in motion that leads to the Commissioners in Lunacy and threatens to bring a Chancery suit. Richard Hardie simply has his son moved to another asylum out of the reach of the commissioners.

Addressing his readers as jurors in the court of public opinion, Reade enjoins them to recognize their own vulnerability to lunacy laws that inflict on his sane, intelligent, and potent hero the full range of its provisions, which render him helpless:

> Chained sane amongst the mad; on his wedding-day; expecting with tied hands the sinister acts of the soul-murderers who had the power to make their lie truth! We can paint the body writhing vainly against its unjust bonds; but who can paint the loathing, agonized, soul in a mental situation so ghastly? For my part I feel it in my heart of hearts; but am impotent to convey it to others; impotent, impotent.
>
> Pray think of it yourselves, men and women, if you have not *sworn* never to think over a novel. Think of it for your own sakes; Alfred's turn to-day, it may be yours tomorrow.[33]

This strategy recalls Reginald Scot's advocacy on behalf of the accused in witchcraft prosecutions, asking readers—among whom Reade, unlike Scot, counts women—to make a sympathetic identification with the victim's plight, and to attach their self-interest to his. By declaring his impotence to paint the particulars of Alfred's mental state, Reade enables his reader/jurors to accept his character's situation as paradigmatic, filling in the details of his suffering from their own (gendered) imaginations.

It is only by means of the implausible coincidences and accidents conventional in sensation fiction, however, that Alfred achieves his day in court. The asylum where Alfred is incarcerated so happens also to house Captain Dodd, and when another inmate, a Fletcher-like young Chancery lunatic, sets fire to the asylum to enable Alfred's escape, Dodd is rescued by Alfred, and he is eventually reunited with his family. Fearful that he will be captured and reincarcerated, Alfred seeks legal help from an honest solicitor, Mr. Compton, through whom Reade makes his case against the lunacy legislation. Compton advises Alfred that "the English statutes of Lunacy are famous monuments of legislational incapacity: and indeed, as a general rule, if you want justice and wisdom, don't you go to Acts of Parliament, but to the Common Law of England" (3: 170). Of a barrister who refuses Alfred's case, Compton declares that "he had taken up the Lunacy Acts, and has forgotten that the rights of sane Englishmen are not the creatures of these little trumpery statutes; no, thank you; our rights are centuries older, and prevail wherever, by good luck, the statutes of the realm are silent; now they are silent about incarcerating sane men" (3: 183).

That Reade's notion of the sane Englishman's rights has fundamentally to do with property is apparent in the legal strategy he works out for Alfred's case. Not only is Reade contemptuous of statute law but he also finds greater likelihood of attaining justice through a civil rather than criminal action, because of the lower standards of proof. Damages awarded against Alfred's uncle, Thomas Hardie, signatory to the lunacy commission, constitute both just retribution and a public sign of Alfred's status as a sane, that is, property-holding, man. What is more, the young barrister who takes on Alfred's case suggests that rather than seeking a lunacy writ from Chancery, they bring a suit in the court of *nisi prius,* where costs would go with the verdict. Alfred's ability to appreciate financial strategy is further evidence of his sanity.

After many delays by the defense, and rulings that allow Reade to cite actual precedents in such cases, *Hardie v. Hardie* goes to trial. Here, once again reminiscent of the strategies of witchcraft prosecution critics, Reade privileges the evidence of common sense, emotion, and patriarchal values over the expert opinions of physicians. Alfred wins the hearts of judge and jury with testimony that is "frank and honest" and has "a certain flavour of Eton and Oxford" (3: 294). When he replies to questions about his suffering in the asylum and his father's financial motives for putting him there, "The jury looked indignant, and the judge looked very grave, and the case very black" (3: 292). Julia, forced to acknowledge her attachment to Alfred before the court, "baffled cross-examination and grammar and everything else," increasing the court's sympathy for Alfred (3: 295–96). The judge reads to the court a letter written to Julia by Alfred's sister, Jane, who has recently died from injuries inflicted by a man driven mad by her father. Jane's dying wish that Julia be assured of Alfred's sanity moves the court: "Many eyes were wet: and the judge himself was visibly affected, and pressed his handkerchief a moment to his eyes" (3: 305).

Reade presents the decisive piece of direct evidence through the testimony of a former American slave, named Vespasian, who had been on board ship with Captain Dodd. Vespasian's companion, the Reverend Fullalove, who has learned of Dodd's fate and Alfred's involvement, interrupts the proceedings: "We heard was a freeborn Briton treated wus than even a nigger in Old Kentuck, decoyed away from his gal, shoved into a darned madhouse—the darbies clapped on him—" "We don't want your comments on this case, sir," declares the judge. "No, nor any other free and enlightened citizen's, I reckon," Fullalove responds. Vespasian is allowed to testify to knowledge of Dodd's £14,000 and his intention to deposit it with the banker, Hardie.

Reade allows only for the feeblest of defenses. The defense claims that Alfred owes his current sanity to those who undertook to put him in an asylum thereby to "preserve his understanding and his property" (3: 306–7). Thomas Hardie's barrister dismisses the plaintiff's evidence as "romantic," whereas their own will be of a class that "does not seduce the imagination, nor play upon the passions; but it is of a much higher character in sober men's eyes, especially in a court of law" (3: 307). That evidence consists not of "the prejudiced sentiments of friends and sweethearts, who always swear from the heart rather than from the head and the conscience," language recalling that of the judge dismissing Maria's deposition in *The Wrongs of Woman,* "but on calm testimony of indifferent men," namely, medical witnesses (3: 307). Reade reveals that mad doctors are anything but indifferent parties; their monetary interests in commissions and asylums are strong motives to collude against any sane man or woman where property is at stake. Under cross-examination by Alfred's barrister, medical expertise is revealed as pseudo-science. The barrister "melted all [Dr. Wycherly's] polysyllables into guess work and hearsay," concluding, "In short, sir, you were retained to make the man out insane, just as my learned friend there is retained" (3: 309). The only evidence that tells against Alfred is that, to compensate for his father's fraud, he has deeded his property to the Dodds: "Fancy a man signing away his property to his wife's relatives!!" a spectator remarks (3: 312).

The Common Law is on the side of common sense—including the sort of sympathetic identification wrought by the affecting narratives of Alfred's suffering, Julia's affection, and Jane's loyalty—over medical testimony, which conceals venal motives and shoddy evidence behind arcane propositions. Traditional values and property rights are preserved in the

Common Law against the fraudulent practices of the market—represented by a speculating banker and mad doctors for hire—which Reade associates with parliamentary legislation. The judge speaks on behalf of those values when he sums up the evidence:

> The representative of evidence and sound reasoning, though accused of insanity, was clear, precise, frank, rational, and dignified in the witness-box. The party [defendant], who relied on hearsay and conjecture, was as feeble as they are; he was almost imbecile, as you observed; and, looking at both parties, it seems monstrous that the plaintiff should be the one confined as a lunatic, and the defendant allowed to run wild and lock up his intellectual superiors. If he means to lock them *all* up, who is safe? (Laughter.) The only serious question, I apprehend, is on what basis the damages ought to be assessed. (3: 337–38)

The jury concurs, awarding Alfred £3,000. The Commissioners in Lunacy prove effective where the law allows them, having protected Alfred's £20,000 inheritance, with which he purchases the Dodds' former home, sold when Capt. Dodd was placed in an asylum. Just as the desperate Richard Hardie prepares to kill himself, he learns that an investment has succeeded, enabling him to repay Dodd's £14,000, while maintaining his innocence and avoiding prosecution. Thus, order is restored when "Mr. Compton rushed to Pembroke Street and put this hard, *Hard Cash* in David Dodd's hands once more" (1: 343).

George Orwell described the closure of *Hard Cash* as "the type of the Victorian happy ending—a vision of a huge, loving family of three or four generations, all crammed together in the same house and constantly multiplying, like a bed of oysters."[34] Orwell's acerbic distillation of Victorian patriarchal desires sharply etches the features of lunacy within the context of Victorian law, as Reade understood it. Richard Hardie's continuing speculating mania constitutes the true instance of insanity in the novel, evidence of his incapacity to manage his property because of his delusional state. Even when he makes money, he remains morbidly fearful of poverty and dies dependent on his son. Alfred and Julia marry, soon producing a son of their own; and for good measure, the senior Dodds produce another son as well. The Hardie bank is restored with Edward Dodd as managing partner. Lunacy law statutes, like witchcraft prosecution, are legal anomalies that threaten the values enshrined in Common Law, principal among them being the right to manage one's own property. Justice is served when the freeborn Englishman is allowed to go about his business unfettered by legislation and regarding the right of his fellows to do likewise.

Whether the exercise of those rights brings about the relentlessly patriarchal domesticity of *Hard Cash*—Orwell's "bed of oysters"—or the individualistic eccentricity of Reade's beneficiary, Mr. Fletcher, they would appear peculiarly unsuited to defending the cause of women incarcerated for lunacy. Yet when Reade, in the wake of publicity over *Hard Cash*, published a request in the *Pall Mall Gazette* for further information regarding private lunatic asylums, he received appeals from both men and women, including Rosina Bulwer Lytton, who viewed her own case as comparable to Alfred Hardie's.

Rosina Bulwer Lytton sent the story of her incarceration in a lunatic asylum in a private letter dated February 10, 1864, to Charles Reade, a story that would later be published as *A Blighted Life* (1880). She requested of Reade "to *tell* the facts herein contained as far, and as wide as you can."[35] Those facts included her husband's infidelity and the conspiracy against her among his literary and political friends, ranging all the way to the queen, whom she described as "our little selfish, sensuous, inane and carnal Queen [who] would not care if all her subjects were equally distributed in madhouses, or pounded in mortars."[36] But despite the broad allegations of vice and injustice she leveled at a wide array of enemies, she was quite specific about her husband's financial motives for persecuting her. She recalled her £350 per annum income, which had qualified Edward for Parliament, and the £1,030 he had settled on her to bar dower. Soon, she remarked, his necessity made him want what little land she had, and though it was tied upon her, she gave it up. After their separation he failed to support her adequately and they fought continually over her debts. And finally, she recorded the sum Edward paid for twenty-five years of Rosina's debts and "to patch up the Madhouse Conspiracy": £3,500.[37] Aspects of this financial abuse had been reported by her allies in the *Somerset County Gazette* and the *Daily Telegraph*, and helped to secure her release from the asylum. But part of the agreement by which Edward raised Rosina's allowance to £500 after her incarceration barred her from pursuing her public campaign against him.

The silence imposed on Rosina Bulwer Lytton robbed her of another source of income: namely, the novels she had written as thinly disguised attacks on her husband, which had included *Cheveley; or, The Man of Honour* (1839) and *Miriam Sedley; or, The Tares and the Wheat. A Tale of Real

Life (1851). She continued to consider herself a wronged party, stymied in her lawsuits against her husband, blocked from disrupting his financial pursuits by public protests, and reduced to accepting an unjust financial settlement. In turning to the author of *Hard Cash,* she hoped to avail herself of the court of public opinion, to which Charles Reade had successfully appealed on behalf of Fletcher. It was not as an aggrieved wife or mother that she hoped to gain support, however, but as someone who had been denied her civil and property rights by a conspiracy of corrupt politicians and literary cronies and the mad doctors they employed. Although she mentions Caroline Norton's case, and the thirty to forty women she saw in the asylum garden, she makes no plea on their behalf and credits the "Somersetshire Yeomanry," who threatened to pull down Edward's house if she were not freed and, ultimately, Prince Albert with bringing to bear the pressure that secured her release. The one female friend, a Miss R——, who first made her incarceration public, is denounced for her "opportunism, vulgarity, [and] ingratitude towards her patron" in seeking personal fame through publishing Bulwer Lytton's case.

It is unclear whether Rosina Bulwer Lytton's consistent emphasis on her husband's economic injustices toward her was merely strategic, or if she understood her plight in terms dictated by the male-centered attacks on the lunacy laws, but in either case the evidence suggests that the reigning paradigm of lunacy in the mid-nineteenth century derived from legal tradition framed to protect property. As such, women protesting the power of the law to render subjects *non compos mentis* were shrewd to avoid explicitly feminist advocacy and focus on financial issues. These are the terms in which female critics of the lunacy laws frame their attacks. In one of the best-known polemics against the lunacy laws, *The Bastilles of England; or, the Lunacy Laws at Work* (1883), Louisa Lowe quoted admiringly from a *New York Times* article on the "Lunacy System in England" by Helen Burnard: "There can be no doubt that the sane, and especially sane women, are constantly incarcerated. The fact seems to be that the Commissioners in Lunacy drive a profitable trade with the superintendents and mad-mongers, by allowing them to incarcerated sane persons or detain patients after recovery."[38] As I noted above, in founding the Alleged Lunatic's Friends Society in 1845, Lowe excluded financially interested doctors and relatives from the assessment of insanity, and relied instead on judicial procedure and jury trials. However, it was a change in the legal and economic status of middle-class women—the Married Women's Property Act of 1882—that enabled women to use the law against the mad doctors and private asylums. Georgina Weldon, whom Louisa Lowe had saved from incarceration as a lunatic by her husband, took advantage of the law and successfully sued not only her husband but also one of Reade's targets in *Hard Cash,* Dr. Forbes Winslow, who had signed her lunacy certificate.

From Wollstonecraft to Weldon, the story of women's legal agency would seem to bear out Pierre Bourdieu's argument, cited at the outset of part 2, that "a performative utterance is destined to fail each time that it is not pronounced by a person who has the 'power' to pronounce it."[39] A drearily consistent futility characterizes the narratives of women decrying their exclusion from legal agency, the defeat of Wollstonecraft's Maria recapitulated in the life accounts of actual women, from the pauper Margaret Walsh to the author Rosina Bulwer Lytton, rendered *non compos mentis* by their very status as women. Literary representations of women's rational discourse, be they authored by women or by men advocating on their behalf, could be ignored (as in the cases of sympathetic lunacy commission visitors) or captured within a commodified literary marketplace, wherein female authors might even be alienated from the very income derived from such publications. The Married Women's Property Act, by admitting women to the Common Law's most potent procedures of agency—those in which to assert their property rights, including their property rights in their own bodies—afforded them a forum in which to demonstrate their capacity for rational discourse and to own their stories in the form of legal arguments.

Enlightenment narrativity did not produce legal agency so much as a whole host of enlightened activism brought about new legal circumstances making it appropriate for women to invoke those legal procedures of contract, bringing lawsuits, and so on, wherein women were procedurally authorized owners of their own stories as *compos mentis* legal agents. The significance of Enlightenment narrativity derives from its position within a more complex matrix, including a literary marketplace, property law as a mechanism of social control of both men and women, and determined activists who asserted not only their reason and discourse but also their bodies against a form of civil death. The role of narrative in bringing about legal recognition for excluded groups is surely to be celebrated. To reduce the dynamic of advocacy to a binary of law and literature, or rule-based reasoning and narrative, however, ignores a far richer account of the struggle for legal recognition. Moreover, exaggerating its significance leaves narrative open to a devastating critique of its limitations, which, in turn, obscures the real contributions it can make. As I will argue in part 3, the metaphorization of legal recognition as "voice" arises in historical circumstances in which narrative production was compensatory for legal agency. But narrative could be turned to another use: modeling for persons denied agency the legal literacy they required to assert it.

PART THREE

Testimony

CHAPTER SIX

Gendered Credibility

Testimony in Fiction and Indecent Assault

"Stuff and nonsense!" said Alice loudly. "The idea of having the sentence first!" "Hold your tongue!" said the Queen, turning purple. "I won't!" said Alice.

"Off with her head!" the Queen shouted at the top of her voice. Nobody moved.

"Who cares for you?" said Alice (she had grown to her full size by this time). "You're nothing but a pack of cards!" At this the whole pack rose up in the air, and came flying down upon her; she gave a little scream, half of fright and half of anger, and tried to beat them off, and found herself lying on the bank, with her head in the lap of her sister, who was gently brushing away some dead leaves that had fluttered down from the trees upon her face.

—Lewis Carroll, *Alice's Adventures in Wonderland*

LEWIS CARROLL'S dystopic legal fantasy, unlike the experiences of women denied legal agency discussed in part 2, resolves into a happy ending. Alice refuses to sit quietly by at the nightmarish Knave of Heart's trial and her words magically release her from the bad dream of legal entanglement. What is more, they reduce the court to silent, agentless objects—a mere pack of cards. Carroll's target certainly includes actual legal practice, but here, law is preeminently a metaphor for the adult world of force thinly disguised by rational procedure. Alice, doubly disenfranchised in the real world as a minor and a female, serves as the repository for adult males' dreams of escape from violence and tyranny. The dream of liberation is dramatized through a potent illocutionary act voiced in the colloquial language of a child: "Stuff and nonsense!" What Carroll's fantasy brackets is the adult world of gender hierarchy into which Alice Lydell, the addressee of the Wonderland stories, is destined to enter. Once she is a wife, restrictions on Alice's speech will guarantee that she does not abuse her magical illocutionary powers by becoming a tyrannical queen. The adult Alice will be "silenced."

"Silencing" has become one of the dominant metaphors for political exclusion in our time. Rather than property ownership, the power of speech has come to signify agency in democracies. To vote is not so much to exercise power, control the distribution of resources, or restructure institutions as it is to "have a voice." To express one's self seems to be an adequate substitute for civil disobedience, or even such forms of material resistance as boycotts. Silencing as metaphor has been adopted more broadly as a kind of shorthand for an array of cultural and material disadvantages suffered by women and minorities. Silence has a particularly rich history in feminist theory, especially in those strands of psychoanalytic criticism wherein language is equated with the symbolic order and the "law of the father." There it has been posited both as the consequence of patriarchalism and as a form of resistance. If all discourse is assumed to be disciplinary, then the only defense is to remain silent. Such theoretical positions do little to address the persistent discrediting of women's testimony. As Jill Tomasson Goodwin has shown, both the demonization and sentimentalization of female witnesses persists in guides to cross-examination in many contemporary works of legal advocacy, implicitly justifying lawyers' hostility or condescension.[1] If there is a traumatic experience with the law that since the Victorian period has fueled a myth of witchcraft prosecutions as a holocaust, then this is likely to be it. It is important for historical narrative jurisprudence to recover the construction of the metaphorization of both law and silence in order to move beyond a conceptual impasse and toward a view of voice that reconnects women's testimony with the social and legal.

This chapter locates the metaphorization of silence and law in a nineteenth-century process that led to the modernist assertion of culture and the aesthetic as categories autonomous from the political. In the introduction I argued that Guyora Binder and Robert Weisberg failed to recognize that this move was itself political. Here I will elaborate on that argument in order to explain how silence was both aestheticized and gendered feminine, leaving female speech available for masculine fantasy and testimony, while law was excluded from aesthetic valorization in part to prevent women from attaining legal literacy and exercising forensic eloquence. I will situate this process within interrelated developments in legal and literary history. The most salient aspect of nineteenth-century legal history is the evolution of trial procedure respecting who may speak in court, specifically (1) the introduction of counsel for the accused and the right of the accused to testify under oath under the Prisoner's Counsel Act (1836), and (2) the extension of competency to more categories of witnesses. In dialectic with these changes are Victorian novelists' attacks on the credibility of legal justice under the increasingly adversarial conditions of trial practice brought about by the Prisoner's Counsel Act, and their efforts to arrogate truth-telling to the disinterested realm of the aesthetic. As I will show, these developments conspired to produce a literary canon strikingly unsuited to feminist advocacy while denigrating (censoring, forgetting, "silencing") an alternative Victorian practice of *literary* advocacy.

Judith Resnick and Caroline Heilbrun waged an early feminist challenge to the Law and Literature movement on the grounds that it ignored writing by women and privileged canonical works by men that merely reproduced the biases of the law.[2] I will argue that under these conditions women's literature was as likely as men's to succumb to the polarization of aesthetic and legal discourses, silencing female witnesses in order to establish the primacy of the literary sphere in which they were granted authority. The literary tradition that we should seek to recover for narrative jurisprudence, therefore, may be one made up of texts dismissed as aesthetic failures in part because they represented women and outsiders as competent legal speakers and directly agitated for their recognition. Such is the case with Charles Reade's sensational historical novel *Griffith Gaunt* (1866), a novel I will argue in chapter 7 enhances women's legal literacy. In this chapter I will identify the ways in which three nineteenth-century realist novelists—Charlotte Elizabeth Tonna, Elizabeth Gaskell, and George Eliot—deployed the silencing of female witnesses in relation to literary and legal histories of gendered testimony. They are (1) as political protest; (2) as psycho-sexual metaphor; and (3) as claim for the priority of the aesthetic over the legal. These examples describe a continuum wherein the eloquence of the female novelist increasingly surpasses that of the female witness with the consequence that a "realistic" view of the law comes to imply rejecting law's authority to credit testimony in favor of aesthetic valorization.

I then turn to depositions in Victorian indecent assault cases in order to assess the significance of gendered categories of narrative aesthetics for men's and women's testimony. In these documents, the power of deponents to "own their stories" is fundamentally implicated in their right of ownership in their own bodies and credible testimony concerning them. Rape prosecutions offer the sine qua non of the silencing effects of gendered rules of evidence. And sodomy is famously remembered as the "crime that dare not speak its name." There are two advantages to considering depositions in indecent assault cases rather than in rape and sodomy cases. First is the relative wealth of materials (rape and sodomy were difficult to prosecute, and records in rape cases were suppressed). And second is the ability to make direct comparisons of testimony by men and women. Indecent assault depositions allow for an analysis of credible testimony that attends to variables of age, class, and sexuality, as well as gender, in the context of legal proceedings in which gender is critical. In these depositions, the gothic and sentimental conventions favored by female realist novelists in their treatments of the law turn out to be accessible to *male* plaintiffs and defendants alike, whereas the testimony of *female* witnesses is characterized by a matter-of-fact quality. Literary and legal histories of testimony are indeed interrelated, but in ways more subtle than "silencing" suggests.

Silent Witnesses

The irony of Alice's queenly command would not have been lost on nineteenth-century feminists. In *Criminals, Idiots, Women, and Minors: Is the Classification Sound? A Discussion on the Laws concerning the Property of Married Women* (1869), Frances Power Cobbe grouped women's legal disabilities along with other categories of persons denied full civil and political rights. Interestingly, though Cobbe's focus is on property rights, among the disabilities common to these classes was their status as witnesses. Rules of evidence barred the mentally incompetent from giving testimony, and imposed tests on the competency of minors.[3] But even the previously excluded testimony of criminals had been allowed since 1843, whereas until 1869 wives were forbidden to witness against their husbands in the very cases that most concerned them—and Cobbe—namely, adultery prosecutions.[4] This disability was famously protested by Caroline Norton, barred from testifying against her husband when he brought a bogus charge of criminal conversation against Lord Melborne.[5] Granted, women's testimony was addressed only indirectly by rules of evidence relating to *spouses:* spouses were deemed competent witnesses in civil trials, excluding adultery, in 1853, but not in criminal cases, and were finally made competent witnesses in adultery cases in the same year as Cobbe's publication. At the time Cobbe constructed her starkly unsentimental list, however, wives' words were deemed less credible in the legal circumstances in which they were most interested than those of criminals. The silencing effect of rules of evidence provided a powerful metaphor that tapped into the paranoia exorcised by Alice's imaginary edict: "Stuff and nonsense!"

Of course, women testified in civil and criminal cases wherein they met ordinary competency criteria, even as they had done in witchcraft trials. As witnesses, women could be the object of particular suspicion and hostility on the part of lawyers, however. In *Harris' Hints on Advocacy* (1879), Richard Harris warned fellow lawyers to "approach [the female witness] as if she were a wild animal ready to tear you if she could get near enough." Female witnesses are the gothic queens of Wonderland; lawyers take on the role of Alice. "You must demolish her, my friend," Harris wrote. "There's a life-and-death struggle in the cross-examination and you must win."[6] Victory in this battle might mean rendering the witness speechless, but more likely it meant discrediting an otherwise competent witness.

The fate of witnesses and defendants regardless of gender took on heightened significance during the nineteenth century by virtue of several procedural changes. The Prisoner's Counsel Act of 1836 afforded defendants the right to legal counsel, while a series of acts expanded the categories of competent witnesses, culminating in the Criminal Evidence Act (1898), which extended to the accused the right to testify under oath. Though both trends have been construed as democratizing legal procedure, they also further professionalized trial proceedings and exacerbated their adversarial character. The adversarial nature of criminal trials in which both defense and prosecution were conducted by lawyers could be seen as a fair fight, preferable to circumstances in which ordinary subjects relied upon the advocacy of the judge, sympathy of the jury, and their own wits, to defend themselves against the legal talents of the Crown. But, as Jan-Melissa Schramm has demonstrated, literary authors for the most part found in the deployment of forensic eloquence on behalf of guilty defendants occasion to decry the venality of the legal profession.[7] What is more, though defendants had access to legal counsel for the purposes of cross-examining witnesses prior to 1836, the attention focused on abuses of forensic eloquence in defense of guilty clients also spurred a sense of outrage at the harsh treatment of witnesses by lawyers on both sides. More people may have been deemed competent to testify, but their credibility was more aggressively assaulted. To be a witness was to be like a woman, denied the right to speak the truth and to be believed.

Furthermore, because the conditions produced by changes in trial procedure coincided with a burgeoning trade in crime and trial reporting, witnesses could become victims in widely published scandals. The professionalization of trial procedure had the general effect of removing the actors of popular legal culture to the sidelines, but the technologies of mass publication added a large audience of readers who consumed sensational testimony in newspapers to the spectators who consumed testimony in the popular theater of the court. Barbara Leckie and Laura Hanft Korobkin have described the consequences of sensationalistic divorce court journalism in nineteenth-century Britain and America, respectively.[8] Women who availed themselves of the right to testify in adultery and divorce cases, whether they sought divorce from adulterous husbands or their husbands had brought suit against their lovers, were rendered marketable commodities by the spectacle of women's testimony about sex, desire, and domestic arrangements. These trends inspired some pointed literary protest, and, as Leckie demonstrates, extensive debates about censorship and cultural values. But they also contributed to the metaphorization of law, along the lines of Carroll's trial of the Knave of Hearts, and of witnesses themselves, as objects of voyeurs or representations gendered abjection.

Alice's power to challenge arbitrary authority represented by the legal system of Wonderland forms a telling contrast with the fortunes of female characters called on to give testimony before English courts of law in Victorian novels by women. Rather like Alice's courtroom nightmare, the extraordinary circumstances of trials allow realist novelists to suspend qualified treatments of social conditions, appealing to gothic, melodramatic, and sentimental conventions. In Charlotte Elizabeth Tonna's *Helen Fleetwood* (1841), Elizabeth Gaskell's *Mary Barton* (1848), and George Eliot's *Felix Holt* (1859), female witnesses experience the trauma of being made a public spectacle and, if not immediately shamed into silence, they suffer the maddening frustration caused by their authorial illegality.[9] Either they are dismissed for transgressing the rules of evidence—that is, the court's preconception of "the facts"—or their testimony will be appropriated for an aestheticized patriarchal plot.

These novelists had experienced women's legal disabilities descried by Cobbe. Charlotte Elizabeth Tonna, who separated from her husband to escape his beatings, was sued by him for the profits from her earliest writings and subsequently published under her Christian name alone in order to avoid further legal entanglements. Biographers have noted William Gaskell's generosity in forgoing his right to Elizabeth's earnings as a writer, but that is because his behavior was the exception, not the rule.[10] "George Eliot" did not escape the lot endured by "Polly Lewes" as the lover of a man legally bound to another woman; even Gaskell wished that *Adam Bede,* which she greatly admired, had not been written by a woman living outside the law.[11] Law enforced each writer's submission to a hostile social order.

Tonna, who died in 1846, did not live to see the sustained and vocal challenge to women's legal oppression launched in the 1850s, but Gaskell and Eliot, who did, were lukewarm in their support. Caroline Norton's *English Laws for Women in the Nineteenth Century* (1854), which complained of the brutal consequences of married women's status as nonentities in common law, was followed in the same year by Barbara Bodichon's *Brief Summary in Plain Language of the Most Important Laws Concerning Women,* paving the way for her petition for a Married Women's Property Act in 1856. Both Gaskell and Eliot signed the petition reluctantly. Though they supported the principle articulated in the act, they remained unconvinced that legislation would provide any genuine reform, for unless individual men were converted to the justice of their cause, the law would be ignored.[12] Rather than a steady progress toward the legal recognition of women's testimony that would parallel their growing influence as novelists, the traumatic backlash against women's agitation for rights can be traced in the declining fortunes of female witnesses in *Helen Fleetwood, Mary Barton,* and *Felix Holt.*

Helen Fleetwood's Protest to the Highest Court

In *Helen Fleetwood,* Tonna's heroine turns to the law to protest her harassment by her factory foreman. As Patricia Johnson has convincingly argued, the device of the hearing enables Tonna to articulate what is probably the first conceptualization in law or literature of sexual harassment as a crime.[13] Because Tonna casts her novel in religious terms as well, contrasting spiritual testimony with its debased counterpart in legal proceedings, there is the sense that the weak will be vindicated in the highest court of divine justice. The novel's principal characters are the Green family—consisting of four orphaned children and their widowed grandmother—and their orphaned cousin, Helen Fleetwood. Victims of both economic and civil laws, Mrs. Green and Helen nevertheless become prophets of social reform by virtue of their biblically privileged status as widow and orphan.[14]

Well before the novel's trial scene, Tonna introduces the injustice of conventional patriarchal social relations which the legal system should redress. The Widow Green is dismissed as a troublesome crank when she complains to the foreman of the immoral conditions of the factory in which Helen and her grandchildren work. The millowner credits her complaint, but angrily dismisses her when he notices his daughter casting compassionate looks at the speaker. He reprimands Mrs. Green "for introducing such improper subjects in the presence of a young lady, whose ears ought not to have been assailed by discourse so unfit for a delicate mind" (560). The threat of feminine solidarity demands the exclusion of this woman's credible testimony. Helen Fleetwood and Mary Green are harassed in the factory for just such solidarity when they defend Katy, a younger Irish girl, from the abuse of the other workers. The overlooker, who intervenes to break up a scuffle after Mary pushes Katy's persecutors away, punishes the innocent Helen for the subversive influence by striking her. Mr. Barlow, the local clergyman, reports the incident to a factory inspector, appointed by Parliament to investigate such abuses and a hearing is scheduled.

Not a trial, wherein Helen would have been represented by counsel, the hearing manifests the power of her speech to establish the truth, but also the inefficacy of law to achieve *de facto* recognition of the justice of her complaint. There is evidence as well of the harassing manner of legal examination and asymmetry of discursive opportunity, the abuse of power made more egregious in that it is directed against children. The magistrate questions Helen's cousin Mary Green first, but when she tries to explain the history of Katy's persecution that led up to her action, he interrupts with a warning that she confine herself to the "facts" of this case. The rules of this investigation allow more freedom to the accused than to the victim, permitting the overlooker John Roy to question Mary, but not the victim her oppressor. Because Mary proves Roy's verbal equal and thwarts his attempts to confuse and contradict her, the magistrate dismisses her as "saucy." Next, Katy herself is called to testify. The foreman manages to provoke Katy by maligning Mary's character, and the court laughs at her stereotypical Irish temper. When the magistrate demands a translation of her ejaculation in Irish, she gladly responds: "It was the verse of a psalm that my father used to say out of the Irish Bible when Helen Fleetwood's character was to be taken away. The English is 'The lying lips shall be put to silence that cruelly, disdainfully, and spitefully speak against the righteous.' 'Are we to have we no decent witnesses . . . ?'" the magistrate inquires (588). Marginalized by race, class, and sex, Katy is rendered incomprehensible in the legal discourse, as her Irish speech illustrates. For Tonna, Scripture promises a deus ex machina more powerful than Alice's "stuff and nonsense" that will one day silence her persecutors.

Helen Fleetwood testifies last. Her emaciated condition makes her appear "almost heavenly," thinks her cousin Richard, and she "modestly, but clearly and distinctly" delivers her testimony. She is indeed the most effective witness. One magistrate acknowledges that she has established Mary's innocence, and the foreman's attempt to discredit Helen backfires. He hopes that by revealing her dependency on the Greens he will taint her as an "interested" witness. But thanks to her reliance on God, Helen enjoys a radical independence. "'If by any dispensation of God,'" Helen tells the court,

> "I was deprived of my best and only friends on earth, I have still one to go to who has said, 'Him that cometh unto me I will in no wise cast out.'"
>
> "That is to say, I suppose, you would turn preacher[,]" [Roy retorts].
>
> Here a murmur of "shame!" was distinctly heard; and one of the gentlemen on the bench said, rather warmly, "Enough of this; it will not shake the clear testimony of the young person before us." (589)

Nevertheless, though the magistrates credit Helen's testimony, it does not change unjust laws. Roy is made to pay a small fine, the girls' persecution at the factory continues. Eventually, Helen Fleetwood dies of illnesses contracted in the mill and Mrs. Green goes to the workhouse.

Tonna's protest is less against the exclusion of female testimony or its discrediting than against the material conditions of factory labor and the legal decision makers who call witnesses before select committees, undertake inspections, establish procedures for hearings, but fail to make substantive changes in the law. Tonna does not dismiss the law as fundamentally resistant to female speech, but dramatizes the gulf between recognizing the truth of women's testimony and making laws that conform to a Christian notion of justice. Like Helen, Tonna might be heard, and believed. But this is merely a *de jure,* not a *de facto,* recognition. Unless lawmakers shared her values, however, nothing would change.

Mary Barton's Traumatic Testimony

In *Lois the Witch,* as we saw in chapter 1, Elizabeth Gaskell creates a historically complex variation on the conventional heroine of sentimental fiction. Lois might strike a contemporary lawyer as the ideal defendant: unassailable integrity, modest manner, sympathetic background, and beautiful, too. When she attempts to speak in her own defense, however, she stumbles—significantly in her recitation of the Lord's Prayer. That her judges fail to see her innocence, are unmoved by her pathos and beauty, evinces their guilt. Yet it is women who witness against her. The credibility of Prudence and Faith as witnesses, however, is part of the corruption of rules of evidence that characterizes witch trials for Gaskell, as it had for many witch trial critics before her. Prudence is not eloquent; she is hysterical. Faith is jealous, perhaps insanely so. Just as the witch trials themselves were often construed as anomalies, so too might these exceptional witnesses be, thereby helping to obscure the history of women as witnesses in the Early Modern period. Nevertheless, Gaskell does insist upon the agency of women as witnesses, if only under extraordinary circumstances. Such was not the case with her first novel, *Mary Barton.*

Like Tonna, Elizabeth Gaskell valued transcendent truth over human judgment, declaring that as "God will cause the errors [of *Mary Barton*] to be temporary[,] the truth to be eternal, . . . I try not to mind too much what people way either in praise or blame."[15] However, Gaskell sees social constructions of truth as posing far greater barriers to women's testimony than Tonna allowed and creates a plot that underscores the inadmissibility of gender difference. While she combines class and sexual exploitation in the novel's dominant plot—Mary Barton's renunciation of Harry Carson in favor of the working-class Jem Wilson, culminating in Jem's trial for the murder of Harry Carson—Gaskell constructs a parallel subplot in which Mary's aunt Esther undergoes her own trial. She is driven outside the law into prostitution, judged guilty by her brother-in-law, John Barton, without an opportunity to defend herself, and left to die. Read together, these plots represent patriarchal law as destroying what it cannot appropriate, and women's testimony as fundamentally out of order.

Though Mary imagines herself "bear[ing] witness" to the truth when she is called to give evidence at Jem's trial, in fact she has been produced merely to deliver the lines already written for her, scripted according to conventions of sentimental and melodramatic literature, as well as salacious trial reporting. Never suspecting that Mary holds the very piece of evidence that could acquit Jem—the gun wadding that implicates her father, John Barton—the prosecutor calls her to tell a love story, her flirtation with Harry Carson that provokes Jem to murder. A crowd presses into the courtroom to see the spectacle of her testimony. A beam of "mellow sunlight streams down . . . on her head, and [falls] on the rich treasure of her golden hair," while her face is "deadly white." As an aestheticized spectacle she possesses "a higher and stranger kind of beauty" than ordinary women, specifically the picturesque beauty one observer associates with "Guido's picture of 'Beatrice Cenci'" (305).

Gaskell narrates the trauma of testifying in terms that suggest rape. When the prosecutor, that "monkeyfied man," demands to know her preferred lover, Mary is shocked that he "should dare so lightly to ask of her heart's secrets[,] . . . to ask her to tell . . . what woman usually whispers with blushes and tears." Meanwhile, she keeps "the tremendous secret [of her father's guilt] imprisoned within her" (306). Alice in Wonderland could reduce the court to a pack of cards and awaken, but Mary is trapped in this nightmare, "conscious that all was real, that hundreds were looking at her, that true-sounding words were being extracted from her . . . by the pert young barrister who was delighted to have the examination of this witness" (305–6).

What is worse, Mary's enforced testimony is a wholly unnecessary performance intended to gratify the court's appetite for spectacle and the desire of Jem's barrister to orchestrate the most dramatic presentation of his own "forensic eloquence" (311). He knows, as we readers do, that Mary has already secured Jem's acquittal by finding the one *man* who can provide him with an alibi, Will Wilson; in the chapters leading up to the trial, we have read the story, which none of the legal authorities will ask to hear, of Mary's heroic pursuit of Will, catching up with him just as his ship is about to set sail from Liverpool. Rather than cross-examine Mary, enabling her to record her heroism into the official account of the trial, Jem's barrister imagines the sentimental version of the story, which he will read into the transcript: "'a gallant tar brought back from the pathless ocean by a girl's noble daring'" (311).

Called to testify, Will literally vaults over the barriers separating accuser from accused, confident "that his tale . . . would be heard by judge and jury." When the prosecutor attempts to discredit him, asking Will how much he has been paid to lie on Jem's behalf, he can call on another man to vouch for his character. Pointing to his ship's pilot in the back of the courtroom, Will asks, "Would somebody with a wig on please to ask him how much he can say for me?" (313). Like Alice in Wonderland, Will has the power to reduce authority to an agentless object: "somebody with a wig on." He possesses the realist novelist's power of demystification. By contrast, Mary is absent when the jury returns a verdict of "Not Guilty."

The jury never hears the principal witnesses: John Barton and Esther, the murderer and the fallen woman. Esther is the source of the "tremendous secret" of the father's guilt; she is the mysterious informer who tells Jem of Mary's attachment to Carson; she even witnesses the confrontation between Jem and Carson. But Esther's testimony is admissible neither in the public space of a courtroom nor in the scripted terms of legal examination, but only in the represented private space and fictionalized autobiography allowed by the novel form. Esther unintentionally bears witness to the wrongs of women by telling her life story, an act she construes as an admission of guilt. Her unsympathetic and self-absorbed audience, Jem Wilson, does nothing to mitigate Esther's sense of shame, but the reader sees in Esther's "confession" to abandonment, poverty, and prostitution a vindication of a victimized woman.[16] Mary, who might comprehend this story properly and speak in Esther's defense, can never hear it because Esther herself is convinced that it is a "discourse unfit for delicate ears." In *Helen Fleetwood*, testimony of women's wrongs is also censored by gendered rules of decorum, but the implications of this failed opportunity for solidarity are more wide-ranging in *Mary Barton*. Here, it is an act of self-censorship coming between two working-class women who already sympathized with one another. Less a realistic account of working-class relations than a metaphor for women's literary testimony, Esther's self-censorship hints at the expectations for women writers in a commercialized literary public sphere as well as courts of law.

Gaskell's novels progressively reveal the importance of a female interpretive community to credit "life worlds" far different from men's. A dissenting minister and a young middle-class woman both speak in defense of the fallen woman in *Ruth* (1853), but her persecutor, Mr. Bradshaw, recognizes the validity of this testimony only when Ruth dies. The vocal and persuasive middle-class heroine of *North and South* (1854–85), having suffered the mortification of ad feminam attacks on her modesty when she acts on moral principle and literally throws herself between the millowner, Thornton, and an angry mob of striking workers, lapses into obedient silence as Thornton's wife. In the *Life of Charlotte Brontë* (1857), Gaskell mounted a defense of a sister author against patriarchal misreadings, making herself the target of all those readers who insisted Brontë behave as a proper lady. With an increasing sense of urgency, Gaskell remained committed in her fiction to voicing women's illegal language: "I'm speaking like a woman," the titular character of *Sylvia's Lovers* (1863) exclaims, "like a woman as finds out she's been cheated by men as she trusted, and as has no help for it. It's me as has been wronged, and as has to bear it."[17] Sylvia's is a generalized complaint about women's vulnerability. Gaskell's trial scene in *Mary Barton,* therefore, does not initiate a sustained engagement with the law, but suggests the extent to which women's legal testimony provided a metaphor both for the experience of the female realist novelists, attempting to address a female audience through the male-dominated, market-oriented mechanism of novel publishing, and for women denied ownership of their own stories.

The Art of Evidence: *Felix Holt*

Tempted as he is by "private motive," "man cannot be defined as an evidence-giving animal," declares the narrator of *Felix Holt* (563). More than any of Eliot's novels, *Felix Holt* directly concerns the law. Eliot agonized over its elaborately researched inheritance plot, set the novel against the backdrop of the 1832 election riots, and included a dramatic murder trial, representing civil, legislative, and criminal law. Yet it is not human law ultimately that interests Eliot, since no rules of evidence, parliamentary investigations, or cross-examinations can overcome people's basic instinct to lie out of self-interest. Jan-Melissa Schramm sees *Felix Holt* as George Eliot's response to the obvious corruption of legal truth-finding entailed by the Prisoner's Counsel Act.[18] Barristers' deployment of forensic eloquence on behalf of guilty clients exceeds even the perfidy of Eliot's Tito Melema in *Romola,* who writes political speeches for the highest bidder and marries a peasant girl in a sham ceremony. It is less the case that George Eliot loses faith in women's ability to achieve legal credibility than that she embraces an aestheticized silence for her female witness. Whereas the heroine of *Felix Holt,* Esther Lyon, retreats into rewarding domesticity after her traumatic testimony on behalf of Felix, the novelist transcends the tainted evidence of commodified, partisan law and popular literature to assert her place in the disinterested aesthetic realm.

In *Felix Holt,* the literary imagination accesses a truer form of law and Eliot promotes a radically different theory of narrative from Robin West's Enlightenment narrativity. She rejects a property-based, individualist understanding of subjectivity and stories. Eschewing the legal system and politics, wherein conflicting individual interests and contradictory testimonies vie for credit, her hero and heroine alike move toward a state in which they relinquish their own stories in favor of an ethical master narrative. Felix has visions of the transcendent law that would reform human hearts, inclining people to cooperation rather than conflict. Esther's principal duty is to recognize the legitimacy of Felix's "law." "He [Felix] was like no one else to her," Esther muses; "he had seemed to bring at once a law, and the love that gave strength to obey the law" (369).

Though Eliot recapitulates criticisms leveled by Tonna and Gaskell in trials scenes, Eliot subjects her heroine to legal persecution in order to reward her with the benefits derived from obedience to a truth transcending individual interests and narratives of self-representation. Esther testifies on behalf of Felix Holt when he is wrongly accused of a murder that takes place during an election riot he tried to defuse. Namesake of the queen who successfully pleaded the Israelites' cause before the Persian king, Esther should possess great oratorical power. This "sweet-voiced Queen Esther" of Malthouse Yard shares more than a name with the biblical queen (160). She too, like Gaskell's Lois, is an orphan brought from her native land (in this case France), to be raised by a foster father. As Queen Esther pleaded for her people, she too will plead before the law of the land to save an innocent man—only to have him rule over her as her husband.

The prosecution's witnesses give damning testimony against Felix, and though the narrator attributes to Felix "the sublime delight of truthful speech" in delivering his defense, he manages only to cheer himself without influencing his judges. From all indication, Harold Transome is correct in deeming Felix's brilliant peroration an abysmal mistake. The jury will misunderstand it and the judge resent it, he tells Esther, and his assessment is borne out. For his part, Harold manages only slightly better in his attempt to impress the judge and jury, and when the questioning turns to his own political activities, Harold's temper gets the better of his oratory. Testimony that might reveal the ambiguous complexities of reality proves to be irrelevant to the legal proceedings, a judgment having been reached even before the trial has begun. With a sinking sense of the futility of this word game as a means for discovering the truth, Esther is inspired to testify.

The description of Esther's thoughts leading up to this decision reveals George Eliot's commitment to the metaphorized feminine—self-effacing, disinterested—as a poetic medium of aesthetic truth.

> When a woman feels purely and nobly, that ardour of hers which breaks through formulas too rigorously urged on men by daily practical needs, makes one of her most precious influences: she is the added impulse that shatters the stiffening crust of cautious experience. Her inspired ignorance gives a sublimity to actions so incongruously simple that otherwise they would make men smile. Some of that ardour which has flashed out and illuminated all poetry and history was burning today in the bosom of sweet Esther Lyon. (571)

Despite Eliot's attempt to celebrate women's contributions to the pursuit of truth as self-effacing disinterested witnesses, one might also read this passage as suggesting that, thanks only to her own marginality, ignorance, and impracticality, a woman can offer credible testimony.

Superficially, Esther's testimony itself follows the model of the female witnesses in *Helen Fleetwood.* Unlike Gaskell's Mary Barton, she is unselfconscious of herself as spectacle, of her own beauty, as well as of the chance that she might look ridiculous. Her speech is sincere and plain: "Her clear voice sounded as it might have done if she had been making a confession of faith" (572), and in a sense, she is. She testifies to the nobility of Felix's sentiments, concluding with her confession of faith in Felix: "He could never have had any intention that was not brave and good." Esther's audience is entranced by her "naive and beautiful" action. She has been transformed from a beautiful "toy or ornament" by bearing witness for Felix. "Some hand had touched the chords, and there came forth music that brought tears." And, like a poet released from her muse, the "acting out of that strong impulse . . . exhaust[s] her energy," so that Esther returns to her place in a daze (573).

Yet, for all its aesthetic effect, the content of Esther's testimony signifies virtually nothing in terms of the verdict she meant to influence. Rather, it is the essentially chivalrous desire to please a "modest, brave, beautiful woman" like Esther that moves a man like Sir Maximus Debarry to exert his influence on Felix's behalf (576). As Harold later tells Esther, "I think your speaking for him helped a great deal. You made all the men wish what you wished" (589). In terms of legal advocacy, this seems a rather sad anticlimax to so "sublime" a speech, yet to move hearts as an artist means more than a legal victory.

Esther's testimony at the trial leads almost without interruption to her union with Felix: "I am weak," she confesses to Felix in her final dialogue;

"my husband must be greater and nobler than I am" (603). The utopian scene of Esther's future provided in the epilogue, which begins with her marriage and ends with the information that she has borne her husband "a young Felix," confirms the wisdom of the heroine's submission. "I will only say that Esther has never repented," the narrator concludes.

George Eliot brings realist ideology to bear on the whole project of legal reform and on the law as metaphorical representation of all institutionalized power. In a novel set during the election riots surrounding the extension of the franchise, she disillusions readers concerning the efficacy of legal testimony and political activism, showing them to be quixotic, when not downright pernicious. Instead, she counsels an aesthetic disengagement with political institutions and substitutes for legal recognition the consolations of sentimental domesticity—or, the happy ending that the literary imagination can uniquely represent. This silence is not imposed by the law, but granted by the novelist to enlightened readers. The objection that this silence has asymmetrical consequences for men and women cannot be meaningfully charged against a novel that discounts political critique and reserves the power of truth-telling for literary narrators. To raise this objection is to engage in the very sort of legalistic debate—to become an "evidence-giving animal"—that George Eliot claims corrupts human action and the realization of true desires and social relations. The law—literally and metaphorically—is unreality; the literary is true.

Aesthetic Appropriations and Silent Bodies in Indecent Assault Testimony

As in the case of narratives of *compos mentis,* discussed in part 2, it is crucial to investigate the effects these literary conventions had upon the ability of actual women to represent themselves within the law and upon legal decision makers' interpretations of them. The literary dynamic I have been tracing in part 4 veers between fantasies of extraordinary female illocutionary force and the axiomatic—even valorized—silencing of women in the law. With regard to *compos mentis,* we saw that realist literary technique, as employed by visitors reporting to the Commissioners in Lunacy, proved inefficacious as a strategy of advocacy on behalf of wrongfully incarcerated women, whereas they might succeed in vindicating propertied males. The indecent assault depositions I discuss here reveal a similar phenomenon, but they also demonstrate an additional valence of gender hierarchy reinforced by sensationalistic and sentimental literary conventions in that these conventions could be deployed by men against *other men*, when they were inaccessible to women victimized by men. Not only are the techniques of nineteenth-century literary narrative unreliable strategies of advocacy for women, they also can be deployed to discipline male sexuality and "feminize" same-sex male desire.

Indecent assault depositions can tell us much about the history of sexuality and social structures in nineteenth-century England that cannot be found in records of the more serious, and more extensively studied, crimes of rape and sodomy. With less stringent rules of evidence and a less draconian punishment, indecent assault was not merely easier to prosecute, but its vague definition also afforded a legal rubric under which a broad range of private sexual behaviors could be brought under public scrutiny and thereby disciplined. In this respect, its anomalous rules of evidence can be compared with those of witchcraft prosecutions. Furthermore, unlike rape and sodomy, indecent assault was charged by both men and women, enabling us to compare their positions as speakers in a public forum. In turn, this comparison necessarily reveals features of the relationship between indictment (law) and indicting (narrative description). By analyzing the discursive strategies deployed by men and women in indecent assault depositions, we can describe the ways in which the law appeals to gendered literary conventions in order to determine legitimacy, authority, guilt, and innocence in policing sexual practices.

Indecent assault prosecutions in the mid-nineteenth century would support Foucault's account in *Discipline and Punish* of the transition from a culture of torture to one of surveillance. The last execution for sodomy occurred in 1836, though it would be another fifteen years before sodomy ceased to be a hanging offense. From 1841 rape no longer carried the death penalty. At the same time, misdemeanor crimes, such as indecent assault, provided a category into which sexual offenses could be placed and by which they were redefined. Rape and sodomy required evidentiary proofs of penetration and emission. Yet as Judge William Brett advised a jury in an 1875 indecent assault case: "I cannot lay down the law as to what is or is not indecent beyond saying that it is what all right-minded men would say was indecent."[19] Any right-thinking man knew indecency when he saw it; therefore, all such men were legitimate supervisors of others' behavior and potential informants.

Within a culture of surveillance, this cadre of amateur detectives performed its duties by turning its observations into discourse: depositions, complaints, medical treatises, conduct literature, domestic fiction, and so forth. In rape and sodomy prosecutions, both the plaintiff and the defendant irrevocably made their bodies objects of public discourse: in other words, they named their privates in public. As Ed Cohen remarks regarding sodomy, the demand for evidence of penetration required "the body to testify against itself."[20] In contrast, the vaguely defined proofs of indecent assault allowed for "cover stories" to protect men's property rights, both to women's bodies and to their own persons. I will discuss this strategy at length in chapter 9. Here I wish to emphasize how indecent assault narratives responded to these difficulties with public representation by contrast with the erasure characteristic of rape and sodomy.

Rape was understood primarily as a violation of a man's right in a woman's body, as his wife, daughter, or servant. A victim's public testimony of her private shame compounded the damage. If, as Carolyn Conley has observed, a woman was willing to announce publicly the loss of sexual innocence, then she probably did not have it in the first place, or if she did, it could not have been of much value to her.[21] Literary texts cooperated to silence so-called fallen women. If we contrast the sharp-tongued and capable Moll Flanders (1722) with Lydia Bennet, the seduced sibling in *Pride and Prejudice* (1813), and, in turn with the woebegone fallen women of Elizabeth Gaskell's *Mary Barton* (1848) and *Ruth* (1853), Charles Dickens' *Oliver Twist* (1837–38) and *Bleak House* (1852–53), or George Eliot's *Adam Bede* (1859), we see a silencing of seduced women that corresponds with rape cases.

If we turn now to sodomy, a crime that can only be named in legal discourse as "unnamable," we find a compelling example of the power of erasure. To designate sodomy as "unspeakable" is to assert society's unanimous abhorrence of a crime so heinous that its very mention inflicts injury. Laws regulating male-male desire underwent a transition in the nineteenth century, as Cohen notes, from criminalizing acts of sodomy to criminalizing a vague range of male interactions as gross indecency under the 1885 Labouchère amendment. These changes, in which indecent assault prosecutions may have played a part, contributed to a homosexual panic—that is, men's "experience [of] their vulnerability to the social pressure of homophobic blackmail," of making their private desires public.[22] According to Dellamora, bourgeois men increasingly felt this fear as their status as gentlemen grew to depend on the homosocial institutions of public schools, universities, clubs, and professions.[23] The task, then, for all "right-thinking men," including magistrates, judges, and legislators, was to bring male-male desire into public representation in such a way as to construct a distinction between "sodomites" and "gentlemen" while protecting privileged homosocial—and homosexual—relationships.

Depositions in indecent assault made by men and women illustrate how gender inflects the construction of narrative authority, agency, victim status, and the like, revealing the interests served by discourses of deviance. Depositions are the statements taken at a police court when a constable has brought in someone he has taken in charge for allegedly committing an indecent assault. In the presence of the prisoner, statements are given by the constable, by the plaintiff (if the plaintiff is not the constable), by witnesses, and by the defendant, if he wishes to respond. The catalogue system for court records in the Public Record Office, which organizes documents according to the court in which a case was heard, and then by the genre of document—affidavit, deposition, ruling, and so on—makes it vastly difficult to follow an individual case from indictment to sentencing. That these depositions appear among King's Bench documents, however, means that deponents against the accused were sufficiently convincing to bring the cases to trial.

The first remarkable characteristic of the depositions given by male plaintiffs is their rather depressing banality. They are unemphatic, detached in tone, devoid of emotional rhetoric. They are set, generally, in common public places—streets, alleys, shops, boarding houses. As the plaintiff and prisoner are usually strangers (or claim to be), there is little in the way of character development. Often, they are almost routine in structure, lacking much in the way of suspense and leading fairly rapidly to their climax: the formulaic expression, "He laid hold of my privates." The deposition of one Thomas Thomas against a George Dawson Lowdes on August 8, 1843, is typical. Thomas, a servant, deponed:

> I was in Oxford Street—looking in at the window of a Jewellers Shop Mr Danieli when the Defendant came up by the side of me and said it is a fine day and he then put his hand on my Private Parts outside my Trowsers I told him to go on he did not but again rubbed his hand down my Trowsers and took hold of my Private Parts and squeezed them he then walked on and I followed him as far as Devonshire Place where I saw a Police Constable and told him what the Defendant had done to me and I gave him his charge. (PRO KB 6.1/1)

What makes this unremarkable deposition interesting is its very narrative impoverishment. The deponent exhibits little anxiety about establishing his credibility by telling a good story, by describing a struggle, or by justifying his presence in a public setting. The prisoner, for his part, declines saying anything in his defense. Thomas, however, has said enough for Lowdes to be charged. Indeed, Lowdes was brought in on similar indecent assault charges three times in the early 1840s (PRO KB 6.1/1).

Lowdes's cases are typical for their cast of characters as well. Thomas, as I noted, was a servant. Lowdes was also accused of indecent assault by Frederick Samuel, a sixteen-year-old bookshop employee, and Henry Martin, a boy employed by a publisher in the Strand. Lowdes is identified as middle-class in Samuel's deposition. As Rob Sindall has determined in a study of middle-class crime in nineteenth-century England, the preponderance of indecent assault defendants were quasi-professionals and businessmen.[24] It was precisely the public's perception that well-to-do adult men were preying upon poor boys, according to Hyde, that so fueled the Cleveland Street scandal, in which Lord Somerset, and other notables, were implicated in a case involving post office errand boys who had been solicited to work in a brothel run by a fake clergyman.[25]

The class inequities in many indecent assault cases do not translate into clear-cut power relationships, however. The relative ease with which an indecent assault charge could be brought made it an attractive means of extortion. In case after case, the plaintiff's deposition ends with the prisoner attempting to bribe his alleged victim to let him go. This is hardly to say that all plaintiffs of inferior age and social status to the men they accused were merely deft manipulators of a gullible audience. Rather, unlike female servants, for example, these deponents were seen as creditable witnesses as to their own abuse, so much so that the legitimacy conferred upon such deponents, and the culture's prejudice against the accused, could be exploited on a large scale.

Finally, with respect to the naming of the crime itself, the phrase "He took hold of my Private Parts" at once speaks and mutes the crime. Fraught with none of the anxious rhetoric employed by female deponents, this appears to be a matter-of-fact statement. The possibility that a man's right to his own private person might be permanently impugned by this temporary trespass remains concealed in order to preserve his freedom as a public person. Indeed, public exposure of male privates, though illegal, might still be seen as a source of pride, given the right audience. Lord Beresford was brought before the Westminster police court on July 8, 1837, by Constable Thomas Stewart Rogers, who witnessed him urinating on a curb at Haymarket. Rogers deposed that Beresford shook his privates at two women who, Rogers surmised, were prostitutes, and said to them, "See how it smokes." Unfortunately for Beresford, Rogers noticed three other women in view, who presumably were not women of the street, and for exposing his genitals (and wit) to them, Rogers took Beresford in charge (PRO KB 6.1/2).

Several examples of female plaintiffs' depositions—one for a rape charge, the others for indecent assault—illustrate important points of comparison with those given by men. Young girls alone in public made plausibly innocent victims. Unlike cases involving boys, however, there is a reluctance to question girls in such a way as to require that they represent their "private parts" in public discourse. Twelve-year-old Lydia Crickmore was sent by her mistress on an errand that took her through the Paddington churchyard in the late afternoon in December 1845. She carried her mistress's child with her. She passed a man named John Watson who called to her, "Here I have got something for you." Crickmore's deposition continues:

> I went up the path with him and he took hold of my hand and then he undid his Trousers in front and placed my hand upon it. He put my hand inside his Trousers. It was the flap of his Trousers that he opened—He pulled up his shirt and put my hand upon his person—He asked me whether I would not like to touch it and I said no—I tried to pull my hand away and he would not let me 'till he saw one coming and then he did—
>
> There was a man about four or five yards from us. . . . I did not stand with him for more than five minutes—It was about three or four Minutes—The Grave Digger jumped up and cried out "Halloo" and I ran away and the Grave Digger ran and stopped me. I did not scream when the Grave Digger ran after me. I was running to the Grave Digger—It was not quite dark. I went with him 4 or 5 Yards from the Public Path. (PRO KB 6.1/1)

We can infer from this deposition the questions that were asked of Lydia Crickmore. She was probably asked what she was doing in the churchyard at twilight, if she was alone, if she tried to resist Watson and, if so, how sincerely. On all points, Crickmore's responses are unassailable. She has been sent on her mistress's business, with a child in arms no less—hardly circumstances suggesting an erotic encounter. Her resistance is immediate and unambiguous, if ineffective without the intervention of a male witness. Finally, she must make clear that she perceived the grave digger as a rescuer, not as a witness to her shameful behavior; she did not run from him but to him, and under these conditions, felt safe to go with him some distance from the "Public Path." The grave digger's testimony corroborates Crickmore's, stating that the prisoner did expose his "private parts" to Crickmore, but adding, interestingly, that he "only touched her waist." Was Crickmore asked if Watson had touched her anywhere besides her hand? Did the grave digger volunteer this information unbidden, or was he responding to a question? Whatever the case—and the various implications are all intriguing—the effect of this specific information is ambiguous. It mitigates Watson's crime because he has left the girl intact, touching *only* her waist. Apparently, her hand is public property (in a period in which factory workers were referred to synecdochically as "hands"); her eyes and waist, however, require legal protection—hence, Watson is brought to trial. Furthermore, there is a connection between Crickmore's genitally inviolate state and her unassailable testimony. If Watson had had the inclination and opportunity to touch Crickmore's genitals, as the grave digger's evidence that he touched her waist implies he intended, would Crickmore have lost her status as a plaintiff *intacta*? Already she needs corroboration, coming ideally from a man whom she instinctively perceived as her protector. Watson left Crickmore intact, however, and so will her questioners—they will not touch on more delicate matters, or further probe into Crickmore's innocence, or ask her to expose her private parts.

According to the deposition of Julia Barnard, a woman had better not stray far from her husband, for his protection was not extensive. Mr. and Mrs. Barnard entered an omnibus on an evening in January 1855. There were only two vacant seats, and Julia Barnard went to the end of the bus, while her husband took a seat further up. On the way to her seat, as Julia Barnard deposed:

> I had to pass the Defendant. I had the greatest difficulty in doing so on account of his knees. In passing he said "Do you know that fellow" pointing to my husband and then said he should like to know me much better, then said "Don't touch me I'm very stiff." I was obliged to take the seat by his side, there was no other. He then placed his hand indecently on my thigh and I pushed him away. A Lady shortly after got out and I removed to that seat which was nearer to my husband. I then named to him what had taken place. (PRO KB 6.2)

The prisoner, Hewitt Bridgeman, cross-examines Julia Barnard, asking if he did not offer his seat to her husband, which she denies. She admits that she did not call out for help, nor did it seem to her that any other passengers noticed the prisoner's behavior. Bridgeman's strategy appears to be to establish that Barnard refused his gentlemanly offer, and must, therefore, not be a lady herself. What is most extraordinary about this incident is the deposition of Julia Barnard's husband, Lyon, who invokes the same kind of chivalric rhetoric as the defendant, while excusing his own failure to defend his wife.

> I saw she was uncomfortable. I saw her once push his hand away. She afterwards came to me and from what she said I told him he was no Gentleman and if he'd been a younger man I'd have thrashed him. He then turned round to my wife and said "Have I insulted you" She said "Yes most grossly" After that I gave him in charge.

Barnard's self-conferred heroism consisted largely in restraining himself from hitting an elderly man, who appeared to be a gentleman, even if he had not acted like one toward Julia Barnard. Finally, it was the law in the form of a police constable who was made to assume patriarchal responsibility—if not to guard women's persons in public, then to defend the husband's honor against ungentlemanly competition.

Apparently any space occupied by a woman might be read as public space in the absence of her husband. In September 1850 Emma Kirkness's own domestic space was violated by a stranger, Edward Denman, while her husband was away. Denman came to her door asking for porter and ham, treating her house like a public. Once seated in her kitchen, Denman forced Kirkness to kiss him, which she did "through fear." "I am a man of old manners, so you need not fear me," he told her. Later, according to Kirkness, Denman "put his hand up my petticoats to the private part of my person, and he pinched them and hurt me very much. I cried out and pushed him away, and called him a Base wretch" (PRO KB 6.1/1). So much for chivalry, though apparently Denman did not perpetrate further violence on Kirkness. Despite this abuse—"he . . . hurt me very much"—it was only on the advice of her husband, Kirkness is careful to note, that she took out a warrant on Denman. Still, a far cry from Robin West's Enlightenment narrativity through which the injunction "don't do that, you're hurting me" is heard.

The ambiguous status of the private and public for women is most effectively institutionalized in the relationship between the master of a house and his female domestics. Anthony Simpson remarks that in the eighteenth and nineteenth centuries, "Sexual exploitation of [female domestics] was taken for granted."[26] The sexual valence of the master-servant relationship was a favorite topic of eighteenth- and nineteenth-century novels, but such fictional representations—many of which "revealed" the hypocrisy of outraged servant girls rather than expose their exploitation—did little to aid women's legal representations as victims of assault.

In June 1834 Caroline Foster brought a complaint against her employer of seven years, Stephen Overy, for indecent assault. According to Foster, having gotten her drunk, Overy

> dragged me into the Room and put me on the Bed and kept me there nearly two hours. he stripped my Clothes all around me and at last I got away and got up in the Garret. When he was in Bed with me he had nothing but his Shirt on—he tried very much to put his person in mine—he said he would give me five shillings if I would lay still and I told him I would not for ten—he kept me there and tore me about a good while and then I got away and went out of the room but he did not effect his purpose. (PRO KB 6.2)

The next day, Overy offered Foster money to keep the previous night's assault a secret, but he could not have feared much from his servant, since he tried again that evening. This attack was noticed by Overy's daughter, who called out to Foster. Shortly thereafter, Foster escaped from the Overy household.

The first thing to note is that Foster stresses her inferior status by testifying that Overy impaired her faculties with drink. She needs this evidence to mitigate any suspicion as to her culpability, but it also undermines her credibility. Second, this was clearly a transaction of domestic economy: it took place in a bedroom in the employer's home and it involved an offer of money to an employee for services rendered. As Overy's inferior in physical strength, and as his dependant trapped in the privacy of Overy's home, Foster was made to pay for her resistance: "He kept me there and tore me about a good while."

More remarkable than Foster's evidence is Overy's reply. Unlike male defendants accused by male plaintiffs, who rarely utter even one sentence in their own behalf, Overy's response goes on for two pages, culminating in a statement succinctly invoking the pervasive structures of bourgeois domestic ideology:

> The long and short of the story is that she [Foster] wanted to be Mistress and I would not let her nor would my wife so she made up this story.

Foster, according to Overy, can be reduced to a cliché. She is first Richardson's Pamela, whom Mr. B represents as a greedy social climber, a construction endorsed in Fielding's *Shamela*. Next, she is the lower-class threat to middle-class female privilege; as such, like Jemima, the raped servant in Wollstonecraft's *The Wrongs of Woman*, she is a figure other women drive out of the domestic sphere. It is heartening that Foster's case was tried, though its verdict remains unknown. Regardless of the verdict, however, Foster lost her job; she had publicly challenged her master's right to her body as a commodity with market value, and she had been cast as a social, sexual, and economic pariah.

Finally, the combined consequences of women's discursive, economic, and sexual handicaps are evident in the case of Elizabeth Walker, who, after agreeing to keep quiet about her master's repeated indecent assaults, was raped. After several delays, beginning with her mistress's injunction that she tell no one and ending with her father's first opportunity to leave his business in order to press charges against William Thornhill, Walker gave her evidence on January 7, 1841. On December 23, Walker deposed, Thornhill

> laid hold of me, and asked me to put the shoes down. I would not—he then pulled his Trousers down. He had hold of me during the time but did not attempt to throw me down. He pulled my petticoats up and put his private parts in mine, and something wet came from him and it dropped on my shoes. I tried to get from him all the time. I began to cry and said I should tell Mrs. Thornhill; he said, if I would not, he would let me go. (PRO KB 6.1/2)

Thornhill released Walker, who immediately went to tell her mistress and to show her the stained shoe. She seemed to have provided herself with the evidence, nearly impossible to obtain, of emission, one of the proofs for a rape charge. Furthermore, as the deposition continues, Walker reveals that not only Mrs. Thornhill but also Mrs. Thornhill's mother were aware of a series of earlier attacks, which Walker goes on to describe, giving dates, times, locations, and Mrs. Thornhill's responses to accounts of these attacks, including her assurance that if Walker screamed, she would come to her aid. On each occasion, including the final attack on December 23, Mrs. Thornhill persuaded Walker to stay, and not "to make any disturbance." Indeed, Walker abided by her mistress's request that she remain in the house until Friday after that last attack, leaving for her parents' home on Friday night. Even then, she told only her mother, and traveled from Derby to Winslow with Mrs. Thornhill and Mrs. Thornhill's mother the next day, returning to her parents' that night. Not until Sunday did she tell her father, whose first opportunity to see a lawyer came several days later.

Thornhill was taken in charge for felony rape, and one would guess that Walker's detailed testimony, her material evidence, and the possibility of corroborating testimony from Mrs. Thornhill gave the prosecution reasons for optimism. In the course of her deposition, however, she contradicts her claim that "he . . . put his private parts in mine" when she asserts: "I am sure his private parts touched mine, and he attempted to penetrate, but did not, I was struggling all the time—." She has material evidence of emission that can be corroborated by another witness, and surely understands its significance, and yet she retracts the testimony about the other proof necessary for a rape conviction: that Thornhill achieved penetration. Is it because she feels that a public admission that she had been penetrated by Thornhill outweighs any possible benefit that could come to her as the result of his conviction? Had Mrs. Thornhill made a deal with Walker? Indeed, when asked by the magistrate if Mrs. Thornhill has put her up to the whole story, presumably to secure a divorce from her husband, she replies in the negative. Walker also has to deny accusations that she was turned out of a previous job for bad conduct. Walker does not suffer from ignorance of the law, extreme reticence born of shame, or simple inarticulateness, which, according to Anna Clark, plagued so many rape victims. Yet she subverts her own testimony to preserve herself intact.

Men alleging indecent assault might also invoke conventions of seduction narratives based on heterosexual models, but with rather different implications. Consider the evidence given by George Quintin against Robert Ward in March 1842. Ward and Quintin had met on the street, and the prisoner had asked Quintin for the location of a pub. As Quintin walked away, Ward chased him. Quintin deposed:

> I had my hand in my Trowsers Pockets—Defendant ran up to me and without speaking he put his Hand inside the flap of my Breeches and caught hold of my Private parts and pinched them in his Hand. He pushed me up against some Railings—I seized hold of his arms. I held him. I called out Police and a Man now present came up. defendant said "don't call the police and I'll give you anything you like to drink" After the Man came up Defendant said "he would give us anything we liked to drink to let him go." (PRO KB 6/1)

Quintin's evidence clearly makes him out to be the innocent and outraged victim of violence. He, like Pamela—or like the scores of female servants, washerwomen, and other female domestics speaking of their assaults—narrates his unambiguous resistance to his attacker. One obvious difference, of course, is that his physical resistance is viable. Yet more than that, his assailant fears his word, begging, "Don't call the police and I'll give you anything you like to drink." Not only does Ward, the assailant, assume that Quintin's narrative will be believed, but he fears being made the subject for which the predicate elicits all the prejudices associated with the crime that does not speak its name. This is in marked contrast to the depositions of female victims of indecent assault, who often testify to the taunts of their assailants that their words would never be believed—that to indite would be futile and self-destructive.

Indeed, in some cases the court's presumption of a male plaintiff's innocence is extraordinarily generous. William McLackie Beresford, a silk broker, gave the following evidence against George Jones on June 16, 1840, at the Worship Street police court. Jones had claimed acquaintance with Beresford in a pub, and when the landlady asked Beresford to take Jones to another house to get a bed, the two men left together. They go to Beresford's room, which he shares with two other men, and Jones convinces him to share the bed, requesting that the deponent lie down near the wall. Once in bed, the prisoner "lays hold of [the deponent's] private parts." Beresford continues, "I did not say a word for I wanted to see what he meant . . . I pretended to be asleep . . . I kept my hand dormant" (PRO KB 6.1/1). This, according to Beresford, continues for three-quarters of an hour, until Jones turns him over and gets on his back, whereupon Beresford "cried out," "gave the alarm," and dragged Jones out to find a policeman. It will be remembered that readers of Elizabeth Gaskell's *Ruth* found incredible the innocence of that seduced, impregnated heroine. Yet a police court found this account sufficiently credible to make Jones stand trial.

Moreover, the combined evocation of seduction and sodomy narratives could function to position the male assailant in the melodramatic role of the desperate fallen woman, and thereby to reinforce his guiltiness. Police Constable Richard Barlett deposed that the prisoner William Hunter, on November 29, 1847, conversed suggestively with him at some length before he

> caught hold of my person & pressed it very hard against my thigh I then shoved him back & asked him what he meant by taking hold of me in that Indecent sort of a manner and also by putting those questions to me he had done. He said he was very sorry & begged my pardon & did not think it any harm & he only did it out of curiosity. I told him I must take him down to the Station. and he begged of me for God's sake not to do it. He said he would give me anything in the World if I did not take him down—
>
> He took his Gold watch from his Pocket & said he would give it me & all he was possessed of if I would not take him to the Station House. He said he would go on his hands and knees to me a thousand times & begged my Pardon & he knelt down & began to cry & then I got him up and got him as far as Harley Street and Devonshire Street He caught hold of the Railing & knelt down again & said he could not go any farther for the World He said Oh Dear what shall I do it will be all published in the Papers—I could not get him away & a Brother Constable came up on the other side of the way & I called him to my assistance He came and asked what was the matter & I told him and the Prisoner begged me for God's sake not to call him. With difficulty we got him down Harley Street he kept kneeling all the way down;—that's all. We took him to the Station. He also asked me what I was going to charge him with and I said he knew what he had done. He said I know very well I am guilty but I thought it no harm. (PRO KB 6.1/1)

One might imagine this incident as a comic routine aimed at the stunning obtuseness of the stolid London bobby. But the police court that heard this deposition took PC Bartlett very seriously, enough so to make William Hunter stand trial. Nor is this sort of incident unique. Rather, it is representative of the law's predisposition to credit both the innocence and the honesty of male deponents alleging indecent assault, and, moreover, to vilify prisoners taken in charge for the offense as at once predatory seducers and, conversely, as pathetic, desperate, and perhaps even hysterical.

A significant disciplinary tool in the mid-nineteenth century, indecent assault is indited—that is, put into words—clearly marked by the gendered signature of its deponents. Their depositions are useful evidence of how law and literature are mutually constitutive and how both discipline sexuality and enforce gender hierarchies. Indecent assault narratives, their points of contact with and departure from rape narratives, mark an important stage in the modern construction of homosexuality, like female sexuality, as difference. Yet, judging from the consequences to men and women of naming privates in public, that difference still clearly admitted of degree in law as well as in literature. The very literary techniques enshrined in canonical literature and embraced by narrative legal theory and much feminist literary theory offered little aid to women—*and men deemed sexual deviant*—who were denied property rights in their own bodies, to advocate on their own behalf. Indeed, as in *Mary Barton* or *Felix Holt,* which privileges the aestheticized silent body, literary conventions might actually both militate against an unaesthetic factual account of victimization and render homosexual men as feminized hysterics. As in the case of *compos mentis* legal and literary narratives discussed in part 2, these sexualized conventions could reduce propertied males to the sort of civil death experienced by women. Clearly, if literary narrative can be construed as affording a strategy for advocacy against such norms, we must look to other literary paradigms, even if they have traditionally been classified as aesthetically flawed.

CHAPTER 7

Women's Legal Literacy and *Pro Se* Representation

From *Griffith Gaunt* to Georgina Weldon

"THE MAN WHO defends himself has a fool for a client" is an old saw, heard whenever some poor sod, or raving lunatic, rejects legal counsel and chooses to exercise his right to represent himself. Unconcerned with the justice of his case, the phrase declares the *pro se* litigant guilty not merely of imprudence, but of unseemly display through a vulgar breach of professional legal etiquette. But type "*pro se* representation" into Google, and you will find hundreds of sites dedicated to disparaging lawyers and all their works and offering advice for the prospective *pro se* litigant. Their central claim is that a democratic justice system must hear the voices of the people, not merely of legal professionals. This view of *pro se* representation would understand "vulgar" in its neutral descriptive sense, meaning the common people, whereas the former view ("fool for a client") associates self-representation with the pejorative sense of the word. That these contradictory views coexist in our popular legal culture, each claiming a kind of common sense authenticity, offers a politically salient example of how the voice of the vulgar—that is, the common people—becomes "vulgar," a coarse, ostentatious, and even offensive sound. This is evident in such popular culture phenomena as the *People's Court* and *Judge Judy* television shows, the success of which spawned a host of similar opportunities for people to "have their day in court," unmediated by legal counsel, while providing a media event for the rest of us. These may be mainly legal "gong shows," but surely they also speak to our fantasy that if only we could address authority in our own voices, justice would be ours. However demonized or trivialized these examples of *pro se* representation are, what American would not construe the elimination of the *pro se* option as a rights violation?

Pro se representation has a different history in English law, one that sheds light on the "vulgarization" of *pro se* and draws our attention to the peculiarly Victorian elements of that phenomenon, including the conflicts democracy, feminism, and mass-circulation print media engendered in popular legal culture. The term "popular legal culture," as coined by Lawrence M. Friedman, refers to the experience ordinary people have of the law when they seek a divorce, serve on a jury, or contest a traffic ticket.[1] Following the lead of scholars of law and society who attend to the role that popular culture, especially the American mass media, plays in shaping people's expectations of the law, I wish to expand the term to encompass not only representations of the law in popular culture but also the uses of popular culture to disseminate legal literacy, to democratize the public sphere.[2] I do so in order to argue that our contradictory attitudes toward *pro se* representation derive in part from the distinctions between high and low culture that arose in response to the emergence of mass culture in the Victorian period and from efforts to resist or bridge those distinctions. Although the dominance of American media in contemporary global legal culture has been remarked upon, in the nineteenth century, influence was more likely to flow from Britain to America, as remains evident in the preoccupation of American legal theorists and criminologists with Shakespeare, Dickens, Conan Doyle, and the Ripper case.[3] Indeed, the novels of Walter Scott were adduced as evidence in nineteenth-century American criminal trials, and Charles Reade's *Griffith Gaunt,* a novel I will discuss in this chapter, figured prominently in the Tildon-Beecher adultery trial, an American cause célèbre parodied by Mark Twain.[4] It should not be surprising, then, that our conflicted popular depictions of *pro se* are yet another legacy of Victorian popular culture. Returning to those origins, I contend that we should be cautious of the tendency to vulgarize *pro se,* not only because that prejudice arises out of legal circumstances quite different from our own, but also because more enabling, democratic options existed even in Victorian popular culture.

The most salient historical difference between American and British law regarding *pro se* representation is that British criminal defendants were denied legal representation until the Prisoner's Counsel Act of 1836. Whereas American law enshrined the citizen's right to self-representation, English statutes from the reign of Mary forbade legal representation for defendants on the grounds that lawyers, as court officials and loyal subjects, could not act in opposition to the Crown. That this logic entailed a presumption of guilt could go unacknowledged thanks to conditions of jury trial procedure that were altogether more "vulgar," in the nonpejorative sense of the word, than those of modern times. As I noted in part 1, historians of early modern law have reminded us that jurymen were chosen on the basis of their intimate knowledge of the characters of defendants, plaintiffs, and witnesses in the cases they considered.[5] Rather than trusting to ignorance to ensure objectivity, early modern trial practice depended upon vulgar knowledge to determine truth. As the practicability of finding jurymen familiar with trial participants waned, another vulgar (again, nonpejoratively speaking) standard of jury decision making emerged: namely, "common sense." In the "accused speaks" theory of criminal procedure that arose in the seventeenth and eighteenth centuries, this communal, ordinary, nonexpert faculty ensured that just verdicts would be rendered by laymen.[6] Under these conditions, it may have seemed reasonable that prisoners should address the court on their own behalf, call and examine witnesses themselves, and look to the judge to act impartially, intervening to question both defense and prosecution witnesses. But as John Langbein has recently demonstrated, lawyers were already acting in a limited fashion on behalf of criminal defendants in the eighteenth century, suggesting that the adversarial model of trial procedure was taking shape in advance of the Prisoner's Counsel Act.[7]

Still, the Prisoner's Counsel Act of 1836, which allowed defendants legal counsel to manage their cases, examine witnesses, and offer closing arguments, is treated as a watershed in British criminal law. On the face of it, this act evened the playing field for defendants and prosecution, but it is also blamed for consolidating the adversarial system of trial procedure, tarnishing the integrity of lawyers who took fees to defend the guilty, professionalizing the criminal justice system, and, as a corollary, excluding the voices of prisoners from their defense. Prisoners who were represented by counsel forfeited any opportunity to speak at their trials. With no provision in English law against self-incrimination, prisoners were not allowed to testify under oath; were they to have alleged their innocence, they would have been subject to a perjury charge if found guilty.[8] As I argued in chapter 6, the Prisoner's Counsel Act gave literary authors ammunition in their battle to wrest political and ethical authority away from lawyers, whom novelists represented as venal, cynical, and unworthy of the public's trust.[9]

In this chapter, I wish to revisit the consequences of the Prisoner's Counsel Act in order to examine how *pro se* defense survived Victorian efforts to squelch the *vox vulgari*. The list of Victorian literary characters used to demonstrate the law's power to silence comes readily to mind: Jo, dismissed from the "inkwich" in Dickens's *Bleak House;* the befuddled and harassed witnesses in Trollope's *Orley Farm,* or his hero Phineas Finn, powerless to defend himself against a charge of murder; Hetty Sorrell, reduced to an inarticulate shriek in Eliot's *Adam Bede;* or Lewis Carroll's Knave of Hearts, rendered speechless by the nonsensical evidence brought against him. All of these characters are in dire need of help from a professional—if not a lawyer, then a literary author. Rather than the popular fear of legal proceedings encouraged by Victorian literature that focused on the exclusionary and combative features of trial procedure after 1836, what I wish to treat here is the powerful popular fantasy of *pro se* representation that arose in apparent defiance of both law and much literature, and which generated a contrasting myth about the criminal trial as a discursive site allowing for a uniquely unmediated, potent, and convincing form of self-representation. There is also a striking group of Victorian characters who act out the fantasy of "having their day in court." As I noted at the outset of part 4, the impotence of the Knave of Hearts contrasts with the extraordinary illocutionary force of Alice herself, who by declaring colloquially, "You're all just a pack of cards," to quote a figure from contemporary popular culture, "makes it so." Additionally, there is William Morris's revisionary "Defense of Guenevere," which, though it places Guenevere's fate in the hands of Lancelot, nevertheless makes her testimony in her own behalf essential to answering an adultery charge, something criminal conversation trial procedure would never have allowed. Most sensationally, we have the lengthy testimony of the murder victim Pomphilia against her husband in Robert Browning's *The Ring and the Book.*

These characters all exercise significant, or even fantastic, verbal agency in a trial context; yet they are hardly unambiguous examples of legally potent self-representation. Only one is defending herself, strictly speaking, and all are circumscribed by gender. It is safe, perhaps, for male authors to ventriloquize forensic eloquence through female characters when women were unlikely to effect such results in or out of a law court. Extraordinary women speaking in extraordinary circumstances, they do little to promote the idea that ordinary speakers could sway a court to their will. Caroline Norton or Frances Power Cobbe they are not. Yet, unlike that list of characters that demonstrate the unmitigated impotence the law imposes upon its subjects, these other characters are at least on a continuum with the literary activism of suffragettes, trade unionists, Irish home rule advocates, and others seeking the right to political representation.

Occupying an intermediate point between the problematic fantasies of female eloquence and the oratorical agitation for democratic rights is Charles Reade's *Griffith Gaunt* (1866). Before turning to this novel, however, I must note that there is no comprehensive statistical evidence of the impact of the Prisoner's Counsel Act. A survey of the *Reports of State Trials, English Reports, Law Reports,* and *Central Criminal Court Sessions Papers* from 1836 to 1900 allows me to draw some generalizations: first, that nearly all defendants in criminal cases were represented by counsel; second, that with the remarkable exception of Georgina Weldon, who represented herself as both defendant and plaintiff in eighty-three cases in the 1880s, most of which she won, women did not undertake *pro se* representation; third, that most of those men who chose to represent themselves did so because, like Feargus O'Connor and Thomas Cooper who were charged with seditious conspiracy, they were challenging the very legitimacy of the British justice system; and fourth, that regardless of their reasons for acting *pro se,* criminal defendants without legal counsel were found guilty.[10] From James Blomfield Rush's spectacular fourteen-hour opening speech in his defense against a murder charge at the Norwich Assizes in 1849, to the obscure case of Robert Henderson, who cross-examined witnesses and entered a defense in his trial for possessing housebreaking implements at the Old Bailey in 1860, *pro se* representation failed.[11] The publication of pamphlet and newspaper accounts of Rush's *pro se* defense promulgated an image of the layperson in court as rambling, inept regarding rules of evidence and trial procedure, harassed by the judge, and ultimately pathetic in his appeals to the jury to "remember his dear little children" and not be led from the facts by the "flowery eloquence" of the prosecutor.[12] In *Phillips v. Phillips* at the Court of Probate and Divorce (1869), a hapless husband who had believed he could represent himself against his wife's petition for divorce on grounds of cruelty, learned from a newspaper report that the decree had been granted in his absence. He hired a lawyer, who won a judgment setting aside the decree.[13] Not even that melodramatic wordsmith W. T. Stead could defend himself against the charges of abduction and indecent assault in 1885.[14] Newspapers, which from the 1850s reached a large audience eager to follow sensational trials, also disseminated courtroom responses in parenthetical remarks—"(Laughter)," "(Sensation in the court)," and the like—which could serve to undermine the public perception of even the most skilled *pro se* litigant.[15] What is more, as Barbara Leckie has demonstrated regarding newspaper accounts of divorce and adultery proceedings, they could encourage readers to identify with a skeptical legal elite on the watch for "a woman's capacity for sexual deception [that] is equated with her capacity for narrative deception."[16]

By contrast, Georgina Weldon's legal advocacy was generally treated with respect by judges and journalists. A *Times* reporter described her opening an 1884 case "with great fluency for more than three hours" and noted that the judge "paid high tribute" to her skills. Nevertheless, her very indefatigability wore on the court, leading Lord Coleridge, before whom she often appeared, to remark during an 1885 case, "I think of you now as I have always thought, as a person who has had wrongs, but who has taken advantage of them to weary the public about matters which are not wrongs." "Oh, my Lord, I know you think me a tiresome and misguided woman," said Weldon. "Mrs. Weldon," replied the judge, "you may be a thought-reader, but I have not said so." Laughter was reported in the court.[17] Weldon's legal success, it would seem, turned her court appearances into a form of popular entertainment rather than models for the viable exercise of *pro se* representation. Would no one champion a Victorian Portia?

As we saw in chapter 5, Charles Reade was an inveterate literary activist, taking up the causes of prison reform and lunacy law reform, to name just two, and not merely in the abstract, but also as an advocate on behalf of actual individuals who had suffered at the hands of the law. He was an incorrigible writer of letters to newspaper editors, compelled to address a broad public on the myriad of social ills that this new mass-medium reported.[18] Unlike his sometime associate, Charles Dickens, however, he maintained faith in the efficacy of British justice. Chancery, pilloried by Dickens, appealed to Reade for many of the reasons that Deiter Polloczek has celebrated the Court of Equity.[19] Contrary to the many popular and literary images of the discursive incompetence of ordinary people in legal contexts, Reade popularizes—in letters to newspapers and a sensation novel—examples of forensic eloquence exercised by nonprofessionals and reasserts a traditional "vulgar" standard of common-sense legal decision making.

In *Hard Cash,* but even more strikingly in *Griffith Gaunt,* not only does Reade argue for the right to self-representation in a court of law as the logical consequence of *habeas corpus,* along with trial by jury as a foundational right deriving from Magna Carta, but he also provides what amounts to a how-to guide to conducting one's own defense. Whereas Dickens, and George Eliot, as Jan-Melissa Schramm contends, arrogated the power of legal representation to novelists in plots that simultaneously disparaged the legal profession and portrayed the futility of laypersons' efforts to exercise forensic eloquence, Reade used the trial scenes in *Griffith Gaunt* to disseminate lessons in advocacy to his readers. As such, his novel was a precursor of our Web sites devoted to instructing *pro se* litigants. Reade's instructions included how to prepare a case by investigating relevant precedents and familiarizing oneself with trial procedure, how to examine witnesses, the rules of evidence, and what made for an effective closing argument—all activities that had been conducted by the prisoner before the Prisoner's Counsel Act, but had been taken over by legal professionals in its wake.

The genre of *Griffith Gaunt* signals Reade's strategic plan to disseminate legal advice. It is a historical romance with large dollops of sensationalism, aimed at a popular audience. That audience had been consolidated through such phenomena as the Tichborne controversy, theatrical and literary melodrama, and sensationalistic journalism and fiction—the political potency of which has been widely discussed.[20] But it is just such a genre that could challenge the sensationalistic trial reporting that ridiculed *pro se* defendants like Rush or Weldon. In Reade's novel, Catherine Gaunt is accused of murdering her husband when an otherwise unidentifiable body is found wearing his clothes. Apart from this superficial forensic evidence, the case against her is circumstantial. The Protestant Gaunt had absconded when he became jealous of his wife's association with her confessor, a Roman Catholic priest. His whereabouts are unknown, and he does not present himself when his wife is charged with murder because he would be subject to a bigamy charge, having married an innkeeper's daughter with whom he has fathered a child.

With advice from the family lawyer, Mr. Houseman, Catherine prepares herself for trial by reading cases. The narrator remarks on the benefits of legal study to this nonprofessional: "Mrs. Gaunt took a line that agreeably surprised the court. It was not for nothing she had studied a hundred trials with a woman's observation and patient docility. She had found how badly people plead their own causes, and had noticed the reasons, one of which is that they say too much, and stray from the point. The line she took, with one exception, was keen brevity."[21] Not only does she use her "woman's observation" to good effect, she proves capable of shrewd analysis of testimony, confusing witnesses and catching them in illogic. Rather than decry legal proceedings as the bête noir of nonprofessionals (women in particular), reserving the pursuit of truth and justice for literary professionals, Reade seeks to demonstrate how they might be made accessible. Though his plot is sensationalistic, he demystifies the law and professional expertise, as any good realist might do.

In fact, Catherine Gaunt does a fairly good impersonation of a professional in attacking the evidence of another professional: the doctor who identified the body as Gaunt's. She succeeds in raising doubts about the doctor's expertise and exposes his false inferences. But the import of this professionalized woman is not unambiguous. Reade displaces onto Catherine's maid, Caroline Ryder, the role of demonized female witness. Ryder, who has been a rival for Gaunt's affection, nearly damns Catherine with her testimony until Catherine catches her in a lie, revealing that she has had an illegitimate child. "'My lord, have pity on me,'" Ryder appeals to the judge. "'I was betrayed, abandoned. Why am I so tormented? *I* have not committed murder.' So, cat-like, she squealed and scratched at once" (301). The judge cautions Catherine, "Prisoner, we make allowances for your sex and your peril, but you must not remark on the evidence at present. Examine as severely as you will, but abstain from comment till you address the jury on your defense." Though Catherine fails in having Ryder disqualified as a witness on the grounds of her "unchastity," the judge grants that she has been impugned. "Our forefathers taught us to call a virtuous woman an honest woman and the law does but follow in that track," he remarks, "still, however, leaving much to the discretion of the jury" (301).

Though it is at the expense in part of a female witness, Reade nevertheless represents a female legal speaker whose authority derives from her command of the law and her *forensic* eloquence, rather than poetic powers or sexualized presence. Indeed, when she does indulge in sentimental language, it is to defend the credibility of another female witness on whom her case depends. Mercy, the woman Gaunt married under an alias, comes forward to testify on Catherine's behalf. As Catherine leads Mercy through her examination, the narrator comments on the spectators' response. At first, sounds of astonishment overwhelm the court. "It went down gradually, as amazement gave way to curiosity; and then there was a remarkable silence; and then the silvery voice of the prisoner, and the mellow tones of the witness, appeared to penetrate the very walls of the building, each syllable of those two beautiful speakers was heard so distinctly" (321). When the prosecutor accuses Mercy of being paid for her testimony, Catherine rises to her defense.

> The woman you insult is as pure as your own mother or mine. She deserves the pity, the respect, the veneration of all good men. Know, my lord, that my miserable husband deceived and married her under the false name he had taken; she has the marriage certificate in her bosom. . . . This is one of those rare women that adorn our whole sex, and embellish human nature: and, so long as you have the privilege of exchanging words with her, I shall stand here on the watch, to see that you treat her with due respect: ay, sir, with reverence; for I have measured you both, and she is as much your superior as she is mine. (326–27)

Catherine, as female legal speaker, resorts to sentimental language, but no more so than did Victorian lawyers. Importantly, Catherine speaks here, not only as a defendant in a murder trial, or a quasi-professional, but also as an advocate on behalf of another woman who, against her own interests, has shown solidarity with her.

Two women have revealed the truth by means of—not in spite of—legal proceedings. As Catherine declares to the judge early in her trial, "Sir, 'tis not mercy I ask, but justice according to law" (302). In the course of the trial, she demonstrates command of the theory of circumstantial evidence, significant precedents, and trial practice, yet she does not conceal the truth, making admissions regarding her marriage that the lawyer Houseman considers fatal. Indeed, he thinks of the whole of her defense that "creditable as it was to a novice, [it] seemed wordy and weak to him, a lawyer; and he was horrified at the admission she had made. In her place he would have admitted nothing he could not thoroughly explain" (311). But in her place, Reade implies, a professional lawyer would not inspire the loyalty of Mercy, who holds the truth. Importantly, once that truth is revealed, the court—judge and prosecutor—willingly abandons the case against Catherine.

The trial concluded, closure in the novel is accomplished by the most sensational and sentimental devices. Gaunt returns and is reconciled to Catherine, saving her from a death from exhaustion by means of a blood transfusion. Mercy's child by Gaunt dies, and she marries a man from her village, with whom she has nine children. Still, for all the sensational events that bring about the trial and its conclusion, Reade chooses to voice his legal argument in *Griffith Gaunt*—including the reliability of circumstantial evidence and expert testimony, methods for examining witnesses, and the ultimate integrity of the judicial system—through a female character.

Arguably, she is "masculinized," especially in her treatment of Caroline Ryder, but she is not "feminized," insofar as her credibility derives from her status in legal proceedings rather than from her status as an object of sentimental regard. In that, she is an unusual example of a female character in Victorian legal fiction. What is more, Catherine Gaunt demonstrates Reade's persistent belief that ordinary people might provide their best defense if armed with a basic legal literacy. They do so because, in Reade's view, the vulgar standard of common sense that had long legitimated the verdicts of English juries remained the most trustworthy guide to justice. In an era of rapidly professionalizing trial procedure, Reade sought to disseminate legal literacy in precisely the form—a sensational novel—that would appeal to the vulgar masses who needed it.

Reade's fiction receives little attention from law and literature scholars, who recur time and again to canonical Victorian novelists for models of literary reasoning as an antidote to the sort of rule-based and rational-choice reasoning that dominate present-day professional legal decision making. Significantly, these scholars address a decision-making elite—judges, legislators, lawyers—contending that transforming their culture of decision making will transform a justice system currently unable to empathize with people whose circumstances, expectations, and constraints differ substantially from their own. They focus, that is, on the construction of a "judicious spectator," to use the term Martha Nussbaum borrows from Adam Smith, rather than on enabling nonprofessionals to address courts in forceful and efficacious manner.[22] In so doing, they recapitulate a high/low culture divide that in the Victorian period was separating out certain novels and novelists from popular mass culture and legitimating them as high art by professional authors, while at the same time asserting a professional monopoly on legal discourse against threats from a populace demanding a meaningful say in politics.

In *Phineas Redux* (1873), a novel roughly contemporaneous with *Griffith Gaunt,* Anthony Trollope suggests how the exclusion of common voices from legal proceedings by the consolidation of a professional legal monopoly becomes a jurisprudential axiom that silences even the male elite. Phineas Finn, a member of Parliament, is tried for a murder of which the reader knows he is innocent. In contemplating his first interview with his client Phineas, the lawyer Chaffenbrass remarks to his clerk, "I hate seeing a client.—What comes of it?" "Of course he wants to tell his own story," Mr. Wickerby replies.

"But I don't want to hear his own story. What good will his own story do me? He'll tell me either one of two things. He'll swear he didn't murder the man—"

"That's what he'll say."

"Which can have no effect upon me one way or the other; or else he'll say that he did,—which would cripple me altogether."

"He won't say that, Mr. Chaffenbrass."

"There's no knowing what they'll say. A man will go on swearing by his God that he is innocent, till, at last, in a moment of emotion, he breaks down, and out comes the truth. In such a case as this I do not in the least want to know the truth about the murder."

"That is what the public wants to know."

"Because the public is ignorant. The public should not wish to know anything of the kind. What we should all wish to get at is the truth of the evidence about the murder. The man is to be hung not because he committed the murder,—as to which no positive knowledge is attainable; but because he has been proved to have committed the murder,—as to which proof, though it be enough for hanging, there must always attach some shadow of doubt. . . . Now the last man to give us any useful insight into the evidence is the prisoner himself."

"His manner of telling you may do something."

"If it do, Mr. Wickerby, it is because I am unfit for my business. If he have the gift of protesting well, I am to think him innocent; and, therefore, to think him guilty, if he be unprovided with such eloquence! I will neither believe or disbelieve anything a client says to me,—unless he confess his guilt, in which case my services can be but of little avail. Of course I shall see him, as he asks it. We had better meet there,—say at half-past ten." Whereupon Mr. Wickerby wrote to the governor of the prison begging that Phineas Finn might be informed of the visit."[23]

Chaffenbrass does win Phineas's acquittal, though he suspects his client is guilty. Trollope's cynicism regarding professional legal actors and trial procedures does not extend to claiming gross miscarriages of justice. Trollope draws our attention to a professional contempt not only for popular eloquence, however, but also for popular notions of justice. That contempt leads to a mode of trial advocacy and understanding of trial procedure that is rationalized as the very sort of rule-based, objective decision making now being called into question by legal theorists who assert that it merely disguises the substitution of dominant-culture norms for genuine engagement with the circumstances of the law's subjects, necessary for truly equitable applications of the law. How odd, then, that these theorists—like the canonical Victorian literary precedents they cite—fail to address a popular audience, leaving it to the vulgar medium of the internet, or Court TV, to inform nonprofessionals about how to manage evidence, legal procedure, and legal language to "tell [their] own stor[ies]."

Griffith Gaunt contributes to the formation of Victorian popular legal culture, not in the manner of Dickens's novels, or much trial reporting, wherein legal and literary professionals wrestled for authority to speak on behalf of the vulgar, but in the manner of the National Society for the Advancement of Social Science, or Emily Faithfull's Victorian Discussion Society. These organizations, contemporaneous with Reade's literary career, offered forums for nonprofessionals, including women, to acquire experience as public orators and debaters. As Janice Schroeder has argued, these venues for public speech helped to democratize the public sphere not only by inviting nonprofessionals to engage in forensic eloquence but also by training audiences to listen respectfully and attentively to voices that were generally met with derision in the courts, and other settings dominated by lawyers, parliamentarians, academics, and the like, who dismissed the *vox populi*.[24] They paved the way for Josephine Butler, Frances Power Cobbe, and Barbara Smith Bodichon to argue publicly—and vocally—for women's rights and the franchise, that is, for substantive legal change. Therefore, we must see the trivialization of *pro se* representation in British legal history as an effort not merely to justify the liberal aspirations of the Prisoner's Counsel Act, but also as a defense against the threat of the *vox populi* to entrenched power: an effort, in short, to neutralize the political force of popular legal culture.

If the gothic terror of being silenced, as dramatized in so many Victorian narratives of trials and imprisonment, is invoked in the popular imagination by the Prisoner's Counsel Act, then so too, paradoxically, is the converse fantasy—that in a courtroom one may become a uniquely charismatic and forceful speaker on one's own behalf. Both fantasies, generated in the dynamic between literature and law, influence popular legal culture. Reporting on an 1884 case involving Georgina Weldon, the *Times* wrote, "In speaking of her having been prosecuted at the Old Bailey for libel, [Mrs. Weldon] said that she had then been urged not to lend any color to the suggestions that she was insane by not employing any counsel to defend her. She thought at the time that the advice was good, but knew now that to have counsel was to commit an act of insanity."[25] Though the court laughed, historians of Victorian literature and law should not. The origins and import of the *pro se* representation fantasy in popular imagination go well beyond both law and literature, pointing to the desires of the individual in an age becoming at once more democratic and more regulated and bureaucratized. As such, the fantasy and its literary dramatizations retain a place in contemporary popular legal culture and, rather than participating reflexively in the trivialization of *vox vulgari,* we should investigate its complex history. Reviewing depictions of the law in our own popular culture—from crime novels to *Law and Order*—we might well ask where models of viable *pro se* representation are to be found. When our own library habits, not to mention telephone conversations, may be the object of obscurely sanctioned surveillance, this is a question we are obliged to pursue.

The literary and legal histories I have traced in parts 2 and 3 reveal a dynamic in which neither discourse is intrinsically progressive, or antidemocratic. Importantly, what enabled Georgina Weldon to bring her first lawsuit against her husband was the passage in 1882 of the Married Women's Property Act, which allowed married women the right to act as legal agents independent of their husbands. The act granted women property rights not just in literal property, then, but in their own persons—and therefore in their own stories. In short, it afforded women the legal recognition manifested in Robin West's ideal of narrativity—ownership of one's own story—and the right to tell that story in a court of law. In turn, newspaper reporting of Weldon's *pro se* representation disseminated a model of forensic eloquence exercised efficaciously by a woman for a wide audience of men and women alike. This model could counteract both the fatalistic silencing of female witnesses dominant in fiction by leading female novelists, and the fantasy of illocutionary force played out by female characters in literature by male authors, threatened with irrelevance by a professionalized legal culture and bureaucratic political culture. Yet literary discourse might also contribute to the democratization of legal literacy, as was the case in *Griffith Gaunt.* Against the trend toward an autonomous aesthetic sphere convincingly described by Leckie, wherein literary authors demonized a politico-legal sphere that devalued them, we can also identify efforts to create what we might term "literary legal aid." Literary discourse, at least that which aimed at a popular audience, might also be seen as a force assisting readers to exercise rights they had won, and, in turn, to embolden unrecognized groups to agitate on their own behalf.

Still, while I have directed attention to a counternarrative of legal literacy in nineteenth-century trial reporting and fiction, forensic eloquence in the absence of substantive legal change could prove counterproductive. In part 5, I will consider an alternative function of literary discourse and forensic eloquence—the construction of "cover stories" to protect victimized groups from legal sanction. In these cases, dramatizing victimization and silencing, as occurred in *Helen Fleetwood, Mary Barton,* and *Felix Holt,* would have exacerbated the law's power not merely to silence but to punish. Instead, literary discourse might be used to deflect attention from sanctioned behaviors, from infanticidal women to homosexual men, and allow for a tacit, extra-discursive solidarity between authors and readers, lawyers and juries—in effect, creating cover stories for jury nullification of the law.

PART FOUR

The Motives of Advocacy

CHAPTER EIGHT

Concealing Women's *Mens Rea*

Advocacy for Female Prisoners and Infanticidal Mothers

A PRIMARY AIM OF narrative legal theory, as has been evident throughout this study, is the use of narrative—with or against legal discourse—to bring unrecognized groups into representation and thereby to win them legal recognition. In this final section, I wish to call into question the central premise of narrative legal theory, *viz.*, that the goal of gender advocacy should always be to bring disenfranchised groups into representation. While this is a compelling agenda, the history of "hyper-representation," beginning with the advent of mass-circulation publications and mass literacy in the nineteenth century, suggests that literary and legal advocacy might be motivated by a desire to shield victimized groups from prosecution by producing "cover stories."

The efficacy of these stories depends less upon what is represented than upon unspoken appeals and tacit agreements, and therefore must be inferred by "reading between the lines" of recorded arguments and imagining what can never be known directly: the responses of individual readers and the decision-making processes of judges and juries. This form of advocacy requires a different strategy for reading literary and legal history, one that is brought into relief by a hallmark of Victorian realist fiction: the omniscient narrator. That wholly fictional device, which has been analyzed as attaining new significance under the pressure of nineteenth-century demands for evidence of *mens rea*, can also point to the reality of what in real life can—and sometimes must—remain unrepresented.

Mens rea, literally the "mind thing," or criminal intent, gained in evidentiary significance in the nineteenth century as the rationale for jury trials evolved. As discussed in part 3, the anonymity of mass culture eroded the early modern reliance on jurymen's knowledge of the character of the accused to determine the plausibility of claims made against her. Character witnesses and eyewitnesses, who had carried significant evidentiary weight into the eighteenth century, gave way to circumstantial evidence.[1] But circumstantial evidence was not only a means of judging the probability of the story proffered by an indictment of the *actus reus;* it could also be used to get at the inscrutability of criminal intent. As Lisa Rodensky has noted, jurisprudence prior to the nineteenth century had demanded evidence of "a wicked soul" for conviction.[2] The rise of expert medical testimony regarding states of mind certainly contributed to increased interest in empirical evidence of criminal intent; however, Rodensky describes a far more complex debate among nineteenth-century jurists, involving liability, negligence, tort law, conspiracy, and grounds for mitigation. And even reflections upon the art of acting might concern theorists of *mens rea:* the jurist J. W. C. Turner felt compelled to answer Dr. Johnson's claim that an actor believing himself to be the murderer he is playing should be hanged.[3] (As we shall see regarding the conspiracy to commit sodomy trial discussed in chapter 9, "play-acting" could be an effective defense.) At the same time, the omnisciently narrated novel created a rich body of representations of interiority and created the illusion of "transparent minds."[4] Together, these forces brought *mens rea* to the fore as a crucial—and contested—element of criminal prosecution.

Literature and law could cooperate to produce "enabling fictions," or cover stories, that allowed legal decision makers, particularly juries, to elude the law with "special verdicts," or what we would term jury nullification. Unlike advocacy for persons wrongfully incarcerated in lunatic asylums, which sought to establish *compos mentis* by bringing victims' rational thought into representation, the form of narrative advocacy I will examine in chapter 9 is predicated upon a tacit recognition that there are instances of *mens rea* that are at once rational and criminal. As such, they require concealment, or pious perjuries, in the face of imminent legal threats. I will illustrate this alternative function of narrative advocacy and the reading strategies they demand by examining two forms of criminal prosecution that, like witchcraft trials and the lunacy scandals, were driven by moral panics and fueled by intrusive forensic medicine and sensationalistic mass reporting: prosecutions for infanticide and sodomy. Those accused of these crimes could be saved by forged identities when eloquent self-representation could prove fatal.

I begin this chapter not with a cover story, but with an example of the pitfalls of constructing gender advocacy according to the very characteristics of literary narrative celebrated in narrative legal theory: the sympathetic identification with others' life worlds supposedly enabled by the access to interiority, or *mens rea,* provided by omniscient narration. My illustration comes from a woman whose authority was recognized by her contemporaries, and whom legal historians credit with a radical shift in both cultural attitudes and legal practices, the Victorian prison reformer Mary Carpenter (1807–77). Significantly, Carpenter's agenda tangentially concerned women, but her primary focus was on children—a group about whom women might have been accorded particular expertise. Yet her strategy would seem to epitomize that recommended by Robin West. It was decidedly empiricist, attacking legal and cultural constructions of children convicted of crimes for their ignorance of scientific evidence of the conditions in which these children lived and of the testimony of the children themselves. But Carpenter insisted that this evidence was counterproductive unless it was read empathically and produced a change of heart. Carpenter's efficacy—with Parliament, prison officials, and reformers across the world—was owing both to her insistence upon scientific investigation and reporting and to her reconception of that evidence in imaginative, *literary* terms. At the same time, she was critical of literary appropriations of children's criminal behavior for sensationalistic commodification. That is to say, Carpenter insisted upon a critical dialectic between empirical and literary forms of evidence and interpretation. Despite her profound knowledge of the results of such investigations as well as her direct experience with children imprisoned, children of the streets, and children in her own "ragged school," Carpenter could nonetheless be gulled by the promise of detecting *mens rea* afforded by the literary convention of the omniscient narrator, because it enabled her to claim a distinctively female empathetic expertise.

The concept of the "juvenile offender" is one of the Victorians' greatest inventions—if by "greatest" is meant broadly influential, though not necessarily beneficial. The process by which the juvenile offender and juvenile delinquent were created was a remarkable feat of literary and legal advocacy spearheaded by Mary Carpenter. An extraordinary public relations effort was required to convince a majority of Victorian decision makers that their ignorance of peculiarly childish motives, desires, and experiences hampered their ability to manage—or serve—this segment of society adequately. Juvenile delinquents had to be constituted as an epistemological problem in order to be dealt with as a social problem. Like other social reforms aimed at groups that deviated from the legal paradigm of the property-holding male, advocacy for reform of penal policies regarding children appealed to the mix of rationalistic and sentimental arguments that typify the legitimating strategies of the bourgeois state.[5] Drawing on sympathy and self-interest, storytelling and statistics, Mary Carpenter addressed herself in articles, pamphlets, and books to the newly emerging authority of "public opinion," calling on this nebulous aggregate to change its corporate mind.

What is more, Carpenter's rise from schoolteacher to internationally recognized expert on juvenile delinquency tells us much about the gendering of advocacy in English political history. The Victorian cult of true womanhood emphasized women's sympathetic and nurturing powers. Not surprisingly, women would come to allege special expertise under the rubrics of sentimental moral theory and empirical observation, particularly when the subject involved children.[6]

The mix of sentimental moral theory, empiricism, aesthetics, gender ideology, and mass culture remain salient features of present-day democratic processes. Indeed, critics who indict contemporary democratic institutions, notably the courts, for their failure to recognize adequately the diverse experiences and needs of our multicultural populations often recur to specifically Victorian modes of representation and argument as ideal means by which decision makers can empathize with people whose circumstances differ from their own. Interestingly, relatively little attention has been focused by narrative legal theory on children as one of those categories of people about whose suffering we need the kind of special, detailed knowledge literature is so adept at providing. Surely, anyone mining Victorian literature for examples of political uses of empathy could hardly miss Oliver Twist, Tiny Tim, Jo in *Bleak House,* or those epitomes of social ills—Ignorance and Want—harbored under the cloak of the Ghost of Christmas Present. To this list we could add the child laborers in Elizabeth Barrett Browning's "The Cry of the Children," and Eliza in *Uncle Tom's Cabin,* or even Peter Pan and Lewis Carroll's Alice, as well as many others contributing to a bourgeois conception of sentimentalized and ideologically potent childhood. Victorian creators of child characters, in short, wrote the book on empathy. Mary Carpenter's career illustrates the powerful—and problematic—mix of fact, fiction, and gender ideology in the politics of empathy.

In our own culture, wherein "poster child" has become synonymous with a paradigmatic representative of a victimized class, we may need to recall the history of legal and literary advocacy that was required to convince decision makers that social status was in any meaningful way inflected by age. The most notable early success for Victorian child advocates was the Ten Hours Movement, and significantly, literary authors were rather behind the curve. Novels such as Frances Trollope's *Michael Armstrong, the Factory Boy* (1839) and Charlotte Elizabeth Tonna's *Helen Fleetwood* (1841) drew on the extensive data that had already been collected by Lord Ashley, leader of the Ten Hours movement in the House of Commons, and that had been published in Parliamentary Blue Books.[7] The Ten Hours Movement was the brainchild of parliamentarians and others of the decision-making elite whose knowledge of factory conditions, gleaned through their investigations over two decades into the effects of previous Factory Acts, convinced them of the need for further reform. Whatever inspired these men to inquire into the lives of child laborers, it is hard to argue that it was imaginative literature, strictly defined. As the sources of Frances Trollope's and Tonna's novels make clear, legislators and social investigators had already turned storytellers. Their reports and expert testimonies were filled with anecdotal evidence, and these novelizers were often at their most powerful when quoting directly from empirical sources. So why were novelists engaged in this movement at all and why were they considered effective?

As Joseph Kestner has argued, from the 1830s the social narrative was increasingly produced by women and in the form of novels. These novels popularized the data and theories of factual sources in a period in which women were looking for engagement in the public sphere and the public sphere was increasingly defined by mass-circulation publications aimed at a broad reading public. Tonna and Elizabeth Gaskell were directly recruited by social reformers to novelize their agendas, as Hannah More had been in an earlier generation.[8] And, as Hannah More had been, they were considered to be especially strategic advocates on behalf of children.

Among the many philanthropists and politicians who devoted their energies to creating the concept of the juvenile offender, Mary Carpenter was the most famous in her own day, and the best remembered in ours. She evolved out of the philanthropic tradition of Unitarianism into an internationally recognized expert on juvenile delinquency, education, and prison reform. Carpenter began her public career in a manner at once peculiarly feminine and practical. At sixteen she began teaching in the school run by her father, Lant Carpenter, a celebrated Unitarian preacher and reformer. In 1827 she went to work as a governess and returned home in

1829, when financial difficulties stemming from her father's illness required the Carpenter women to open a girls' school. In 1831 she undertook a Sunday school and, under the influence of Rammohun Roy and Joseph Tuckerman, began a visiting society in 1835. Her father died in 1840, and in her grief Mary Carpenter proceeded not only to write a memoir of Lant Carpenter, which she would issue in her first publication, *Morning and Evening Meditations,* but also to open a Ragged School in the Bristol slum of Lewin's Mead.

Consistent with the reform tradition of her day, practical sympathy went hand in hand with rational analysis, and she set about to master the subject of juvenile delinquency. Like many philanthropists, Carpenter read Parliamentary Blue Books (first sold to the public in 1836) and prison returns, as well as the growing body of pamphlet literature and journalism arguing for legislative reform. Carpenter brought an active and sympathetic imagination to her reading, finding moving drama in the stories of children recorded in prison reports, but also identifying intensely with their authors. Years later she would confess in a letter to her friend Frances Power Cobbe that she always "devour[ed]" prison reports "as many people do the last new novel."[9] And she expressed to Cobbe a profound sense of bonding with authors of juvenile reform literature, describing as kindred spirits even those writers whom she had never met. Though it may be difficult for us to appreciate the literary value of prison reports or Parliamentary Blue Books, for Carpenter, like many pious women of the period who dedicated themselves to social reform, nothing was more moving or a more reliable guide to their spiritual duty than what they took to be unadorned representations of the truth. As much as her direct experience with juvenile delinquents, then, Carpenter's reading habits are key to understanding her sense of vocation, a calling to do the "Heavenly Father's work," as she put it. Not surprisingly, that vocation would come to include a literary element, writing by which she could move others to action through sympathetic identification with her and her children.

In 1835 the Duke of Richmond's committee produced the first parliamentary report on transportation to distinguish between juvenile and adult offenders. Earlier, as in Peel's Gaol Acts of 1823 and 1824, there had been some effort to distinguish classes of prisoners, yet no mention had been made of juvenile offenders as a distinct class, and the Poor Law of 1834 had lumped all classes of criminals together. But the report of the Duke of Richmond's committee was indicative of change, brought about, arguably, by the same mechanisms that had spurred Lord Ashley's Ten

Hour Movement. The Acts of 1823 and 1824, though they made no provision for juvenile offenders, set in place an inspection system that brought the stories of juvenile offenders to the attention of Parliament. Often including allegedly verbatim interviews with juvenile offenders, these inspectors' reports did much to create the concept of juvenile offender as a distinct category. Nevertheless, they did not necessarily argue for lighter or distinct forms of treatment for children, but merely for their segregation within existing prisons. Indeed, precisely because prison inspectors were aware of the "miserable circumstances that drove boys to crime," they warned that separate prisons for juveniles would be ineffective unless they were made too harsh to present an attractive alternative to the conditions under which criminal children enjoyed freedom.[10] The result was the act of 1838 founding the Parkhurst Reformatory, an institution that Carpenter would attack for attempting to combine what she believed to be the incompatible goals of punishment and character reformation.

Carpenter made her first contribution to the literature on juvenile delinquency with an 1849 tract entitled "Ragged Schools," and in 1851 her book *Reformatory Schools for the Perishing and Dangerous Classes* gained her immediate national recognition as an expert on the reform of child convicts. These works combined utilitarian arguments regarding the causes of childhood criminality and the most efficacious means of its prevention with graphic accounts of child convicts, taken both from personal experience and from the reports of prison inspectors who had solicited young convicts' stories. In 1849 and 1850, Richard Monkton Milnes (later Lord Houghton) had introduced juvenile offenders bills, which had failed. Carpenter put these failures down to public ignorance. In the preface to her next work, *Juvenile Delinquents, Their Condition and Treatment* (1853), Carpenter complained that "the mass of society are better acquainted with the actual condition of remote savage nations, than with the real life and the springs of action of these children, whose true nature is less visible to the public eye when collected in a Ragged School, or swarming in the by-streets, than is the state of little heathen children as exhibited in the Reports of Missionaries." Her goal in writing *Juvenile Delinquents* was "to offer a full and clear picture of the actual condition of Juvenile Delinquents, to consider their various characteristics, to trace out their mode of life, so see their homes, and thence to learn their early influences."[11]

Carpenter was instrumental in attracting public attention to her cause, in 1851 organizing with Matthew Davenport Hill the first Birmingham Conference on juvenile delinquency. Her role in that conference, along with the popularity of her books, led a parliamentary committee of inquiry on juvenile delinquency to call her to testify. She had not even addressed the Birmingham Conference, but she testified before the select committee with an authority and polemical conviction that in retrospect alarmed her. Nonetheless, she was well on her way to becoming the principal spokesperson for juvenile penal reform.

Carpenter opened another school at Kingswood in 1852, and in 1854 she founded the first reformatory school for girls, Red Lodge, which she superintended until her death in 1877. In 1853 she participated in the second Birmingham Conference on juvenile delinquency, attended by 3,000 and chaired by Lord Shaftesbury. Yet parliamentary support was still slow in coming. Several measures were introduced in these years, only to be rejected. Carpenter and her colleagues had kept Parliament and the press focused on the need for reformatories for juvenile delinquents, but had not managed to overcome the long-standing belief in the efficacy of the deterrence afforded by prison sentences. Indeed, at the same time segments of the press were joining Carpenter's cause, soliciting public sympathy for juvenile delinquents, they were also fueling public anxiety regarding the effect of the 1853 Penal Act, which allowed for the release of ticket-of-leave men into the community in lieu of transportation. Before this act provoked a backlash against criminals, Parliament passed, in 1854, the Youthful Offenders Act establishing reformatory schools. This act authorized the home secretary to issue certificates to private reformatory schools and to contribute to maintenance of convicted children. Magistrates were empowered to send any offender under age 16 to a reformatory school for not less than two and no more than five years, but their admission to reformatory school had to be preceded by imprisonment for a minimum of fourteen days. Carpenter was deeply dissatisfied with this bill, preserving as it did what she believed to be the wholly counterproductive element of a preliminary prison sentence. Her work was hardly at an end, but it would be carried out under significantly changed conditions of public discourse, some of her own making.

The next decade saw the growth of two apparently unrelated phenomena: the reformatory school movement and the new journalism, the latter spurred by the repeal of the stamp tax in 1855. Carpenter's original goal of reformatory sentencing for juvenile convicts was expanded to include a preventative element: the creation of schools for children whose social circumstances made it likely that they would commit crimes if not removed from their irresponsible, criminal, or simply destitute families. Twenty-seven reformatory schools were established in the first three years of the Youthful Offenders Act. Further parliamentary action was spurred by the public attention focused on these schools, both by parliamentary reports and by the press. In 1857 Parliament passed the Industrial Schools Act as a supplement to an 1854 act aimed at an estimated 50,000 vagrant children. Justices were empowered to send any vagrant child between the ages of 7 and 14, whose parents could not give sureties of his or her good behavior, to a certified industrial school for as long as was thought necessary, but not beyond age 15. Carpenter complained in 1859 that of thirteen industrial schools reporting, only fourteen children had been committed by magistrates.[12] In 1860 responsibility for industrial schools was transferred from the Education Committee of the Privy Council to the Home Office, and in the same year there were forty-eight certified reformatories, housing 4,000 offenders. An 1861 amending act to the Industrial Schools Act widened the category of children to include any child under age 14 found begging or receiving alms or found vagrant, or who "frequents the Company of reputed Thieves." Also, parents were allowed to commit children they could not control. The reformatory movement crested in the 1860s. Still, there were never more than fifty-three; annual admissions peaked at 1,570 boys and girls. Facilities were concentrated in Yorkshire, Lancashire, Middlesex, Surrey, and Warwickshire—a fact that depended on the chance efforts of private benevolence rather than systematic social policy. The acceptance of industrial schools was slow. Nevertheless, it would seem that Carpenter had won an extraordinary public relations victory in little over a decade. Yet those gains would soon be linked in the dialectic of public sympathy manufactured by means problematically similar to those Carpenter had herself exploited.[13]

The concept of "public opinion" was transformed under the conditions of mass-circulation journalism after 1855. Historians of journalism have thoroughly documented the effect on editorial policies, driven now by profit motive, rather than the desire for political influence.[14] Crime reporting was the undisputed key to sales. The very Blue Books and inspectors' reports that had fueled legislation now became fodder for exposés, and the perennial favorites of crime fiction, such as Jack Sheppard and Dick Turpin, were overshadowed by the real-life criminals whose stories newspaper writers culled from police reports. The underworld of child criminals that had been so dramatically—and lucratively—represented by, for example, Charles Dickens in *Oliver Twist* and in *Household Words* articles, could also provide a rich source for sensationalizing journalism.

Indeed, as these new material conditions foregrounded, the line between empathy and sensationalism in forming public opinion was never clear.

The first crime panic of the newspapers' making came in the year following the repeal of the Stamp Act, and three years after the 1853 Penal Act. Major papers, such as the *Times,* helped to create a myth of the ticket-of-leave men as the perpetrators of a garroting epidemic. Crime statistics of the period are for various reasons difficult to interpret, but legislators undeniably responded to the newspapers as newly powerful organs of public opinion with amazing alacrity, passing the Penal Servitude Act of 1857, tightening up the provisions and administration of the 1853 act. The papers turned their attention elsewhere. But in 1862 the papers once again raised the cry against crime after Mr. Pilkington, the MP for Blackburn, was attacked by a garroter. This was the incident that served as Trollope's model for the attack on Mr. Kennedy in *Phineas Finn.* The newspapers turned it into a full-fledged moral panic, provoking a legislative backlash against the penal reform movement. Public outrage against ticket-of-leave men is credited with securing royal assent to the Security from Violence Act, which reintroduced flogging for robbery with violence.[15] And in 1864 the Penal Servitude Act marked a fundamental change of public opinion away from reform of criminals to punishment. Minimum sentences were increased from three years to five, and the 1865 Prisons Act reestablished harsh prison regimes aimed at punishing rather than reforming criminals.[16]

It is in this climate that Mary Carpenter produced her final major work on prison reform, *Our Convicts* (1864). For more than a decade she had lectured to and corresponded with politicians, social scientists, authors, and philanthropists and had become the most widely recognized expert on the subject of juvenile crime. Carpenter had even addressed the 1860 meeting of the Statistical Section of the British Association, opened by the Prince Consort. Who better to bring a reasoned experienced perspective to the crime panic? She began *Our Convicts* by acknowledging the panic: "The events of the last two years have filled every one with consternation and fear for personal safety," she wrote.[17] Yet, as it had been throughout her career, empathetic identification was the only principled and practical response to crime. "Our Convicts!" she exclaimed in the book's first sentence,

> They are part of our society! They belong to ourselves! They are not only subjects with us of the same great British Empire on which the sun never sets, but they belong to the same British Isles, the same small

> centre of civilization, the same heart of all the world's life, the same Island, small in geographical extent, infinitely great in its influence on the nations,—whence must go forth laws, principles, examples, which will guide for better or for worse the whole world! (1: 1)

Furthermore, addressing adult crime was impossible without attending to the very issue to which Carpenter had devoted her life—juvenile delinquency. So, in one last great effort to secure the goals of a lifetime, to turn the tide of public opinion yet again, Carpenter asked her readers to look to the children.

Carpenter drew evidence not only from her own experience as a teacher in ragged schools but also from the extensive literature that had been produced by the newly created reformatory school and prison inspection system. These bureaucratic empiricist documents provided her with a wealth of stories of children raised up in crime by their parents, abandoned and forced to steal food, or co-opted into criminal gangs by older children. But in addition to such sources, Carpenter now drew as well on the very newspapers that had helped to cause the panic and, most problematically, on two works that impugn the method by which she had established her own expertise and influenced public policy: *Female Life in Prison* (1862) and *Memoirs of Jane Cameron, Female Convict* (1864), both written ostensibly by a prison matron.

Female Life in Prison is a series of character sketches of female prisoners illustrating the sentiment that "to see some of these women hour by hour, and listen to them in their mad defiance, rage and blasphemy, is almost to believe that they are creatures of another mould and race, born with no idea of God's truth, and destined to die in their own benighted ignorance. . . . One is almost skeptical of believing that there was ever an innocent childhood or a better life belonging to them."[18] Mad infanticides, unrepentant thieves, and hardened juvenile convicts are sketched by the Prison Matron, who characteristically checks her expressions of sympathy with a worldly-wise fatalism regarding these women's reform. In *Jane Cameron,* the Prison Matron records the life story of a prisoner raised up in crime by her own mother, brought to repentance by the Prison Matron's sympathy and moral influence only to fall into bad company after her release and finally to commit a transportable offense.

These books were great popular sensations, offering, as they claimed to do, the intimate details of female prisoners' lives such as would be uniquely available to a prison matron. As Carpenter's biographer Jo Manton describes them, "Books catering so delectably to feelings of prurient curiosity and moral superiority at the same time were sure of a sale; the second [*Jane Cameron*] ran through three editions in a year."[19] "The Prison Matron's narrative has been so extensively read," wrote Carpenter in *Our Convicts,* "that acquaintance with it may here be assumed" (1: 2). There is evidence in *Our Convicts* of Carpenter's concern to authenticate the Prison Matron's testimony, though she does not directly question the identity of their author. After all, anonymous publication by women was conventional, a sign of the writer's sense of decorum. Indeed, Carpenter herself was suspected of having been the author. But Carpenter was also concerned that the Prison Matron had revealed facts about female convicts' degeneracy that threatened to put them beyond the pale of reclamation, feeding the growing public sentiment to lock criminals up and throw away the key. Still, she could not deny the value of testimony that appeared to satisfy perfectly the very epistemological criteria she had urged as fundamental to sound penal policy. The prison matron was the ideal investigator of female convicts' lives: her position gave her access to these women, but her superior feminine sympathies also drew prisoners out, softened their hearts, and encouraged them to speak not only of their criminal exploits but also, more important, of their childhoods and of their own children. These were precisely the kinds of stories Carpenter had always claimed would enable the higher classes to empathize with convicts so as better to understand that proper treatment of child criminals—and potential child criminals—was the key to preventing crime.

As she wrote in *Our Convicts,*

> The condition in which the young of our country are growing up, or as it has been truly expressed, are dragged up, to take the place of the present generation in the ranks of crime and pauperism, should especially engage the attention of society, and enlist extensive voluntary effort. It is not known to the bulk of the middle and upper classes of society;—it cannot be known, for no word can give an adequate idea of it to those who have not *personally* [my emphasis] witnessed it. (2: 378–79)

Mary Carpenter herself had witnessed these conditions, and so too, she believed, had the Prison Matron and the charges whose stories she told. Defending the Prison Matron's narratives as evidence superior to that of official reports, Carpenter wrote in *Our Convicts:*

> Such is the only insight which we can obtain into the general working of the Female Convict Prisons from official sources. Vague rumours, of course, from time to time, give some insight in the "secrets of the prison house;" the volumes of the Prison Matron give a vivid picture of their internal working. Respecting the reliable nature of this work we cannot entertain any doubt, as it is referred to by the Royal Commissioners in their interrogations of the Chief Director, and no doubt is expressed by them or him of the truth of the statements it contains; no suspicion appears to be entertained in it of serious faults in the system, and the greatest deference and respect is everywhere shown to the Directors, to one of whom the book is dedicated. (2: 228)

Viewed cynically—or, merely with hindsight—the Prison Matron's "deference and respect" to the prison directors, indeed, the book's dedication to a director, appear to be self-authenticating devices designed to forestall skepticism. They worked.

What seemed not to occur to Carpenter was that she was reading a fictionalized version of the very information that she and other reformers, and now the newspapers, had popularized, a fiction that exploited the thrilling sensation of identifying with the criminal class. Clearly, if the Prison Matron's narratives simply reproduced official reports already rich in narratives of the lives of convicts, including those of juvenile convicts, it is unlikely that Carpenter would have relied on them so extensively, despite their popularity. The Prison Matron's narratives also provide the kind of information about *mens rea* that could only be known—or rather created—by a novelist. Carpenter would have encountered many scenes in *Female Convicts* and *Jane Cameron* in which characters' states of mind were represented, or unwitnessed events narrated, and she often cited such scenes. One is particularly notable both for its melodrama and its use of omniscient narration. Speaking of outbreaks of disruptive behavior at female prisons, Carpenter remarked, "Though the official testimony already given, fully proves in general terms the violence of the outbreaks, yet as it is well to realize the kind of evil involved in them, and the difficulties the officials have to contend with, we copy the following scene from 'Jane Cameron.' It is evidently sketched from life" (2: 233). In that scene, we are given Jane's thoughts as she sits alone in her cell, the memories and regrets that drive her to madness. Then follows a series of observable events: Jane tears her blanket, leaps on the table, batters at the window with her cup, and screams. Other prisoners respond in kind, and Jane continues screaming and singing the whole night, "with satisfaction," the Prison Matron tells us. Carpenter knowingly comments on this scene, "These fits of uncontrolled and desperate passion sometimes end in insanity; attempts, either real or feigned, at self-destruction are not uncommon" (2: 234).

This incident gets to the heart of Mary Carpenter's need for the Prison Matron's narratives. Carpenter had won success as an advocate for juvenile delinquents because she had established the legitimacy of a peculiar form of expertise that depended on the unique powers of women's empathy, and these narratives provided the logical end point of that expertise: the omniscience we know is enjoyed only by creators of fiction. And that is precisely what the Prison Matron's narratives turned out to be. They had been written by Frederick William Robinson, the author of scores of pulp novels, none of which ever achieved the popularity or sales of the Prison Matron's narratives.

Should it matter that the kind of evidence deemed foundational to juvenile delinquents' reform by the foremost Victorian expert on the subject was not merely fictional, rather than factual, but the product of a man writing for commercial motives rather than a woman offering her empathetic experiences out of the kindness of her heart? We cannot know how Mary Carpenter herself would have answered this question, since the identity of the Prison Matron was not revealed in Carpenter's lifetime. In one respect she might have welcomed the news, since she had sought to counteract the Prison Matron's grimly fatalistic view of prisoners, raised up to be criminals since infancy, hardened by their teens, and hopelessly corrupt as adults. This was the very process of human development in which Carpenter believed society was obliged to intervene with the measures she had devoted her life to realizing. Two years after writing *Our Convicts,* Carpenter wrote to Frances Power Cobbe not only defending her own work on the grounds "that it was necessary for *me* to write 'Our Convicts' two years ago, because I saw that the public *ought* to know certain things . . . wch those who *could* tell them would not," but also urging her friend to produce a similar book on behalf of workhouse reform. "Your philosophic mind & literary talents combined with your womanly and loving nature," Carpenter wrote, "would enable you to do an infinitely greater good to the country . . . by writing. If you devote yourself to produce for the paupers system such a book, only better, as 'Our Convicts,' this system will be doomed, for the public will understand it. . . . Do think of this; no one *can* do it as you could."[20]

Yet the success of the Prison Matron's narratives—both as a commercial venture and as a literary fraud—does, I believe, significantly impugn

Carpenter's own methods. She had attacked the penal system for basing policy on abstract notions of human nature, on deterrence and retributive theories of punishment, policy which she found both inhumane and counterproductive. Only firsthand experience of individual juvenile delinquents provided by the sympathetic reformers who worked with them could offer the foundation for effective penal policy. And, as we have seen, while Carpenter believed that argument had to be addressed to legislators, it had also to be aimed at the hearts of the people, for it was their moral duty as well as their self-interest that must compel them to own their convicts.

They took an interest, but not in ways that Carpenter and her supporters could control. Indeed, their interest became a desire that might be better satisfied by a fiction mimicking her own stories without troubling readers with claims on their benevolence.[21] We do know that Carpenter was hostile to fictions that inflamed and corrupted the imaginations of the poor. At several points in *Our Convicts,* she recounted the stories of juvenile prisoners who blamed popular crime novels for leading them astray. She turned this evidence on novelists, writing,

> We trust this avowal may be taken to heart by those who pander to the vitiated tastes of our depraved classes. Surely the bad influence to which youths are exposed in the wretched haunts among which our sin-bred populace first draw breath, need no aggravation from the pens of men of intellect and imagination. May our popular novelists learn a lesson from this occurrence, and if they deal in criminal subjects at all, state facts as they are, with the veracious accompaniments of the criminal's habitual, trembling, apprehensive dread of discovery, his frequent subjection to poverty, hunger, cold and fatigue, ending in the privation of personal liberty and severe discipline, or still more severe monotony of prison life. No more suggestive lesson than this can be needed by the philanthropist. (1: 75)

It is ironic that this exhortation should exist cheek by jowl with Carpenter's citations of texts that followed her own formula for "proper" crime writing in order to pander to the vitiated tastes of the middle class. Carpenter's method of legitimating her authority had helped to create this taste and contributed to the success of those who would exploit it. Like many Victorian reformers who in appealing to public sentiment engendered a newly powerful political force, Carpenter found herself competing with narratives far more influential over volatile public opinion than her own.

In 1872 Carpenter would tell the International Penitentiary Congress that statistics were inadequate to show the progress that had been made: "Juvenile crime, as it existed 20 years ago has been *absolutely annihilated,*" she said.[22] It is undeniable that Carpenter's methods were influential. The legislative changes predicated on a new conception of juvenile delinquency were no doubt achieved thanks in part to the stories of individual children Carpenter brought to light. Harriet Martineau, reviewing *Our Convicts,* applauded her friend for apprehending juvenile delinquents—especially girls—where all others had failed. "No one understands them," Martineau exclaimed, "neither judge nor jury, chaplain nor matron, neither doctor nor warder, can enter into the mind and feeling of a being who seems to be made up of the idiot and the intriguer, the infant and the devil, the ferocious animal and the idolater."[23] Yet we know that even Mary Carpenter believed that Frederick William Robinson—the Prison Matron—had done so, and that his creation had lent power to Carpenter's own representation.

Mary Carpenter's reading practices, applied not only to Robinson's fraud but also to Blue Books and prison reports, closely resemble those celebrated by many narrative legal theorists. While we may be inclined to dismiss Carpenter and her heirs as naïve readers, we could instead see an opportunity for a robust engagement on the part of literary historians with the project of narrative jurisprudence. Carpenter's literary advocacy, which remains influential in constructing the category of the juvenile delinquent, demands a critical perspective rather than outright dismissal. In turning to infanticide prosecutions in the remainder of this chapter, and sodomy prosecutions in chapter 9, we find alternative uses of literary advocacy that foreground the ethical stakes involved in contextualizing literary genres and narrative techniques in wider questions of inequity, recognition, and political representation.

Forensic Medicine and Sentimental Advocacy in Infanticide Prosecutions

Countering the quest for knowledge of other minds supplied by the problematic literary device of omniscient narration was an alternative strategy of literary advocacy that sought to conceal subjectivity by means of plausible cover stories. This alternative approach to *mens rea* was also centrally concerned with gender. On no topic was this more evident in the nineteenth century than infanticide, which was typically prosecuted not as outright murder, but under the 1624 Act to Prevent the Destroying and Murthering of Infant Bastards, which criminalized *concealment* of birth. In the absence of reliable medical evidence of an infant's cause of death, that its birth had been concealed was taken as presumptive evidence that its mother had not merely killed the infant, but done so with evil intent and the desire to escape punishment. The competency of the mother to form an evil intent to kill her child was proven by her decision to conceal its birth. As in early modern witchcraft law, this presumption of guilt classified infanticide as a *crimen exemptum*—another anomaly in Common Law wherein *mens rea* appeared unproblematic.

As Josephine McDonagh has established in her comprehensive study of infanticide, *Child Murder and British Culture, 1720–1900,* eighteenth-century writers such as Mandeville, Swift, and Defoe so readily accepted the transparently rational motives for infanticide that they used it as a trope by which to address the new structures of rationality brought into being by capitalist economics. In the nineteenth century, fueled by journalistic and medical hysterias over perceived infanticide epidemics, however, sympathy for infanticidal mothers grew. Legal reforms, decisions by judges and juries, doctors' testimony, and later, police practice, all betrayed a desire to shield women from prosecution and punishment.[24] Historians agree on this point, but do not attempt to account for how this sentiment was formed, promulgated, or put into effect.[25] Literary treatments of infanticide contributed to this effort to protect women from the state by elaborating a representation of infanticide that insisted on its private character—a strategy that remains successful, if limiting, in securing reproductive rights today.[26] Moreover, texts indebted to a tradition of representation stretching back to sixteenth-century ballads, broadsides, and romances, including Wordsworth's "The Thorn" (1798) and Scott's *Heart of Mid-lothian* (1818), located infanticide in pastoral settings in order to render mothers as rural innocents inhabiting a sacrosanct natural space.[27] The privatization and pastoralization of infanticide aimed at placing women who killed their infants in a virtually supernatural space, outside the state's jurisdiction. At the same time, mystifying maternal motives for infanticide and denying access to women's decision-making processes deflected attacks on capitalist social relations, such as Swift's in *A Modest Proposal,* by concealing the conditions under which infanticide could be a rational choice.

The success of this representational strategy, demanding cooperation among members of the professions of law, medicine, and literature—professions that have been theorized as constituting themselves through the disciplinary objectification of women—complicates arguments regarding the violence of representation.[28] Thanks in large part to Foucault's analyses of nineteenth-century medical and legal discourses and their broad impact on social policies, we are well aware of the power of what Mary Poovey has termed "anatomical realism" to objectify, scrutinize, and discipline the social body.[29] Nevertheless, Poovey allows for the possibility that "the social investigator cannot measure what people will not allow him to see, especially, as in the case of illegitimacy, when laws are also insufficient to identify every person who commits this crime."[30] Resistance to prosecutorial investigations of the social body came not only from the disenfranchised but also from within institutions and privileged classes defending traditional and local customs against intrusion by what Wordsworth in "The Thorn" called "public justice." This form of literary advocacy forms a striking contrast with Mary Carpenter's empathic expertise.

Nineteenth-century reforms of infanticide laws produced a readerly version of rules of evidence. Lord Ellenborough's 1803 Offenses Against the Person Act repealed the unique presumption of guilt imposed by the 1624 act on infanticide defendants who had given birth to stillborns.[31] What is more, in order to prove murder in an infanticide case, the prosecution needed to establish the separate existence of the infant, a concept remarkably malleable in the hands of judges, medical witnesses, and juries sympathetic to the accused. If even a foot remained in the birth canal at the time of an infant's death, the corpse could not be the object of a murder charge.[32] The lesser charge of concealment of birth, which the 1828 Offenses Against the Person Act affirmed was applicable to stillbirths and exempt from the separate existence rule, nevertheless still left considerable leeway for judges and juries. For example, if the concealment were on a public highway where the body was likely to be found, juries were reluctant to convict.[33]

Debates over the likely consequences of the 1834 Bastardy Law illustrate how representations of infanticide, illegitimacy, and sexual behavior were contested over questions of maternal *mens rea*. Supporters of the reform, which eliminated an unmarried woman's right to maintenance of a bastard child from a man simply by naming him as its father, argued that "maternal feelings and natural timidity" would counterbalance economic motives for infanticide. Opponents held up a seduced innocent as the representative unmarried mother, driven in desperation to kill her child.[34] As Ann R. Higginbotham's survey of Victorian infanticide cases indicates, judges and juries typically sanctioned—if not credited—affecting stories of defendants' circumstances over forensic evidence: of forty-one indictments in the twelve years Higginbotham surveyed between 1839 and 1906, no woman was convicted of murdering her infant under one year of age—and many cases never made it past the grand jury.[35] Though conviction rates for concealment were relatively high—a mean of 73 percent between 1845 and 1900—Mary Beth Wasserlein Emmerichs concludes from her review of Assize records for these years that concealment convictions were "pious perjuries" accomplished by juries in the face of forensic evidence.[36]

Medical reformers complained that their testimony was often discredited by other medical witnesses, or by expert medical opinion cited by judges on behalf of defendants, all susceptible to literary sentimentalization.[37] T. R. Beck and John B. Beck, in their seventh edition of the *Elements of Medical Jurisprudence* (1842), voiced their frustration with the sentiments that typically mitigated infanticide cases in terms parodically echoing the literary tradition that I shall examine:

> That a young female of character and reputable connexions may be betrayed by the arts of a base seducer, and when reduced to a state of pregnancy, to avoid the disgrace which must otherwise be her lot, may stifle the birth of the womb, or after it is born, in a state of frenzy imbrue her hands in the infant's blood, in the expectation of throwing the mantle of oblivion over her crime, is a case which too frequently occurs; but even such a case, with all its palliations, cannot be considered as less than willful murder, and as such demands exemplary punishment.[38]

Such sentimental stories as the Becks bemoaned were still swaying judges and juries in the 1850s. During the 1859 trial of Agnes Bradley for infanticide, the judge reportedly "became painfully affected, so much so, that at one time he buried his face in his note-book and shed tears, and seemed almost unable to proceed with the evidence. The youthful and interesting appearance of the prisoner, who was also much affected, added considerably to the interest which was excited throughout the court."[39] The jury acquitted Bradley, on the ground of insanity. The Reverend William Scott, writing in the *Saturday Review,* August 1856, complained of a dozen recent infanticide trials resulting in acquittals. Juries "will not convict under any circumstances," he asserted. His case in point was the trial of Celestine Sumner at the Dorchester Assizes. Scott notes that the courtroom atmosphere was charged by "sympathetic girls." When the not guilty verdict was announced in a courtroom packed with country girls, "a general demonstration of applause took place in Court and the girls left town boasting that 'now they might do what they liked.'"[40]

What exactly were these powerfully affecting images of infanticidal mothers that brought judges to tears and frustrated unsentimental medical witnesses? Since verbatim transcripts of trials were rarely made in the nineteenth century, court records are an inadequate source of information. But even if such records did exist, they would not disclose the decision-making processes of judges or juries, which remain tacit. We can turn with some confidence, however, to the tradition of literary representations targeted by the medical reformers who sought to establish their unique authority to represent infanticide.

The ballad tradition offered a source of narrative devices and potent images of wronged womanhood adaptable to a representational strategy aimed at blocking infanticide prosecutions and convictions. "The Thorn" (1798), an exaggerated example of Wordsworth's distancing strategies in *Lyrical Ballads*, demonstrates the correspondence between this literary mode of constructing infanticide and legal and medical tactics on behalf of defendants.[41] Characterizing the treatment of fallen women in the ballad tradition, Hilary Schor notes that "the abandoned women poems all focus on the difficulty of reading the meaning of the woman: her story is hard to elicit; her appearance is hard to describe; her voice is difficult to hear." As a device for denying the fallen woman the power to state her case, to own her story, the "pedantic narrator" of "The Thorn," Schor is right to complain, "can never quite size up the object in front of him."[42] In David Simpson's reading of "The Thorn," Wordsworth intends to provoke irritation with his narrator in order "to invite a critical response without quite demanding it."[43]

The case can be put more strongly, however. Paul D. Sheats argues that "'The Thorn' forcefully disciplines a response to human suffering itself" by "deflect[ing] the reader's attention from its putative object, the incidents of Martha's story."[44] I would add that the poem's explicit references to the infanticide prosecution threatening this particular fallen woman suggest that the poet's distance from his subject can be read as refusing the narrator and the reader the authority to investigate and police her *mens rea,* what should be known only "to every star / And every wind that blows."[45] The very inscrutability of Wordsworth's fallen woman, which Schor reads as silencing, might be read instead as a defensive obscuring and poeticizing, a sympathetic revision of contemporary ballads, such as William Taylor's "Lass of Fair Wone," which had included graphic descriptions of infanticide.[46] This literary defense of infanticidal mothers lends a specificity and urgency to what Simpson identifies as Wordsworth's general critique of urban, commercial culture and artificial, enlightenment speech: Martha Ray must be defended by poetic justice against intrusion by an inquisitorial criminal justice system.[47]

Wordsworth prevents his narrator/poet from interrogating Martha Ray, the fallen woman, directly. Instead, he provides a mediating figure to field his "pedantic narrator's" questions, a character he identified in a note of 1800 as a retired sea captain. The sea captain has had only one accidental encounter with Martha Ray beside the thorn. While observing ships through his telescope from the shore, the captain is caught in a storm, and losing his way, comes near enough to hear her repeated cry, "Oh misery, oh misery!" and see her distraught expression. The captain's instrument of observation, the telescope, unlike the speculum—a technology literalizing the equation of penetrating inspection with masculine power—enforces distance on future observations, bringing only the image, not the body, near. In the 1798 version of the poem, this speaker is responsible for the notorious clunker, referring to the pond beside the thorn: "I've measured it from side to side: / 'Tis three feet long, and two feet wide" (lines 32–33). Sheats persuasively demonstrates that the bathetic quality of these lines both discredits measurement as inane and traps the reader into exposing prejudices against ordinary speech and incident. But this speaker becomes more fully complicitous in the effort to preserve the fallen woman's secrecy in the 1820 version where the offending couplet is replaced with the vague and more "poetic" description: "Though but of compass small, and bare / To thirsty suns and parching air."

Under interrogation by the poem's other speaker, the sea captain relates Martha Ray's history: her betrothal to and abandonment by Stephen Hill; her pregnancy and madness; her retreat into nature and restored faculties; and, finally, the circumstantial evidence (motive, opportunity, and means) that she murdered her child. But, as Susan Wolfson notes, his testimony aims at deflecting closer investigation of the crime and reinforcing the symbolic privacy that has afforded sanctuary to the suspect for twenty years.[48] The questioner's inquisitorial behavior, like that of zealous prosecutors and medical examiners later in the century, betrays a failure of imagination and political wisdom of the sort that made the same figure in "Resolution and Independence" the target of Lewis Carroll's wit. As

Wolfson puts it, "Wordsworth makes the tale of Martha Ray less an explanation for a mystery than an expression of the imagination's reach after fact and reason in the face of mystery."[49]

What is more, anyone who would inquire further into the fate of Martha Ray's baby sets himself against nature, at least as the sea captain tells the tale. First, despite the evidence pointing to infanticide, the captain objects: "But kill a new-born infant thus, / I do not think she could!" (lines 212–13). Beliefs about womanly nature and maternal instinct posed formidable obstacles to establishing *mens rea* for infanticide convictions, and like a shrewd defense witness, the captain inserts his appeal to feminine nature to shape the surrounding material evidence. In that evidence, nature itself resists an inquest. According to the legend, in the pond beside the thorn, where Martha may have drowned her child, a baby's face substitutes for an investigator's reflection, returning his gaze. For its part, the earth conceals the infant in its own womblike hill of moss. Lest there be any doubt that Wordsworth specifically opposes legal intervention into infanticide, he stages an inquest foiled by supernatural agency:

And some had sworn an oath that she
Should be to public justice brought;
And for the little infant's bones
With spades they would have sought.
But instantly the hill of moss
Before their eyes began to stir!
And, for full fifty yards around,
The grass—it shook upon the ground!
Yet all do still aver
The little Babe lies buried there,
Beneath that hill of moss so fair. (lines 221–31)

Wordsworth's limits do not substantially circumscribe circumstantial evidence against Martha; rather, they restrict the jurisdiction of "public justice" by describing a boundary around Martha that would be dangerous to transgress. Wordsworth's reconstruction of the sentimental narrative of the fallen woman serves as an effective cover story to thwart prosecutorial examinations of her body and history for as evidence of *mens rea*.

Features of Wordsworth's strategy in "The Thorn" inform two well-known novelistic treatments of infanticide in the nineteenth century: Walter Scott's *The Heart of Mid-lothian* (1818) and George Eliot's *Adam Bede*

(1859). Both novels cast the unwed mother as a country girl; both babies are concealed in nature; both infanticide trials include males rather more sympathetic toward the defendants than Wordsworth's sea captain, who are nonetheless powerless to resist the ineluctable requirements of the law to investigate, interrogate, and convict. Both novels make use of retrospective settings to reflect on the contemporary politics of infanticide. Scott's 1739 setting shows judge and spectators shedding tears over the obligation to enforce a draconian law against a pathetic prisoner, thereby approving the latitude afforded juries reluctant to convict by the more lax laws in force in 1818. Eliot's novel bears the marks of the long controversy over changes in the Bastardy Laws, particularly in its representation of Hetty as the desperate victim of seduction by a thoughtless aristocrat.

Like "The Thorn," *The Heart of Mid-lothian* and *Adam Bede* maintain that infanticide should be set outside the realm of legal representation. Whereas the law is associated with urban male institutions—specifically, the Assizes at Edinburgh and Stoniton—infanticide is removed to the pastoral, feminine, private, and, overwhelmingly, the natural realm. As such, it becomes literally unspeakable in legal discourse. At her infanticide trial, Scott's character Effie Dean shrieks when the defense counsel proposes that whoever carried off her child may have murdered it:

> Her counsel availed himself of the tragical interruption, to close his pleading with effect.
>
> "My Lords," said he, "in that piteous cry you heard the eloquence of maternal affection, far surpassing the force of my poor words—Rachel weeping for her children! Nature herself bears testimony in favour of the tenderness and acuteness of the prisoner's parental feelings. I will not dishonour her plea by adding a word more."[50]

In *Adam Bede,* Hetty Sorrel is likewise reduced to an insensible shriek when confronted with her guilt in the courtroom. However, whereas this failure to act as effective speaking subjects at their trials relies on the fallen woman tradition, which Schor argues renders the woman an inscrutable icon, Scott and Eliot attribute this failure to the law, allowing fallen women to speak their minds in literary spaces.

Effie is saved by the simple moving rhetoric of her loyal sister and a royal pardon from the queen, that is, by a female partnership working around and above the law. Not only does this prove a more merciful mode of dealing with the crime, but also one that more accurately corresponds with the truth: Effie's child, stolen by the "natural," Madge Wildfire, was never murdered. Instead, he has become a savage child of nature, the subject of a broadside legend, who at last disappears into a tribe of American Indians. As I argued in chapter 6, Eliot's critique of the law focuses on its gendered discursive practices. What Hetty cannot reveal about the death of her child in response to questions that recall those of Wordsworth's pedantic narrator, she can describe in a discourse Eliot fashions as peculiarly female. In the privacy of a prison cell, Hetty unburdens her heart with a tragic, pastoral tale—strikingly similar in its details to "The Thorn"—confessed to Dinah Morris, the sisterly representative of a forgiving God rather than a hanging judge. Here again, the methods of legal interrogation have proven useless in discovering a crime steeped in the mysteries of nature, the female body, and private motives.

Stories like these enabled judges and juries to acquit women of infanticide (perhaps to cover over their tacit rejection of the law) and as such became the target of medical reformers. But before turning to the strategies aimed at changing attitudes toward infanticide, I wish to consider two different sorts of literary representation. The logic of the pastoral representation of infanticide could lead to rather more radical conclusions than those of Wordsworth, Scott, or Eliot. That possibility was taken up by Frances Trollope in her novel denouncing the 1834 Poor Law, *Jessie Phillips, A Tale of the Present Day* (serialized between 1842 and 1843) and by Elizabeth Barrett Browning in her deployment of an infanticide narrative against slavery in "The Runaway Slave at Pilgrim's Point" (1848). Like Hetty Sorrel, Jessie Phillips is a cottager seduced by a squire's son, Frederic Dalton. The 1834 bastardy clause prevents Jessie from claiming support from Frederic as the father of her child, and she herself is wrongly accused of infanticide. Unlike Tonna's *Helen Fleetwood* or Gaskell's *Mary Barton,* discussed in chapter 6, in *Jesse Phillips,* middle-class women, including the culprit's own sister, come to the fallen woman's defense, in this case revealing Frederic as the murderer. Frederic drowns himself and Jessie dies before she hears that she has been acquitted—two plot developments that blunt the critique of patriarchy implicit in the story of an infanticidal father, and reflect Trollope's own changing position on the bastardy clause in the course of serialization. However, as Joseph Kestner points out, Trollope's treatment of the bastardy clause is part of her general denunciation of what her character the Reverend Mr. Rimmington calls "the hateful Frenchified principle of centralization."[51] Barrett Browning, on the other hand, could not be accused of prevarication in "Runaway Slave at Pilgrim's Point," a poem she described as "fierce." The poem's appeals to the convention I have been describing—the unwed mother as rural girl violated by a socially superior man, its setting in nature, nature's apparent collusion in the child's burial, its formal ballad qualities—make Barrett Browning's revision all the more powerful. Dorothy Mermin credits Barrett Browning with being one of the first women writers in Britain to take up slavery as a feminist issue, "recognizing that the oppression of black women (especially in sexual terms) offered a grim commentary on the angelic purity that was supposed to enshroud white women."[52] Additionally, Barrett Browning should be acknowledged for imagining how features of the pastoral representation of infanticide could be persuasively deployed by an infanticide defendant insisting upon her rational motives.

As dramatic monologue, "The Runaway Slave at Pilgrim's Point" allows its speaker to represent herself, neither mediated by a sympathetic presence nor interrogated by a hostile examiner. She testifies against the law of slavery, which has determined her relationship to nature, desire, motherhood, God, and history. Whereas Wordsworth's Martha Ray may find some refuge in her spot beside the thorn, for the slave woman the landscape has already been inscribed by the oppressing race. White men have denied her the pleasure of "natural" sexual and maternal bonds as well, separating her from her beloved and raping her. The child she bears reflects the master's face: "A child and mother Do wrong to look at one another / When one is black and one is fair."[53] That face unnaturally repels a bond with its mother, a maddening situation that can be remedied only by removing the child from the conditions defining its life: smothering it, removing its body from the white man's house, and returning it to nature by burying it in the black ground. Barrett Browning makes explicit what pastoral representations of infanticide left implicit, namely, the naturalization of infanticide. But what is even more damning is the Runaway Slave's repeated declaration "I am not mad." Slavery makes infanticide her rational choice. Not surprisingly, the indictment of white patriarchy explicit in Barrett Browning's statement of *mens rea*, not as evil intent but rational choice, would be expunged from these new sensationalistic representations.

Efforts to counter literary defenses of infanticide began in earnest when, in 1839, West Middlesex elected Thomas Wakley, the nation's first medical doctor as coroner, thereby handing medical men a significant political victory over lawyers. Wakley made no secret of his contempt for the literary profession either, and as an MP he was a vociferous opponent of the 1842 copyright reforms, arguing that literary authors were the medical equivalents of quacks. His anti-infanticide campaign was intensified by his successor, the second in an uninterrupted line of medical coroners for Central Middlesex extending into the 1880s.[54] This movement drew on the growing number of medical societies in London following the 1858 Medical Act, which lent clout to doctors' challenges of the legal profession, particularly regarding the qualifications of coroners.[55] These London physicians sought to stir up public wrath against infanticide by asserting a link between infanticide and the city as the site of vice, disease, and decay. Their representational strategy exploited phenomena peculiar to Victorian London over which they claimed particular expertise through the growing public health bureaucracy. Among them were urban sanitation, public parks, and the paradoxical combination of intimacy and anonymity produced by growing population density. And finally, the technologies by which urban spectatorship could be mass produced, including cheap newspapers, promulgated readings of the city as a feminized reproductive body to be penetrated by heroic explorers, a diseased womb from which innocent babies must be delivered.[56]

For almost a century infanticide had peculiarly pitted legal and medical experts against one another, and methods for detecting the crime had become a focal point in the development of medical jurisprudence. The success of medical reformers depended upon shifting the law's traditional focus from *mens rea* to forms of evidence observable by medical techniques. Proof of live birth for an infanticide conviction was in fact unobtainable with nineteenth-century diagnostic techniques. In a paper entitled *On the Uncertainty of Signs of Murder in Bastard Children,* read before the Medical Society in 1783, Dr. William Hunter had discredited the hydrostatic test as a means of determining live birth by floating the lungs of an infant corpse. Physicians as well as defense attorneys called on Hunter's authority to ambiguate evidence of live birth, to the dismay of those medical men committed to elevating their professional expertise. In an 1825 work aimed at coaching medical witnesses, John Gordon Smith bemoaned that fact that

> the errors of William Hunter are enforced from the judgment-seat, while those among us who choose to follow the guidance of scientific truth, in preference to the dogmas of a great name, are pronounced to be deficient in respectability, and are not allowed to give evidence that may tend to correct the mistakes or supply the deficiencies of one who,

> unhappily for us and for our science, did not live to see the introduction of forensic medicine as an important and well-digested branch of political and philosophic study.[57]

Alfred Taylor went further in condemning the sentimental, mystifying motives behind appeals to Hunter's skepticism that persisted in 1836 and decried the affronts to medical witness's dignity that had resulted:

> The cases of infanticide which [Hunter] brings forward as illustrations, are stated in terms to excite our pity,—to make us forget the murderess in our compassion for the mother; in short, in a manner altogether unbecoming a professedly physiological disquisition.[58]

That is to say, in a manner relying on aesthetic, particularistic, subjective standards of evidence.

The medical coroners of Middlesex countered with images of a brave new urban world where pastoral representations of infanticide could not apply. In the years immediately following the 1858 Medical Act and the formation of a medical office within the Privy Council, Dr. Thomas Wakley, coroner for Middlesex, began to return an appreciably higher number of murder verdicts on infants, substantially exceeding those of East Middlesex where a nonmedical coroner, John Humphreys, served. Of the 316 inquests Wakley conducted in 1861 on children under two years of age, 39 murder verdicts were returned; for Humphreys, it was 17 murder verdicts out of 421 inquests. Wakley's figures prompted the Home Secretary to review statistics for the whole of London, with the result that only Middlesex appeared to be suffering from an infanticide epidemic. Wakley died in 1861 and was succeeded by Dr. Edwin Lankester, who quickly spearheaded the campaign against infanticide. During the 1860s, Lankester typically returned between 58 and 70 murder verdicts on infant corpses annually, and those statistics were for the smaller Central Middlesex division carved in 1862 out of the division Wakley had served. Lionel Rose concludes that the "impression was to be firmly fixed in people's minds in the 1860s that Middlesex was the national hotbed for infanticide, and that the Marylebone and Paddington parishes of central Middlesex were, as the *British Medical Journal* puts it in March 1861, 'especially infamous as seats of such massacres of the innocents.'"[59]

What made Lankester particularly effective in attracting attention had nothing to do with his superior forensic technique. Little progress had been made in methods for detecting live birth. Rather, Lankester was adept at representational strategy and publicity. To this end, he shrewdly used the resources provided him by the streets of London. Wakley had tended to classify infant corpses found in the streets as having died of natural causes, despite signs of possible violence or neglect, using his verdict to cover the corpse. Lankester, by contrast, seems to have viewed these bodies as a neglected resource, a ready supply of evidence that he was loath to bury. The *Times* for August 15, 1861, reported that "in the last five years within the metropolitan district alone, at least 178 infants were murdered; above 60 were found dead in the Thames or the canals or ponds about London and many more than 100, at all events were found dead under railway arches, on doorsteps, in dustholes, cellars and the like."[60] The mild shock of the *Times* to the Registrar General's report would swell into a tabloid sensation fed by Lankester's representations of infanticide statistics.

Lankester returned 79 murder verdicts on 361 infant inquests in 1867, over half the total of 149 murder verdicts for all of England and Wales. Rather than claim that his district was especially prone to baby dropping, Lankester accused the legal establishment of turning a blind eye to the crime. He argued that accurate infanticide rates for England could be extrapolated from Central Middlesex: the figure he reached for 1866 was 1,420. Still more could be made of this number by conjuring up the specters of corpses that never came to light, the burials of live-borns as stillborns, and decomposed subjects on whom a conclusive verdict was impossible.[61] He estimated that in 1866 London harbored 16,000 women who had destroyed their babies.[62]

Central Middlesex division was particularly suited to Lankester's investigations and speculations. Unlike such slum areas as St. Giles, Marylebone and Paddington had a large population of domestic servants (the most prone to infanticide prosecutions), many water closets (as opposed to privies and cesspools), and relatively orderly public spaces. Judging from infanticide depositions I have reviewed from the 1820s to the 1850s, privies had offered both the favored mode of disposing of infant corpses and a highly effective defense if the corpse was discovered. Judges and juries were generally willing to accept a defendant's claims that she was unaware of her pregnancy, and indeed that what had passed from her into the privy was a fetus, or that the baby had dropped from her and drowned before she could do anything to save it. Water closets eliminated this strategy for concealing *mens rea*, meaning that more corpses would end up in public places, to be discovered and brought to Dr. Edwin Lankester. Because the culture, geography, and technology of the slums were more resistant to discovery made it a better—not worse—site of speculation in Lankester's view. Anything was possible.

Lankester's strategy appealed to medical societies, social scientists, and urban journalists. Dr. William Burke Ryan's *Infanticide: Its Law, Prevalence, Prevention, and History* (1862) suggested that the modern urban landscape—its parks, streets, canals, public transport, and domestic spaces—veritably sprouted infant corpses. Emphasizing the frequency of infanticide in London, Ryan wrote:

> The feeble wail of murdered childhood in its agony assails our ears at every turn, and is borne on every breeze. The sight is horrified as day after day, the melancholy catalogue of murders meets the view, and try as we may, still are we met by the evidence of a wide spread crime. In the quiet of the bedroom we raise the box-lid, and the skeletons are there. In the calm evening walk we see in the distance the suspicious-looking bundle, and the mangled infant is within. By the canal side, or in the water, we find the dead child. In the solitude of the wood we are horrified by the ghastly sight; and if we betake ourselves to the rapid rail in order to escape the pollution, we find at our journey's end that the mouldering remains of a murdered innocent have been our travelling companion; and that the odour from that unsuspected parcel truly indicates what may be found within.[63]

Although the urban landscape may have been dotted with infant corpses, their source became more difficult to trace. Emmerichs notes that of the 221 dead infants found in 1865, only 120 resulted in indictments against women. The effect of Lankester's "spectral" evidence was to make normative a representation of infanticide at once urban and anonymous and ubiquitous, which erased the subjectivity of the infanticidal mother in favor of the infant corpse.

The proliferation of London newspapers after mid-century helped to expose and spread this representation of urban baby dropping. Parish papers, such as the *Marylebone Mercury,* provided a steady supply of accounts of skeletons dug up in local gardens and fresh bodies discovered on doorsteps, along the paths of Regent's Park and Primrose Hill, or in the Regent's Canal—all in or adjacent to Lankester's Central Middlesex division.[64] Apparently untroubled by doubts about their "capacity to read the city and to sustain a coherent vision of a structured public landscape," such as Judith Walkowitz attributes to men of letters in the 1880s, journalists set out to explore the world of infanticide, where lesser explorers had failed.[65] More than a decade before W. T. Stead would earn a place in the history of investigative journalism with his exposé of child prostitution, "The Maiden Tribute of Modern Babylon," Ernest Hart, editor of the *British Medical Journal* and member of the Harveian Society, commissioned Dr. Albert Wheeler to undertake the fieldwork in an investigation to "take the lid off the nether world of midwife-abortionists and baby-farmers," which resulted in a series of articles running February through September 1868.[66] Notably, the *Times* investigation was carried out by a woman, who signed her articles "A.B." The *Clerkenwell News* attempted to draw out participants in the baby-dropping system with ads offering children for adoption. In concert, these groups castigated the police and Palmerston's government for their apparent inability to see clearly what was before their eyes, reversing the tactics used by lawyers to discredit medical witnesses who had claimed to see with certainty what no one else could—including the contents of an accused woman's mind.

Under public pressure, the Metropolitan Police were forced to respond with undercover investigations of their own. Significantly, these operations focused not on Lankester's district but on South London, where the system of baby farming was centered. While few middle-class women were likely to abandon unwanted infants in Regent's canal, they were known to make use of baby farmers along with poorer women. Discovery of decomposed corpses in Brixton led police to the baby farming operation of Margaret Waters, who was tried at the Central Criminal Court in July 1870, convicted of murder, and hanged on October 11, 1870.[67] The courts had been the target of a barrage of criticism for several years. Between the last hanging of a woman for infanticide in 1849 and 1864, only thirty-nine women had been convicted, and the Home Secretaries had reprieved them all. Waters believed herself to be a scapegoat, and a number of prominent politicians agreed. But her motives being transparently economic, none could save her.

The immediate legislative consequence of the Waters case was a diluted version of an elaborate inspection scheme proposed in 1871 by the Select Committee on Infant Life Protection, the 1872 Infant Life Protection Act. Its administration in London fell to the Metropolitan Board of Works, the same body that oversaw drains and sewers and had become involved in slum clearance, street widening, park acquisition, and so forth. Feminists were among those opposed to the scheme. Lydia Becker tried to revive the image of maternity as private and extralegal to preserve women from the consequences of an intrusive new bureaucracy, writing that this bill,

> dealing with women in the performance of that domestic office which is, by common consent, regarded as peculiarly their own—namely the nursing of infants—. . . places the entire supervision, regulation, and authority in these matters in the hands of men. *Men only* are to grant the licenses—*men only* are competent to certify to the qualifications of the licensee—*men only* are to visit the babies in their own nurses' charge. This minute and galling supervision by men of the domestic and nursery arrangements of women, would be felt as grievously vexatious by the women of this nation, especially by the poorer classes.[68]

Evidence can be found as late as 1890 of the persistence of the pastoral representation of infanticide as a mitigating force in infanticide prosecutions. The National Society for the Prevention of Cruelty to Children complained of the compassion, tinged with gallantry, that misled middle-class, male jurors into judging female instincts by standards of their own class, and rejecting the idea of a woman willfully killing her child.[69] But these sentiments persisted as an overdetermined phenomenon, largely unaided, however, by fresh images from literary authors. In the midst of the rising infanticide hysteria of the 1860s, the most memorable literary statement on infanticide had been Matthew Arnold's terse quotation from a newspaper story, "Wragg is in custody."[70] Whereas urban prostitution occasioned fairly brave treatments by Elizabeth Gaskell, Charles Dickens, and Felecia Skene, urban infanticide was not represented in bourgeois literature—at least until Hardy's spectacular conflation of Darwinian nature and Malthusian urban crowding in Father Time's infanticide-suicide in *Jude the Obscure* (1895).[71] When infanticide was treated at all, as in Emma Woods's *Sorrows on the Sea* (1868), it was embodied by a villainous female baby farmer. G. W. M. Reynolds brought the representational tradition I have been examining full circle in his 1884 novel *The Days of Hogarth; or, The Mysteries of Old London*. Taking William Hogarth's eighteenth-century street scenes as his inspiration, Reynolds supplied a Romantic, pastoral biography for the drunken woman featured in "Gin Lane," whose baby drops from her arms as she sucks from a gin bottle. This "drunken beast in female shape," he wrote, was once "the fairest of God's creatures," tempted to her ruin by a young man who offered her gin in a tea-garden.[72] As such, she was now doubly incapable of forming criminal intent.

What neither legislator nor novelist, neither physician nor poet, was eager to spotlight was the testimony of women accused of infanticide, or the female witnesses who were so often called to testify against them. Many such cases heard at Assizes and the Old Bailey were summarized in the *Times,* often with fragments of testimony. Depositions in these cases—at once graphic and tragic—resist the representational categories available in the official discussion of the crime. Take, for example, the suicide note of Eliza Clark, entered into evidence by Eliza Gorman at her niece's trial at the Central Criminal Court on May 15, 1846, for the murder of her children. Clark had been discovered preparing to jump off of Battersea Bridge, from which she had just thrown her three children. The note was addressed to Clark's husband:

> Now my *Jemmy,* you need not give me any more of your threats, because I do not need them, and I hope the next wife you get, you will know how to use *them,* and not act a brute to them as you have to me, and bid me good-bye in the morning, and come home at night and knock my head through the panel of the door, and break my rest the whole night, and swear in the morning that he would come home drunk and kill me, and I would rather prefer seeing my children go before me, and then I shall know that they did not starve. And if you go to Battersea bridge you will find the children there.[73]

Clark was declared not guilty—but by reason of insanity, thereby concealing the rationality of her infanticidal motives. The courts may have tended toward mercy, the reforming medical community toward prosecution, but neither would openly acknowledge Medea.

By the late nineteenth century, some women's organizations embraced the empiricist representational strategies and urban, bureaucratic political model employed earlier by the infanticide hunters. The decline in infanticide prosecutions in the last decades of the century have been attributed to the dissemination of sound birth control information to poor women, though police and court attitudes toward prosecuting infanticide have not been fully investigated. Roy Porter and Lesley Hall note that Havelock Ellis's success in gathering evidence for his *Studies in the Psychology of Sex* (1910) indicates that respectable women were not entirely barred from speaking of their own sexual experiences.[74] Regenia Gagnier has concluded that the 1913 Working Women's Co-Operative Guild, in demanding an end to the conspiracy of silence surrounding women's bodies, pregnancy, and "mothercraft," broke down middle-class boundaries between private and public: "Women who had been isolated by their subjective experiences of pain learned as Guildswomen to articulate that pain as part of a narrative of progressive demands on behalf of a 'we,' finding community and voice simultaneously."[75] It would be the representation of motherhood as private, subjective, and therefore extralegal, however, on which the legal decision for abortion rights would be founded. And, at the same time, we instinctively envision corpses in urban dumpsters when we think of infanticide.

In an argument about Victorian attitudes toward children marked by thorough and provocative self-reflection, James Kincaid nevertheless feels confident in declaring, "First of all, the law is always several generations behind the feeling of the public."[76] His remark is apropos of the prosecution over Charles Knowlton's groundbreaking treatment of birth control, *Fruits of Philosophy* (1877). However, with respect to infanticide, the prevalent form of birth control earlier in the century, I would be hard-pressed to position the law relative to public feeling. Courts and judges, at least, seemed to be working in concert with many medical experts and literary writers, first to encourage sympathy for infanticide defendants—especially after the 1834 Bastardy Law—and then to stave off reformers' efforts to bring such women to justice. To do so, they relied on a cover story with a long and distinguished history. Yet those cover stories of natural innocence and melodramatic seduction concealed such stories such as that told by Eliza Clark in her suicide note. Should those stories have been voiced instead? Could they have been comprehended even if they had been spoken? And if they had been spoken, would they excuse or mitigate murder?[77]

These questions connect the efficacy of narrative to provide cover stories with the larger context of feminist advocacy, narrative theory and literary history described throughout this study, thus far. As I have argued respecting witchcraft trials, advocacy for women's legal recognition, and forensic eloquence in previous chapters, narrative reasoning is better understood in strategic terms dependent upon the historically specific status of speakers constructed in dialectic with law than as an intrinsically efficacious antidote to an overly narrow understanding of positivist rules of legal reasoning. Eliza Clark lacked Georgina Weldon's status to alter conceptions of *mens rea* not merely because she was poor and uneducated, nor because she was prosecuted before the Married Women's Property Act. She could not claim ownership of her story in the manner of Robin West's "Enlightenment narrativity" because, as with Wollstonecraft's Maria, her story radically challenged a whole system of gendered social and economic relationships. Without the capacity to bring about radical change, the law could, at best, admit legal fictions to mitigate its violence. Legal decision makers could employ the very sentimental narratives used to shore up gendered social arrangements to exclude the alterity of disenfranchised women's rational decision making, or *mens rea,* from direct legal scrutiny. They denied Eliza Clark's agency in order to avoid the consequences to patriarchy of acknowledging her rationality, but also in a pragmatic effort to shield her from even more draconian consequences than she already suffered as a woman. Their strategy on Clark's behalf, it must be said, was more efficacious than either the advocacy of lunacy commissioners or the testimony of female indecent assault victims had been.

Literary history can alert us to a form of narrative advocacy that depends not upon securing legal recognition, but upon deploying convincing cover stories. It challenges the theorization of a monolithic carceral state. Nevertheless, predicated on an all-or-nothing construction of agency in relation to narrative and legal representation, this episode in legal history, as well as Mary Carpenter's advocacy for juvenile delinquents, cannot reveal how the production and interpretation of narrative could function to enable subjugated groups and individuals to exercise agency within the law. Without such evidence, it would seem that narrative is unduly emptied of progressive force and relegated to a subsidiary role with respect to law. If narrative is ever in meaningful dialectic with law, then it must be possible to demonstrate an oppositional narrative agency operating in legal decision making. That agency, however, will necessarily be difficult to detect, precisely because it must rely not merely on "cover stories," as we have seen in infanticide verdicts, but also on the tacit reading strategies of legal decision makers who are themselves members of subjugated groups. In the next chapter I will offer a reading strategy by which to identify the "secret agency" of jurors who nullified legal prosecutions, not out of a sense of chivalry, but out of a sense of solidarity. Significantly, this chapter will deal, necessarily, with men tried by juries of their peers.

CHAPTER NINE

The Secret Agency of Juries

Forging Resistance against Sodomy Prosecution

NARRATIVE JURISPRUDENCE aims at influencing legal decision making, yet legal decision making itself is stubbornly opaque. Whereas judges' written decisions cite precedents and principles, the more complex motivations of those decisions are not made evident in documents. What is more, in the cornerstone of Anglo-American legal procedure, the trial by jury, decision making is even more obscure, what Barbara Shapiro has termed the great "black box" of legal history.[1] And as Carol J. Clover has remarked, "The rules of evidence and protocol that are designed at the point of production to maximize fairness are, at the point of reception, a veritable machine for the production of paranoid speculation far beyond the trial's official parameters."[2]

That paranoia has permeated cultural criticism of the law. Nineteenth-century Britain's criminal justice system has been so cogently—and repeatedly—described as the apogee of the carceral state that it is easy to forget that defendants sometimes succeeded in winning acquittals. This is not to say that the legal process did not disadvantage the accused. But, as infanticide prosecutions illustrate, mid-nineteenth-century trials could also enable juries—and even judges and prosecutors—to cooperate with defense counsel in authoring stories to protect not merely privileged defendants, but those whom the law has been blamed for demonizing. In this chapter I will consider how these strategies may have been employed in defense of homosexual men. The example of sodomy prosecutions against homosexual men offers the opportunity to explore a distinctive possibility in the history of jury decision making in that, unlike women, homosexual men in the nineteenth century may have been tried by juries of their peers. Speculation about a subjected solidarity being realized in a jury verdict—a sort of "secret agency"—requires attention to a more subtle deployment of narrative advocacy and its tacit reading by jurors. Carlo Ginzburg's directive to read between the lines of witchcraft trials in order to appreciate the agency of accused women is useful here.[3] To explore how this secret agency is forged, I will argue that we may look to the intersection of institutional and popular legal cultures by reading two texts across one another: Anthony Trollope's 1862 novel *Orley Farm,* about a woman guilty of forgery and perjury but twice acquitted, and the 1871 trial of Boulton, Park, and others, who were acquitted of the charge of conspiracy to commit sodomy. These texts suggest a self-conscious, willed opposition, carried out in courts of law by literary means, against statute law and speculatory discourses and technologies. They offer counterexamples to theories of both the novel and law that treat each as devoted wholly to producing disciplined subjects for the bourgeois state. And they help us to see that the opacity of legal decision making does not always conceal "sinister interests," as legal theorists from Bentham to the Critical Legal Studies movement have alleged, but might also signal the secret agency of citizens quite capable of forging solidarity with defendants, whose circumstances may *or may not* have diverged substantially from their own.

While the Boulton and Park trial has come to attract the attention that historians of sexuality long devoted to the Cleveland Street scandal or the Wilde trials, read in the light of *Orley Farm,* it offers unique insight into a stubborn problem in Queer History: how and why the homosexual juridical subject was created in the latter decades of the nineteenth century.[4] Unlike more celebrated trials, a verbatim court transcript exists of the Boulton proceedings. We have, therefore, not only a clearer sense of what was said in this trial but also what was not said. It is precisely the gaps in reasoning, non sequiturs, and omitted evidence that may suggest not the poststructuralist ruptures of discourse or the incoherence of bourgeois ideology, but the strategic formation of tacit agreements among gentlemen.

Reading between the lines of the transcript of the Boulton trial, wherein the defendants were forbidden by law to testify under oath, may help us to perceive another agency, that of queer decision makers within legal institutions—if not defendants, then judges, jurors, defense counsel, and even prosecutors. Just as Ginzburg corrects a historiographic model that emphasized female victimization to the exclusion of female agency, this reading strategy encourages us to ask whether historians have not overlooked the resistance by queer legal agents in their attention to the emergence of homosexuals as juridical subjects.

Indeed, entertaining the possibility of queer legal argument and its place in the dialectic of legal history may enable us better to understand the causes that led to the witch hunts authorized by the Labouchère Amendment. The almost accidental quality of the addition of the Labouchère Amendment to the Criminal Law Amendment Act of 1885 raises questions about its status as the manifestation of a widespread homosexual panic. The convictions of men charged with gross indecency in the 1880s and 1890s occur within a larger context of an ongoing assault on legal fictions, tacit agreements, judicial activism, and forensic eloquence, the means by which Boulton and Park were acquitted. Defense counsel, first allowed in 1836, had won many sensational victories by the 1860s, including on behalf of some defendants who had confessed guilt to their advocates. As a result, the press had launched campaigns against "lying lawyers."[5] Concurrently, the pious perjuries of juries who authored "special verdicts," most notoriously to shield women from infanticide convictions, were coming under assault. Reformers sought procedural changes to drag juries out of their "black box" by limiting their discretionary powers. And, above all, England's unique system of Equity jurisdiction, authorizing an activist Court of Chancery in effect to set aside statute law in the interest of conscience, as it had energetically done with respect to women's property, was the target of positivist legal reformers, for whom it represented the most egregious example of judge-made law. Their goals were realized four years after the Boulton and Park acquittal with the Judicature Act of 1875, bringing Chancery under the heel of a unitary High Court.[6]

When Law and Literature scholars Richard Delgado and Jean Stefancic urge humanists to ransack the stories of our culture for what they call "saving narratives," texts by which the interests of outsiders—women, racial and ethnic minorities, gays and lesbians, the poor—can be recognized and defended, do they understand that they are calling us back to the future?[7] I wish to suggest that the efficacy of saving narratives, so evident in mid-Victorian law, depended upon a legal culture that allowed the tacit complicity of judges, lawyers, and juries to author and credit legal forgeries, or cover stories: not stories that brought subjectivities into representation, but ones that protected an extralegal space for criminalized subjectivities. When that culture was itself demonized, the cover stories of law became proofs of guilt. If this was the case, is it any wonder that, as Joseph Bristow has remarked, Oscar Wilde's eloquence was his undoing?[8]

This argument relies on a substantial revision in paradigms of the relationship of literature to law held by many narrative legal scholars. "Narrative [legal] scholars," Kathryn Abrams writes, "take the . . . position that what persuades decision makers to embrace new legal rules is not, or not only, the abstract elegance of a proposed solution. They may also be moved to action by a more visceral response: a response animated by a particularized depiction of the lives of those affected by a legal rule. Because of its pungency and particularity, its inflection with the emotional resonances and factual minutiae of life, narrative may elicit this visceral understanding in a way that more abstract propositions rarely can."[9] It should not be surprising that in this paradigm, which causally connects empathy with representation, certain forms of Victorian fiction have been cited as exemplary. But I wish to question the assumption that it is the power to reveal subjectivities rather than the power to create plausible fictions that produces such "visceral understanding."

Whereas Dickens has been used to illustrate many scholars' claims for the empathic contribution literature can make to law, Dickens may be the worst illustration of my claim.[10] Rather, I would look to Dickens's Victorian critics, notably Anthony Trollope, who skewered Dickens as the scandal-mongering Mr. Popular Sentiment in *The Warden*. Like Sir James Fitzjames Stephen, the legal theorist and vitriolic critic of the baleful influence of Dickens's sensationalism on public discourse, Trollope deplored the persecutions carried out by journalists and editors—including Dickens—against public servants.[11] Whereas Dickens associates relentless probing with the law, as represented, for example, by Tulkinghorn in *Bleak House*, Trollope identifies this vice with vulgar journalists, embodied in the "h"-dropping scoundrel of the Palliser novels, Mr. Quintius Slide. He derides Slide's claim that journalists act in the public interest, assigning him motives of venality, self-promotion, and revenge. Conversely, when Trollope treats the law, he is generally more interested in the defense than the prosecution—indeed, even in prosecutors' reluctance to perform their duty. In short, Trollope rejects the fundamental claim of Benthamite legal reform: that publicity secures justice. Instead, he sees the public interest as served by Bentham's bête noir: gentleman's agreements—the tacit, unrecorded, and opaque decision-making processes of the trial by jury.

As John Kucich remarks in *The Power of Lies*, the strategies of concealment that arose in response to Victorian mechanisms of surveillance "cannot be reduced to Foucauldian notions of disciplinary self-production, nor should they blind us to the real creativity that Victorian writers celebrated in those who used discretion to defeat the prying of official eyes."[12] Even Trollope, Kucich contends, who represents for many the quintessential bourgeois novelist, endorses lying as a form of resistance against the disciplinary technologies of knowledge.[13] In *Orley Farm,* plausible stories and the tacit solidarities they cover provide a way of conceptualizing resistance within the very bourgeois institutions identified with the production of deviance, ubiquitous surveillance, and other disciplinary technologies. Only in a fiction could such fiction-making practices of the law be brought into representation and defended. In law, fictions are efficacious only insofar as their fictionality is tacitly denied.

Significantly, the legal scholar Anne B. Goldstein, in a discussion of her strategies for defending lesbian clients, proposes a similar use for literary narrative. "The work of a lawyer," Goldstein writes, "is, in some respects, like the work of a novelist. Litigation is a storytelling contest. To win, a lawyer must tell a compelling story." She insists, however, that "the story is not fiction, because the lawyer is obligated to present the truth, but truth is a conclusion. . . . Six witnesses to the same event will swear to six different versions of it, and none will be lying. The lawyer's job is to take these various, conflicting, accounts and by selection and emphasis construct a version that will convince the finder of fact. The lawyer is a technician of the truth."[14] Goldstein describes her use of lesbian-authored novels in defending a client she calls "Mary Charmichael," who was dismissed from her job for making what a female co-worker interpreted as sexual overtures. Goldstein writes: "One might ordinarily assume that lesbian novels are engaged in the project of liberating lesbians by breaking an enforced silence. In fact, however, although this is true about some aspects of lesbian existence, it is not generally true of lesbian sexuality. Perhaps the novelists' strategies and my own were similar because our goals were similar: to deflect attention away from an area of vulnerability to something 'more relevant.'" Whatever the strength of the strategy in novels, it worked for Mary Charmichael: she got her job back. Goldstein's appeals to stereotypes formed and promulgated in literary texts closely resembles the defense strategies in *Orley Farm,* and which, I will argue, we might detect in the Boulton and Park trial, wherein the truth-telling potential of narrative is not deconstructed, but tacitly set aside.

In choosing to write a novel about a forger, Trollope was evoking a complex history of epistemology in which novels and law were directly implicated in one another's practices. Murder cases may have offered the best opportunities for exercising Victorian methods of detecting, prosecuting, and judging crime.[15] But abuses of discourse—the crimes of forgery, perjury, and personation—enabled a writer to examine laws and legal processes as discursive practices integral to a system of beliefs by which political, economic, and sexual relationships were organized. In his *Principles of Morals and Legislation* (1789), Jeremy Bentham classified forgery along with perjury and personation as offenses by falsehood. "Offenses by falsehood, however diversified in other particulars," he wrote, "have this in common, that they consist in some abuse of the faculty of discourse . . . of influencing the sentiment of belief in other men, whether by discourse or otherwise. The use of discourse is to influence belief, and that in such manner as to give other men to understand that things are as they are really. Falsehoods, of whatever kind they be, agree in this: that they give men to understand that things are otherwise than as in reality they are."[16]

Wholesale skepticism might be appropriate to particular fields of endeavor, but trust is necessary for the orderly conduct of everyday life. So cautioned the barrister Richard Whitcombe in *An Enquiry into Some of the Rules of Evidence, Relating to the Incompetency of Witnesses,* published in 1824. Responding to Bentham and James Mill on the competency of witnesses, Whitcombe wrote:

> In science and all matters of abstract speculation, scepticism and distrust are, perhaps, necessary and natural: in the common transactions of life, they are not merely dangerous impediments, but so widely are they opposed to the natural constitution of the human mind, as very rarely to occur, unless where they are the offspring of a perverse discipline, or of a vicious organization of the judgment. Improbability, and that of a very high degree, is the only rational, indeed the only possible ground, on which the belief of one man is suspended or withheld from the assertion of another.[17]

Novelists in the realist tradition from Fielding onward were, in Alexander Welsh's words, "quick . . . to forge chains of circumstances," that is, to construct stories that inspired trust, but not necessarily for prosecutorial use.[18] Like the "Man of Candor" admitted behind the curtain of nature in Fielding's *Tom Jones,* Trollope is interested in questions of judgment, but in his view good judgment may mean knowing when to leave a misrepresentation intact, the curtain drawn. To that end, he admits a very different purpose for legal and literary discourses, what Ruth apRoberts termed "Situation Aesthetics" to correspond to his Situation Ethics.[19] *Orley Farm*'s forger is female, evoking ancient fears of women's deceitfulness, but Trollope is careful to plot Lady Mason's forgery as the only course of action available to effect a mother's selfless devotion to her son in a social system which severely circumscribes women's agency. Jane Nardin notes that some critics of *Orley Farm* have "display[ed] an interesting unwillingness to admit how limited Lady Mason's freedom of action really is."[20] I would concur with Nardin and apRoberts that the novel is unambiguous on the point of Lady Mason's motives and constraints. Mary Johnson assumes the title Lady Mason when she marries the widower Sir Joseph Mason, who employs her in his household after he has bought out her bankrupt father. Just as Mary's father failed to provide for her, Sir Joseph fails in his will to provide for their son, Lucius, leaving all his property to the son of his first marriage. Caught in a conflict between the duties entailed by her roles and wife and mother, Lady Mason warns the dying Sir Joseph that unless he does his duty toward Lucius she will be forced to forge a codicil bequeathing Orley Farm to him. Significantly, she transcribes the entire will when the attorney's gout prevents him from holding a pen. As wife, she acts as amanuensis. But as mother, she is the author of a forged codicil that provides land—real wealth—for her son.

The opening chapter summarizes the events I have just recounted, describing Lady Mason's guilt, her successful defense against a forgery charge brought by the young Joseph Mason, and the twenty years she has lived a forged identity as a respectable widow. Since Trollope has already involved the reader in the conspiracy with Lady Mason by his sympathetic revelation of her guilt, the plot focuses not on the detection of crime, but instead on the communal act of constructing saving narratives in the law. Lady Mason is brought to trial a second time when new evidence is discovered by a solicitor, Dockwrath, a tenant of Orley Farm with a grudge against Lucius Mason. While the second Joseph Mason may find Dockwrath's vulgarity distasteful, he embraces the project to bring Lady Mason to justice and avenge them both. He regrets only that the Forgery Act of 1837 has robbed him of the pleasure of seeing her hanged.

Counterpoised to the competitive energies of Lady Mason's opponents is Sir Peregrine Orme, an aged standard bearer of fading chivalrous values. James Kincaid comments that Sir Peregrine "dramatizes the passing away of the old and coherent world and its dependence on the final justice of communal instinct."[21] Sir Peregrine declares Mason's action against Lady Mason to be "unmanly," and, acting the gentleman, he offers her marriage. But Sir Peregrine ultimately poses an obstacle to Trollope's version of communal justice in *Orley Farm* almost as dangerous as that of commercially driven individualism or primal vengeance. When Lady Mason confesses her guilt to Sir Peregrine to save his reputation, she devastates him, not simply because she disappoints his desire, but because her forgery and fraudulent self-representation threaten his confidence in the transparency of natural law that rationalizes his own status. His first instinct is to cast out her out, to sacrifice her to his "old and coherent world."

Sir Peregrine's identity is compromised because it is relational to the feminine ideal equally well represented by Lady Mason and his authentically blameless daughter-in-law, Mrs. Orme. Without Lady Mason's confession, the credulous Sir Peregrine would never have detected the difference. Unlike Sir Peregrine, who would have abandoned Lady Mason, Mrs. Orme—a faultless widow and mother, a genuine version of what Lady Mason claims to be—remains loyal to Lady Mason when she has confessed her guilt, reading Lady Mason as Fielding claimed the "Man of Candour" would do. Urging Christian forgiveness, Mrs. Orme views Lady Mason from the perspective of one admitted behind the curtains of the social theater, though she lacks the institutional authority to enforce her merciful judgment.

It is left to Lady Mason's attorney, Mr. Furnival, to accomplish that end. Furnival's decision-making processes demonstrate the ethical and psychological operations by which communal justice is effected in the compromised world of *Orley Farm.* Trollope narrates the evolving lawyer-client relationship as a seduction plot: Lady Mason's strategic shows of dependence and desirability, and Furnival's efforts to rationalize his devotion despite his growing realization of her guilt.[22] Eventually, Furnival is convinced that the woman he has desired for twenty years is not innocent, and Lady Mason perceives his discovery, but not a word is said by either. Their legal relationship depends as much upon this unspoken text as on their unconsummated sexual relationship.

Trollope has Furnival leave the positivistic National Society for the Promotion of Social Science conference in Birmingham to answer Lady Mason's request for his assistance. The imbricated cause he is about to enter points up the distance between the practice of lawyering and the abstractions of rationalistic reform under discussion at Birmingham, where the great Rustums of the British legal system were "inquiring with energy, solemnity, and caution, with much shaking of ponderous heads and many sarcasms from those which were not ponderous, whether any and what changes might be made in the modes of answering that great question, 'Guilty or not guilty?' and that other equally great question, 'Is it meum or is it tuum?'"[23]

Unlike the novel's young idealistic lawyer, Felix Graham, whose rationalistic extremes (he tries, unsuccessfully, to raise up an orphan girl to be his ideal wife) gradually give way with experience, Furnival has never been able to put principles above individuals, and as a result has always been compromised by his personal loyalties. But never before has Furnival been unable to reconcile loyalty with the truth, or more precisely, with a plausible fiction. Over the course of many passages, Trollope details Furnival's self-examination, discontinuous motives, partial goods, and repressed desires. One such passage is worth quoting at length:

> Mr. Furnival again raised his eyes from the papers on the table, and leaning back in his chair, gave himself up to further consideration of the Orley Farm case. Crabwitz he knew was a sharp, clever man, and now the opinion formed by Crabwitz . . . tallied with his own opinion. Yes; it was his own opinion. He had never said as much, even to himself, with those inward words which a man uses when he assures himself of the result of his own thoughts; but he was aware that it was his own opinion. In his heart of hearts, he did believe that that codicil had been fraudulently manufactured by his friend and client, Lady Mason.
>
> How beautiful had she looked while she stood in Sir Peregrine's library, leaning on the old man's arm—how beautiful and how innocent! That was the form which his thoughts chiefly took. And then she had given him her hand, and he still felt the soft silken touch of her cool finger. He would not be a man if he could desert a woman in such a strait. And such a woman! If even guilty, had she not expiated her guilt by deep sorrow? And then he thought of Mr. Mason of Groby Park; and he thought of Sir Peregrine's strong conviction, and of Judge Staveley's belief; and he thought also of the strong hold which public opinion and twenty years of possession would still give to the cause he favoured. He would still bring her through! Yes; in spite of her guilt, if she were guilty; on the strength of her innocency, if she were innocent; but on account of her beauty, and soft hand, and deep liquid eye. So at least he would have owned, could he have been honest enough to tell himself the whole truth. (1: 340–41)

This could serve as a catalogue of the mitigating situational forces that reformers sought to exclude from the law by replacing the authority of tradition and precedent with a positivistic analytical model of law. Kincaid reads such deconstructions of legal decision making as evidence of

Trollope's bleak irony regarding the dissolution of communal life, wherein "rigid principles are . . . now seen to be absurd, floating rules."[24] We may be more inclined to concur that justice is the product of rather more complex processes involving individual desire, public opinion, precedent, and aesthetics, as well as logic and evidence. Ultimately, Furnival comes to rationalize his defense of Lady Mason as loyalty to a friend, not so far removed, perhaps, from the loyalties that preserve an open secret in the Boulton trial, to which I will shortly turn.

The grand jury in *Mason v. Mason* hands down a bill indicting Lady Mason not for forgery but for perjury, suppressing her authorship in favor of the lesser crime of a spoken misrepresentation. At her trial, Furnival and his leader, the barrister Mr. Chaffanbrass—who specializes in defending dubious clients (for example, Phineas Finn)—discredit the eyewitness testimony of the two household servants who witnessed Sir Joseph Mason's will, and present instead a representation of Lady Mason's character that, though it contradicts factual evidence in the case, is consistent with the culture's cover story about gender. "'Look at her!'" Furnival urges the jury.

> "Was she a forger? Was she a woman to deceive the sharp bloodhounds of the law? Could she, with that young baby on her bosom, have wrested from such as him"—and as he spoke he pointed with his finger, but with a look of unutterable scorn, to Joseph Mason, who was sitting opposite to him—"that fragment of his old father's property which he coveted so sorely? Where had she learned such skilled artifice? Gentlemen, such ingenuity in crime as that has never yet been proved in a court of law, even against those who have spent a life of wretchedness in acquiring such skill; and now you are asked to believe that such a deed was done by a young wife, of whom all that you know is that her conduct in every other respect had been beyond all praise!" (2: 329)

Indeed, the entire court is convinced of her guilt—"The judge in this case did his work with admirable skill," Trollope comments, "blowing aside the froth of Mr. Furnival's eloquence, and upsetting the sophistry and false deductions of Mr. Chaffanbrass" (2: 360–62)—and yet she is acquitted. The only injustice that merits the narrator's scorn is the abuse of witnesses by judge, prosecution, and defense, when they alone are by legal definition wholly disinterested bearers of the truth. Trollope makes palatable this account of law as a means of mitigating the pragmatic forgeries required for bourgeois social organization to function by invoking the higher law of conscience, but restricts its action to the private sphere. Mrs. Orme insists that Lady Mason confess her guilt to Lucius, who relinquishes Orley Farm to Joseph Mason. His cold dutifulness to his mother makes for her cruelly appropriate punishment. It likewise authorizes the narrator's persistent sympathy for Lady Mason and demands that his readers, too, remain loyal to the end.

Orley Farm enables us to read between the lines to detect the peculiar literary and legal strategies employed in the Boulton and Park trial, a decade after Trollope's novel. On the night of April 29, 1870, Ernest Boulton and Frederick Park were brought before the Bow Street Police Court on a charge of disturbing the peace.[25] The two men, who performed female roles in amateur theatrical productions, were dressed in women's clothing, described minutely by the constable who took them in charge. While they were in custody, a police surgeon, James Thomas Paul, conducted an unauthorized examination of their bodies for evidence of sodomy. Claiming to have found such evidence, Paul insisted that the prisoners be charged instead with the felony crime of sodomy. As a felony case, it was sent on to the attorney general, who, on the grounds that the physician's examination was unauthorized, charged Boulton and Park, along with six other defendants, not with sodomy but with conspiracy to commit sodomy. What had been a case based on observation and forensic evidence, wherein, to use Ed Cohen's phrase, the body was forced to testify against itself, became a crime of discourse and intention—conspiracy—not a physical act.[26] The surgeon Paul's original deposition was not entered into evidence during the trial; instead, the case was to be tried on largely textual evidence—the thousands of letters exchanged between Boulton and his friends—and called for a peculiarly literary judgment as to probable narratives.

At the request of counsel for the defense, the trial was moved from the Old Bailey to the more rarified Queen's Bench at Westminster Hall. Though the one nobleman named in the indictment, Lord Arthur Clinton, MP, had died before the trial began—probably by his own hand—nevertheless the court also granted the defense request that the case be tried before a special jury, that is, a jury made up of gentlemen, generally reserved for prosecutions against noblemen. The attorney general opened his case with a note of regret that the Crown was compelled to try these well-educated young men of good character. In decidedly sympathetic terms he described their family backgrounds and noted that Mr. Park had been "educated for the profession of the law . . . [and was] now articled to a respectable firm of solicitors." Putting aside his obvious desire to serve as a character witness for the defendants, the attorney general nevertheless charged "that the defendants and other persons mentioned in the Indictment, and also I regret to say other persons whose names have not been discovered, associated together, spoke to and wrote to each other, in such a manner as to indicate that relations subsisted between them such as are only permissible between men and women." He accused the defendants of behaving "with a studied air of effeminacy, powdering their necks, painting their faces, by amatory airs and gestures they endeavored to excite each other's passions, and to make themselves objects of desire to persons of their own class," and also "that they addressed each other in terms of endearment, such as men only address to women and that they wrote to each other in the language of love."

Significantly, the defense agreed with the prosecution's account of the defendants' behavior and language but, like Furnival in his defense of Lady Mason, argued that the prosecution had constructed an implausible narrative from this evidence. They reemphasized the defendants' class status and family backgrounds. Speaking of their talents as female impersonators in theatricals, counsel reminded the jury men of their own days at public school where they had donned female costume in plays. Their behavior was all impersonation, forgery, "a lark." This argument implies that to believe otherwise would threaten to expose the role of the gentleman as the forgery. They went on to discredit the prosecution's main eyewitness, a man who had entertained Boulton and Park at a restaurant, believing them to be women. Under cross-examination, he is reduced to admitting that he had no empirical evidence of their sex, but, tautologically, that he treated them as women because he believed them to be women. Finally, defense counsel accused the attorney general of unpatriotic libel when he suggested that a plague of sodomy was upon the nation. "You will pronounce your Verdict in this case at all events with regard to these facts," the defense concluded, "that London is not cursed with the sins of Sodom, or Westminster tainted with the vices of Gamorrah [*sic*]."

If this were not enough to authorize the jurymen's tacit solidarity with the defendants, in his charge to the jury the Lord Chief Justice Alexander Cockburn construed the medical evidence in a manner favorable to the defense and also instructed the jurors to read the defendants' letters in terms of the values they—judge, jury, and defendants—shared as classically educated gentleman. "The learned, the wise, and the good in every age," argued the Lord Chief Justice, "have come to the belief that the sentiment which undoubtedly Socrates entertained for the youths with whom he delighted to associate was one of a spiritual and ethereal character in which no sensual desire was mired."[27] Whether or not this claim was disingenuous, like the defense counsel's reminder to the jury of their days in public school theatricals, it suggests that the cultural experiences Linda Dowling argues helped to form a positive homosexual identity extended into legal institutions.[28] The defendants were acquitted on the conspiracy charge.

In his fascinating analysis of the Boulton and Park trial as a paradigmatic Victorian scandal, William Cohen rightly emphasizes the ideological role of publicity—the sensational and controversial reporting of the case in the newly powerful mass-circulation press of the 1870s—in the verdict. "While the verdict resulted from the Crown's failure to establish a persuasive link between public persona and private criminality," Cohen argues, "the scandal functioned to the extent that plausible explanations—provisional fictions—could be sustained and proliferated."[29] He accepts Neil Bartlett's interpretation of the Boulton verdict, however, as the jury's refusal to admit that they could read the defendants' language, preferring instead to "silenc[e], not punish . . . , the sodomites."[30] Cohen shrewdly reads evidence of tacit complicity between the press and its audience—both claiming to be horrified by what they crave, the "winking," insinuating methods by which the attorney general presented evidence from the defendants' amorous letters, and even defense counsel's strategic silences as instances of how "tacit precepts of the normative accrete authority."[31] But why should we not read the jury's verdict as a tacit acknowledgement of solidarity with the defendants? Can we be so sure, as Cohen suggests, that the only "in" audience was *outside* the law? What *was* all that winking about—not to mention the hilarity the letters occasioned in the courtroom—if all the legal parties were as ignorant of "drag" and "camp" as they claimed?

Indeed, Cohen might have extended his analysis of privacy and publicity in the sex scandal to the debates over judicial reform in the 1870s. He remarks on the "scandal's counterhegemonic potential: protogay men and would-be transvestites, otherwise ignorant of their brethren's existence, might discover in the news reports [of the Boulton trial] positive lessons about the coded language the defendants used, the places they consorted, and the ways they behaved."[32] But he also notes that the strategies used to defend Boulton and others would be rendered tragically ineffectual in the following decades, through the Dublin Castle affair (1884), the Cleveland

Street scandal (1889–90), and finally the Wilde trial of 1895. One reason for this is the victory scored against legal fictions as rival to statute law.

In his *Handbook of Forensic Medicine,* a frequently cited authority in English medical jurisprudence translated from German in 1861–64, Johann Ludwig Casper wrote the following about sodomites: "In all the large towns of Europe this vice glides about enshrouded in darkness, impenetrable to *the uninitiated;* but there seems to be no inhabited spot where it is not to be found. Unknown to the uninitiated, I say, for even in ancient times the brotherhood had their private means of recognition . . . These men *recognise one another*, and are even at this day found in *all* classes of society without exception." He cites as his authority the claim of such a man that "'We discover each other at once . . . at a single glance, and by exercising a little caution, I have never been deceived. Upon the Righi, at Palermo, in the Louvre, in the Highlands of Scotland, in St. Petersburg, on landing at Barcelona I observed parties who I had never before seen, and whom I recognised in a second.'" Casper continues, "But this kind of subjective diagnosis has no existence for the physician or the Judge."[33]

Casper deftly narrates a position within two solidarities, one in which an extensive community is represented to itself, and another, in which his profession authorizes a cover story, dismissing from medical and legal consideration such subjective diagnoses. Like Trollope, who withholds his characters' subjectivities from fact-finding and discovery by ungentlemanly, vengeful eyes, the judge and attorneys on both sides of *R. v. Boulton* rejected the evidence of the police surgeon as "unauthorized." Historians of sexuality have argued that the transition from antisodomy legislation to gross indecency should not be interpreted as a sign of growing toleration for homosexual behavior, but rather as a shift in disciplinary strategies along a continuum from sanction to surveillance.[34] Undeniably, the Labouchère amendment made not only cultural but economic currency out of spying on men: shortly after its passage in 1885 it came to be known as the blackmailer's charter. But it is easy to overlook evidence that Victorian institutions did not move inevitably and unanimously toward ever more efficient forms of discipline, and that classes of defendants were caught up with jurists and jurymen in the battles over legal fictions precisely because those fictions had proven successful. To symbolize the triumph of positivistic legal reforms, the newly unitary High Court moved in 1882 from its quarters in Westminster Hall, where Boulton and Park were tried, to its new buildings on the Strand, where Wilde's case was heard, cheek by jowl with the newspaper offices in Fleet Street.

Having decriminalized sexual relationships between consenting male adults in 1967, almost a century after Boulton and Park, Parliament in 2000 refused to bring the consenting age for homosexuals in line with that for heterosexuals. As a consequence of the adoption of the European Union's bill of rights, the British courts are likely to see a wave of suits brought for discrimination on the basis of sexual orientation, affording new opportunities for activist jurisprudence to do what Parliament has proven unwilling to do. When legal theorists of our own day urge us back to the future, to restore narrative evidence to legal decision making on behalf of outsiders, we may well inquire which Victorian past they would have in mind: Dickens's or Trollope's? My sense is that Professor Goldstein, defending other "Mary Charmichaels," would opt for Trollope.

Conclusion

Conflating the titles of two superb detective novels, Umberto Eco's *The Name of the Rose* and Dorothy Sayers's *Gaudy Night,* Teresa de Lauretis titled the chapter of *Technologies of Gender* dealing with gendered epistemology "Gaudy Rose."[35] De Lauretis returns us to the figure of the witch—where this study began—to argue that until feminist epistemology succeeds in deconstructing masculinist norms and categories of knowing, women's knowledge will remain both incomprehensible to and demonized within male-dominated social and political systems. The screams of the woman burned as a witch in *The Name of the Rose* are gibberish to Eco's monkish narrator, just as her testimony was to the Inquisitor who condemned her. A native peasant, she literally does not speak the language of the cosmopolitan male elite. For de Lauretis, this condition and the violence it enables are paradigmatic of the condition of feminist advocacy under the reign of masculine power. *Gaudy Night,* a novel of female-perpetrated crime against other women, and accessible only to detection informed by women's knowledge, offers an alternative paradigm in de Lauretis's view. Set in a fictionalized version of Oxford's first women's college, *Gaudy Night* presents a double argument for feminist epistemology, both arguing for women's education and presenting a mystery that can be solved only if men take seriously women's knowledge of family life. Significantly, the female dons who have embraced masculinist disciplinary knowledge have cut themselves off from such knowledge, even when it is the subject of their scholarly inquiries. They fail to perceive that a woman in their midst—a menial "scout," the widow of a scholar, who seeks revenge for her husband's suicide after his exposure for falsifying scholarly evidence—is the nemesis threatening their fragile hold on intellectual recognition. Only a male detective working in league with a female detective can discover the truth. And even Harriet Vane, Sayers's fictionalized alter ego—who, as a detective novelist, brings scholarly and narrative expertise, as well as experience of female desire, to bear on solving the problem of her alma mater's poltergeist—cannot comprehend alone what the disinterested Lord Peter Wimsey finally brings to light. Wimsey does a better job of thinking as a woman than do women under patriarchy. De Lauretis's target is empiricism itself, insofar as the process of detection is governed by a gender-biased construction of what counts as evidence. Unlike Elizabeth Gaskell, who in *Lois the Witch* insisted upon forensic evidence as the transparent testimony of women's persecution, de Lauretis would have us acknowledge forensic evidence as one more technology by which violence against women is rationalized. The principal weapon against these technologies, as de Lauretis sees it, is a distinctively literary, specifically deconstructive strategy of reading and representation.

De Lauretis's argument is representative of much subsequent feminist criticism, including feminist criticism of law. It is a particularly apt argument to recall at the conclusion of *Reading for the Law* because it reminds us of the persistence of the witchcraft trial as historical trauma and because it is a compelling critique of the structures of power and discourse that rendered tragic so much feminist advocacy I have treated throughout this study. Nevertheless, it is also representative of a genre of argument pitting narrative against legal reasoning on behalf of women against which literary and legal history affords so many counterexamples.

Gender advocacy, like other forms of advocacy aimed at ensuring equitable treatment for alternative rationalities, must be carried out on multiple fronts, employing diverse means. Victorian legal and literary history demonstrates that this practice is not merely strategic, but inescapable. As I have argued, Victorian literature appeals to narrative jurisprudence not because of its superior empathic or emancipatory potential, but because it is so thoroughly embedded in law, history, journalism, economics, forensic science, political activism, all of which contribute to the formation of democratic structures of social organization. Law and literature is limited insofar as it is constituted as an interdiscipline, rather than a multidisciplinary practice attentive to the synergies among a wide range of cultural practices.

Julie Stone Peters, in a critique of law and literature, likens the interdiscipline to a hall of mirrors, paradoxically "exaggerat[ing] disciplinarity, caricaturing disciplinary difference through each discipline's longing for something it imagined the other to possess."[36] By contrast, a multidisciplinary account of gender advocacy calls for cooperative and mutually critical difference, aimed at progressive goals, but not assuming that any one discipline, be it law or literature, has superpowers. *Reading for the Law* does not insist on the dissolution of disciplines, but rather the common ground of reading underlying the differentiation of reading skills. It is, perhaps, understandable that my practice should arise out of engagements with the nineteenth century, since, as Andrew Elfenbein has recently outlined, it is in the nineteenth century that differentiated professions first give rise to claims of differentiated reading skills.[37] If, in the words of Percy Shelley so often invoked by narrative legal theorists, "poets are the unacknowledged legislators of mankind," so too are ordinary defendants and witnesses, social activists, third-rate novelists, unsung jurors, antiquarians, newspaper writers, asylum inmates, and a host of others. To read for the law is also to read literature, history, science, economics, aesthetics, newspapers and blue books, ballads and arias, speeches and sermons. I am confident that this practice will not, in A. V. Dicey's words, "tend . . . to quench the confident enthusiasm necessary for carrying out even the most well approved and the most beneficial among democratic innovations." Rather, it is an innovative practice of democratic teaching and scholarship.

Notes

Abbreviations

PRO ASSI	Public Records Office, London, Assizes
PRO KB	Public Records Office, London, Kings Bench
PRO MH	Public Records Office, London, Mental Health

Introduction

1. For a contrasting view of the interdiscipline as a codependency relationship between lawyers seeking to escape dehumanization and literary critics seeking relevance, see Peters, "Law, Literature," 448.

2. See, for example, Balkin and Levinson, "Law as Performance," and Weisberg, "Literature's Twenty-Year Crossing."

3. West, *Narrative, Authority, and Law,* 21.

4. Coombe, "Contingent Articulations," 64.

5. Welsh, *Strong Representations,* and Bourdieu, *Language and Symbolic Power.*

6. Z. Eisenstein, *Female Body,* 187.

7. Poovey, *Social Body,* 74.

8. Habermas, *Inclusion of the Other,* 208.

9. Dicey, *Lectures,* 461.

10. S. R. Maitland to Dicey, fall 1896, Gen MS 508(14), Glasgow University Library, quoted in Cosgrove, *Rule of Law,* 177. Dicey's quarrel with Maitland over the utility of legal history is recounted in Cosgrove, *Rule of Law,* 176–79. For a discussion of constitutional narrative and historical agency, see Vernon, *Politics and the People,* 295–98. In *Public Moralists,* Stefan Collini remarks of Dicey's *An Introduction to the Study of the Law of the Constitution* (London: Macmillan, 1885) that it "managed to make the ordinary operations of the common law central to the characterization of the distinctive identity of the English nation. In so doing, [Dicey] achieved the improbable fusion of the Whig interpretation of English his-

tory, the Austinian analysis of law, and the Individualist conception of the state, the whole amalgam presented as the dispassionate conclusion of academic legal science" (287).

11. Baron makes this point cogently in "Interdisciplinary Legal Scholarship."

12. Binder and Weisberg, *Literary Criticisms,* 539.

13. Habermas uses this term to describe the meta-legal motivation of "constitutional patriotism," whereby citizens of various cultural and ethnic origins give loyalty to a constitutional state, recognizing that as an entity dependent upon their actions and behaviors, it is the product of their corporate history ("Reply," 398). For a discussion of the decline of jurists as social commentators in Britain from its apogee in the nineteenth century, see Cosgrove, *Scholars of the Law,* 4–11, 211–12.

14. In *Overcoming Law,* Posner writes, "Emotion can clarify as well as fog understanding. If, for example, an advocate's appeal to the emotions induces in the judge or juror an empathetic understanding of a victim's or an accused wrongdoer's motives, drives, and beliefs, the appeal may enable the tribunal to form a more accurate impression of essential facts and so render a more just judgment" (511).

15. Nussbaum, *Poetic Justice,* xvi. Nussbaum dedicates this book to her "intellectual adversary," Richard A. Posner, "who was in many ways [the first Rosenthal] lecture's Mr Gradgrind" (xi).

16. See, for example, Weisberg, *Poethics,* 143–87, and *Vichy Law.*

17. Binder and Weisberg, *Literary Criticisms,* 539.

18. Binder and Weisberg's examples might best be classified as cultural history and sociology after the linguistic turn. Examples included Halley, "Equivocation"; Clifford, *Predicament of Culture;* W. Miller, *Bloodtaking and Peacemaking;* and Polanyi, *Great Transformation.*

19. For a recent discussion of origins of cultural criticism, especially its relationship to nineteenth-century literary and historical studies, see Kucich and Sadoff's introduction to a special issue of *Nineteenth-Century Contexts* on Postmodern Victorians.

20. Binder and Weisberg, *Literary Criticisms,* 477–79.

21. Binder and Weisberg follow George E. Marcus and Michael M. J. Fischer in identifying these forms of twentieth-century cultural criticism in *Anthropology as Cultural Critique,* 538–39.

22. Binder and Weisberg base their version of literary Romanticism largely on M. H. Abram's *The Mirror and the Lamp: Romantic Theory and the Critical Tradition* (New York: Oxford University Press, 1953), through which they emphasize its "expressive" and "subjective" qualities, and Raymond Williams's *Marxism and Literature* (Oxford: Oxford University Press, 1977), from which they take an account of the emergence of literature as a category separated from letters on the grounds of its claims to transcendent values. A rather different sense of Romanticism emerges from the work of later scholars influenced by Williams, including Gilmartin, *Print Politics,* and D. Simpson, *Romanticism,* or by feminist theory, such as Mellor, *Romanticism and Gender.*

23. Binder and Weisberg, *Literary Criticisms,* 7–16.

24. In "Victorian Narrative Jurisprudence," I offer a critique of the ahistoricism of narrative legal scholarship. For an excellent formulation of narrative ethics, drawing on the philosophies of intersubjectivity of Emanuel Levinas, Stanley Cavel, and Jürgen Habermas, see A. Newton, *Narrative Ethics.*

25. Habermas, *Structural Transformation.*

26. See, for example, McGowan, "Modernity and Culture."

27. Ferguson, *Law and Letters;* B. Thomas, *Cross-examinations;* and *American Literary Realism;* Dimock, *Residues of Justice;* and Korobkin, *Criminal Conversations.*

28. Welsh, *Strong Representations;* Polloczek, *Literature and Legal Discourse;* Dolin, *Fiction and the Law;* and Leckie, *Culture and Adultery.*

29. Examples of such criticism must begin with Ian Watt's *The Rise of the Novel,* wherein Watt tied "formal realism" to the rise of the middle class. Watt's materialist analysis has been extended through Foucault's *Survellier et punir* (1975; *Discipline and Punish: The Birth of The Prison,* 1977) by, among others, Bender, *Imagining the Penitentiary;* Armstrong, *Desire and Domestic Fiction;* and D. A. Miller, *Novel and the Police.* See also the essays in Armstrong and Tennenhouse, *Violence of Representation.*

30. Brooks, "Storytelling without Fear," 114–34.

31. Walkowitz, *City of Dreadful Delight,* 20.

32. See, for example, Douzinas and Warrington, *Postmodern Jurisprudence.* For evidence of the growing skepticism regarding the political viability of narrative by two leading advocates of narrative jurisprudence, see Delgado and Stefancic, *Failed Revolutions.*

33. Simpson is speaking specifically of the continuities of deployments of history and theory between the 1790s in England and 1990s America (*Romanticism,* 16). I trust I do not violate the spirit of his astute observation.

34. Dolin, *Fiction and the Law,* 10.

35. Recent examples of scholarship pushing the origins of the Habermasian public sphere into early periods include Raymond, "Newspaper, Public Opinion," and Lake, "Deeds against Nature."

36. Abrams, "Hearing the Call."

37. Roscoe, *Observations,* n.p.

38. McGowen, "Punishing Violence," 142.

39. Joyce, "Constitution and the Narrative," 187–88.

40. McKeon, *Origins,* 20.

41. Weisberg, *Poethics,* 35.

42. Rorty, *Contingency,* xvi.

43. Nussbaum, *Poetic Justice,* xvi.

44. Examples of feminist narrative scholarship include Abrams, "Narrative and the Normative"; Heilbrun and Resnik, "Convergences"; Resnik, "Feminism and the Language"; and Minow, *Not Only for Myself.* For examples of Critical Race theorists,

see Bell, *Faces;* Williams, *Alchemy of Race;* and Delgado and Stefancic, *Failed Revolutions.* For discussions of nineteenth-century working-class writers, see Webb, *British Working Class Reader;* Vicinus, *Industrial Muse;* and Vincent, *Literacy and Popular Culture.* Women writers of nineteenth-century social discourse are discussed in Kestner, *Protest and Reform;* J. Newton, *Women;* and Krueger, *Reader's Repentance.*

45. Carlyle, *Chartism,* 26.

46. Friedman, "Law, Lawyers," 1584.

47. Clover, "Law and the Order," 97–98.

48. Alexis de Tocqueville, *Democracy in America,* 2 vols. (New York: Vintage, 1990), 2: 280, quoted in Clover, "Law and the Order," 101.

49. Wahrman, "Public Opinion," 113–14. Wahrman traces the rise of a trans-class discourse of public opinion to the sentiment aroused on behalf of Queen Caroline when George IV brought an adultery suit against her in 1820. In the case of the Tichborne claimant, one Arthur Orton claimed to be the long-lost Sir Roger Tichborne. Working-class people figured prominently in the popular support for Orton, who was nonetheless exposed in two celebrated trials between 1871 and 1874. The Tichborne cause grew into a full-scale media event, with Tichborne newpapers, pamphlets, and the founding of the Magna Charta Association to defend Orton's claim. For a detailed discussion of this case, see McWilliam, *Tichborne Claimant.* Walkowitz treats W. T. Stead's "Maiden Tribute of Modern Babylon" and the Armstrong case in *City of Dreadful Delight,* 121–34.

50. Hay, "Prosecution and Power," 394.

51. Vicinus, *Industrial Muse,* 2.

52. Coombe, "Contingent Articulations," 64.

53. Habermas, "Reply," 398.

CHAPTER ONE. Historiographies of Witchcraft for Feminist Advocacy

1. On eighteenth- and nineteenth-century historical fiction by women, see Doody, "George Eliot." For a discussion of Gaskell as a writer of historical fiction, see Krueger, "'Female Paternalist.'"

2. James Sharpe, *Instruments of Darkness,* 173.

3. Rosenthal, *Salem Story,* 7, 8.

4. Krueger, "'Female Paternalist.'"

5. Uglow, *Elizabeth Gaskell,* 476.

6. Ennemoser, *History of Magic,* 1: v.

7. See Uglow, *Elizabeth Gaskell,* 216–18.

8. Gaskell, *Lois the Witch,* 175. Page references hereafter will be given in the text.

9. See, for example, Cornell, "Toward a Modern/Postmodern Reconstruction" and *Feminism as Critique;* Unger, *Knowledge and Politics,* 232.

10. Levine, *Realistic Imagination,* 8, 21.

11. See, for example, Gallagher, *Industrial Reformation,* and McKeon, *Origins.*

12. Orwell, *Homage to Catalonia,* xi, 241.

13. See Daly, "Witches Return"; Hester, *Lewd Women.*

14. Purkiss, *Witch in History,* 10.

15. Coombe, "Contingent Articulations," 57–58.

16. Klein, "Emergence of Memory," 145.

17. Cohn, Foreword, ix.

18. See Sharpe, *Instruments of Darkness,* 176, and Holmes, "Women: Witnesses."

19. Barstow, "On Studying Witchcraft."

20. Willis, *Malevolent Nurture,* 241–42.

21. Larner, *Witchcraft and Religion,* 80.

22. J. Scott, *Gender,* 211. Page references hereafter will be given in the text.

23. Quoted in J. Scott, *Gender,* 215.

24. Larner, *Witchcraft and Religion,* 91.

25. See, for example, Weisberg, *Vichy Law.*

26. For an exposition of this phenomenon, see Bonnie Smith, *Gender of History.*

27. Murray, *God of the Witches.*

28. Kerwin Lee Klein similarly cautions academic practitioners of memory discourse in "Emergence of Memory."

29. Michelet, *La Sorcière,* 37.

30. Ginzburg, "Checking the Evidence," 294–95.

31. Sharpe, *Instruments of Darkness,* 7–9.

32. Ibid., 9.

33. Gage, *Women, Church, and State,* 247.

34. Sharpe, *Instruments of Darkness,* 106.

35. Sharpe notes that before 1645 even Home Circuit records are hardly complete, estimating that a quarter are missing (ibid., 107).

36. See Herrup, *Common Peace,* and Ewen, *Witch Hunting.*

37. See Dolan, *Dangerous Familiars,* 171–236, and Sharpe, *Instruments of Darkness,* 106–7.

38. Sharpe cites Larner's work as the methodological model for future investigations of English witchcraft prosecution (*Instruments of Darkness,* 12, 32).

39. Even a basic chronology of the statutes criminalizing witchcraft can be misleading. Ewen documents earlier examples of witchcraft noticed in secular and ecclesiastical courts in England as early as the seventh century (*Witch Hunting,* 1–12), and Owen Davies traces the persistence of legal interest in witchcraft into the twentieth century in *Witchcraft, Magic and Culture.*

40. For estimates of witchcraft executions in Europe, see Sharpe, *Instruments of Darkness,* 5; for England, see C. L'Estrange Ewen, quoted in K. Thomas, *Religion and the Decline,* 451–52.

41. K. Thomas, *Religion and the Decline,* 451–52.

42. Shapiro, *Culture of Fact,* 165, 168.

43. Jackson, "Narrative Theories," 30.

44. Davies, "Newspapers."

45. Green, *Crisis of Truth.*

46. de Lauretis, *Technologies of Gender,* 54–57.

CHAPTER TWO. Witchcraft Precedents as Literary History

1. Pollock and Maitland, *History of English Law,* 2: 556.

2. E. Eisenstein, *Printing Press,* 1: 76.

3. Shapiro, *Culture of Fact,* 210.

4. Herrup, *Common Peace,* 70.

5. Ibid., 68.

6. For evidence that juries resisted judges' counsel, in favor of both acquittal and conviction, see Holmes, "Popular Culture," 87–89. Brian P. Levack cites trial by jury as one of the reasons for the "relative mildness of British witch-hunting" (*Witch-hunt,* 184).

7. Levy, "How Information Spread," 13.

8. See Holmes, "County Community," and Levy, "How Information Spread."

9. Sharpe, "'Last Dying Speeches,'" 147.

10. Quoted in Sharpe, *Instruments of Darkness,* 160.

11. Henry Peacham, *The Worth of a Penny* (London, 1641), sig. D1, quoted in T. Watt, *Cheap Print,* 11.

12. S. Clark, *Elizabethan Pamphleteers,* 108.

13. Ibid., 110.

14. Davies, *Witchcraft,* 122.

15. S. Clark, *Elizabethan Pamphleteers,* 22.

16. Holmes, "County Community," 59–60.

17. Wiltenburg cites the fact that ballads and cheap pamphlets were preserved by "elite" collectors as evidence of their dissemination across class lines (*Disorderly Women,* 30).

18. Dolan, *Dangerous Familiars,* 85–86.

19. Davies, *Witchcraft,* 61.

20. Holmes, "Popular Culture," 89, 100, 101.

21. Wiltenburg, *Disorderly Women,* 39.

22. *Examination and Confession,* in Rosen, *Witchcraft in England,* 72–82. Page references hereafter will be given in the text.

23. Sharpe, "'Last Dying Speeches,'" 162, 157–58.

24. See Rodrick, "'Only a Newspaper Metaphor,'" 2–3.

25. Johns, *Nature of the Book,* 630.

26. Sharpe, *Instruments of Darkness,* 50.

27. Scot, *Discoverie of Witchcraft,* B.v. Section and page references hereafter will be given in the text.

28. Sharpe, "Women, Witchcraft," 112–13.

29. Holmes, "Women: Witnesses."

30. Rosen, *Witchcraft in England,* 57.

31. Sharpe, *Instruments of Darkness,* 48–49.

32. Dolan, *Dangerous Familiars,* 210–11.

33. See Braunmuller, Introduction to *Macbeth.*

34. Dolan, *Dangerous Familiars,* 217.

35. Shapiro, *Culture of Fact,* 58, and chapter 3.

36. Bernard, *Guide,* 1–11. Page references hereafter will be given in the text.

37. Sharpe, "Women, Witchcraft," 111.

38. Holmes, "Popular Culture."

39. Sharpe notes that female examiners had been used in ecclesiastical courts to verify charges of impotency in annulment proceedings and were appointed to detect evidence of rape and incest, as well as pregnancy in female convicts pleading their bellies ("Women, Witchcraft," 112).

40. Notestein, *History of Witchcraft,* 154–55.

41. K. Thomas, *Religion and the Decline,* 451–52.

42. N. Smith, *Literature and Revolution,* 23–24.

43. Joad Raymond lists Elizabeth Alsop, Mary Constable, Jane Coe, and Sarah Griffin, as active printers in this period (*Invention of the Newspaper,* 250).

44. Johns, *Nature of the Book,* 78.

45. Ibid., 413–14, 418.

46. Hunter, *Before Novels,* 198.

47. K. Thomas, *Religion and the Decline,* 451–52.

48. Hopkins, *Discovery of Witches;* Holmes, "Women: Witnesses," 71.

49. Sharpe, "Women, Witchcraft," 110.

50. Bostridge, *Witchcraft and Its Transformations,* 13–14, 21.

51. Ibid., 23.

52. Ady, *Candle in the Dark,* sig. A3. Page references hereafter will be given in the text.

53. Holdsworth, *Historians of Anglo-American Law,* 52.

54. Gage, *Woman, Church and State,* 276.

55. Bostridge, *Witchcraft and Its Transformations,* 65.

56. Johns, *Nature of the Book,* 415.

57. Quoted in K. Thomas, *Religion and the Decline,* 462.

CHAPTER THREE. The Historical Turn in Witchcraft Literature

1. Hutchinson, *Historical Essay,* 60–61. Page references hereafter will be given in the text.

2. Pollock and Maitland, *History of English Law,* 2: 556.

3. Quoted in K. Thomas, *Religion and the Decline,* 459.

4. Clery, *Rise of Supernatural Fiction.*

5. Davies, *Witchcraft,* 10.

6. Blackstone, *Commentaries on the Laws,* 4: 60.

7. Davies, *Witchcraft,* 8.

8. Clery, *Rise of Supernatural Fiction,* 18–19.

9. For a discussion of Godwin's intense interest in history, but his devotion to political writing, see Marshall, *William Godwin,* 35–38.

10. Godwin, *Lives of the Necromancers,* v. Page references hereafter will be given in the text.

11. W. Howitt, *Popular History of Priestcraft,* 175.

12. M. Howitt, *Popular History of the United States,* 2: 352.

13. Linton, *Witch-Stories,* 182.

14. Quoted in Helsinger, Sheets, and Veeder, *Woman Question,* 2: 209.

15. For a discussion of this incident and an examination of witchcraft in Scott's novels, see Parsons, *Witchcraft and Demonology.*

16. Ibid., 140–44.

17. Kerr, *Fiction against History,* 8.

18. W. Scott, *Letters on Demonology,* 224. Page references hereafter will be given in the text.

19. Foss, *Judges of England,* 7: 105, 108.

20. The anonymous author of *Law and Lawyers,* who noted that Hale's Victorian reputation was principally as an author, described him as a "friend of moderation in religion and politics." This writer applies a relativistic analysis to Hale's role in a witchcraft conviction, complaining that Hale should not be condemned because "he was not superior to his age in discrediting the existence of posers in those days generally believed; which were recognized by laws not repealed for seventy years afterwards; to which Lord Bacon and Addison have added the suffrage of their opinions; which have been asserted also by Dr Johnson and Sir William Blackstone; and which his friend, Baxter, wrote a book expressly to defend" (1: 305).

21. Campbell, *Lives,* 1: 170–71.

22. Welsby, *Lives,* 16–17.

23. Ritso, *Introduction,* 37–38.

24. Mill, *Essays on Equality,* 30.

25. Phillimore, *History and Principles,* 260–61.

26. Ryan, *Manual of Medical Jurisprudence,* 127.

27. J. G. Smith, *Analysis of Medical Evidence,* 197.

28. Mackay, *Memoirs,* xv.

29. Ibid., xvi.

CHAPTER FOUR. Theories and Histories of Agency

1. See Rhode, *Justice and Gender.* For a discussion of the history of reasonable person and reasonable woman standards of proof in American jurisprudence, see Unikel, "'Reasonable' Doubts."

2. For a defense of a reasonable woman standard of proof, see Lahey, "Reasonable Women."

3. See, for example, MacKinnon, *Sexual Harassment,* and Ehrenreich, "Pluralist Myths."

4. For a critique of alternatives to a universalized standard of reasonable proof, see Kelman, "Reasonable Evidence."

5. Habermas, *Inclusion of the Other,* 208.

6. Habermas, *Between Facts and Norms,* 421.

7. Habermas, *Inclusion of the Other,* 209.

8. Ibid.

9. See Habermas, *Structural Transformation.*

10. Bourdieu, *Language and Symbolic Power,* 111.

11. West, *Narrative,* 21.

12. West, "Relativism," 1483.

13. West, *Narrative,* 19–20.

14. Ibid., 22.

15. Pateman, *Sexual Contract;* Horkheimer and Adorno, *Dialectic of Enlightenment.*

16. Habermas, *Structural Transformation,* 160–61.

17. Cvetkovich, *Mixed Feelings,* 25. For an extended treatment of sentimental fiction as a form of disciplinary ideology, see Armstrong, *Desire and Domestic Fiction.*

18. Barker-Benfield, *Culture of Sensibility,* 95.

19. See, for example, D. Simpson, *Romanticism,* 106–7.

20. Mary Wollstonecraft, *The Female Reader; or Miscellaneous Pieces in Prose and Verse; Selected from the Best Writers; and Disposed under Proper Heads; for the Improvement of Young Women* (London: J. Johnson, 1789), quoted in D. Simpson, *Romanticism,* 107.

21. Conger, *Mary Wollstonecraft,* 175–76.

22. Ibid., 106.

23. Poovey, *Proper Lady,* 105.

24. See Johnson, *Equivocal Beings.*

25. Shawn Lisa Maurer succinctly makes the point that "rational as they might be, Maria's 'feelings' can find no place in a legal system that classifies a wife as her husband's property" ("Female (as) Reader," 47).

26. Marquis d'Argens, cited in Aram Vartanian, *Diderot and Descartes* (Princeton, NJ: Princeton University Press, 1952), 31, quoted in D. Simpson, *Romanticism,* 111. See also Maurer, "Female (as) Reader," 36–54.

27. James MacKintosh, *A Discourse on the Study of the Law of Nature and Nations* (London: 1799), quoted in D. Simpson, *Romanticism,* 138.

28. D. Simpson, *Romanticism,* 120, 137.

29. Godwin, *Caleb Williams,* 1.

30. Wang, "Other Reasons," 143.

31. Ibid., 133–34.

32. Ernesto Laclau and Chantal Mouffe, *Hegemony and Socialist Strategy: Towards a Radical Democratic Politics* (London: Verso, 1985), 154, quoted in Wang, "Other Reasons," 132.

33. Choi, "Feminine Authority," 649.

34. Ibid., 658.

35. Wollstonecraft, *Wrongs of Woman,* 74. Page references hereafter will be given in the text.

36. In *Family Fictions,* Christopher Flint remarks that Wollstonecraft's skepticism about the effects of her political instruction is underscored by Maria's addressing her memoirs to her infant, "a pre-verbal figure who represents latent political understanding" (302).

37. *Trials for Adultery; or, The History of Divorces* (London: S. Bladon, 1779–80).

38. Belcher, *Address to Humanity,* advertisement. Belcher published essays on religion, politics, metaphysics, and science. On the title page of *Intellectual Electricity* (London: Lee and Hurst, 1798), Belcher termed himself a "Rational Mystic."

39. Conger, *Language of Sensibility,* 198.

40. Staves, *Married Women's Separate Property,* 226.

41. For a discussion of the impact of seditious libel trials on radical discourse, see Gilmartin, *Print Politics,* 115–19.

42. Mellor, *Mothers of the Nation,* 86–87.

43. Ibid., 99–102.

44. West, *Caring for Justice,* 37.

45. Ibid., 217.

46. For a discussion of the connections between various forms of "civil death" in Victorian feminist argument, see Shanley, *Feminism, Marriage, and the Law,* 9–10.

47. Staves, *Married Women's Separate Property,* 221.

CHAPTER FIVE. Agency, Equity, Publicity

1. Unikel, "'Reasonable' Doubts," 327.

2. William Jones, *An Essay on the Law of Bailments* (London: J. Nichols, 1781), quoted in Unikel, "'Reasonable' Doubts," 330, n. 35.

3. Rodensky, *Crime in Mind.*

4. Smith, *Trial By Medicine,* 67.

5. Rowbotham and Stevenson, "Causing a Sensation," 45.

6. Ratcliffe elaborates this theory in *Rhetorical Listening.*

7. McCandless, "Liberty and Lunacy," 368. On the Tichborne Claimant scandal, see McWilliam, *Tichborne Claimant.* On adultery in Victorian novels and newspapers, see Leckie, *Culture and Adultery.*

8. K. Jones, *Lunacy,* 221–22.

9. Polloczek, *Literature and Legal Discourse,* 17–18.

10. Parry-Jones, *Trade in Lunacy* 69.

11. Holcombe, "Victorian Wives," 7.

12. Dicey, *Lectures,* 376.

13. Defoe, *Review of the State,* 327, 353–56.

14. Parry-Jones, *Trade in Lunacy,* 9.

15. Quoted in K. Jones, *Lunacy,* 32.

16. Ibid., 35.

17. For the repercussions of George III's madness, see Byrd, *Visits to Bedlam,* 120–21, and K. Jones, *Lunacy,* 41–42.

18. K. Jones, *Lunacy,* 111.

19. Quoted in McCandless, "Liberty and Lunacy," 368.

20. Ibid., 368.

21. Winslow, "On Medico-Legal Evidence," 111.

22. Ibid., 105.

23. Mellett, "Bureaucracy and Mental Illness," 222. See also K. Jones, *Lunacy,* and Parry-Jones, *Trade in Lunacy,* for detailed accounts of lunacy law reforms and the roles played by inspectors, doctors, and the press.

24. K. Jones, *Lunacy,* 223.

25. Mellet, "Bureaucracy and Mental Illness," 235.

26. See Byrd, *Visits to Bedlam.*

27. Porter, *Social History of Madness,* 118.

28. See Gagnier, *Subjectivities.*

29. K. J. M. Smith, *James Fitzjames Stephen,* 16–18, 47.

30. Sutherland, *Victorian Fiction,* 80.

31. Burns, *Charles Reade,* 203.

32. Reade, "Our Dark Places," in *Readiana,* 114. Page references hereafter will be given in the text.

33. Reade, *Hard Cash,* 2: 289. Page references hereafter will be given in the text.

34. George Orwell, quoted in Burns, *Charles Reade,* 53.

35. Lytton, *Blighted Life,* 75.

36. Ibid., 42.

37. Ibid., 78.

38. Lowe, *Bastilles of England,* 75.

39. Bourdieu, *Language and Symbolic Power,* 111.

CHAPTER SIX. Gendered Credibility

1. Goodwin, "'Final Struggle.'"

2. Heilbrun and Resnick, "Convergences."

3. Peake, *Compendium,* 81.

4. Allen, *Law of Evidence,* 183.

5. Poovey, *Uneven Developments,* 63.

6. Harris, *Harris' Hints*, 76, 74.

7. Schramm, *Testimony and Advocacy.*

8. Leckie, *Culture and Adultery;* Korobkin, *Criminal Conversations.*

9. Page references to these novels will be given in the text.

10. Gérin, *Elizabeth Gaskell*, 261.

11. When Elizabeth Gaskell heard the rumor that *Adam Bede*, which she had praised in a letter to "Gilbert Eliot," had been written by Marian Evans, she wrote to George Smith: "It is a noble grand book, whoever wrote it,—but Miss Evans' life taken at the best construction, does so jar against the beautiful book that one cannot help hoping against hope. But two people have directly assured me they have seen the assertion of her authorship in her own handwriting . . . Oh do say Miss Evans did *not* write it—" (August 4 [1859], *Letters*, 566–67). For examples of Eliot's ostracism from her family and society, see Uglow, *George Eliot*, 69–70, 144–145, and Haight, *George Eliot*, 231–33, 336–37, 393–95.

12. Burton, *Barbara Bodichon*, 65.

13. P. Johnson, *Hidden Hands.*

14. Catherine Gallagher interprets the "feminization" of working-class characters as a way of ensuring their dependence in a paternalistic view of social reform (*Industrial Reformation*, 128–29).

15. Gaskell to Miss Lamont, January 5, [1849] (*Letters*, 39).

16. In this exchange Gaskell upsets the hierarchy between confessor and the confessing described by Michel Foucault in *The History of Sexuality*, 1: 61–62.

17. Gaskell, *Sylvia's Lovers*, 443–44.

18. Schramm, *Testimony and Advocacy.*

19. Conley, "Rape and Justice," 523.

20. E. Cohen, *Talk on the Wilde Side*, 188.

21. Conley, "Rape and Justice," 536.

22. Sedgwick, *Between Men*, 89.

23. Dellamora, *Masculine Desire*, 195.

24. Sindall, "Middle-Class Crime," 24.

25. Ibid., 28.

26. A. Simpson, "Vulnerability," 198.

CHAPTER SEVEN. Women's Legal Literacy and *Pro Se* Representation

1. Friedman, "Law, Lawyers," 1584.

2. Clover, "Law and the Order," 104.

3. Two of the founding works of the Law and Literature movement—James Boyd White's *Justice as Translation* and Richard Weisberg's *Poethics*—relied exclusively on canonical literary texts, including works by Shakespeare (White) and Dickens (Weisberg). Dickens's exemplary status in diverse arguments regarding literary reasoning in political philosophy is evident in Richard Rorty's *Contingency,*

Irony, and Solidarity and Martha Nussbaum's *Poetic Justice.* For a recent discussion of the continuing influence of Holmes stories not merely on Law and Literature scholarship but also on contemporary criminology and FBI profiling, see Lonsdale, "Rounding Up the Usual Suspect."

4. Korobkin, *Criminal Conversations.*

5. Shapiro, *Culture of Fact;* Herrup, *Common Peace.*

6. On the "accused speaks" theory, see Schramm, *Testimony and Advocacy,* and Langbein, *Origins of Adversary.*

7. Langbein, *Origins of Adversary.*

8. The Criminal Amendment Act of 1898 first allowed defendants to testify under oath. See Parker, "Prisoner in the Box," and Langbein, "Historical Origins."

9. Schramm, *Testimony and Advocacy.*

10. For an account of nineteenth-century law reports and their status, see Baker, "Records."

11. *Trial of James Blomfield Rush; Regina v. Robert Henderson, Central Criminal Court Sessions Papers* (1st session, 1860–61).

12. *Trial of James Blomfield Rush,* 185.

13. *Law Reports,* 1: 169–75.

14. *Regina v. W. T. Stead, Central Criminal Court Sessions Papers* (12th session, 1884–85); see also Walkowitz, *City of Dreadful Delight,* 105–13.

15. See Schroeder, "Speaking Volumes," and A. Jones, *Powers of the Press.*

16. For a discussion of the impact of newspaper reports of adultery trials on Victorian literature, especially the formulations of theories of "high culture" and aestheticism meant to elude censorship, see Leckie, *Culture and Adultery,* 76.

17. *Times,* November 11, 1885, 3.

18. Reade, *Readiana;* Burns, *Charles Reade.*

19. Polloczek, *Literature and Legal Discourse.*

20. On the Tichborne Claimant, see McWilliam's "Liberalism Lite?" and his *Tichborne Claimant;* on melodrama, see Hadley, *Melodramatic Tactics,* and Voskuil, *Acting Naturally;* on sensationalism and the law, see my "Victorian Narrative Jurisprudence," as well as Ledger's *Dickens and the Popular Radical Imagination.*

21. Reade, *Griffith Gaunt,* 293. Page references hereafter will be given in the text.

22. Nussbaum, *Poetic Justice,* 72–77.

23. Trollope, *Phineas Redux,* 2: 177–79.

24. Schroeder, "Speaking Volumes."

25. *Times,* March 22, 1884, 4.

CHAPTER EIGHT. Concealing Women's *Mens Rea*

1. See Welsh, *Strong Representations.*

2. Rodensky, *Crime in Mind,* 17.

3. Ibid., 28.

4. Dorrit Cohn, quoted in Rodensky, *Crime in Mind,* 10.

5. See, for example, Eagleton, *Ideology of the Aesthetic;* D. Simpson, *Romanticism;* Warhman, "Public Opinion."

6. D. Simpson, *Romanticism,* ch. 5.

7. Kestner, *Protest and Reform,* 52.

8. Krueger, *Reader's Repentance,* 94–124.

9. Mary Carpenter to Frances Power Cobbe, July 9, 1859, Frances Power Cobbe Papers.

10. Radzinowicz, *History,* 5: 148–49.

11. Carpenter, *Juvenile Delinquents,* v, iv.

12. Radzinowicz, *English Criminal Law,* 5: 178–79.

13. Ibid., 5: 179–81.

14. See, for example, A. Jones, *Powers of the Press;* Sindall, *Street Violence.*

15. Sindall, *Street Violence,* 51, 89, 137.

16. Ibid., 136–40.

17. Carpenter, *Our Convicts,* 1: 4. Page references hereafter will be given in the text.

18. Robinson, *Female Life in Prison,* 1: 45–46.

19. Manton, *Mary Carpenter,* 180.

20. Mary Carpenter to Frances Power Cobbe, January 22, 1865, Frances Power Cobbe Papers.

21. Peter Brooks connects narrative desire with capitalist consumerism in *Reading for the Plot.*

22. Radzinowicz, *English Criminal Law,* 225.

23. Harriet Martineau, *Edinburgh Review,* October 1865, quoted in Manton, *Mary Carpenter,* 189.

24. See Emmerichs, "Trials of Women," 108; Higginbotham, "'Sin of the Age,'" 323; Hoffer and Hull, *Murdering Mothers,* 71–75; and Rose, *Massacre of the Innocents,* 73–74.

25. Along with Higginbotham, "'Sin of the Age,'" and Emmerichs, "Trials of Women," see Beattie, *Crime and the Courts,* 113–23.

26. Zillah R. Eisenstein makes a similar argument regarding contemporary American laws governing reproduction (*Female Body,* 187).

27. For a discussion of sixteenth- and seventeenth-century ballads treating infanticide, see Dolan, *Dangerous Familiars,* 159–64.

28. A very partial bibliography of such works would include, on law: MacKinnon, *Feminism Unmodified* and *Only Words;* and Minow, *Not Only for Myself.* On medicine: Jordanova, *Sexual Visions;* and Poovey, *Uneven Developments* and *Social Body.* On poetry: Richardson, "Romanticism." On the novel: Armstrong, *Desire and Domestic Fiction;* Davis, *Resisting Novels;* and D. A. Miller, *Novel and the Police.* For a more complex account of gender and representation in law, see West, *Caring for Justice.*

29. Poovey, *Social Body,* 74.

30. Ibid., 84.

31. Behlmer, "Deadly Motherhood," 412.

32. Rose, *Massacre,* 70–72.

33. Ibid., 71.

34. Ibid., 25, 29.

35. Higginbotham, "'Sin of the Age,'" 324, 328, 331–33.

36. Emmerichs, "Trials of Women," 105–6.

37. J. G. Smith, *Analysis,* 46; Taylor, *Elements,* 12–13.

38. Beck and Beck, *Elements,* 341.

39. *Times,* March 28, 1859.

40. Quoted in Rose, *Massacre,* 75.

41. D. Simpson, *Romanticism,* 29.

42. Schor, "Plot," 162.

43. D. Simpson, *Romanticism,* 7.

44. Sheats, "'Tis Three Feet Long," 98.

45. Wordworth, "The Thorn," lines 63–64. Line references hereafter will be given in the text.

46. Schor, "Plot," 162.

47. D. Simpson, *Romanticism,* 61–62, 100.

48. Wolfson, *Questioning Presence,* 56–58.

49. Ibid., 56.

50. Scott, *Heart of Mid-lothian,* 242.

51. Kestner, *Protest and Reform,* 107.

52. Mermin, *Elizabeth Barrett Browning,* 157.

53. "Runaway Slave," lines 138–40, in Barrett Browning, *Complete Works,* 3: 160–70.

54. Rose, *Massacre,* 62.

55. Behlmer, "Deadly Motherhood," 402.

56. These issues are discussed by Behlmer (*Child Abuse,* 17), Poovey (*Social Body,* 74–76), and Walkowitz (*City,* 18–19).

57. Smith, *Analysis,* 46.

58. Taylor, *Elements,* 12–13.

59. Rose, *Massacre,* 64.

60. Quoted in Rose, *Massacre,* 38.

61. Ibid., 68.

62. Behlmer, *Child Abuse,* 23.

63. Quoted in Behlmer, "Deadly Motherhood," 404.

64. Rose, *Massacre,* 37.

65. Walkowitz, *City of Dreadful Delight,* 39.

66. Rose, *Massacre,* 45.

67. Behlmer, *Child Abuse,* 29.

68. Quoted in Behlmer, *Child Abuse,* 34.

69. Rose, *Massacre,* 74.

70. Arnold, "Function of Criticism," 3: 274.

71. For an insightful discussion of the related issue of the interdependent activities of reading cities and reading Victorian novels, see Richard L. Stein, "Street Figures: Victorian Urban Icnonography," in *Victorian Literature and the Victorian Visual Imagination,* edited by Carol T. Christ and John O. Jordan, 233–263 (Berkeley and Los Angeles: University of California Press, 1995).

72. Reynolds, *Days of Hogarth,* 53–54.

73. Testimony of Eliza Gorman, *Central Criminal Court Sessions Papers,* Session 24: 28.

74. Porter and Hall, *Facts of Life,* 179.

75. Gagnier, *Subjectivities,* 62.

76. Kincaid, *Child-Loving,* 40.

77. Sandra Gilbert, Susan Gubar, Sherri Hallgren, and Annette Kolodny are among the feminist critics who endorse the position put forward in Susan Glaspell's 1917 short story, "A Jury of Her Peers"—that women's social position entitles them to a parallel system of justice, in this instance one in which women are justified in colluding in the cover-up of one woman's murder of her husband. See Glaspell, "Jury of Her Peers"; Gilbert and Gubar, *No Man's Land,* 1: 91; Hallgren, "'The Law is the Law,'" 204, 216; and Kolodny, "Map for Rereading," 463–64.

CHAPTER NINE. The Secret Agency of Juries

1. Shapiro, *"Beyond Reasonable Doubt,"* xi–xii.

2. Clover, "Law and the Order," 104.

3. Ginzburg, "Checking the Evidence."

4. For a recent analysis of the Boulton and Park trial, see W. Cohen, *Sex Scandal,* 73–129. Major contributions to the analysis of the homosexual juridical subject include Dollimore, *Sexual Dissidence;* E. Cohen, *Talk on the Wilde Side;* Foldy, *Trials of Oscar Wilde;* Moran, *Homosexual(ity) of Law;* and Sinfield, *Wilde Century.*

5. For a discussion of this scandal, see Schramm, *Testimony and Advocacy,* 123–30.

6. For a discussion of the significance of the Judicature Act to Victorian literature and law, see Polloczek, *Literature and Legal Discourse,* esp. 134.

7. See Delgado and Stefancic, *Failed Revolutions.*

8. Bristow, *Effeminate England,* 36–43.

9. Abrams, "Narrative and the Normative," 53.

10. Among the many arguments featuring Dickens, see Weisberg, *Poethics,* 35; Rorty, *Contingency,* xvi; Nussbaum, *Poetic Justice,* xvi.

11. Sutherland, "Trollope," 72–73.

12. Simmel, *Sociology,* 321; Welsh, *George Eliot,* 73, 75; Kucich, *Power of Lies,* 21.

13. Kucich, *Power of Lies,* 41–42.

14. Goldstein, "Representing the Lesbian," 357.

15. Alexander Welsh notes that James Fitzjames Stephen, in his *Introduction on*

the Principles of Judicial Evidence (1872), illustrated his exposition of circumstantial evidence exclusively with murder cases (*Strong Representations,* 162).

16. Bentham, *Introduction*, 203.

17. Whitcombe, *Enquiry,* 2.

18. Welsh, *Strong Representations,* 42.

19. apRoberts, *Moral Trollope,* 52.

20. Nardin, *He Knew She Was Right,* 223, n. 3.

21. Kincaid, *Novels of Anthony Trollope,* 81.

22. R. D. McMaster points out the peculiarity of such intimacy existing between a barrister and his client (who would normally deal with a solicitor) in *Trollope and the Law* (33–38).

23. Trollope, *Orley Farm,* 1: 115. Page references hereafter will be given in the text.

24. Kincaid, *Trollope,* 80.

25. Case descriptions and quotations are from PRO KB 6.

26. E. Cohen, *Talk on the Wilde Side,* 106.

27. PRO KB 6, quoted in W. Cohen, *Sex Scandal,* 115.

28. Dowling, *Hellenism and Homosexuality.*

29. W. Cohen, *Sex Scandal,* 94, 96.

30. Bartlett, *Who Was That Man?* 141–42.

31. W. Cohen, *Sex Scandal,* 101.

32. Ibid., 95.

33. Capser, *Handbook of Forensic Medicine,* 3: 331.

34. E. Cohen, "Legislating the Norm"; Weeks, *Sex, Politics, and Society.*

35. de Lauretis, *Technologies of Gender,* 51–69.

36. Peters, "Law, Literature," 449.

37. Andrew Elfenbein, unpublished talk, North American Victorian Studies Association, University of Virginia, September 2005.

Bibliography

Abrams, Kathryn. "Hearing the Call of Stories." *California Law Review* 79 (July 1991): 1014–15.

———. "The Narrative and the Normative in Legal Scholarship." In *Representing Women: Law, Literature, and Feminism,* edited by Susan Sage Heinzelman and Zipporah Batshaw Wiseman, 44–56. Durham, NC: Duke University Press, 1994.

Ady, Thomas. *A Candle in the Dark: or, A Treatise concerning the Nature of Witches & Witchcraft.* London: Thomas Newberry, 1656.

Allen, C. J. W. *The Law of Evidence in Victorian England.* Cambridge: Cambridge University Press, 1997.

apRoberts, Ruth. *The Moral Trollope.* Athens: Ohio University Press, 1971.

Armstrong, Nancy. *Desire and Domestic Fiction: A Political History of the Novel.* Oxford: Oxford University Press, 1987.

Armstrong, Nancy, and Leonard Tennenhouse, eds. *The Violence of Representation: Literature and the History of Violence.* New York: Routledge, 1989.

Arnold, Matthew. "The Function of Criticism at the Present Time." In *Lectures and Essays in Criticism,* vol. 3 of *Complete Prose Works,* edited by R. H. Super, 258–85. Ann Arbor: University of Michigan Press, 1962.

Baker, J. H. "Records, Reports and the Origins of Case-Law in England." In *Judicial Records, Law Reports, and the Growth of Case Law,* edited by J. H. Baker, 15–46. Berlin: Duncker and Humbolt, 1989.

Balkin, J. M., and Sanford Levinson. "Law as Performance." In *Law and Literature,* Current Legal Issues 2, edited by Michael Freeman and Andrew D. E. Lewis, 729–51. Oxford: Oxford University Press, 1999.

Barker-Benfield, G. J. *The Culture of Sensibility: Sex and Society in Eighteenth-Century Britain.* Chicago: University of Chicago Press, 1992.

Baron, Jane B. "Interdisciplinary Legal Scholarship as Guilty Pleasure: The Case of Law and Literature." In *Law and Literature,* Current Legal Issues 2, edited by

Michael Freeman and Andrew D. E. Lewis, 21–45. Oxford: Oxford University Press, 1999.

Barstow, Anne Llewellyn. "On Studying Witchcraft as Women's History: A Historiography of the European Witch Persecutions." *Journal of Feminist Studies in Religion* 4 (1988): 7–19.

Bartlett, Neil. *Who Was That Man? A Present for Mr. Oscar Wilde*. London: Serpent's Tail, 1988.

Beattie, John. *Crime and the Courts in England, 1660–1800*. Princeton, NJ: Princeton University Press, 1986.

Beck, Theodric Romeyn, and John B. Beck. *Elements of Medical Jurisprudence*. 7th ed. London, 1842.

Behlmer, George K. *Child Abuse and Moral Reform in England, 1870–1908*. Stanford, CT: Stanford University Press, 1982.

———. "Deadly Motherhood: Infanticide and Medical Opinion in Mid-Victorian England." *Journal of the History of Medicine and Allied Sciences* 34 (October 1979): 403–27.

Belcher, William. *Address to Humanity*. London: Allen and West, 1798.

Bell, Derrick. *Faces at the Bottom of the Well: The Permanence of Racism*. New York: Basic Books, 1992.

Bender, John. *Imagining the Penitentiary: Fiction and the Architecture of the Mind in Eighteenth-Century England*. Chicago: University of Chicago Press, 1987.

Bentham, Jeremy. *An Introduction to the Principles of Morals and Legislation*. Edited by J. H. Burns and H. L. A. Hart. New York: Methuen, 1982.

Bernard, Richard. *A Guide to the Grand-Jury Men*. London, 1627.

Binder, Guyora, and Robert Weisberg. *Literary Criticisms of the Law*. Princeton, NJ: Princeton University Press, 2000.

Blackstone, William. *Commentaries on the Laws of England*. Oxford: Clarendon Press, 1766–67.

Bostridge, Ian. *Witchcraft and Its Transformations, c. 1650–c. 1750*. Oxford: Clarendon Press, 1997.

Bourdieu, Pierre. *Language and Symbolic Power*. Edited with an introduction by John B. Thompson. Translated by Gino Raymond and Matthew Adamson. Cambridge, MA: Harvard University Press, 1991.

Braunmuller, A. R. Introduction to *Macbeth*, by William Shakespeare. New Cambridge Shakespeare. Cambridge: Cambridge University Press, 1997.

Bristow, Joseph. *Effeminate England: Homoerotic Writing after 1885*. New York: Columbia University Press, 1995.

Brooks, Peter. *Reading for the Plot: Design and Intention in Narrative*. Cambridge, MA: Harvard University Press, 1992.

———. "Storytelling without Fear? Confession in Law and Literature." In *Law's Stories: Narrative and Rhetoric in the Law*, edited by Peter Brooks and Paul Gewirtz, 114–34. New Haven, CT: Yale University Press, 1996.

Browning, Elizabeth Barrett. *The Complete Works of Elizabeth Barrett Browning*. Edited by Charlotte Porter and Helen A. Clarke. New York: AMS Press, 1973.

Burns, Wayne. *Charles Reade: A Study in Victorian Authorship*. New York: Bookman Associates, 1961.

Burton, Hester. *Barbara Bodichon, 1827–1891*. London: John Murray, 1949.

Byrd, Max. *Visits to Bedlam: Madness and Literature in the Eighteenth Century*. Columbia: University of South Carolina Press, 1974.

Campbell, John. *Lives of the Chief Justices*. 2nd ed. 2 vols. London: J. Murray, 1858.

Capser, Johann Ludwig. *A Handbook of Forensic Medicine*. Translated by George William Balfour. 3rd ed. 3 vols. London, 1861–64.

Carlyle, Thomas. *Chartism*. In *The Collected Works of Thomas Carlyle*, 9: 3–68. London: Chapman and Hall, 1858.

Carpenter, Mary. *Juvenile Delinquents, Their Condition and Treatment*. London: W. and F. G. Cash, 1853.

———. Letters to Frances Power Cobbe. Frances Power Cobbe Papers. Huntington Library, San Marino, California.

———. *Our Convicts*. 2 vols. London, 1864. Reprint, Montclaire, NJ: Patterson, Smith, 1969.

———. *Reformatory Schools for the Children of the Perishing and Dangerous Classes and for Juvenile Offenders*. London, 1851. Reprint, London: Woburn Press, 1968.

Carroll, Lewis. *Alice in Wonderland*. Edited by Donald Gray. New York: Norton, 1971.

Chapple, J. A. V., and Arthur Pollard, eds. *The Letters of Mrs. Gaskell*. Manchester: Manchester University Press, 1966.

Choi, Julie. "Feminine Authority? Common Sense and the Question of Voice in the Novel." *New Literary History* 27, no. 4 (Autumn 1996): 641–62.

Clark, Anna. *Women's Silence, Men's Violence: Sexual Assault in England, 1770–1845*. London: Pandora, 1987.

Clark, Sandra. *The Elizabethan Pamphleteers: Popular Moralistic Pamphlets, 1580–1640*. Rutherford, NJ: Fairleigh Dickinson University Press, 1983.

Clery, E. J. *The Rise of Supernatural Fiction, 1762–1800*. New York: Cambridge University Press, 1995.

Clifford, James. *The Predicament of Culture: Twentieth-Century Ethnography, Literature, and Art*. Cambridge, MA: Harvard University Press, 1988.

Clover, Carol J. "Law and the Order of Popular Culture." In *Law in the Domains of Culture*, edited by Austin Sarat and Thomas R. Kearns, 97–98. Ann Arbor: University of Michigan Press, 1998.

Cobbe, Frances Power. *Criminals, Idiots, Women and Minors: Is the Classification Sound?* Manchester: A. Ireland, 1869.

Cohen, Ed. "Legislating the Norm: From Sodomy to Gross Indecency." In *Displacing Homophobia: Gay Male Perspectives in Literature and Culture*, edited by Ronald R. Butters, John M. Clum, and Michael Moon, 169–205. Durham, NC: Duke University Press, 1989.

———. *Talk on the Wilde Side: Towards a Genealogy of a Discourse on Male Sexualities*. London: Routledge, 1993.

Cohen, William A. *Sex Scandal: The Private Parts of Victorian Fiction*. Durham, NC: Duke University Press, 1996.

Cohn, Norman. Foreword to *Enemies of God: The Witch-Hunt in Scotland*, by Christina Larner. Baltimore, MD: Johns Hopkins University Press, 1981.

Collini, Stefan. *Public Moralists: Political Thought and Intellectual Life in Britain, 1850–1930*. Oxford: Clarendon Press, 1991.

Conger, Syndy. *Mary Wollstonecraft and the Language of Sensibility*. Rutherford, NJ: Fairleigh Dickinson University Press, 1994.

Conley, Carolyn. "Rape and Justice in Victorian England." *Victorian Studies* 29 (1986): 519–36.

Coombe, Rosemary J. "Contingent Articulations: A Critical Cultural Studies of Law." In *Law in the Domains of Culture*, edited by Austin Sarat and Thomas R. Kearns, 21–64. Ann Arbor: University of Michigan Press, 1998.

Cornell, Drucilla. *Feminism as Critique: On the Politics of Gender*. Minneapolis: University of Minnesota Press, 1987.

———. "Toward a Modern/Postmodern Reconstruction of Ethics." *University of Pennsylvania Law Review* 133 (1985): 291–380.

Cosgrove, Richard A. *The Rule of Law: Albert Venn Dicey, Victorian Jurist*. Chapel Hill: University of North Carolina Press, 1980.

———. *Scholars of the Law: English Jurisprudence from Blackstone to Hart*. New York: New York University Press, 1996.

Cvetkovich, Ann. *Mixed Feelings: Feminism, Mass Culture, and Victorian Sensationalism*. New Brunswick, NJ: Rutgers University Press, 1992.

Daly, Mary. "The Witches Return: Patriarchy on Trial." In *Radically Speaking: Feminism Reclaimed*, edited by Diane Bell and Renate Klein, 551–56. Victoria, Australia: Spinifex Press, 1996.

Davies, Owen. "Newspapers and the Popular Belief in Witchcraft and Magic in the Modern Period." *Journal of British Studies* 37, no. 2 (April 1998): 139–65.

———. *Witchcraft, Magic and Culture, 1739–1951*. Manchester: Manchester University Press, 1999.

Davis, Lennard J. *Resisting Novels: Ideology and Fiction*. New York: Methuen, 1987.

Defoe, Daniel. *A Review of the State of the English Nation*. London: B. Bragg, 1706.

de Lauretis, Theresa. *Technologies of Gender: Essays on Theory, Film, and Fiction*. Bloomington: Indiana University Press, 1987.

Delgado, Richard. "Storytelling for Oppositionists and Others: a Plea for Narrative." *Michigan Law Review* 87 (August 1989): 2412–41.

Delgado, Richard, and Jean Stefancic. *Failed Revolutions: Social Reform and the Limits of Legal Imagination*. Boulder, CO: Westview Press, 1994.

Dellamora, Richard. *Masculine Desire: The Sexual Politics of Victorian Aestheticism*. Chapel Hill: University of North Carolina Press, 1990.

Dicey, A. V. *Lectures on the Relation between Law and Public Opinion in England*. London: Macmillan, 1905; reprint, 1962.

Dimock, Wai-Chee. "Cognition as a Category of Literary Analysis." *American Literature* 67, no. 4 (December 1995): 25–31.

———. *Residues of Justice: Literature, Law, Philosophy*. Berkeley: University of California Press, 1996.

Dolan, Frances E. *Dangerous Familiars: Representations of Domestic Crime in England, 1550–1700*. Ithaca, NY: Cornell University Press, 1994.

Dolin, Kieran. *Fiction and the Law: Legal Discourse in Victorian and Modernist Literature*. Cambridge: Cambridge University Press, 1999.

Dollimore, Jonathan. *Sexual Dissidence: Augustine to Wilde, Freud to Foucault*. Oxford: Clarendon Press, 1991.

Doody, Margaret Anne. "George Eliot and the Eighteenth-Century Novel." *Nineteenth-Century Fiction* 35 (1980): 260–91.

Douzinas, Costas, and Ronnie Warrington, with Shaun McVeigh. *Postmodern Jurisprudence: The Law of Text in the Texts of Law*. London: Routledge, 1991.

Dowling, Linda. *Hellenism and Homosexuality in Victorian Oxford*. Ithaca, NY: Cornell University Press, 1994.

Eagleton, Terry. *The Ideology of the Aesthetic*. Oxford: Basil Blackwell, 1990.

Ehrenreich, Nancy S. "Pluralist Myths and Powerless Men: The Ideology of Reasonableness in Sexual Harassment Law." *Yale Law Journal* 99 (April 1990): 1177–234.

Eisenstein, Elizabeth. *The Printing Press as an Agent of Change: Communications and Cultural Transformations in Early-Modern Europe*. 2 vols. Cambridge: Cambridge University Press, 1979.

Eisenstein, Zillah R. *The Female Body and the Law*. Berkeley: University of California Press, 1988.

Eliot, George. *Adam Bede*. Edited by Stephen Gill. Baltimore, MD: Penguin, 1980.

———. *Felix Holt*. Edited by Peter Coveney. Harmondsworth, UK: Penguin, 1973.

———. *Romola*. Edited by Andrew Brown. New York: Oxford University Press, 1993.

Emmerichs, Mary Beth Wasserlein. "Trials of Women for Homicide in Nineteeth-Century England." *Women and Criminal Justice* 5 (1993): 99–109.

Ennemoser, Joseph. *The History of Magic*. Translated by William and Mary Howitt. 2 vols. London: Henry G. Bohn, 1854.

Ewen, C. L'Estrange. *Witch Hunting and Witch Trials: The Indictments for Witchcraft from the Records of 1373 Assizes held for the Home Circuit A.D. 1559–1736*. London: Kegan Paul, Trench, Trubner, 1929.

Farr, Samuel. *Elements of Medical Jurisprudence*. London, 1788.

Ferguson, Robert A. *Law and Letters in American Culture*. Cambridge, MA: Harvard University Press, 1984.

Filmer, Robert. *An Advertisement to the Jury-men of England, Touching Witches*. London: Angel in Ivy Lane, 1653.

Flint, Christopher. *Family Fictions: Narrative and Domestic Relations in Britain, 1688–1798*. Stanford, CT: Stanford University Press, 1998.

Foldy, Michael S. *The Trials of Oscar Wilde: Deviance, Morality, and Late-Victorian Society*. New Haven, CT: Yale University Press, 1997.

Foss, Edward. *The Judges of England.* 9 vols. London: Longman, 1864.

Foucault, Michel. *Discipline and Punish: The Birth of the Prison.* Translated by Alan Sheridan. New York: Vintage, 1979.

———. *The History of Sexuality.* 3 vols. Translated by Robert Hurley. New York: Pantheon, 1978–86.

Friedman, Lawrence M. "Law, Lawyers, and Popular Culture." *Yale Law Journal* 98 (1989): 1579–606.

Gage, Matilda Joslyn. *Women, Church, and State.* New York: Truth Seeker Co., 1893.

Gagnier, Regenia. *Subjectivities: A History of Self-Representation in Britain, 1832–1920.* Oxford: Oxford University Press, 1991.

Gallagher, Catherine. *The Industrial Reformation of English Fiction: Social Discourse and Narrative Form, 1832–1867.* Chicago: University of Chicago Press, 1985.

Gaskell, Elizabeth. *The Letters of Mrs. Gaskell.* Edited by J. A. V. Chapple and Arthur Pollard. Manchester: Manchester University Press, 1966.

———. *Life of Charlotte Brontë.* Harmondsworth, UK: Penguin, 1975.

———. *Lois the Witch.* In *Cousin Phillis and Other Tales,* edited by Angus Easson, 105–93. Oxford: Oxford University Press, 1981.

———. *Mary Barton.* London: Everyman, 1971.

———. *North and South.* New York: Oxford University Press, 1973.

———. *Ruth.* London: Chapman and Hall, 1853.

———. *Sylvia's Lovers.* London: Smith, Elder, 1863.

Gérin, Winifred. *Elizabeth Gaskell.* Oxford: Oxford University Press, 1980.

Gilbert, Sandra M., and Susan Gubar. *No Man's Land: The Place of the Woman Writer in the Twentieth Century.* 2 vols. New Haven, CT: Yale University Press, 1988.

Gilmartin, Kevin. *Print Politics: The Press and Radical Opposition in Early Nineteenth-Century England.* Cambridge: Cambridge University Press, 1996.

Ginzburg, Carlo. "Checking the Evidence: The Judge and the Historian." In *Questions of Evidence: Proof, Practice, and Persuasion across the Disciplines,* edited by James Chandler, Arnold I. Davidson, and Harry Harootunian, 290–303. Chicago: University of Chicago Press, 1994.

Glaspell, Susan. "A Jury of Her Peers." In *American Voices, American Women,* edited by Lee R. Edwards and Arlyn Diamond, 359–81. New York: Avon, 1973.

Godwin, William. *Lives of the Necromancers.* London: Frederick J. Mason, 1834.

———. *Things As They Are; or, The Adventures of Caleb Williams.* Edited with an introduction by David McCracken. New York: Norton, 1977.

Goldstein, Anne B. "Representing the Lesbian in Law and Literature." In *Representing Women: Law, Literature, and Feminism,* edited by Susan Sage-Heinzelman and Zipporah Batshaw Wiseman, 356–84. Durham, NC: Duke University Press, 1994.

Goodcole, Henry. *The Wonderfull Discoverie of Elizabeth Sawyer a Witch, Late of Edmonton.* London: William Butler, 1621.

Goodwin, Jill Tomasson. "The 'Final Struggle': A Discoursal, Rhetorical and Social

Analysis of Two Closing Arguments." In *Law and Literature,* Current Legal Issues 2, edited by Michael Freeman and Andrew D. E. Lewis, 301–22. Oxford: Oxford University Press, 1999.

Green, Richard Firth. *A Crisis of Truth: Literature and Law in Ricardian England.* Philadelphia: University of Pennsylvania Press, 1999.

Greenberg, David F. *The Construction of Homosexuality.* Chicago: University of Chicago Press, 1988.

Habermas, Jürgen. *Between Facts and Norms: Contributions to a Discourse Theory of Law and Democracy.* Translated by William Rehg. Cambridge: MIT Press, 1998.

———. *The Inclusion of the Other: Studies in Political Theory.* Edited by Ciaran Cronin and Pablo de Greif. Cambridge, MA: MIT Press, 1998.

———. "Reply to Symposium Participants." In *Habermas on Law and Democracy,* edited by Michel Rosenfield and Andrew Arato, 381–452. Berkeley and Los Angeles: University of California Press, 1998.

———. *Structural Transformation of the Public Sphere: An Inquiry into a Category of Bourgeois Society.* Translated by Thomas Burger and Frederick Lawrence. Cambridge, MA: MIT Press, 1989.

Hadley, Elaine. *Melodramatic Tactics: Theatricalized Dissent in the English Marketplace, 1800–1885.* Stanford, CT: Stanford University Press, 1995.

Haight, Gordon S. *George Eliot.* Oxford: Oxford University Press, 1968.

Halley, Janet E. "Equivocation and the Legal Conflict over Religious Identity in Early Modern England." *Yale Journal of Law and the Humanities* 3 (1991): 33–52.

Hallgren, Sherri. "'The Law is the Law—and a Bad Stove is a Bad Stove': Subversive Justice and Layers of Collusion in 'A Jury of Her Peers.'" In *Violence, Silence, and Anger: Women's Writing as Transgression,* edited by Deirdre Lashgari, 203–18. Charlottesville: University Press of Virginia, 1995.

Halperin, David M. *One Hundred Years of Homosexuality.* New York: Routledge, 1990.

Harris, Richard. *Harris' Hints on Advocacy.* London: Waterlow Bros. and Layton, 1879.

Harvey, A. D. "Prosecutions of Sodomy in England at the Beginning of the Nineteenth Century." *Historical Journal* 21 (1978): 939–48.

Hay, Douglas. "Prosecution and Power: Malicious Prosecution in the English Courts, 1750–1850." In *Policing and Prosecution in Britain, 1750–1850,* edited by Douglas Hay and Francis Snyder, 343–95. Oxford: Oxford University Press, 1989.

Heilbrun, Carolyn, and Judith Resnik. "Convergences: Law, Literature, and Feminism." *Yale Law Journal* 99 (1990): 1913–56.

Helsinger, Elizabeth, Robin Lauterbach Sheets, and William Veeder, eds. *The Woman Question: Society and Literature in Britain and America, 1837–1883.* 3 vols. New York: Garland, 1983.

Herrup, Cynthia. *The Common Peace: Participation and the Criminal Law in Seventeenth-Century England.* Cambridge: Cambridge University Press, 1987.

Hester, Marianne. *Lewd Women and Wicked Witches: A Study of the Dynamics of Male Domination*. London: Routledge, 1992.

Higginbotham, Ann R. "'Sin of the Age': Infanticide and Illegitimacy in Victorian London." *Victorian Studies* 32 (Spring 1989): 319–37.

Hoffer, Peter C., and N. E. H. Hull. *Murdering Mothers: Infanticide in England and New England, 1558–1803*. New York: New York University Press, 1981.

Holcombe, Lee. "Victorian Wives and Property: Reform of the Married Women's Property Law, 1857–1882." In *A Widening Sphere: Changing Roles of Victorian Women*, edited by Martha Vicinus, 3–28. Buffalo: University of Toronto Press, 1983.

Holdsworth, W. S. *The Historians of Anglo-American Law*. New York: Columbia University Press, 1928.

Holmes, Clive. "The County Community in Stuart Historiography." *Journal of British Studies* 19, no. 2 (Spring 1980): 54–73.

———. "Popular Culture? Witches, Magistrates, and Divines in Early Modern England." In *Understanding Popular Culture: Europe From the Middle Ages to the Nineteenth Century*, edited by Steven L. Kaplan, 85–111. New York: Mouton, 1984.

———. "Women: Witnesses and Witches." *Past and Present* 140 (1993): 45–78.

Hopkins, Matthew. *The Discovery of Witches*. London, 1647.

Horkheimer, Max, and Theodor W. Adorno. *Dialectic of Enlightenment*. Translated by John Cumming. New York: Herder and Herder, 1972.

Howitt, Mary. *Popular History of the United States of America*. 2 vols. London: Longman, 1859.

Howitt, William. *A Popular History of Priestcraft in All Ages And Nations*. London: E. Wilson, 1833.

Hunter, J. Paul. *Before Novels: The Cultural Contexts of Eighteenth-Century English Fiction*. New York: Norton, 1990.

Hutchinson, Francis. *An Historical Essay concerning Witchcraft*. London, 1718.

Hyde, H. Montgomery. *The Cleveland Street Scandal*. London: Allen, 1976.

———. *The Other Love: An Historical and Contemporary Survey of Homosexuality in Britain*. London: Heinemann, 1970.

Jackson, Bernard S. "Narrative Theories and Legal Discourse." In *Narrative in Culture: The Uses of Storytelling in the Sciences, Philosophy, and Literature*, edited by Christopher Nash, 163–65. London: Routledge, 1990.

James I. *Daemonologie in the Forme of a Dialogue*. Edinburgh: Robert Waldegrave, 1597.

Johns, Adrian. *The Nature of the Book: Print and Knowledge in the Making*. Chicago: University of Chicago Press, 1998.

Johnson, Claudia L. *Equivocal Beings: Politics, Gender, and Sentimentality in the 1790s*. Chicago: University of Chicago Press, 1995.

Johnson, Patricia. *Hidden Hands: Working-Class Women and Victorian Social-Problem Fiction*. Athens: Ohio University Press, 2001.

Jones, Aled. *The Powers of the Press: Newspapers, Power and the Public in Nineteenth-Century England.* Aldershot, UK: Scolar Press, 1996.

Jones, Kathleen. *Lunacy, Law, and Conscience, 1744–1845: The Social History of the Care of the Insane.* London: Routledge, 1955.

Jones, Nancy A. "The Rape of the Rural Muse: Wordsworth's 'The Solitary Reaper' as a Version of Pastourelle." In *Rape and Representation,* edited by Lynn A. Higgins and Brenda R. Silver, 263–77. New York: Columbia University Press, 1991.

Jordanova, Ludmilla. *Sexual Visions.* Hemel Hempstead, UK: Harvester, 1989.

Joyce, Patrick. "The Constitution and the Narrative of Victorian Politics." In *Re-Reading the Constitution: New Narratives in the Political History of England's Long Nineteenth Century,* edited by James Vernon, 179–203. Cambridge: Cambridge University Press, 1996.

Kelman, Mark. "Reasonable Evidence of Reasonableness." In *Questions of Evidence: Proof, Practice, and Persuasion Across the Disciplines,* edited by James Chandler, Arnold I. Davidson, and Harry Harootunian, 169–88. Chicago: University of Chicago Press, 1994.

Kerr, James. *Fiction against History: Scott as Storyteller.* Cambridge: Cambridge University Press, 1989.

Kestner, Joseph. *Protest and Reform: The British Social Narrative by Women, 1827–1867.* Madison: University of Wisconsin Press, 1985.

Kincaid, James R. *Child-Loving: The Erotic Child and Victorian Culture.* New York: Routledge, 1992.

Klein, Kerwin Lee. "On the Emergence of Memory in Historical Discourse." *Representations* 69 (Winter 2000): 127–50.

Kolodny, Annette. "A Map for Rereading: Or, Gender and the Interpretation of Literary Texts." *New Literary History* 11 (1980): 451–67.

Korobkin, Laura Hanft. *Criminal Conversations: Sentimentality and Nineteenth-Century Legal Stories of Adultery.* New York: Columbia University Press, 1998.

Krueger, Christine L. "'The Female Paternalist' as Historian: Elizabeth Gaskell's My Lady Ludlow." In *Rewriting the Victorians: Theory, History, and the Politics of Gender,* edited by Linda M. Shires, 166–83. London: Routledge, 1992.

———. *The Reader's Repentance: Women Writers, Women Preachers and Nineteenth-Century Social Discourse.* Chicago: University of Chicago Press, 1992.

———. "Victorian Narrative Jurisprudence." In *Law and Literature,* Current Legal Issues 2, edited by Michael Freeman and Andrew D. E. Lewis, 437–61. Oxford: Oxford University Press, 1999.

———. "Witnessing Women: Trial Testimony in Novels by Tonna, Gaskell, and Eliot." In *Representing Women: Feminism, Literature, and Law,* edited by Susan Sage Heinzelman and Zipporah Batshaw Wiseman, 337–55. Durham, NC: Duke University Press, 1994.

Kucich, John. *The Power of Lies: Transgression in Victorian Fiction.* Ithaca, NY: Cornell University Press, 1994.

Kucich, John, and Diane F. Sadoff. Introduction to special issue of *Nineteenth-Century Contexts: An Interdisciplinary Journal* 22, no. 1 (2000): 5–6.

Lahey, Kathleen A. "Reasonable Women and the Law." In *At the Boundaries of Law: Feminism and Legal Theory,* edited by Martha Albertson Fine and Nancy Sweet Thomadsen, 3–21. New York: Routledge, 1991.

Lake, Peter. "Deeds against Nature: Cheap Print, Protestantism and Murder in Early Seventeenth-Century England." In *Culture and Politics in Early Stuart England,* edited by Kevin Sharpe and Peter Lake, 257–84. Houndmills, Basingstoke, UK: Macmillan, 1994.

Landry, Donna, and Gerald MacLean. *Material Feminisms.* Cambridge, MA: Blackwell, 1993.

Langbein, John. "The Historical Origins of the Privilege Against Self-Incrimination at Common Law." *Michigan Law Review* 92 (1993–94): 1047–85.

———. *The Origins of Adversary Criminal Trial.* Oxford: Oxford University Press, 2003.

Larner, Christina. *Enemies of God: The Witch-hunt in Scotland.* Baltimore, MD: Johns Hopkins University Press, 1981.

———. *Witchcraft and Religion: The Politics of Popular Belief.* Oxford: Blackwell, 1984.

Law and Lawyers; or Sketches and Illustrations of Legal History and Biography. 2 vols. London: Longmans, 1840.

Law Reports: Courts of Probate and Divorce. Edited by James Redford Bulwer, Q.C. 3 vols. Michaelmas-Trinity, 1869; London: Council of Law Reporting, 1869.

Laws Respecting Women, as They Regard Their Natural Rights or Their Connections and Conduct. London: J. Johnson, 1737.

Leckie, Barbara. *Culture and Adultery: The Novel, Newspaper, and the Law, 1857–1914.* Philadelphia: University of Pennsylvania Press, 1999.

Ledger, Sally. *Dickens and the Popular Radical Imagination.* New York: Cambridge University Press, 2007.

Leps, Marie Christine. *Apprehending the Criminal: The Production of Deviance in Nineteenth-Century Discourses.* Durham, NC: Duke University Press, 1992.

Levack, Brian P. *The Witch-hunt in Early Modern Europe.* London: Longmans, 1987.

Levine, George. *The Realistic Imagination: English Fiction from Frankenstein To Lady Chatterley.* Chicago: University of Chicago Press, 1981.

Levy, F. J. "How Information Spread among the Gentry, 1550–1640." *Journal of British Studies* 21 (1982): 11–34.

Linton, Eliza Lynn. *Witch-Stories.* London: Chapman and Hall, 1861.

Lonsdale, Kate. "Rounding Up the Usual Suspect: Echoing Jack the Ripper." In *Functions of Victorian Culture at the Present Time,* edited by Christine L. Krueger, 97–114. Athens: Ohio University Press, 2002.

Lowe, Louisa. *The Bastilles of England; or, The Lunacy Laws at Work.* London, 1883.

Lytton, Rosina Bulwer. *A Blighted Life.* Introduction by Marie Mulvey Roberts. Bristol: Thoemmes Press, 1994.

Mackay, Charles. *Memoirs of Extraordinary Popular Delusions and the Madness of Crowds.* London: R. Bentley, 1841.

MacKinnon, Catherine. *Feminism Unmodified: Discourses on Life and Law.* Cambridge, MA: Harvard University Press, 1987.

———. *Only Words.* Cambridge, MA: Harvard University Press, 1993.

———. *Sexual Harassment of Working Women: A Case of Sex Discrimination.* New Haven, CT: Yale University Press, 1979.

Manton, Jo. *Mary Carpenter and the Children of the Streets.* London: Heinemann Educational, 1976.

Marcus, George E., and Michael M. J. Fischer. *Anthropology as Cultural Critique: An Experimental Moment in the Human Sciences.* Chicago: University of Chicago Press, 1986.

Marshall, Peter. *William Godwin.* New Haven, CT: Yale University Press, 1984.

Maurer, Shawn Lisa. "The Female (as) Reader: Sex, Sensibility, and the Maternal in Wollstonecraft's Fictions." *Essays in Literature* 19 (Spring 1992): 36–54.

McCandless, Peter. "Liberty and Lunacy: The Victorians and Wrongful Confinement." *Journal of Social History* 11 (Spring 1978): 366–86.

McDonagh, Josephine. *Child Murder and British Culture, 1720–1900.* Cambridge: Cambridge University Press, 2003.

McGowan, John. "Modernity and Culture, The Victorians and Cultural Studies." *Nineteenth-Century Contexts* 22, no. 1 (2000): 21–49.

McGowen, Randall. "Punishing Violence, Sentencing Crime." In *The Violence of Representation: Literature and the History of Violence,* edited by Nancy Armstrong and Leonard Tennenhouse, 140–56. New York: Routledge, 1989.

McKeon, Michael. *The Origins of the English Novel, 1600–1740.* Baltimore, MD: Johns Hopkins University Press, 1987.

McMaster, R. D. *Trollope and the Law.* New York: St. Martin's Press, 1986.

McWilliam, Rohan. "Liberalism Lite?" *Victorian Studies* 48, no.1 (2005): 103–11.

———. "Radicalism and Popular Culture: The Tichborne Case and the Politics of 'Fair Play.'" In *Currents of Radicalism: Popular Radicalism, Organised Labour, and Party Politics in Britain, 1850–1914,* edited by E. F. Biagini and A. J. Reid, 44–64. Cambridge: Cambridge University Press, 1991.

———. *The Tichborne Claimant: A Victorian Sensation.* London: Hambledon Continuum, 2007.

Mellett, D. J. "Bureaucracy and Mental Illness: The Commissioners in Lunacy, 1845–90." *Medical History* 25 (1981): 221–50.

Mellor, Anne K. *Mothers of the Nation: Women's Political Writing in England, 1780–1830.* Bloomington: Indiana University Press, 2000.

———. *Romanticism and Gender.* New York: Routledge, 1993.

Mermin, Dorothy. *Elizabeth Barrett Browning: The Origins of a New Poetry.* Chicago: University of Chicago Press, 1989.

Michelet, Jules. *La Sorcière.* Paris: E. Dentu, 1862.

Mill, John Stuart. *Essays on Equality, Law, and Education.* Vol. 21 of *Collected Works.* Edited by John M. Robson. Toronto: University of Toronto Press, 1989.

———. *On Liberty*. London: Longman, Roberts and Green, 1869.

Miller, D. A. *The Novel and the Police*. Berkeley: University of California Press, 1988.

Miller, William Ian. *Bloodtaking and Peacemaking: Feud, Law, and Society in Saga Iceland*. Chicago: University of Chicago Press, 1990.

Minow, Martha. *Not Only for Myself: Identity, Politics, and the Law*. New York: New Press, 1997.

Moran, Leslie J. *The Homosexual(ity) of Law*. London: Routledge, 1996.

Morris, Polly. "Sodomy and Honor: The Case of Somerset, 1740–1850." In *The Pursuit of Sodomy: Male Homosexuality in Renaissance and Enlightenment Europe*, edited by Kent Gerard and Gert Hekma, 383–406. London: Haworth, 1989.

Mort, Frank. *Dangerous Sexualities: Medico-moral Politics in England since 1830*. London: Routledge, 1987.

Murray, Margaret. *The God of the Witches*. Oxford: University Press, 1970.

Nardin, Jane. *He Knew She Was Right: The Independent Women in the Novels of Anthony Trollope*. Carbondale: Southern Illinois University Press, 1989.

Newton, Adam Zachary. *Narrative Ethics*. Cambridge, MA: Harvard University Press, 1995.

Newton, Judith Lowder. *Women, Power, and Subversion: Social Strategies in British Fiction, 1778–1860*. Athens: University of Georgia Press, 1981.

Notestein, Wallace. *A History of Witchcraft in England from 1558 to 1718*. New York: Russell and Russell, 1965.

Nussbaum, Martha C. *Poetic Justice: The Literary Imagination and Public Life*. Boston: Beacon, 1995.

Orwell, George. *Homage to Catalonia*. London: Secker and Warburg, 1938.

Parker, Graham. "The Prisoner in the Box--The Making of the Criminal Evidence Act, 1898." In *Law and Social Change in British History*, edited by J. A. Guy and H. G. Beale, 156–75. London: Royal Historical Society, 1984.

Parry, Ann. "Sexual Exploitation and Freedom: Religion, Race, and Gender in Elizabeth Barrett Browning's *The Runaway Slave at Pilgrim's Point*." *Studies in Browning and His Circle* 16 (1988): 114–26.

Parry-Jones, William Llywelyn. *The Trade in Lunacy: A Study of Private Madhouses in England in the Eighteenth and Nineteenth Centuries*. London: Routledge and K. Paul, 1972.

Parsons, Coleman O. *Witchcraft and Demonology in Scott's Fiction*. Edinburgh and London: Oliver and Boyd, 1964.

Pateman, Carole. *The Sexual Contract*. Stanford, CT: Stanford University Press, 1988.

Peake, Thomas. *A Compendium of the Law of Evidence*. London, 1801.

Perkins, William. *Discourse of the Damned Art of Witchcraft So Farre Forth as It Is Revealed in the Scriptures, and Manifest by True Experience*. Cambridge: Cantrel Legge, 1608.

Peters, Julie Stone. "Law, Literature, and the Vanishing Real: On the Future of an Interdisciplinary Illusion." *PMLA* 120 (March 2005): 442–53.

Phillimore, John George. *History and Principles of the Law of Evidence*. London: William Benning, 1850.

Polanyi, Karl. *The Great Transformation: The Political and Economic Origins of Our Time*. Boston: Beacon, 1957.

Pollock, Frederick, and Frederic William Maitland. *The History of English Law before the Time of Edward I*. 2 vols. Cambridge: Cambridge University Press, 1923.

Polloczek, Deiter. *Literature and Legal Discourse: Equity and Ethics from Sterne to Conrad*. Cambridge: Cambridge University Press, 1999.

Poovey, Mary. *Making of the Social Body: British Cultural Formation, 1830–1864*. Chicago: University of Chicago Press, 1995.

———. *The Proper Lady and the Woman Writer: Ideology as Style in the Works of Mary Wollstonecraft, Mary Shelley, and Jane Austen*. Chicago: University of Chicago Press, 1984.

———. *Uneven Developments: The Ideological Work of Gender in Mid-Victorian England*. Chicago: University of Chicago Press, 1988.

Porter, Roy. "Rape--Does It Have a Historical Meaning?" In *Rape*, edited by Sylvana Tomaselli and Roy Porter, 216–36. Oxford: Blackwell, 1986.

———. *A Social History of Madness: The World through the Eyes of the Insane*. New York: Weidenfeld and Nicholson, 1987.

———. "A Touch of Danger: The Man-Midwife as Sexual Predator." In *Sexual Underworlds of the Enlightenment*, edited by G. S. Rousseau and Roy Porter, 206–32. Manchester: Manchester University Press, 1987.

Porter, Roy, and Lesley Hall. *The Facts of Life: The Creation of Sexual Knowledge in Britain, 1650–1950*. New Haven, CT: Yale University Press, 1995.

Posner, Richard A. *Law and Literature: A Misunderstood Relation*. Cambridge, MA: Harvard University Press, 1988.

———. *Overcoming Law*. Cambridge, MA: Harvard University Press, 1995.

Potts, Thomas. *The Wonderfull Discoverie of Witches in the Countie of Lancaster*. London: W. Stansby, 1613.

Purkiss, Diane. *The Witch in History: Early Modern and Twentieth-Century Representations*. New York: Routledge, 1996.

Radzinowicz, Leon. *A History of English Criminal Law and Its Administration from 1750*. Vol. 5. London: Stevens and Sons, 1986.

Ratcliffe, Krista. *Rhetorical Listening: Identification, Gender, Whiteness*. Carbondale: Southern Illinois University Press, 2005.

Raymond, Joad. *The Invention of the Newspaper: English Newsbooks 1641–1649*. Oxford: Clarendon Press, 1996.

———. "The Newspaper, Public Opinion, and the Public Sphere in the Seventeenth Century." In *News, Newspapers, and Society in Early Modern Britain*, edited by Joad Raymond, 109–40. London: Frank Cass, 1999.

Reade, Charles. *Griffith Gaunt; or, Jealousy*. New York: AMS Press, 1970.

———. *Hard Cash*. 3 vols. London, 1863.

———. *Readiana: Comments on Current Events*. London: Chatto and Windus, 1883.

Resnik, Judith. "Feminism and the Language of Judging." *Arizona State Law Journal* 22 (1990): 31–38.

Rey, Michael. "Police and Sodomy in Eighteenth-Century Paris: From Sin to Disorder." In *The Pursuit of Sodomy: Male Homosexuality in Renaissance and Enlightenment Europe,* edited by Kent Gerard and Gert Hekma, 129–46. London: Haworth, 1989.

Reynolds, G. W. M. *The Days of Hogarth; or, The Mysteries of Old London.* London: J. Dicks, 1884.

Rhode, Deborah L. *Justice and Gender: Sex Discrimination and the Law.* Cambridge: Harvard University Press, 1989.

Richardson, Alan. "Romanticism and the Colonization of the Feminine." In *Romanticism and Feminism,* edited by Anne K. Mellor, 13–25. Bloomington: Indiana University Press, 1988.

Ritso, Frederick. *An Introduction to the Science of the Law.* London: W. Clark and Sons, 1815.

Robinson, Frederick William. *Female Life in Prison, by a Prison Matron.* 2 vols. London, 1862.

———. *Memoirs of Jane Cameron, Female Convict.* 2 vols. London, 1864.

Rodensky, Lisa. *The Crime in Mind: Criminal Responsibility and the Victorian Novel.* Oxford: Oxford University Press, 2003.

Rodrick, Anne Baltz. "'Only a Newspaper Metaphor': Crime Reports, Class Conflict, and Social Criticism in Two Victorian Newspapers." *Victorian Periodicals Review* 29 (1996): 1–18.

Rorty, Richard. *Contingency, Irony, and Solidarity.* Cambridge: Cambridge University Press, 1989.

Roscoe, William. *Observations on Penal Jurisprudence and the Reformation of Criminals.* London: n.p., 1819.

Rose, Lionel. *The Massacre of the Innocents: Infanticide in Britain, 1800–1939.* London: Routledge and Kegan Paul, 1986.

Rosen, Barbara, ed. *Witchcraft in England, 1558–1618.* Amherst: University of Massachusetts Press, 1969.

Rosenthal, Bernard. *Salem Story: Reading the Witch Trials of 1692.* Cambridge: Cambridge University Press, 1993.

Rousseau, G. S. "The Pursuit of Homosexuality in the Eighteenth Century: 'Utterly Confused Category' and/or Rich Repository?" *Eighteenth Century Life* 9 (1985): 132–68.

Russett, Cynthia Eagle. *Sexual Science: The Victorian Construction of Womanhood.* Cambridge, MA: Harvard University Press, 1989.

Ryan, Michael. *A Manual of Medical Jurisprudence.* London: Renshaw and Rush, 1831.

Schor, Hilary. "The Plot of the Beautiful Ignoramus: *Ruth* and the Tradition of the Fallen Woman." In *Sex and Death in Victorian Literature,* edited by Regina Barreca, 158–77. Bloomington: Indiana University Press, 1990.

Schramm, Jan-Melissa. *Testimony and Advocacy in Victorian Law, Literature, and Theology.* Cambridge: Cambridge University Press, 2000.

Schroeder, Janice. "Speaking Volumes: Victorian Feminism and the Appeal of Public Discussion." *Nineteenth-Century Contexts* 25, no. 2 (June 2003): 97–117.

Scot, Reginald. *The Discoverie of Witchcraft.* London: William Brome, 1584.

Scott, Joan Wallach. *Gender and the Politics of History.* Revised edition. New York: Columbia University Press, 1999.

Scott, Walter. *The Heart of Mid-lothian.* London: J. M. Dent and Sons, 1980.

———. *Letters on Demonology and Witchcraft.* London: J. Murray, 1830.

———. *Letters on Demonology and Witchcraft.* New York: J. & J. Harper, 1831.

Sedgwick, Eve Kosofsky. *Between Men: English Literature and Male Homosocial Desire.* New York: Columbia University Press, 1985.

———. *Epistemology of the Closet.* Berkeley: University of California Press, 1990.

Shanley, Mary Lyndon. *Feminism, Marriage, and the Law in Victorian England, 1850–1895.* Princeton, NJ: Princeton University Press, 1989.

Shapiro, Barbara J. *"Beyond Reasonable Doubt" and "Probable Cause": Historical Perspectives on the Anglo-American Law of Evidence.* Berkeley: University of California Press, 1991.

———. *A Culture of Fact: England, 1550–1720.* Ithaca, NY: Cornell University Press, 2000.

Sharpe, James. *Instruments of Darkness: Witchcraft in England 1550–1750.* London: Hamish Hamilton, 1996.

———. "'Last Dying Speeches': Religion, Ideology and Public Execution in Seventeenth-Century England." *Past and Present* 107 (May 1985): 144–67.

———. "Women, Witchcraft, and the Legal Process." In *Women, Crime and the Courts in Early Modern England,* edited by Jenny Kermode and Garthine Walker, 106–24. London: UCL Press, 1994.

Sheats, Paul D. "'Tis Three Feet Long, and Two Feet Wide': Wordworth's 'Thorn' and the Politics of Bathos." *Wordsworth Circle* 22 (Spring 1991): 92–99.

Showalter, Elaine. *The Female Malady: Women, Madness, and English Culture, 1830–1980.* New York: Penguin, 1985.

Simmel, Georg. *The Sociology of Georg Simmel.* Edited and translated by Kurt H. Wolff. Glencoe, Ill.: Free Press, 1950.

Simpson, Anthony E. "Vulnerability and the Age of Female Consent." In *Sexual Underworlds of the Enlightenment,* edited by G. S. Rousseau and Roy Porter, 181–205. Manchester: Manchester UP, 1987.

Simpson, David. *Romanticism, Nationalism, and the Revolt against Theory.* Chicago: University of Chicago Press, 1993.

———. *Wordsworth's Historical Imagination: The Poetry of Displacement.* New York: Methuen, 1987.

Sindall, Rob. "Middle-Class Crime in Nineteenth-Century England." *Criminal Justice History* 4 (1983): 23–40.

———. *Street Violence in the Nineteenth Century: Media Panic or Real Danger?* Leicester: Leicester University Press, 1990.

Sinfield, Alan. *The Wilde Century: Effeminacy, Oscar Wilde, and the Queer Moment.* New York: Columbia University Press, 1994.

Smart, Carol. *The Ties That Bind: Law, Marriage, and the Reproduction of Patriarchal Relations.* London: Routledge, 1984.

Smith, Barbara Bodichon. *Brief Summary in Plain Language of the Most Important Laws concerning Women.* London: John Chapman, 1854.

Smith, Bonnie G. *The Gender of History: Men, Women, and Historical Practice.* Cambridge, MA: Harvard University Press, 1998.

Smith, Elton E. *Charles Reade.* Boston: Twayne, 1976.

Smith, John Gordon. *Analysis of Medical Evidence: Comprising Directions for Practitioners in the View of Becoming Witnesses in Courts of Justice.* London: T. and G. Underwood, 1825.

Smith, K. J. M. *James Fitzjames Stephen: Portrait of a Victorian Rationalist.* Cambridge: Cambridge University Press, 1988.

Smith, Nigel. *Literature and Revolution in England, 1640–1660.* New Haven, CT: Yale University Press, 1994.

Smith, Roger. *Trial By Medicine: Insanity and Responsibility in Victorian Trials.* Edinburgh: Edinburgh University Press, 1981.

Staves, Susan. *Married Women's Separate Property in England, 1660–1833.* Cambridge, MA: Harvard University Press, 1990.

Sutherland, John. "Trollope, the *Times,* and *The Warden.*" In *Victorian Journalism: Exotic and Domestic,* edited by Barbara Garlick and Margaret Harris, 62–74. Queensland: University of Queensland Press, 1998.

———. *Victorian Fiction: Writers, Publishers, Readers.* London: Macmillan, 1995.

Taylor, Alfred S. *Elements of Medical Jurisprudence.* London, 1836.

Thomas, Brook. *American Literary Realism and the Failed Promise of Contract.* Berkeley: University of California Press, 1997.

———. *Cross-examinations of Law and Literature: Cooper, Hawthorne, Stowe, and Melville.* Cambridge: Cambridge University Press, 1987.

Thomas, Keith. *Religion and the Decline of Magic.* New York: Charles Scribner's Sons, 1971.

Tonna, Charlotte Elizabeth. *Works.* Introduction by Harriet Beecher Stowe. New York: M. W. Dodd, 1852.

Trial of James Blomfield Rush. Edited by W. Teignmouth Shore. Edinburgh: William Hodge, 1928.

Trollope, Anthony. *Orley Farm.* Edited by David Skilton. Oxford: Oxford University Press, 1985.

———. *Phineas Redux.* Oxford: Oxford University Press, 1973.

Trollope, Frances. *Jessie Phillips: A Tale of the Present Day.* London: Colburn, 1844.

Trumbach, Randolph. "London's Sodomites: Homosexual Behavior and Western Culture in the Eighteenth Century." *Journal of Social History* 11 (1977): 1–33.

———. "Sodomitical Assaults, Gender Role, and Sexual Development in Eighteenth-

Century London." In *The Pursuit of Sodomy: Male Homosexuality in Renaissance and Enlightenment Europe,* edited by Kent Gerard and Gert Hekma, 407–32. London: Haworth, 1989.

Uglow, Jenny. *Elizabeth Gaskell: A Habit of Stories.* London: Faber and Faber, 1993.

Unger, Roberto Mangabeira. *Knowledge and Politics.* New York: Free Press, 1976.

Unikel, Robert. "'Reasonable' Doubts: A Critique of the Reasonable Woman Standard in American Jurisprudence," *Northwestern University Law Review* 87 (1992): 326–75.

United Kingdom. London. *Central Criminal Court Sessions Papers.*

Upham, Charles Wentworth. *Lectures on Witchcraft, Comprising a History of the Delusion in Salem, in 1692.* Boston: Carter, Hendee and Babcock, 1831.

Vernon, James. *Politics and the People: A Study in English Political Culture, c. 1815–1867.* Cambridge: Cambridge University Press, 1993.Vicinus, Martha. *The Industrial Muse: A Study of Nineteenth Century British Working-Class Literature.* London: Croom Helm, 1974.

———, ed. *A Widening Sphere: Changing Roles of Victorian Women.* Buffalo: University of Toronto Press, 1983.

Vincent, David. *Literacy and Popular Culture: England, 1750–1914.* Cambridge: Cambridge University Press, 1989.

Voskuil, Lynn M. *Acting Naturally: Victorian Theatricality and Authenticity.* Charlottesville: University of Virginia Press, 2004.

Wahrman, Dror. "Public Opinion, Violence and the Limits of Constitutional Politics." In *Re-Reading the Constitution,* edited by James Vernon, 83–122. New York: Cambridge University Press, 1996.

Walkowitz, Judith R. *City of Dreadful Delight: Narratives of Sexual Danger in Late-Victorian London.* Chicago: University of Chicago Press, 1992.

———. *Prostitution and Victorian Society.* Cambridge: Cambridge University Press, 1980.

Wang, Orrin N. C. "The Other Reasons: Female Alterity and Enlightenment Discourse in Mary Wollstonecraft's *A Vindication of the Rights of Woman.*" *Yale Journal of Criticism* 5, no. 1 (1991): 129–49.

Ward, Cynthia V. "A Kinder, Gentler Liberalism? Visions of Empathy in Feminist and Communitarian Literature." *University of Chicago Law Review* 61 (Summer 1994): 929–55.

Watt, Ian. *The Rise of the Novel: Studies in Defoe, Richardson, and Fielding.* London: Chatto and Windus, 1957.

Watt, Tessa. *Cheap Print and Popular Piety, 1550–1640.* Cambridge: Cambridge University Press, 1991.

Webb, R. K. *The British Working Class Reader, 1790–1848: Literacy and Social Tension.* London: Allen and Unwin, 1955.

Weeks, Jeffrey. *Sex, Politics, and Society: The Regulation of Sexuality since 1800.* London: Longman, 1981.

Weisberg, Richard. "Literature's Twenty-Year Crossing into the Domain of Law: Continuing Trespass or Right by Adverse Possession?" In *Law and Literature,*

Current Legal Issues 2, edited by Michael Freeman and Andrew D. E. Lewis, 47–61. Oxford: Oxford University Press, 1999.

———. *Poethics, and Other Strategies of Law and Literature.* New York: Columbia University Press, 1992.

———. *Vichy Law and the Holocaust in France.* New York: New York University Press, 1996.

Welsby, W. N. *Lives of the Eminent English Judges.* London: S. Sweet, 1846.

Welsh, Alexander. "Burke and Bentham on the Narrative Potential of Circumstantial Evidence." *New Literary History* 21 (1990): 607–28.

———. *George Eliot and Blackmail.* Cambridge, MA: Harvard University Press, 1985.

———. *Strong Representations: Narrative and Circumstantial Evidence in England.* Baltimore, MD: Johns Hopkins University Press, 1992.

West, Robin. *Caring for Justice.* New York: New York University Press, 1997.

———. *Narrative, Authority, and Law.* Ann Arbor: University of Michigan Press, 1993.

———. "Relativism, Objectivity, and Law." *Yale Law Journal* 99 (1990): 1473–501.

Whitcombe, Richard. *An Enquiry into Some of the Rules of Evidence, Relating to the Incompetency of Witnesses.* London, 1824.

White, James Boyd. *Justice as Translation: An Essay in Cultural and Legal Studies.* Chicago: University of Chicago Press, 1990.

Williams, Patricia J. *The Alchemy of Race and Rights.* Cambridge, MA: Harvard University Press, 1991.

Willis, Deborah. *Malevolent Nurture: Witch-hunting and Maternal Power in Early Modern England.* Ithaca, NY: Cornell University Press, 1995.

Wiltenburg, Joy. *Disorderly Women and Female Power in the Street Literature of Early Modern England and Germany.* Charlottesville: University of Virginia Press, 1992.

Winslow, Forbes. "On Medico-Legal Evidence in Cases of Insanity." *Journal of Psychological and Mental Pathology* 21 (January 1855): 94–131.

Wolfson, Susan. *The Questioning Presence: Wordsworth, Keats, and the Interrogative Mode in Romantic Poetry.* Ithaca, NY: Cornell University Press, 1986.

Wollstonecraft, Mary. *A Vindication of the Rights of Woman.* Boston: Peter Edes, 1792.

———. *The Wrongs of Woman.* Edited by Gary Kelly. Oxford: Oxford University Press, 1980.

Wood, Emma. *Sorrow on the Sea.* London, 1868.

Wordsworth, William. "The Thorn." In *Lyrical Ballads and Other Poems, 1797–1800,* edited by James Butler and Karen Green, 77–85. Ithaca, NY: Cornell University Press, 1992.

Index

Recent Books in the Victorian Literature and Culture Series

Linda Dowling
The Vulgarization of Art: The Victorians and Aesthetic Democracy

Tricia Lootens
Lost Saints: Silence, Gender, and Victorian Literary Canonization

Matthew Arnold
The Letters of Matthew Arnold, vols. 1–6
Edited by Cecil Y. Lang

Edward FitzGerald
Edward FitzGerald, Rubáiyát of Omar Khayyám: A Critical Edition
Edited by Christopher Decker

Christina Rossetti
The Letters of Christina Rossetti, vols. 1–4
Edited by Antony H. Harrison

Barbara Leah Harman
The Feminine Political Novel in Victorian England

John Ruskin
The Genius of John Ruskin: Selections from His Writings
Edited by John D. Rosenberg

Antony H. Harrison
Victorian Poets and the Politics of Culture: Discourse and Ideology

Judith Stoddart
Ruskin's Culture Wars: Fors Clavigera and the Crisis of Victorian Liberalism

Linda K. Hughes and Michael Lund
Victorian Publishing and Mrs. Gaskell's Work

Linda H. Peterson
Traditions of Victorian Women's Autobiography: The Poetics and Politics of Life Writing

Gail Turley Houston
Royalties: The Queen and Victorian Writers

Laura C. Berry
The Child, the State, and the Victorian Novel

Barbara J. Black
On Exhibit: Victorians and Their Museums

Annette R. Federico
Idol of Suburbia: Marie Corelli and Late-Victorian Literary Culture

Talia Schaffer
The Forgotten Female Aesthetes: Literary Culture in Late-Victorian England

Julia F. Saville
A Queer Chivalry: The Homoerotic Asceticism of Gerard Manley Hopkins

Victor Shea and William Whitla, Editors
Essays and Reviews: The 1860 Text and Its Reading

Marlene Tromp
The Private Rod: Marital Violence, Sensation, and the Law in Victorian Britain

Dorice Williams Elliott
The Angel out of the House: Philanthropy and Gender in Nineteenth-Century England

Richard Maxwell, Editor
The Victorian Illustrated Book

Vineta Colby
Vernon Lee: A Literary Biography

E. Warwick Slinn
Victorian Poetry as Cultural Critique: The Politics of Performative Language

Simon Joyce
Capital Offenses: Geographies of Class and Crime in Victorian London

Caroline Levine
The Serious Pleasures of Suspense: Victorian Realism and Narrative Doubts

Emily Davies
Emily Davies: Collected Letters, 1861–1875
Edited by Ann B. Murphy and Deirdre Raftery

Joseph Bizup
Manufacturing Culture: Vindications of Early Victorian Industry

Lynn M. Voskuil
Acting Naturally: Victorian Theatricality and Authenticity

Sally Mitchell
Frances Power Cobbe: Victorian Feminist, Journalist, Reformer

Constance W. Hassett
Christina Rossetti: The Patience of Style

Brenda Assael
The Circus and Victorian Society

Judith Wilt
Behind Her Times: Transition England in the Novels of Mary Arnold Ward

Daniel Hack
The Material Interests of the Victorian Novel

Frankie Morris
Artist of Wonderland: The Life, Political Cartoons, and Illustrations of Tenniel

William R. McKelvy
The English Cult of Literature: Devoted Readers, 1774–1880

Linda M. Austin
Nostalgia in Transition, 1780–1917

James Buzard, Joseph W. Childers, and Eileen Gillooly, Editors
Victorian Prism: Refractions of the Crystal Palace

Michael Field
The Fowl and the Pussycat: Love Letters of Michael Field, 1876–1909
Edited by Sharon Bickle

Dallas Liddle
The Dynamics of Genre: Journalism and the Practice of Literature in Mid-Victorian Britain

Christine L. Krueger
Reading for the Law: British Literary History and Gender Advocacy